SELECTED PROSE OF
ALEXANDER POPE

Alexander Pope was the foremost poet of early eighteenth-century England, but he was also a prolific prose writer. This anthology is intended to make Pope's major prose works more widely available. It includes the critical prefaces to his *Works*, to Homer, and to Shakespeare; the mock critical treatises, *A Key to the Lock* and *The Art of Sinking in Poetry* which deride the poetry and criticism of Pope's opponents, and raise important questions about the principles of writing and interpretation; maliciously comic pamphlets attacking John Dennis, Stephen Duck, Edmund Curll, and Lord Hervey; and a selection from Pope's wide-ranging correspondence, which illustrates his genius for friendship, and his opinions on literature, politics, and religion.

The volume complements the critical and moral concerns of Pope's poetry, documenting the controversies in which he was continuously engaged. Pope emerges as a gifted critic and a complex mixture of integrity and deviousness, a man concerned both for the culture of his day and for his public image.

SELECTED PROSE OF
Alexander Pope

Edited by
PAUL HAMMOND

Lecturer in English, University of Leeds

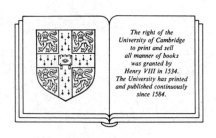

The right of the
University of Cambridge
to print and sell
all manner of books
was granted by
Henry VIII in 1534.
The University has printed
and published continuously
since 1584.

Cambridge University Press

CAMBRIDGE

LONDON   NEW YORK   NEW ROCHELLE

MELBOURNE   SYDNEY

13424014

Published by the Press Syndicate of the University of Cambridge
The Pitt Building, Trumpington Street, Cambridge CB2 1RP
32 East 57th Street, New York, NY 10022, USA
10 Stamford Road, Oakleigh, Melbourne 3166, Australia

First published 1987

Printed in Great Britain at
the University Press, Cambridge

British Library cataloguing in publication data
Pope, Alexander
Selected prose of Alexander Pope.
I.Title   II Hammond, Paul
828'.508   PR3622

Library of Congress cataloguing in publication data
Pope, Alexander, 1688-1744.
Includes index
I. Hammond, Paul, 1953–   II. Title.
PR3622. H35   1987   828'.508   86-8295

ISBN 0 521 25011 0

Contents

Preface

When Matthew Arnold remarked that Pope was one of the classics of our prose, he was not being complimentary. Pope's poetry has recovered from such disparagement, but his prose is less well known, and less accessible. The aim of the present volume is to offer a selection of the literary criticism, pamphlets and letters, both for their intrinsic interest, and for the light which they cast upon Pope's poetry and the literary world in which it was composed and first read.

The texts which follow are drawn for the most part from originals in the Brotherton Collection at the University of Leeds, and I am grateful to the staff there for their ready and courteous assistance. I have been continually endebted to the work of previous students of Pope, especially to the editions and studies which are cited hereafter by abbreviations.

I am also grateful to Dr Howard Erskine-Hill for his comments on the typescript of this edition.

PAUL HAMMOND

Leeds
August 1985

Abbreviations

Ault	*The Prose Works of Alexander Pope,* newly collected and edited by Norman Ault. Vol. I. The Earlier Works, 1711-1720 (Oxford, 1936)
Poems	*The Twickenham Edition of the Poems of Alexander Pope,* edited by John Butt *et al.*, 11 vols. (1939-68)
E-C	*The Works of Alexander Pope,* edited by Whitwell Elwin and J.W. Courthorpe, 10 vols. (1871-89)
Corr.	*The Correspondence of Alexander Pope,* edited by George Sherburn, 5 vols. (Oxford, 1956)
Guerinot	J.V. Guerinot, *Pamphlet Attacks on Alexander Pope 1711-1744: A Descriptive Bibliography* (1969)
Mack	Maynard Mack, *Alexander Pope: A Life* (New Haven, 1985)
Erskine-Hill	Howard Erskine-Hill, *The Social Milieu of Alexander Pope: Lives, Example and the Poetic Response* (New Haven, 1975)

Chronology

1688	21 May	Pope born in London
c.1700		Pope's family moves to Windsor Forest
c.1705		Pope begins to become acquainted with London literary figures
1709	2 May	*Pastorals*
1711	15 May	*An Essay on Criticism*
	20 June	John Dennis's *Reflections Critical and Satyrical upon a late Rhapsody call'd, An Essay upon Criticism*
	? July	*The Critical Specimen*
1711-12		Pope contributes essays to *The Spectator*
1712	20 May	*The Rape of the Locke* (two-canto version)
		Pope becomes acquainted with Gay, Swift, Arbuthnot and Parnell, the Scriblerians
1713		Pope contributes to *The Guardian*
	7 March	*Windsor-Forest*
1714	4 March	*The Rape of the Lock* (five-canto version)
	1 August	Death of Queen Anne; accession of George I
1715		Pope becomes acquainted with Lady Mary Wortley Montagu
	April	*A Key to the Lock*
	6 June	*The Iliad* vol. i
	8 June	Tickell's rival translation of *Iliad* 1
1716	22 March	*The Iliad* vol. ii
	26 March	Curll publishes *Court Poems*
	31 March	*A Full and True Account*
	1 May	Curll publishes *State Poems*, including Pope's *The Worms*
	? November	*A Further Account*
1717	3 June	*The Iliad* vol. iii
	3 June	*Works of Mr. Alexander Pope*

	23 October	Death of Pope's father
1718	28 June	*The Iliad* vol. iv
1720	? Late March	*A Strange but True Relation*
	12 May	*The Iliad* vols. v-vi
1721	3 April	Walpole appointed First Lord of the Treasury
1723	? January	Pope's edition of *The Works of John Sheffield, Earl of Mulgrave*
	May	Atterbury's trial in the House of Lords, at which Pope testifies
1725	12 March	Pope's edition of *The Works of Shakespear*
	23 April	*The Odyssey* vols. i-iii
1726	March	Theobald's *Shakespeare Restored*
	June	*The Odyssey* vols. iv-v
	October	Swift's *Gulliver's Travels*
1727	June	Pope–Swift *Miscellanies in Prose and Verse*, vols. i-ii
	12 June	Death of George I; accession of George II
1728	8 March	Pope–Swift *Miscellanies. The Last Volume* (dated 1727); includes *The Art of Sinking*
	18 May	*The Dunciad...In Three Books*
1729	10 April	*The Dunciad Variorum*
1730	19 November	*Of the Poet Laureate* in *The Grub-street Journal*
1731	December	*Of Taste. An Epistle to the...Earl of Burlington*
1732	4 October	Pope–Swift *Miscellanies. The Third Volume*
	4 December	Death of Gay
1733	15 January	*Of the Use of Riches, An Epistle to...Lord Bathurst*
	15 February	*The First Satire of the Second Book of Horace, Imitated*
	February-May	*An Essay on Man*, Epistles I-III.
	9 March	Lady Mary Wortley Montagu's *Verses Address'd to the Imitator of the First Satire of the Second Book of Horace*
	7 June	Death of Pope's mother

Chronology

	10 November	Lord Hervey, *An Epistle from a Nobleman to a Doctor of Divinity*
	30 November	*A Letter to a Noble Lord* [not printed]
1734	16 January	*An Epistle to…Viscount Cobham*
	24 January	*An Essay on Man*, Epistle IV
	4 July	*Imitations of Horace, Sat.* II ii
	28 December	*Sober Advice from Horace*
1735	2 January	*Epistle to Dr. Arbuthnot*
	8 February	*Of the Characters of Women: An Epistle to a Lady*
	27 February	Death of Arbuthnot
	23 April	*Works*, vol. ii
	12 May	Curll's edition of Pope's letters
1737	28 April	*Imitations of Horace, Ep.* II ii
	19 May	Pope's official edition of his letters
	25 May	*Imitations of Horace, Ep.* II i
1738	23 January	*Imitations of Horace, Ep.* I vi
	7 March	*Imitations of Horace, Ep.* I i
1742	20 March	*The New Dunciad* (i.e. Book IV)
1743	29 October	*The Dunciad* (revised four-book version)
1744	30 May	Death of Pope

Introduction

On 3 June 1717 there appeared a handsome quarto volume entitled *The Works of Mr. Alexander Pope*. The claim which this book makes for Pope's status is conveyed in a variety of ways. The very title, 'Works', implies bulk and value, a definitive collection. There is a large engraved frontispiece portrait of Pope. On the title page, a quotation from Cicero; it is not translated or identified, and one wonders how many of Pope's readers recognised it as a passage from *Pro Archia* which might be rendered thus: 'These studies nourish youth and divert old age; they are an adornment when affairs are flourishing, and provide a refuge and consolation in adversity; they give delight at home, and are no encumbrance in public affairs; they pass the night hours with us, travel with us, and accompany us into our country retreats.' Will the ensuing works be this classic and versatile companion? There follows a preface which opens with an engraved ornament showing Apollo surrounded by the nine Muses; the initial letter of the preface just happens to be 'I', and is a decorative initial showing the winged horse Pegasus, symbol of poetic inspiration. After the preface come laudatory verses from authors including John Sheffield, Duke of Buckingham; Anne Finch, Countess of Winchilsea; and William Wycherley. The works actually collected here comprise *Pastorals, Windsor-Forest, An Essay on Criticism* and *The Rape of the Lock,* together with various translations and minor poems. The book appeared a couple of weeks after Pope's twenty-ninth birthday.

As we turn the pages of this lavish volume we may murmur that modesty was not one of Pope's virtues. But we are not simply looking at an example of poetic vanity; rather, it is a stage in the creation of an image of himself, which Pope worked at throughout his life. Many means were employed to fashion this image. Careful control over the way his works were published (extending to the details of typography) helped to create a visual style of elegance and classical authority. The poses adopted in his poems – the humble man devoted to his parents and his God, the disinterested critic of life and letters, bearing no grudges and concerned only to uphold moral and literary standards – these are important strategies defining the position of the writer, and placing the work of the critic and satirist in a realm apparently free from private and party malice. And yet this strategy was not without recourse to outrageous mendacity and the scandalous misrepresentation of honest men.

The prose works collected in the present anthology illustrate various aspects of Pope's self-image. There are formal critical essays, on pastoral poetry, on Homer and on Shakespeare. But there are also works which look like literary criticism yet turn out to be devious and challenging critical jokes: *A Key to the Lock* and *The Art of Sinking* take standard critical forms and use them in disconcerting ways. Then there are the scurrilous, mocking attacks on Dennis and Curll and Duck, which delight in inversion and practical jokes. Finally, we have Pope's letters. Some were composed or revised for publication, and carefully project the desired image of the man of letters; others included here are more intimate pieces which allow us to see a different side to the mask, and sometimes even the face itself.

The preface to the *Works* of 1717 is a curious exercise in the creation of an image and a role. It begins with a sentence which sounds modest and tentative, but which is also quite firm in its delineation of the relationship between writer and reader: 'I am inclined to think that both the writers of books, and the readers of them, are generally not a little unreasonable in their expectations.' Though the sentence appears to admit the unreasonableness of authors, this admission is subordinate to the superior defining position of the 'I', this particular author who can see the errors of both writers and readers. The sentences which follow are oddly weighted, with the antitheses unequal: writers are said to desire fame, approval, and power over the opinions of others; readers seek pleasure and entertainment. If there is over-ambition in writers, there is mere frivolity in readers. Pope disingenuously lowers the status of writing, saying that poetry and criticism are 'by no means the universal concern of the world, but only the affair of idle men who write in their closets, and of idle men who read there'. Now the writer/reader antithesis becomes that of poet and critic, and in contrast to the languid state previously evoked, Pope identifies intemperate zeal as a characteristic of critics: 'a bad Author deserves better usage than a bad Critic; a man may be the former merely thro' the misfortune of an ill judgment, but he cannot be the latter without both that and an ill temper'. A careful sleight of hand is at work. Pope suggests that 'even the worst authors might endeavour to please us, and in that endeavour, deserve something at our hands'. Here the 'us' and 'our' align Pope with the readers who are to be charitable to bad authors, thus creating a distance between this author and 'bad authors', who are now 'they'. Then the identity of 'us' changes again, and at the end of this paragraph 'we' are every man whose reputation 'generally depends upon the first steps he makes in the world'.

This sympathetic point conceded, Pope changes the point of view once more and introduces a new character, the good poet, who 'no sooner communicates his works with the same desire of information, but it is imagin'd he is a vain young creature given up to the ambition of fame'. The reading public becomes divided into three groups: 'were he sure to be commended by the best and most knowing, he is as sure of being envy'd by the worst and most ignorant'; and then 'there is a third class of people who make the largest part of mankind, those of ordinary or indifferent capacities; and these (to a man) will hate, or suspect him: a hundred honest gentlemen will dread him as a wit, and a hundred innocent women as a satyrist'. This sentence dismisses the vast majority of readers; it may say that they are honest and innocent, yet dread of wits and satirists can only be attributed to fools and knaves, so the terms 'honest' and 'innocent' are called into question. The paragraph continually plays with conditional clauses, but a succession of 'if's and subjunctives does not hide the underlying insistence that 'a fine Genius' is derided by those who fear or fail to understand it. And so, adverse criticism is turned into an inadvertent acknowledgement of Genius.

The rhetoric continues to claim both modesty and greatness. 'The life of a Wit is a warfare upon earth; and the present spirit of the world is such, that to attempt to serve it (any way) one must have the constancy of a martyr, and a resolution to suffer for its sake': if there is an element of self-deprecation in calling oneself a 'Wit' (rather than a 'Genius') it is almost obliterated by the appropriation of religious language. Just enough facetiousness is preserved to forestall outrage at this gambit, and the word 'martyr' is thus dexterously slipped past the reader's guard. But lest this appear too solemn a development, Pope moves into a sentence which offers a self-deprecating account of how he came to write and to publish: 'I writ because it amused me; I corrected because it was as pleasant to me to correct as to write; and I publish'd because I was told I might please such as it was a credit to please.' The separation of the activities of writing, correcting and publishing into discrete stages is important: the first two are governed by the desire to please himself, the third only by a desire to please a select few. There has been no intention to become a public man of letters, no vocation to instruct and please readers at large, and the implication that this was all a kind of pleasant accident distances momentarily the grand claims made by the rhetoric of this preface and the typography of the *Works*. But even in this parenthesis Pope advances a claim to social prestige: he will please such as it is a credit to please, as, earlier, one of the advantages of having a 'Genius to Poetry' was said to be the 'privilege of being admitted into the best company'.

The modesty topos wears thin, and Pope forestalls the reader's recognition of this by remarking: 'If anyone should imagine I am not in earnest...'. Yet what follows this, offered as a further demonstration of humility, is actually a comparison with the Ancients. The moderns are limited by writing in an insular and transitory language. But then, commending the imitation of the Ancients, Pope asserts that 'the highest character for sense and learning has been obtain'd by those who have been most indebted to them', and procedes to draw attention to his own extensive debt. The distinguishing characteristic of the Ancients was their dedication to correctness, for 'it was the business of their lives to correct and finish their works for posterity'. Here Pope touches upon a subject of recurrent concern to him, that of erasure and correction. This is not only a zeal for stylistic excellence, but forms part of Pope's attitude to life, part of his notion of how one creates a self. His own works were compulsively revised both before and after publication: pages of manuscript drafts and hundreds of small alterations to the wording and typography of his poems testify to his continual desire to erase and re-create. Pope also redraws the boundaries of his own canon, and in this preface he distances himself from, without actually denying, some verses of which he is not proud, by saying: 'look upon no verses as mine that are not inserted in this collection'. This continual process of revision also extends to the moral life, for he wished to 'make each Day a *Critick* on the last' (*An Essay on Criticism* 571). 'For what I have publish'd, I can only hope to be pardon'd; but for what I have burn'd, I deserve to be prais'd': the destruction of some early, imperfect work invites praise, partly for the moral reason that it has entailed a sacrifice of self-love. Yet this sits oddly with other areas of the egoistic rhetoric of the *Works*, such as the insistence on the early date at which the *Pastorals* were composed. For all that Pope talks of a sacrifice of self-love, and erases parts of his past, the self is never erased, or even diminished, but only reinforced. The persona of the man of letters is built up from a series of strategies which proscribe

Introduction

criticism: Pope is precocious (and so judgement of his early work must be merciful); he is modest (and does not claim to have produced perfect works); he is a classic (and is so steeped in the good sense of the Ancients that his thoughts are more theirs than his own); and, above all, he is the servant of nature, but far from this being a deprecation of his artistry, it is the appropriation of the ultimate talisman in the eighteenth century's moral vocabulary. Every one of these strategies which appear to diminish the author actually erases his figure only temporarily, to bring it back in a more powerful form.

Whatever moral view we may take of these tricks, they do amount to a potent enabling strategy. Pope himself was triply disabled, by his physical deformity, his Roman Catholicism, and his lack of formal education. These strategies enable him to take command of the literary and moral language of his age. His early work appropriates the literary traditions: the *Pastorals* and *Windsor-Forest* announce a new Virgil who can recreate the *Eclogues* and *Georgics*; the translations announce a new Dryden, whose *Fables* are continued by this gifted successor; while the *Essay on Criticism* places Pope in the tradition of poet–critics such as Horace, Vida and Boileau as one who will re-shape the literary heritage and redefine the age's key terms, 'wit', 'sense' and 'nature'.

Pope's concern with re-writing, with making perfect, and his employment of deceit and rhetorical tricks, seems to be part of that dual vision of chaos and stability which informs much of his work. There is a stable truth, he insists, a common fund of good sense shared by us and the Ancients; Nature is 'One *clear, unchang'd*, and *Universal* Light' (*An Essay on Criticism* 71), and yet the constructs of human reason are precarious, and the world of letters corrupt and desperately fragmented. For us to spell out the antithesis in that way makes it seem clear and tolerable, makes it into a rational proposition subject to analysis and amendment. But for Pope the instruments of analysis and reform have themselves been corrupted, with language and the cultural institutions damaged by the dunces. A perception of the instability of language haunts Pope's own language; words have an unstable half-life, imaged in troubling shifts between the inanimate, the animal and the human:

> How hints, like spawn, scarce quick in embryo lie,
> How new-born nonsense first is taught to cry,
> Maggots half-form'd in rhyme exactly meet,
> And learn to crawl upon poetic feet.
>
> (*The Dunciad* B i 59-62)

5

Terror and facetiousness are held together in Pope's poetry, and while the prose works at a lower pressure, there are still many unsettling shifts of tone which trip up the reader, keeping him alert and troubled.

The image offered by the visual appearance of the *Works* is confident, even over-weening; but the strange turns in the rhetoric of the preface disclose a deep uncertainty, suggesting that any self is unstable, including the self of the author, and that of the reader as he experiences a text. Each self is continually erased and re-composed.

Four years before the publication of his *Works,* Pope had contributed to *The Guardian* an essay on dedications (no.4). Hyperbolic flattery had long been a feature of dedications, but Pope draws attention to its deep implications. First, it is 'a Deceit upon the Gross of Mankind, who take their Notion of Characters from the Learned'. But besides deceiving their public, the men of letters are also destroying their own language. Even if an author is sincere, he 'can find no Terms to express it, but what have been already used, and rendered suspected by Flatterers. Truth itself in a Dedication is like an Honest Man in a Disguise or Vizor-Masque, and will appear a Cheat by being so drest like one.' The persona has become intrinsically fallacious, so that there is no way of expressing the truth which does not call it into question. Pope then moves on to a paragraph of unsettling implications. He treats with great respect 'the least Instances or Remains of Ingenuity' wherever they are found, and has often discovered 'unvalued Repositories of Learning in the Lining of Bandboxes. I look upon these Pasteboard Edifices, adorned with the Fragments of the Ingenious, with the same Veneration as Antiquaries upon ruined Buildings, whose Walls preserve divers Inscriptions and Names, which are no where else to be found in the World.' This is a complex passage, despite its facetious tone. Is learning in this society only to be found in the lining of bandboxes, reduced to an adjunct of trade and vanity? Or can this writer not distinguish discarded rubbish from real learning? Are antiquarians and archaeologists equally indiscriminate, as *The Dunciad* will suggest? Awkward and oscillating as it is, the passage is also poignant and troubling in its image of art destroyed and then haphazardly collected with an almost childlike labour. Ironically, this fragmentary and partly erased writing which is reconstructed after so much effort turns out to be just another example of the destruction of language by writers themselves.

A way out of this sad labyrinth is fashioned by Pope in a further ironic twist: make a dedication which actually spells out that message which is the sub-text of all other dedications – praise not of the patron but of the poet. This new dedication is also double-edged, revealing writers' simultaneous subservience and pride. Once more, Pope's troubled contemplation of the vulnerability of art is presented inextricably with a proud assertion of the writer's own importance. Pope's solution to the problem of how to write about such a state of affairs is one which will recur: into an accepted literary form he inserts subject matter which is entirely out of place by normal standards, but which is the only suitable subject in the conditions which now prevail. The same strategy will produce the ironic critical treatise in *The Art of Sinking* and the ironic epic in *The Dunciad*.

If we turn to Pope's formal literary criticism from reading these strangely convoluted and almost desperate images of the writer and his art, we may wonder how Pope manages to work with the languages and assumptions permitted by the critical decorum of his time.

Pope's first critical essay (if we are to believe his dating of it to 1704) was the *Discourse on Pastoral*, an essay which reveals with particular clarity some of the chief assumptions of his criticism. 'The original of Poetry', he says, 'is ascribed to that age which succeeded the creation of the world', and the pastoral poetry which flourished then was 'afterwards improv'd to a perfect image of that happy time; which by giving us an esteem for the virtues of a former age, might recommend them to the present'. Here we see the need for some notion of origin; poetry is ascribed to a happy state, a golden age from which any Christian idea of the fall of man has been elided. Pope knows that this account is a myth: the words 'ascribed', 'seems' and 'imagine' point to this explanation as a fiction, and one which serves a social function. Pastoral poetry is to image the tranquillity of the country life, so it should not represent the lives of shepherds as they 'at this day really are, but as they may be conceiv'd then to have been; when a notion of quality was annex'd to that name, and the best of men follow'd the employment'. Hence Theocritus himself, the original writer of pastoral, is rebuked for a lack of decorum: his manners are defective, for 'his swains are sometimes abusive and immodest, and perhaps too much inclining to rusticity'. The expression should instead be humble but pure, and 'comparisons drawn from the most agreeable objects of the country'. There is a great difference 'betwixt simplicity and rusticity, so the expression of simple thoughts should be plain, but not clownish'. This requires a rigorous selectivity in writing English, for many country phrases used by Spenser were 'spoken only by people of the basest condition'. Finally, 'that Air of piety to the Gods should shine thro' the Poem, which so visibly appears in all the works of antiquity'. The word 'all' here may be a pardonable exaggeration, but it is interesting that Pope uses the word 'piety' (which, though Latin in origin, has strong Christian connotations) to describe Greek and Roman religion, implying a continuity of religious devotion across the centuries and across cultures.

And all this is 'natural', for Pope begins his account of the elements of pastoral with the words, 'If we would copy Nature'. He assumes that Nature is 'there' to be copied; moreover, that it is unchanging and accessible via these different cultures. 'Nature' here is a carefully edited version of the country and of human society, and becomes an authentication of social organization. The form of poetry which images the original of Nature shows us a happy world of shepherds (Pope interestingly censures Theocritus for including reapers and fishermen, workers whose tasks are in fact more dangerous) who are pious and genteel, and the eighteenth-century notion of social rank ('quality', 'the best') is endorsed by the ascription of this arrangement to Nature, and to mankind's origins. Pope's essay is a curious piece of writing, aware that pastoral is a myth, but conscious of only some elements in that myth, leaving other crucial concepts unexamined.

But more significant than pastoral as an example of cultural origins was Homer. For Pope, as for Virgil, '*Nature* and *Homer* were, he found, the same' (*An Essay on Criticism* 135). The preface to Pope's translation of the *Iliad* begins by describing Homer's great distinguishing characteristic as his *invention*. This is a classical rhetorical term (*inventio*) for the first of the elements of composition, and its etymology implies that the writer does not make up but discovers material, which is thus thought to be there waiting to be used. Accordingly, Homer as the greatest poetic inventor is the writer who is closest to Nature; invention 'furnishes Art with all her Materials... For Art is only like a prudent Steward that lives on managing the Riches of Nature.' (The economic, regulatory function of art betrayed by that image is noteworthy.) Pope is concerned to praise not so much the judgement (that faculty which organizes and orders, pre-eminently represented by Virgil) as the invention, represented by Homer. Critics, says Pope, are uneasy when confronted by this kind of writer, 'because they find it easier for themselves to pursue their Observations through an uniform and bounded Walk of Art, than to comprehend the vast and various Extent of Nature'. Homer's work is 'a wild Paradise'.

Pope himself has difficulty judging Homer by the rules of neo-classical criticism, and is compelled to think about the function of these rules. He offers us an explanatory image: in an ordered garden the flowers produced by Nature are arranged by art so that they are set off to advantage in the eyes of a human onlooker; the rules are therefore principles of arrangement. '*True Wit* is *Nature* to Advantage drest' (*An Essay on Criticism* 297), where 'drest' is as much a metaphor from gardening as from tailoring: true wit does not dress up Nature, but arranges it. False wit, by contrast, smothers it in all manner of flashy ornaments (ibid., 292-6). Homer is Nature unadorned and unarranged, like a great tree, or like the Nile.

Homer was remarkable for his invention in several areas. First, in the area of fable, where he originated a number of human stories which have supplied his successors; but he also created allegorical fables, and this is another instance of his close proximity to Nature, showing 'those innumerable Knowledges, those Secrets of Nature and Physical Philosophy which *Homer* is generally suppos'd to have wrapt up in his *Allegories*'. He also excelled in the variety of his characters and the appropriateness of speech to speaker. Perhaps most characteristic is his use of images from nature, where he brings disparate things together: 'each Circumstance and Individual of Nature summon'd together by the Extent and Fecundity of his Imagination; to which all things, in their various Views, presented themselves in an Instant'. For Homer 'found out *Living Words*', as Pope puts it: 'An Arrow is *impatient* to be on the Wing, a Weapon *thirsts* to drink the Blood of an Enemy', and Pope sees the use of compound epithets as a further example of 'the Fruitfulness of his Invention', since they are 'a sort of supernumerary Pictures of the Persons or Things they are join'd to'. Finally, Homer is full of sublime thoughts; this was recognized by Longinus, but is also demonstrated by his ideas having 'so remarkable a Parity with those of the Scripture'. He has defects, but these are wholly attributable to the times in which he lived.

The inventive use of nature in Homer's language is brought out in many of Pope's notes to the *Iliad*. He points to the exactitude with which Homer makes his similes, such as the comparisons of an army to cranes in flight, to waves beating against a rock, or clouds poised in the sky. But also remarkable, says Pope, is Homer's habit of breaking off the simile, so as to allow the reader to complete the comparison for himself: this makes reading an activity, forcing the reader to think and respond, not just to absorb. And yet there are images from nature (or perhaps we should say, from country life) which disturb Pope, such as the comparison of Greek soldiers to a swarm of flies round a shepherd's cottage, or the suggestion that a hero has the boldness of a fly. In both these cases Pope points to how changing social organization and values have altered the way we look at the natural world. 'Our present Idea of the Fly is indeed very low, as taken from the Littleness and Insignificancy of this Creature', but 'there is really no Meanness in it'. Homer was writing at a time when 'Agriculture was the Employment of Persons of the greatest Esteem and Distinction'. Pope's notion of this dignity in agriculture is shaped in part by his importation into the Homeric period of eighteenth-century ideas of nobility and social quality, and yet an attentive reading of Homer also forces Pope to articulate, and sometimes to challenge, the values of contemporary art. He knows that readers will be offended by certain similes, so he explains that our perception of nature is socially conditioned; indeed at one point he uses language of incisive honesty to define the change which has taken place in the social valuation of art: Homer was writing 'before Politeness had rais'd the esteem of Arts subservient to Luxury, above those necessary to the Subsistence of Mankind'.

This question of decorum is raised again in the Postscript to the *Odyssey*. Noting that the *Odyssey* is more concerned than the *Iliad* with domestic and everyday matters, Pope asks how a poet should handle a *'low action'*. The 'representations of common, or even domestic things, in clear, plain, and natural words, are frequently found to make the liveliest impression on the reader'. But the language used must be plain and not figurative, since 'the *low actions of life* cannot be put into a figurative style without being ridiculous, but *things natural* can'. In view of his careful use of inappropriate figurative language in *The Rape of the Lock* and *The Dunciad*, the reasons which Pope gives for this are worth attention. Laughter implies censure, but only rational beings are the object of censure; so inanimate aspects of nature lie outside the sphere of moral judgement and may therefore be treated with lofty figurative language. But when human beings, who are rational creatures, are represented 'above their real character' this is 'ridiculous in Art, because it is vicious in Morality'. The 'because' in that phrase is worth pondering; so too is Pope's assumption that men have some 'real character', some absolute position in the social order which cannot be misrepresented without committing an error which is at once moral and artistic. A fly has no 'real' meanness, but men do have a 'real'

Introduction

character: Pope perceives the social construction of value in one case but not in the other.

As Homer was an 'original', so too was Shakespeare. Indeed, 'he is not so much an Imitator, as an Instrument, of Nature; and 'tis not so just to say that he speaks from her, as that she speaks thro' him'. Pope's starting-point here is Dryden's remark in his *Essay of Dramatic Poesy* that 'All the Images of Nature were still present to him...he needed not the spectacles of Books to read Nature; he look'd inwards, and found her there.' But Pope's formulation of the idea indicates a further degree of mythologizing, so that Nature is more strongly personified, and Shakespeare separated more clearly from other writers. Pope's essay is endebted to a tradition of Shakespearean criticism which had found its first formulation in Dryden's brief but seminal paragraph. To Dryden, Shakespeare was 'naturally learned', and Pope suggests that he was gifted with great intuition, not only in respect of the passions but also 'in the coolness of Reflection and Reasoning'. 'This', says Pope, 'is perfectly amazing, from a man of no education or experience in those great and publick scenes of life which are usually the subject of his thoughts.' Shakespeare is, indeed, 'the only Author that gives ground for a very new opinion, that the Philosopher and even the Man of the world, may be *Born*, as well as the Poet'. Here Pope is compelled to recognize a kind of artist quite unlike himself. Pope had carefully made himself a man of the world, a philosopher and a poet, by cultivating the friendship of leading writers, politicians and aristocrats, and by extensive reading; that conversation and reading he laboriously made into new works of art, which he then laboriously remade.

But if in this respect Pope admits that Shakespeare, like Homer, was an irregular genius, in other instances he remakes the traditional image of Shakespeare into that of a writer less exceptional in his habits. The players had reported that Shakespeare never blotted a line, but Pope argues that he did actually revise several of his plays (as modern Shakespearean scholarship now also believes). And as for Shakespeare being unlearned, Pope draws a distinction between learning and languages. Even if (in Jonson's notorious phrase) Shakespeare had 'small *Latine*, and lesse *Greeke*' he nevertheless read widely, and Pope attributes to him 'a taste of natural Philosophy, Mechanicks, ancient and modern History, Poetical learning and Mythology'. If Pope is sensibly refuting a commonplace exaggeration, he is also partially remaking Shakespeare in another image, that of the great 'original' who has wide knowledge of many branches of human activity, as Homer was credited with having by readers in the ancient world. And yet Shakespeare remained defective in 'knowledge of the best models, the Ancients', and although Pope recognizes that Shakespeare is not to be judged by Aristotle's rules, he nevertheless argues that the plays are imperfect because they respond too closely to the demands of the Elizabethan theatre-going public. At the outset Shakespeare wrote to please the people, and only later did he receive 'patronage from the better sort' and 'the encouragement of the Court', whereupon his plays improved. Pope is right in saying that Shakespeare did write for both town and court, and did try to please different kinds of audience, but what is particularly revealing here is his assumption that art written for court patrons will be better, for 'players are just such judges of what is *right*, as Taylors are of what is *graceful*'. Here the word '*right*' elevates into a universal principle the taste of one privileged section of one insular society, however much it may be bolstered by invocation of 'the Ancients'. It is therefore easy for Pope (notwithstanding what he has just said about not trying a man by the laws of another country) to use a firmly judgemental vocabulary in speaking of Shakespeare's 'Errors', his 'wrong choice', 'wrong conduct' and 'false thoughts'. From here it is a simple step for Pope to remake Shakespeare's plays, cutting out lines, speeches and even scenes which do not suit the taste of his age. Some of these passages Pope will not accept as coming from the hand of Shakespeare at all; others are explained as the result of Shakespeare trying to please 'the meaner sort of people': word-play and clowning in comedy, bombast and exaggerated thoughts in tragedy were aimed at this audience, as were 'the most strange, unexpected, *and consequently most unnatural*, Events and Incidents' (my italics). What displeases Pope is attributed to the influence of the meaner sort and at the same time labelled unnatural. Once again we see Pope freeing himself from many contemporary assumptions through his exposure to a very different kind of writer, while at the same time partly remaking the author so that he becomes explicable by Pope's own ideology.

Some of Pope's prose works look like formal critical essays but are not. *Guardian* no.40 can be read almost throughout as a straight attack on Pope's way of writing pastoral poetry, and in praise of Ambrose Philips, for only on a couple of occasions does the ironic mask slip. *The Critical Specimen* preserves the format of a critical prospectus, but imports obviously satirical material into that struc-

Introduction

ture; in mocking the pretensions of John Dennis it presents the critic as epic hero, anticipating *The Dunciad* in simultaneously preserving and subverting a familiar form.

This interest in subverting a genre (and with the genre, the assumptions which it offers about how to read) is taken further in *A Key to the Lock*. The 'key' was a well-established critical genre, offering a clear guide through long and difficult romances, or a political reading of an apparently innocent text. The strategy adopted by Pope in his *Key* is complex: it is in part a defensive move, for by offering a bizarre political interpretation of *The Rape of the Lock* he pre-empts other attempts to give it dangerous topical implications. And yet, by suggesting a political significance for *The Rape of the Lock*, however absurd, Pope alerts his reader's attention to the possibility that the poem might indeed have such a meaning, albeit one which is less schematic. The self-confident wrong-headedness of *A Key*'s complete explanation itself suggests that any sensible reading of the poem must instead be alert to occasional and fragmentary political implications. This particular key, then, far from explaining the difficulties of a work, actually makes the act of reading more complex, and it also sets the reader thinking about some larger, theoretical questions. How do poems 'mean'? Why do we recognize these two proposed allegorical readings of *The Rape of the Lock* as ridiculous? Are there legitimate and illegitimate readings of a work? Is our knowledge of the writer's life and opinions a guide to the work's meaning, as *A Key* at one point claims? It seems that the process by which Pope has defined how his poem is to be read is typically paradoxical: by adopting the stance of an enemy, Pope has proscribed a hostile way of reading and prompted another method in which the reader has to be alert for echoes and hints and intermittent allegory, in effect a way of reading which allows the author control without responsibility.

Pope's games with critical genres reach a climax in *The Art of Sinking*. We are made continually uneasy by its not being a work whose satire proceeds simply and in one direction. The title suggests a comic reversal of Longinus's treatise, and yet we cannot read very far without losing our bearings. The language used suggests both praise and blame: a lofty kind of art seems to be indicated by 'profund' (and the Ancients, we are told, had but one word for height and for depth), yet it is also 'the downhill way...the Bottom, the End'. Is this poetry profound or abysmal? and how do we tell? The remark that 'The Taste of the *Bathos* is implanted by Nature itself in the Soul of Man' seems to be a comment on man's instinct for the depth of spiritual experience, and simultaneously for the crass and banal; and when the sentence continues: "'till perverted by Custom or Example he is taught, or rather compell'd, to relish the *Sublime*' we think we know where we are, until we are again disturbed by being told that 'unprejudiced Minds of Children delight only in such Productions, and in such Images'. A childish taste, or a child-like innocence? The main thrust of the satirical strategy is of course clear enough, but there remains a disturbing undertow which prevents us from simply reading praise as blame and *vice versa*, a complexity also created by Erasmus in *The Praise of Folly*.

Pope compounds our unease in his discussion of the relationship between art and nature. The new art of the bathos is said to replace not an artistic code but the natural world: readers have 'long been weary of natural Things'. Harlequins and magicians delight an audience by turning a 'Coach... into a Wheel-barrow, a Conjurer into an Old Woman, or a Man's head where his Heels should be'. So the master of the bathos should 'render himself Master of this happy and antinatural way of thinking' so as to provide for each object ideas which are 'infinitely below it'. But the bathos is not the exclusive sphere of artists, for any scientist can excel in his own way – 'an active Catcher of Butterflies, a careful and fanciful Pattern-drawer, an industrious Collector of Shells...'. Like the collectors in *The Dunciad* (B iv 397-458) these artists and collectors suffer from a lack of perspective, by minute attention to particulars without attention to their origins in Nature or God. If the sublime can be thought of as art leading the reader towards a sense of life's divine origins, then the bathos is the reverse, the use of art and science to obscure this awareness by fixing the attention on the extravagant surface of objects and images. Those who practice this art destroy nature like the harlequins and conjurors who produce monsters; and they are themselves monsters, for Pope classifies them as various kinds of sub-human creatures, flying-fish, swallows, ostriches, parrots, didappers, porpoises, frogs, eels and tortoises. Appropriately, this taxonomy is itself bizarre and contradictory: not only is the selection of creatures peculiar, but the categories are unclear, since many of these are amphibious (flying-fish, frogs) or on the boundaries between genera (is an eel a fish or a reptile, is a parrot rational if it has speech?). Moreover, some writers are assigned to more than one category. The bathos, it seems, is not just bad art: it is a transgression of nature, and a destruction of the human capacity to order and understand nature.

Introduction

While suggesting this radical disturbance in which bad writers are participating, Pope is at the same time developing notions of linguistic propriety which he had aired in his comments on Homer. Blackmore is seen as a master of the bathos partly because of his penchant for low objects, as in the case of his elaboration of the idea that Job washed his feet in butter, 'a Circumstance some Poets would have soften'd, or past over'. But the bathos is not only produced by breaches of decorum, it is a misuse of language which has several characteristics – the imitation of a celebrated writer's blemishes, or of his quirks of vocabulary and spelling, and the 'Variegating, Confusing, or Reversing *Tropes* and *Figures*'. In his examples of catachresis, metonymy and synecdoche, Pope draws attention to an affected style which is a corruption of language because it pursues linguistic tricks as an end in themselves.

But Pope is anxious that this treatise should not simply be read as an attack on bad writers: it is, more importantly, a disturbing enquiry into the way we all use language and the ways in which society encourages these abuses. Chapter X on metaphorical language questions the very basis of our habitual metaphorical speech. As for its encouragement by society, the bathos 'is already so much relish'd, encourag'd, and rewarded, by the Nobility and Gentry of *Great Britain*'; but many of the best examples of the abuse of language are provided by tradesmen. All that is needed for the perfection of the bathos is its encouragement by such regulations as are applied to other trades: the new economic structures of English society will serve the bathos admirably. As in *The Dunciad*, Pope shows that the destruction of language and culture, and the obliteration of nature by fantasy, are becoming established as the nation's predominant, indeed, official, culture.

From this part of Pope's work it requires only a small step to pass on to the scurrilous pamphlets. At first sight the attacks on Curll and Dennis may seem strange marginal caricatures in the intervals of Pope's more serious achievements, but the transformation of his opponents into caricatures or quasi-mythological forms is a recurring part of Pope's poetic technique. All readers could compile their own lists of examples, from the sub-human imagery which translates Hervey into Sporus in the *Epistle to Dr. Arbuthnot,* to the ventriloquism which fashions a figure of Richard Bentley in *The Dunciad.* Some of these caricatures pay off personal grudges, yet none has quite the malice and spite which are so evident in the many attacks on Pope himself, and for the most part these grotesque images in Pope's art serve serious purposes.

The attacks on Dennis and Curll are part of an attempt to exhibit the chaotic and destructive side of the literary world. In the case of Dennis it is hard to discover any literary difference of opinion which would account for him being singled out for this treatment: he was a good critic. But Dennis's temper had got the better of him, and he had allowed some rude lines in *An Essay on Criticism* to provoke him into a series of attacks on Pope's work, character and shape. This violated one of the cardinal principles which Pope laid down for literary criticism (and often broke himself), that it should be disinterested. In the preface to his *Works* Pope remarks that bad criticism is less excusable than bad poetry because it has been compounded by ill temper. Similarly Pope's jibes against Addison (for instance, in the character of Atticus in the *Epistle to Dr. Arbuthnot*) are motivated chiefly by a feeling that Addison had allowed his critical judgement to be swayed by flattery and jealousy. So it is that in *The Narrative of Dr. Robert Norris* Pope depicts Dennis as one whose ill temper and unbalanced judgement have degenerated into madness.

Curll's offence was of a different kind. An unscrupulous bookseller who published illicit editions of biography and poetry, he was obviously engaged in the hack trade which turned literature into a desperate and often scandalous device for making money. We can therefore see Pope reacting against Curll's debasement of culture. But another way of understanding what irritated Pope about Curll would be to suggest that Curll's offence was to offer a different image of Pope from the one which Pope himself was busily creating. Sometimes Curll did this by publishing abusive pamphlets; but, more insidiously, he also printed poems which Pope had indeed written but did not want published, or he associated Pope and Lady Mary Wortley Montagu together as social satirists when Pope wanted that friendship seen differently. Curll was therefore making an alternative image, and one which was difficult to refute as it was close to what a sceptical public or jealous rivals might wish to believe, and, moreover, was often constructed out of authentic material.

Just as Pope had displaced Dennis from the rational discipline of letters by portraying him as mad, so he marginalises Curll by a purge which makes him a sick man, and then by having him join the Jews (a group yet more marginal than the Roman Catholics) where by a slip of the knife he is made impotent. Pope would have Curll lose his power to create images. The strategies of these pamphlets, their use of madness, purgation and castration, belong to a world of carnival and subversion. Techniques which in communal ritual and popular tales had been ways of challenging and subverting the established social order are here deployed in defence of high culture. This suggests that Pope felt the established literary and political world to be a world turned upside down, a distorted and monstrous image of the ideal, one whose true character can only be revealed in this way. But the tactics may also disclose Pope's sense of his own marginality. For the leading writer of his day to resort to the traditional methods of the voiceless and dispossessed is itself an eloquent comment on Pope's relation to contemporary power-structures – while no doubt being another clever piece of self-characterisation. In *The Dunciad* this relationship between order and subversion becomes even more complex: like *The Art of Sinking*, *The Dunciad* shows Pope's interest in subverting a genre, not merely inverting its normal significance but using it with subtle and disturbing twists of irony, and treating the bizarre material with an imaginative relish which leaves the reader deeply uneasy, as well as deeply pleased. Pope's pamphlets began by being marginal, ephemeral pieces, but were made classic and canonical by being reprinted in his collected works; this is a development which, like *The Dunciad*, makes the destruction of culture the dominant subject of that culture's art.

Of all Pope's attempts to create an image for himself, the most remarkable was the way in which he deployed his correspondence. Enormous vanity and mendacity went into this project, but good precedents for a writer publishing his own letters had been provided by Cicero and Erasmus, precedents which themselves contributed powerfully to the image thus created. Pope not only edited and revised his letters for publication, he also assigned letters to new (and usually more prestigious) recipients and fabricated some letters completely to fill important gaps (such as the deteriorating relationship with Addison, which had to be seen from Pope's standpoint). Pope also made a point of arranging the letters carefully, not chronologically but by correspondent, so that the 1737 edition opens with letters to and from the great writers of the previous age (Walsh and Wycherley), proceeds to contemporary men of letters (Addison and Steele), exhibits his friendship with the nobility (Bolingbroke and Burlington) and commemorates the important friendships with Gay, Arbuthnot and Swift. The early letters show Pope as a precocious critic, stressing the need for naturalness and simplicity, discussing good and bad imitation and the principles of versification. We also see Pope revising Wycherley's poetry, and suggesting that it might be better as prose. One letter to Wycherley even refers to a comment made by Dryden in conversation, implying that they had been privy to the great man's leisure hours. Another, on Crashaw, defines the revolution in taste which has left Crashaw's wit behind, and observes severely that no man can expect to be a good poet who writes only for diversion.

Pope's religious and political views are aired also, but circumspectly. Several letters on religion stress his dislike of bigotry, and his inclination for religious toleration, views which were courageous rather than expedient since they made him suspected of betrayal by his co-religionists and of duplicity by his protestant enemies. But they have the ring of sincerity, and in one letter to Swift declining to change his religion Pope manages an admirable blend of humour and firmness. As for politics, he once told Allen: 'I never in my life wrote a Letter on these subjects: I content myself as You do, with honest wishes, for honest men to govern us, without asking for any Party, or Denomination, beside' (*Corr.* iv 386-7). This is almost literally true: Pope rarely makes explicit political comments in his letters, but there is plenty of implicit commentary, as, indeed, in that very wish for honest rulers. His political views are signalled by the substantial section of letters which he printed to and from Atterbury, showing his loyalty to the memory of his exiled friend; by the letter to Gay on his rejecting a minor court office; and by the frequent remarks in his letters to Swift that caution is required because their letters are being intercepted. Moreover, Pope's very silence about politics, coupled with his eloquence on the subject of retirement, is itself a clear statement of values.

Swift told Pope that from his letters 'there might be collected...the best System that ever was wrote for the Conduct of human life, at least to shame all reasonable men out of their Follies and Vices' (*Corr.* iv 77). This opinion must have gratified Pope deeply, for his letters both depict and sustain the moral life, particularly through their emphasis on friendship. We may not wish to accept without reservation the picture which they draw of the poet as moral guardian and example; but they are an impressive epitome of Pope's life-long attempt to show that despite the degeneration of language, the frivolity of art and the indifference of government, a few individuals can still fashion for themselves a kind of civilization, if only by making that corruption and betrayal the constant concern of their living and their art.

1. *The Critical Specimen*

John Dennis (1657-1734), poet, dramatist and critic, was embroiled in a dispute with Pope which lasted for twenty years. Dennis took violent exception to Pope's *Essay on Criticism* (1711), probably on account of lines 585-7:

> But *Appius* reddens at each Word you speak,
> And *stares, Tremendous*! with a *threatning Eye,*
> Like some *fierce Tyrant* in *Old Tapestry*!

Six weeks after the publication of Pope's *Essay*, Dennis published his *Reflections Critical and Satyrical, upon a Late Rhapsody, Call'd, An Essay upon Criticism*, a pamphlet which combined astute criticism with malicious abuse. He followed this with *A True Character of Mr. Pope, and His Writings* (1716), *Remarks upon Mr. Pope's Translation of Homer* (1717), *Remarks on Mr. Pope's Rape of the Lock* (1728) and *Remarks upon Several Passages in the Preliminaries to the Dunciad* (1729). There were occasional, but not lasting, reconciliations between the two men. Dennis's attacks on Pope are reprinted in *The Critical Works of John Dennis*, edited by E.N. Hooker, 2 vols. (Baltimore, 1939).

The Critical Specimen was published anonymously in 1711, and attributed to Pope by Ault, who argued that it probably appeared in response to Dennis's *Reflections*, and pointed out links with Pope's later attack on Dennis, *The Narrative of Dr. Robert Norris* (1713). *The Critical Specimen* is aimed chiefly at Dennis's *The Grounds of Criticism in Poetry*, which was published in peculiar circumstances, as E.N. Hooker relates:

A considerable portion of the work was written during 1703, and what was finally printed [in 1704] was but a fragment of the whole which Dennis outlined in his Proposal. The completed opus was to have comprised a full exposition of the nature of poetry and of the sublime, an account of the poetic *genres* and of the essential rules of each, and a criticism of all the '*English* Poets, who have written anything that comes near to Heroick Poetry.'... The *Grounds of Criticism* was the first work of English criticism to be published by subscription and the reason why the whole ambitious undertaking was not finished, lies in the fact that only seventy-seven gentlemen in England were willing to pay a guinea for a folio volume of critical remarks.　　　　　　　　　　　　　(*Critical Works* i 506-7)

The 1704 publication consisted of a preface and proposal, outlining the scope of the work, a specimen, consisting of chapters discussing heroic poetry, including Milton, and a postscript relating the failure of his attempt to publish by subscription. *The Critical Specimen* makes play with various features of Dennis's enterprise: the failed plan to publish by subscription;

Selected prose of Alexander Pope

Dennis's praise of Milton; his analysis of the parts played by the angels and devils in *Paradise Lost*; and his interest in Longinus and the sublime. Part of Dennis's essay is concerned with 'enthusiasm', which he defines as 'a Passion which is moved by the Ideas in Contemplation, or the Meditation of things that belong not to common Life'; he also enumerates six 'Enthusiastick Passions', namely 'Admiration, Terror, Horror, Joy, Sadness, Desire', and he explores the first two at some length (*Critical Works* i 338-63). Pope alludes to other works by Dennis: his play *Rinaldo and Armida* (1699); his poem on the death of William III, *The Monument* (1702) with its preface defending blank verse; and his critical *Essay on the Opera's* (1706). There is also a reference (Ch. 29) to the new method of imitating thunder in the theatre which Dennis introduced in his *Appius and Virginia* (performed in 1709), which is mentioned again in *The Dunciad* (A) ii 218 and note.

Text: *The Critical Specimen* (1711).

THE
CRITICAL
SPECIMEN

Ipsa ingens Arbos, faciemque simillima lauro;
Et si non Alium late jactaret odorem,
Laurus erat.—   Virg.[1]

A
SPECIMEN
OF THE
PREFACE

When I first resolv'd to write the Life of the Renown'd Rinaldo Furioso, *Critick of the Woful Countenance, my Inclinations naturally led me to* Blank Verse, *and to lay a Scheme for a Poem of the* Epick *kind; but I was soon brought off from such an Undertaking when I consider'd, that the* Critick's *Life was made up of such a Medly of Adventures, that though some of them might appear very Noble in the true* Sublime, *yet others were so indifferent that they would have made but a very odd Figure in that Dress: Another prevailing Argument against an* Epick Poem *was, that the* Criticks *Extravagancies could be reduc'd into no manner of Time, for his Whimsical Notions began from his Cradle, and have continued with him ever since.*

There are several Similies, *that are in great Reputation at this present, which are attributed to the Productions of his Youth; by which, it was conjectur'd by his Nurse, and some others of as sound Judgment, that, with his Years, he would arrive to be a famous Poet. 'Tis reported, that he was the first that compared the* Moon *to a* Green Cheese, *an* Ugly Fellow *to an* Owl *in an* Ivy-Bush, *and introduced that general* Simile *now so much in Vogue amongst the* Beau Monde, *as like, as any thing, with several others that are now Exstant in Conversation.*

Another Reason against the Epick Poem, *was, that the* Critick's *Actions did not tend towards bringing about one great Design; for it is manifest by several of his Pranks, that he aimed at being both a* Critick *and a* Poet; *and besides, I could not have raised him to any Degree of Eminency in Either, without deviating from the Truth.*

I must confess, I should have been at very little Loss for the Machinary of the Poem, and that Angels and Devils might have been introduced with very little trouble: I had a Design to have made the Devil make his first Appearance at the Critick's *reading* Milton *backwards, which I concluded would have been a very natural Incident, and not have hauled him in by Head and Shoulders. Upon my communicating this thought to a Friend, I was easily persuaded that a Repetition of some of his own Lines would have raised him altogether as properly; upon which, I immediately made choice of some for that purpose.*

I only mention this, to satisfie the Reader *that I had some Thoughts of writing an* Epick *Poem upon this Subject: But I hope my Reasons against it, have fully convinced him that my digesting the* Critick's *Life in the following manner, as is to be seen in the Contents of the Chapters, will be most Advantagious for the* Critick, *and for the Diversion of all my* Candid Readers.

Before I alter'd my first Design, I had made two Descriptions of the Morning, one of the Evening, another of Midnight; with a Simile, *and some other Sketches which I resolv'd to Embellish when I finish'd the* Epick *Poem I have been before speaking off. I hope the* Reader *will pardon my inserting the* Simile, *being very loath to lose so beautiful a* Fragment: *I would have introduc'd it just before the* Critick *utter'd the ever Memorable Sentence as is now related in the 17th Chapter: Having first describ'd him frowning and swelling with Anger and Resentment, as ready to burst with Passion. I would have proceeded thus,*

> So on *Mæotis'* Marsh, (where Reeds and Rushes
> Hide the deceitful Ground, whose waving Heads
> Oft' bend to *Auster's* blasts, or *Boreas'* Rage,
> The Haunt of the voracious *Stork* or *Bittern,*
> Where, or the *Crane,* Foe to *Pygmæan* Race,
> Or Ravenous *Corm'rants* shake their flabby Wings,
> And from soak'd Plumes disperse a briny Show'r,
> Or spread their feather'd Sails against the Beams,
> Or, of the Rising or *Meridian* Sun)
> *A baneful *Hunch-back'd Toad,* with look Maligne,
> Glares on some Traveller's unwary steps,
> Whether by Chance, or by Misfortune led
> To tread those dark unwholsome, misty Fens,
> Rage strait Collects his Venom all at once,
> And swells his bloated Corps to largest size.

I shall trouble the Reader *no farther with an Account of my first Design, but say something of my present Undertaking.*

I am not without some Apprehensions of having this Work taken out of my Hands, since a false Cervantes, *and Counterfeit* Bickerstaffs *have already endeavoured to impose upon Mankind. But how far the True ones surpass the Impostors, I shall not insist upon; least some envious* Critick *should from thence infer that I by* innuendo *was Haranguing in praise of my own Productions. I shall say only this, That if such Upstarts should arise, take the Advice of Dr.* Case, *which you will find at every Corner*

The Critical Specimen

throughout the City; READ, TRY, JUDGE, AND SPEAK AS YOU FIND.

Before I proceed farther, it is necessary that I say something of the different Kinds of Criticks, range them in their several Orders, and speak to them seperately, &c.

A
SPECIMEN
OF
A Treatise in *Folio*, to be printed by Subscription,
ENTITLED,
The Mirror of Criticisme:
OR,
The History of the Renown'd *Rinaldo Furioso*, Critick of the Woful Countenance.
With a further Comparison of the Renown'd *Rinaldo Furioso*, Critick of the Woful Countenance, and the valiant Restorer of Chivalry Don *Quixote de la Mancha.*

This Work containing *several New Discoveries, never made before*; and being of a very curious and uncommon Nature, will ('tis hop'd) deserve a particular encouragement from the Critical Part of the Town. It will be publish'd either by single Chapters, or in the whole, as the Majority of Subscribers shall please to Appoint; who are desir'd to pay half a Guinea down, and the other half when the Book is delivered. The Author gives Notice, that when his Subscriptions are full, he will (like most of his Contemporaries) begin the Work, or *at least Print a fair List of the Subscribers Names, Titles, and Places of Abode*, so curiously, and in so fair a Letter, that *no Reasonable Man shall grudge his Money for it.* He will in a short time give Information by an Advertisement in the *Spectator* where Subscriptions are to be taken in, being at present much divided in his Opinion, whether to prefer the every way excellent Mr. *Jacob Tonson*, Junior, or Mr. *Bernard Lintot* to be his Bookseller, for the latter of whom he has had a particular consideration since he received from his Honoured Friend *Isaac Bickerstaff*, Esq; the *Eulogium* of –[2] That Eminent and Worthy Citizen Mr. *Bernard Lintot.*

Selected prose of Alexander Pope

CHAPTER, 4TH.

Of the Critick's *first Extravagance, How he took a*
Hobby-Horse *for* Pegasus, *with some other Conceits, not
unworthy Attention, being the shortest Chapter in the whole
Book.*

Cervantes has been very Particular in the Description of Don
Quixote's Horse, 1. though I find, by his own Confession, that he has
omitted several passages relating to the Adventures of that serviceable Creature, which *Cid Hamet Benengeli* thought very material to
the better illustrating his History.

The *Don* was so cursedly pester'd with Enchanters, that he very
often by the height of Imagination, or rather by the delusion of some
envious Necromancers, mistook Appearances, so that, to his Sight,
Windmills appeared *Briareuses*, and *Puppets* real Kings and Queens;
but by all the Accounts I can meet with, *Rosinante* seems to be a real
Horse of Flesh and Bones, and not a wooden Machine endow'd with
any hidden Magical Power. In this respect, I mean in the difference
of their Horses, the *Critick*'s Extravagance, goes beyond the *Don*'s;
for 'tis credibly Attested, that one Day, collecting all his Courage,
He, his adventrous Leg with bold Essay, rais'd from the ground, and
(Oh presumptuous Deed!) an *Hobby-Horse* bestrode, while the *Great
Youth*, that rein'd *Bellerophon*, proud chaumping Steed, prompted
Ambition, and his Breast inspir'd with Emulating Ardor; so have I
often seen in *Bethlem College* a poor unhappy Mortal, whose turn'd
Brains, or Pericranium crack'd or overladen with wild Ideas, which
confus'dly jumble and shatter his disappointed Judgment, Uniting
all his Force at once, with Looks that show high thoughts and daring
Enterprise, bound o'er some slender Chip, or straw Minute. *The
Mirror of Criticisme* being thus mounted without a Saddle, (for he
scorn'd to make use of one of his Father's making) 2. thrice
scamper'd o'er the Floor, whilst, as he scowr'd along, the Stick with
sinuous Trace pursu'd, though ne'er to overtake his wandring steps.
He fancy'd that he was now mounted on *Pegasus*, and that he had
travelled several Leagues through the Air towards Mount *Parnassus*;
during his Imaginary Flight, he was heard to repeat with great
vehemence the following Rhapsody.

> ☞ *Fly* Pegasæan *Steed, thy Rider bear,*
> *To breath the Sweets of pure* Parnassian *Air,*
> *Aloft I'm swiftly born, methinks I rise,*
> 3. *And with my Head* Sublime *can reach the Sky.*

The Critical Specimen

Large Gulps of Aganippe's *streams I'll draw,*
And give to Modern Writers Classic *Law;*
In Grecian Buskins *Tragedy shall Mourn,*
And to its Ancient *Mirth the* Comic *Sock return.*

After he had utter'd the Preceeding Lines several times with a thund'ring Voice, he put himself into distorted Figures, and screw'd his Visage into New Grimaces, crying aloud, *s'Death*, I'm 4. *Roscius*, I'm *Roscius*, I'm *Roscius*. He travels at least once a Week in this manner to make a Visit to the Muses. It happen'd, as he was one Day bestriding his Hobby-Horse, to come into his Head that he had never read in *Milton*, or any of *the Ancients*, that *Pegasus* wore *Bells*; upon which, he in a very great rage tore the *Bells* from his Hobby-Horse, wisely imagining *Pegasus* to be like a Millers Horse, that while he listned to their gingling he slacken'd his Pace, and he has rid him without *Bells* ever since.

Here it will be necessary to inform the Reader of the *Criticks* Chimærical Notions of the *Muses*. He always maintain'd that the *Muses* were a Company of Book learn'd Country Wenches, that liv'd upon a High Hill that reach'd above the Clouds, not unlike the Peak of *Tenariff*; that they had very Hoarse Voices, and had an utter Aversion to all kinds of Musick, that their Mien was Stiff, without the least mixture of the Stately or Janty, that though most of them were lame, yet they always Scamper'd the Plains like Rural Hoydens who on rustick Heel and with uneven Hobling, frisk and bound o'er the Champaign. He held further, that their Faces were homely and without Ornament, that they were of a Brawny Strong Complexion, that they understood the Art of Flying, which they had communicated to himself *Milton*, 5. and two or three others: that they were the Inventers of the Dumb Bell, which is put in Motion with much Labour, but makes no manner of *Musick*: That they had great Skill in Opticks, and had instructed him to see faults in others, and Beautys in himself that could be discover'd by no body else, with some other Notable Inventions which will more naturally imbellish some of the Following Chapters.

The Contents of the Chapters.

Chapter 1.

Of the Criticks Nativity, and how he was oblig'd to the Stars, not for the good fortune or sense they gave him, but for the many *Sublime Similes* they supply'd him with.

Chapter 2.

Of his Education, Person, Parts, and *other inconsiderable Matters*; with some Reflections *very Critical and Satyrical, but nothing to the Purpose.*

Chapter 3.

How after leaving the College, he generously despis'd the *Narrow Soul'd Principles*, taught there, and fell in with the *Modern, free and daring Principles* of the Town, as favouring much more of *Publick Spirit*, together with his *Private Reasons* for so doing.

Chapter 4.

Of the Criticks first Extravagance, How he took a *Hobby-Horse* for *Pegasus*, with some other conceits not unworthy Attention, being the shortest Chapter in the whole Book.

Chapter 5.

How the *Critick* was dub'd a Poet by a conceited frolicksome Country Lass call'd *Moria*[3] which he fancy'd to be one of the *Muses*, with a dissertation upon the *Laurel*, the *Ivy* and *Bays*, and some other Matters very surprizing.

Chapter 6.

How the *Critick* read *Milton* Backward.

Chapter 7.

How he found out that a Minister's Cassock might make two pair of Breeches, and of his Printing a *Probation Sermon*, to make it Manifest that he was *out of* Holy Orders.

Chapter 8.

Of the *Criticks* excellent expedient not to be seen in Dirty Shoos, which was to be carried in a Chair.

The Critical Specimen

Chapter 9.

How when some People were displeas'd at the shortness of his Coat, he made an ample satisfaction with the length of his Sword.

Chapter 10.

How he wrote a Dialogue, which he fancy'd to be a Comedy.

Chapter 11.

Of the Bombarding of *Gibraltar*, and how several of the Cheifs engaged in this dreadful enterprise were contrary to the Law of Arms, almost pelted to Death with *Apples* and *Orange-Peel*.

Chapter 12.

Of the *Criticks* mortal aversion to the *Catt-call*.

Chapter 13.

How the *Critick* was taken up for a *Plotter*, and his being discharg'd as not Guilty, upon a diligent search amongst all his Papers.

Chapter 14.

How he took it in his Head that he had made something like a Tragedy, and how C[*ibbe*]r the *Pantomine* read the First Page *all over*. Of the *Blind Critick who* judg'd at sight.

Chapter 15.

How C[*hristophe*]r R[*i*]ch, Esq; having perus'd the whole, intreated the Author with great Civility to acquaint him *whether it were one of your Tragedys or your Comedys?* and likewise by what Argument he induced C[*hristophe*]r R[*i*]ch, Esq; to believe it really was a Tragedy.

Chapter 16.

How by the *Wonderful force of Magick* he prevail'd with *one* Mr. W[*il*]ks to believe he might pass for an Honourable *Roman Senator*, and with one Mr. *B[oo]th* that he represented a *Roman Tyrant*, and possess'd several others with the like imaginations.

Chapter 17.

Of the Heinous and Unparalell'd Affront offer'd to the most perfect Tragedy since *Euripides*, and how, to the great dishonour of the stage, and without the least regard to their illustrious Characters the aforesaid *Roman Tyrant* and others of very little inferior Dignity were surpris'd in a Brandy Shop, which occasioned that ever Memorable Sentence of the *Criticks*. *Immortal Gods, how can it be, that those who are Brandy Drinkers in the Morning, should become Noble Romans at Night!*

Chapter 18.

Of the Success of the *What d'ye call'um* and the *Criticks Third Night*.

Chapter 19.

The Manner of his buying a pair of Breeches, and what they Cost him *besides Coach Hire*, with other particulars worthy Remark.

Chapter 20.

Of the Manner of Wearing his Breeches, with a short Essay to show that the most Natural Position of *Rolls for Stockings* is about ones Heels.

Chapter 21.

Of the Duel design'd to be fought on Horseback between the *Critick* and a certain *Colonel*, and how it was deferr'd by reason the *Critick* was not vers'd in the *Manage*, and could not procure a War Horse.

Chapter 22.

How the *Critick* fell into a swoon at hearing an *Opera* and what he said at his Recovery. An Extract of his Dissertation against *Operas*.

The Critical Specimen

Chapter 23.

A Discourse of the *Critick* concerning the exact *Contraction* and *Extension* of the *Muscles* of a True *Hypercritical* Countenance, the most learned manner of *Frowning*, as it were with judgment; together with the *whole Art of Staring*.

Chapter 24.

Of the Difficulties he found in attaining to a *C[la]p*, his Discourse with *Hippocrates*, and how at last he was enabled to get one.

Chapter 25.

How *Hippocrates* generously refus'd to take any Fees for the said *C[la]p*.

Chapter 26.

How he writ upon occasion (*vide Spect.* 47.) two good Lines, being the most wonderful and surprizing Adventure in the whole Book.

Chapter 27.

How the *Critick* ingeniously drew *Three Cherubims*, and several *Myriads* of *Subaltern Spirits* out of *Paradise*, which since enter'd into the service of my *L[or]d M[arlbr]o*, and how some of Satan's Angels deserted to the Duke of *Bavaria*.

Chapter 28.

Of the most *amazing Discovery* the *Critick* ever made, showing how and in what manner the *Soul* of a *Late King* was chang'd into a *Seraphim*.[4]

Chapter 29.

Of his Invention of a wonderful *Mustard Bowl* of a prodigious Size for the Players to make *Thunder* with, and the *Tremendous Effects* it had on the *Child* of an Eminent *Citizen*.

Chapter 30.

Of the near Resemblance of Mr. *D[ur]fy* and the *Critick*, both in their Persons and Writings, so that they were often taken one for the other.

Chapter 31.

How the *Critick* had Fourscore Guineas from a certain Nobleman for a Dedication; and how he made a Lady Miscarry at one of his Things that he call'd Tragedy's; with a Discourse upon *Æschylus*, or the *Power of Fustian*.

Chapter 32.

How the *Critick* was invited aboard a Ship at the *Buoy* and *Oar* by an *Officer of the Custom-House*, and how notwithstanding all his *Specious Complements*, he discovered that there was a Design to *Trapan him into* France.

Chapter 33.

The *Critick*'s Reasons for his Suspicion, showing the Extream desire of the *French King* to have him in the *Bastile*, because the sharpness of his *Satyr* (next to Dr. *Partridge*'s) had most provok'd that Monarch, and impair'd his Health more than all the Ill Success of his Armies.

Chapter 34.

A Contention in Civility and good Breeding between the Critick and a little Gentleman of *W[indso]r F[ore]st*, in which the little Gentleman had some Advantage.

Chapter 35.

How, and what Year, Month, and Day, the Critick is to dye, what Will he is to Make, and what dying Words he shall utter, where, and by whom he is to be buried, and what Funeral Orations and Elegies will be made upon him, with his Epitaph a Prophecy, by the *True Individual* Isaac Bickerstaff, *Esq*;

The Critical Specimen

N.B. *For the greater Beauty and Variety of the Impression, the Subscribers are desired to take Notice that the Vertues of the* Critick *are to be printed in a very small neat* Elzevir *Character, and his* Extravagancies *in a Noble large Letter, on Royal Paper.*

To the Reader from the Bookseller.

By the Author's Leave *least I should give the Renown'd* Rinaldo Furioso the Fatigue *of Playing the* Critick *upon this single Chapter,* I have employ'd *one of my Authors to make the following short Remarks.*

Remarks on the Foregoing Chapter.

*The Author has been very just in the Application of this Simile, though he has not dealt so ingeniously with Mankind as to own that he took the Hint from Mr. *Dennis*'s Critical and Satyrical Reflections. *vid.* Crit. and Sat. Reflections. 1 *vide* Don *Quixote.* 2 *Numero Deus impare gaudet* vid. Virg. 3 *Sublimi feriam Sydera Vertice.* vid. Hor. ☞ The Author has made the *Critick* Speak his *Rhapsody* in Rhime, which seems to deviate from his Character, but this, in my Opinion, wants no Excuse, since it was before he had taken the Bells off his *Hobby-Horse.* 4 *Roscius* was a *Roman* Player, *vid. Hor.* 5 Several Judicious *Criticks* of my Acquaintance seem here to doubt the Matter of Fact, since it cannot be sufficiently prov'd from any of his Writings, that he ever allow'd any Proficient in this Art of Flying Except himself and *Milton.*

ADVERTISEMENT.

There is in the Press and will speedily be publish'd Two Dissertations, The first by the Reverend Dr. *B[ent]ly* proving from *Æsop's Fables* that the Author of them was not *Crooked* but *Strait,* The second by Mr. *Dennis* making it plain from the late *Essay* upon *Criticisme* that the Author is by no means *Strait* but *Crooked.*

Price of this Specimen to all but Subscribers Two Pence. And for the Encouragement of such well dispos'd Persons as will give it about in Charity 20s. *per* Hundred.

2. Contributions to
The Spectator

The Spectator, edited by Joseph Addison (1672-1719) and Richard Steele (1672-1729), ran from 1 March 1711 to 6 December 1712. Three contributions were acknowledged by Pope, and Ault attributed to him a further nine. Number 406 was included by Pope in his collected correspondence in 1735 as a private letter to Steele under the date of 18 June 1712, and number 532 was assigned to Pope by Steele in *The Spectator*.

Text: from the original parts.

Contributions to *The Spectator*

406

Monday, June 16, 1712

ON A CITY AND COUNTRY LIFE

Dear Sir,

You have obliged me with a very kind Letter; by which I find you shift the Scene of your Life from the Town to the Country, and enjoy that mixt State which wise Men both delight in, and are qualified for. Methinks most of the Philosophers and Moralists have run too much into Extremes in praising entirely either Solitude or publick Life; in the former Men generally grow useless by too much Rest, and in the latter are destroy'd by too much Precipitation: As Waters lying still, putrify and are good for nothing; and running violently on, do but the more Mischief in their Passage to others, and are swallow'd up and lost the sooner themselves. Those who, like you, can make themselves useful to all States, should be like gentle Streams, that not only glide through lonely Vales and Forests amidst the Flocks and Shepherds, but visit populous Towns in their Course, and are at once of Ornament and Service to them. But there is another sort of People who seem design'd for Solitude, those I mean who have more to hide than to shew: As for my own Part, I am one of those of whom *Seneca* says, *Tam Umbratiles sunt, ut putent in turbido esse quicquid in luce est.*[1] Some Men, like Pictures, are fitter for a Corner than a full Light; and I believe such as have a natural Bent to Solitude, are like Waters which may be forc'd into Fountains, and exalted to a great Height, may make a much nobler Figure and a much louder Noise, but after all run more smoothly, equally, and plentifully, in their own natural Course upon the Ground. The Consideration of this would make me very well contented with the Possession only of that Quiet which *Cowley* calls the Companion of Obscurity[2]; but whoever has the Muses too for his Companions, can never be idle enough to be uneasy. Thus, Sir, you see I would flatter my self into a good Opinion of my own Way of living: *Plutarch* just now told me, that 'tis in humane Life as in a Game at Tables, one may wish he had the highest Cast, but if his Chance be otherwise, he is e'en to play it as well as he can, and make the best of it.[3]

I am,

SIR,

Your most obliged,

and most humble Servant.

33

532
Monday, November 10, 1712.

ON THE LAST WORDS OF ADRIAN

Mr. SPECTATOR,

I Was the other Day in Company with five or six Men of some Learning; where chancing to mention the famous Verses which the Emperor *Adrian* spoke on his Death-bed, they were all agreed that 'twas a Piece of Gayety unworthy that Prince in those Circumstances. I could not but dissent from this Opinion: Methinks it was by no Means a gay, but a very serious Soliloquy to his Soul at the Point of his Departure; in which Sense I naturally took the Verses at my first reading them when I was very young, and before I knew what Interpretation the World generally put upon them.

> *Animula vagula, blandula,*
> *Hospes Comesque corporis,*
> *Quæ nunc abibis in loca?*
> *Pallidula, rigida, nudula,*
> *Nec (ut soles) dabis Joca!*[4]

Alas, my Soul! thou pleasing Companion of this Body, thou fleeting Thing that art now deserting it! whither art thou flying? to what unknown Region? Thou art all trembling, fearful, and pensive. Now what is become of thy former Wit and Humour? thou shalt jest and be gay no more! I confess I cannot apprehend where lies the Trifling in all this; 'tis the most natural and obvious Reflection imaginable to a dying Man; and if we consider the Emperor was a Heathen, that Doubt concerning the future Fate of his Soul will seem so far from being the Effect of want of Thought, that 'twas scarce reasonable he should think otherwise; not to mention that here is a plain Confession included of his Belief in its Immortality. The diminutive Epithets of *Vagula*, *Blandula*, and the rest, appear not to me as Expressions of Levity, but rather of Endearment and Concern; such as we find in *Catullus*, and the Authors of *Hendeca-syllabi* after him, where they are used to express the utmost Love and Tenderness for their Mistresses—If you think me right in my Notion of the last Words of *Adrian*, be pleased to insert this in the *Spectator*; if not, to suppress it.

I am, &c.

3. Contributions to
The Guardian

After *The Spectator* came to an end, Steele started *The Guardian*, which ran from 12 March to 1 October 1713. Pope acknowledged eight contributions to this journal, of which all but one are printed here, the exception being no.78, *A Receipt to make an Epic Poem*, which later formed chapter xv of *The Art of Sinking in Poetry* and is printed there. A modern edition of *The Guardian* has been produced by John Calhoun Stephens (Lexington, 1982).

Text: from the original parts.

4

Monday, March 16, 1713.

ON DEDICATIONS

It matters not how false or forc't,
So the best things be said o' th' worst;
It goes for nothing when 'tis said,
Only the Arrow's drawn to th' head,
Whether it be a Swan or Goose
They level at: So Shepherds use
To set the same Mark on the Hip
Both of their sound and rotten Sheep.   Hudibras.[1]

Though most Things which are wrong in their own Nature are at once confessed and absolv'd in that single Word the *Custom*; yet there are some, which as they have a dangerous Tendency, a thinking Man will the less excuse on that very Account. Among these I cannot but reckon the common Practise of *Dedications*, which is of so much the worse Consequence, as 'tis generally used by People of Politeness, and whom a Learned Education for the most part ought to have inspired with nobler and juster Sentiments. This Prostitution of Praise is not only a Deceit upon the Gross of Mankind, who take their Notion of Characters from the Learned; but also the better Sort must by this means lose some part at least of that Desire of Fame which is the Incentive to generous Actions, when they find it promiscuously bestowed on the Meritorious and Undeserving: Nay, the Author himself, let him be supposed to have ever so true a Value for the Patron, can find no Terms to express it, but what have been already used, and rendered suspected by Flatterers. Even Truth itself in a Dedication is like an Honest Man in a Disguise or Vizor-Masque, and will appear a Cheat by being drest so like one. Tho' the Merit of the Person is beyond Dispute, I see no reason that because one Man is eminent, therefore another has a right to be impertinent, and throw Praises in his Face. 'Tis just the Reverse of the Practise of the Ancient *Romans*, when a Person was advanced to Triumph for his Services: As they hired People to rail at him in that Circumstance, to make him as humble as they could, we have Fellows to flatter him, and make him as Proud as they can. Supposing the Writer not to be Mercenary, yet the great Man is no more in Reason obliged to thank him for his Picture in a Dedication, than to thank the Painter for that on a Sign-Post; except it be a less Injury to touch the most Sacred Part of him, his Character, than to make free with his Countenance

only. I shou'd think nothing justified me in this Point, but the
Patron's Permission before-hand, that I shou'd draw him as like as I
cou'd; whereas most Authors proceed in this Affair just as a Dawber
I have heard of, who not being able to draw Portraits after the Life,
was used to paint Faces at Random, and look out afterwards for
People whom he might persuade to be like them. To express my
Notion of the Thing in a Word: To say more to a Man than one
thinks, with a Prospect of Interest, is dishonest; and without it,
foolish. And whoever has had Success in such an Undertaking, must
of necessity at once, think himself in his Heart a Knave for having
done it, and his Patron a Fool for having believed it.

I have sometimes been entertained with considering Dedications
in no very common Light. By observing what Qualities our Writers
think it will be most pleasing to others to compliment them with,
one may form some Judgment which are most so to themselves; and,
in consequence, what sort of People they are. Without this View one
can read very few Dedications but will give us cause to wonder,
either how such things came to be said at all, or how they were said
to such Persons? I have known an Hero complimented upon the
decent Majesty and State he assumed after Victory; and a Nobleman
of a different Character applauded for his Condescention to Inferiors. This would have seemed very strange to me, but that I
happened to know the Authors. He who made the first Compliment
was a lofty Gentleman, whose Air and Gait discovered when he had
published a new Book; and the other tippled every Night with the
Fellows who laboured at the Press while his own Writings were
working off. 'Tis observable of the Female Poets and Ladies
Dedicatory, that here (as elsewhere) they far exceed us in any Strain
or Rant. As Beauty is the thing that Sex are piqu'd upon, they speak
of it generally in a more elevated Style than is used by the Men. They
adore in the same manner as they would be adored. So when the
Authoress of a famous Modern Romance begs a young Nobleman's
Permission to pay him her *Kneeling Adorations*, I am far from
censuring the Expression, as some Criticks would do, as deficient in
Grammar or Sence; but I reflect, that Adorations paid in that
Posture are what a Lady might expect herself, and my Wonder
immediately ceases. These, when they flatter most, do but as they
would be done unto; for as none are so much concerned at being
injured by Calumnies, as they who are readiest to cast them upon
their Neighbours; so 'tis certain, none are so guilty of Flattery to
others, as those who most ardently desire it themselves.

What led me into these Thoughts, was a Dedication I happened upon this Morning. The Reader must understand that I treat the least Instances or Remains of Ingenuity, with respect in what Places soever found, or under whatever Circumstances of Disadvantage. From this Love to Letters I have been so happy in my Searches after Knowledge, that I have found unvalued Repositories of Learning in the Lining of Bandboxes. I look upon these Pasteboard Edifices, adorned with the Fragments of the Ingenious, with the same Veneration as Antiquaries upon ruined Buildings, whose Walls preserve divers Inscriptions and Names, which are no where else to be found in the World. This Morning, when one of Lady *Lizard*'s Daughters was looking over some Hoods and Ribbands, brought by her Tirewoman, with great Care and Diligence, I employed no less in examining the Box which contained them; it was lined with certain Scenes of a Tragedy, written (as appeared by a part of the Title there extant) by one of the Fair Sex. What was most legible was the Dedication; which, by reason of the Largeness of the Characters, was least defaced by those *Gothick* Ornaments of Flourishes and Foliage, wherewith the Compilers of these sort of Structures do often industriously obscure the Works of the Learned. As much of it as I could read with any Ease, I shall communicate to the Reader, as follows.

'**** Though it is a kind of *Prophanation* to approach your Grace with so poor an *Offering*, yet when I reflect how acceptable a *Sacrifice* of First-Fruits was to *Heaven*, in the earliest and *purest Ages of Religion*, that they were honour'd with *solemn Feasts*, and *consecrated to Altars* by a *Divine Command*, **** upon that Consideration, as an Argument of particular *Zeal*, I dedicate. ***'Tis impossible to behold you without *Adoring*; yet dazled and aw'd by the *Glory* that surrounds you, Men feel a *sacred Power*, that refines their Flames, and renders them pure as those we ought to offer to the Deity. ***** The *Shrine* is worthy the *Divinity* that inhabits it. In your Grace we see what Woman was before she fell, how nearly allied to the *Purity* and *Perfection* of *Angels*. And WE ADORE AND BLESS THE GLORIOUS WORK!'

Undoubtedly these, and other Periods of this most Pious Dedication, could not but convince the Dutchess of what the Eloquent Authoress assures her at the End, that she was her Servant *with most ardent Devotion*. I think this a Pattern of a new Sort of Stile, not yet taken Notice of by the Criticks, which is above the Sublime, and may be called *the Celestial*; that is, when the most sacred Phrases appropriated to the Honour of the Deity are applied to a Mortal of good Quality. As I am naturally emulous, I cannot but endeavour, in Imitation of this Lady, to be the Inventor, or, at least, the first Producer of a new kind of Dedication, very different from hers and most others, since it has not a Word but what the Author religiously thinks in it. It may serve for almost any Book, either Prose or Verse, that has, is, or shall be published, and might run in this manner.

The AUTHOR to HIMSELF.

Most Honoured Sir,
THESE Labours, upon many Considerations, so properly belong to none as to you: First, as it was your most earnest Desire alone that could prevail upon me to make them publick: Then, as I am secure (from that constant Indulgence you have ever shown to all which is mine) that no Man will so readily take them into Protection, or so zealously defend them. Moreover, there's none can so soon discover the Beauties; and there are some Parts, which 'tis possible few besides your self are capable of understanding. Sir, the Honour, Affection and Value I have for you are beyond Expression; as great, I am sure, or greater, than any Man else can bear you. As for any Defects which others may pretend to discover in you, I do faithfully declare I was never able to perceive them; and doubt not but those Persons are actuated purely by a Spirit of Malice or Envy, the inseparable Attendants on shining Merit and Parts, such as I have always esteemed yours to be. It may perhaps be looked upon as a kind of Violence to Modesty, to say this to you in Publick; but you may believe me, 'tis no more than I have a thousand times thought of you in Private. Might I follow the Impulse of my Soul, there is no Subject I could launch into with more Pleasure than your Panegy-rick. But since something is due to Modesty, let me conclude by telling you, that there's nothing so much I desire as to know you more thoroughly than I have yet the Happiness of doing. I may then hope to be capable to do you some real Service; but 'till then can only assure you, that I shall continue to be, as I am more than any Man alive,

> *Dearest Sir,*
> *Your Affectionate Friend, and*
> *The greatest of your Admirers.*

40

Monday, April 27, 1713.

ON PASTORALS

Compulerantque Greges Corydon & Thyrsis in unum.
Ex illo Corydon, Corydon est tempore nobis.[1]

I designed to have troubled the Reader with no farther Discourses of *Pastorals*, but being informed that I am taxed of Partiality in not mentioning an Author, whose Eclogues are published in the same Volume with Mr. *Philips*'s; I shall employ this Paper in Observations upon him, written in the free Spirit of Criticism, and without Apprehension of offending that Gentleman, whose Character it is, that he takes the greatest Care of his Works before they are published, and has the least concern for them afterwards.[2]

I have laid it down as the first Rule of Pastoral, that its Idea should be taken from the Manners of the *Golden Age*, and the Moral form'd upon the Representation of Innocence; 'tis therefore plain that any Deviations from that Design degrade a Poem from being true Pastoral. In this View it will appear that *Virgil* can only have two of his Eclogues allowed to be such: His First and Ninth must be rejected, because they describe the Ravages of Armies, and Oppressions of the Innocent; *Corydon*'s Criminal Passion for *Alexis* throws out the Second; the Calumny and Railing in the Third are not proper to that State of Concord; the Eighth represents unlawful Ways of procuring Love by Inchantments, and introduces a Shepherd whom an inviting Precipice tempts to Self-Murder. As to the Fourth, Sixth, and Tenth, they are given up by *Heinsius, Salmasius, Rapin,*[3] and the Criticks in general. They likewise observe that but eleven of all the *Idyllia* of *Theocritus* are to be admitted as Pastorals; and even out of that Number the greater Part will be excluded for one or other of the Reasons abovementioned. So that when I remark'd in a former Paper, that *Virgil*'s Eclogues, taken all together, are rather *Select Poems* than *Pastorals*; I might have said the same thing, with no less Truth, of *Theocritus*. The Reason of this I take to be yet unobserved by the Criticks, *viz. They never meant them all for Pastorals.* Which it is plain *Philips* hath done, and in that Particular excelled both *Theocritus* and *Virgil*.

As Simplicity is the distinguishing Characteristick of Pastoral, *Virgil* hath been thought guilty of too Courtly a Stile; his Language is perfectly pure, and he often forgets he is among Peasants. I have frequently wonder'd that since he was so conversant in the Writings of *Ennius*,[4] he had not imitated the Rusticity of the *Doric*, as well, by the help of the old obsolete *Roman* Language, as *Philips* hath by the antiquated *English*: For Example, might he not have said *Quoi* instead of *Cui; Quoijum* for *Cujum; volt* for *vult*, &c. as well as our Modern hath *Welladay* for *Alas, Whilome* for *of Old, make mock* for *deride*, and *witless Younglings* for *simple Lambs*, &c. by which Means he had attained as much of the Air of *Theocritus*, as *Philips* hath of *Spencer*.

Mr. *Pope* hath fallen into the same Error with *Virgil*. His Clowns do not converse in all the Simplicity proper to the Country: His Names are borrow'd from *Theocritus* and *Virgil*, which are improper to the Scene of his Pastorals. He introduces *Daphnis, Alexis* and *Thyrsis* on *British* Plains, as *Virgil* had done before him on the *Mantuan*; whereas *Philips*, who hath the strictest Regard to Propriety, makes choice of Names peculiar to the Country, and more agreeable to a Reader of Delicacy; such as *Hobbinol, Lobbin, Cuddy*, and *Colin Clout*.

So easie as Pastoral Writing may seem, (in the Simplicity we have described it) yet it requires *great Reading*, both of the *Ancients* and *Moderns*, to be a Master of it. *Philips* hath given us manifest Proofs of his Knowledge of Books; it must be confessed his Competitor hath imitated some single Thoughts of the Ancients well enough, if we consider he had not the Happiness of an University Education; but he hath dispersed them, here and there, without that Order and Method which Mr. *Philips* observes, whose whole third Pastoral is an Instance how well he hath studied the fifth of *Virgil*, and how judiciously reduced *Virgil*'s Thoughts to the Standard of Pastoral; as his Contention of *Colin Clout* and the *Nightingale* shows with what Exactness he hath imitated *Strada*.[5]

When I remarked it as a principal Fault to introduce Fruits and Flowers of a Foreign Growth, in Descriptions where the Scene lies in our Country, I did not design that Observation should extend also to Animals, or the Sensitive Life; for *Philips* hath with great Judgement described *Wolves* in *England* in his first Pastoral. Nor would I have a Poet slavishly confine himself (as Mr. *Pope* hath done) to one particular Season of the Year, one certain time of the Day, and one unbroken Scene in each Eclogue. 'Tis plain *Spencer* neglected this Pedantry, who in his Pastoral of *November* mentions the mournful Song of the Nightingale:

Sad Philomel *her Song in Tears doth Steep*.[6]

Selected prose of Alexander Pope

And Mr. *Philips*, by a Poetical Creation, hath raised up finer Beds of Flowers than the most industrious Gardiner; his Roses, Lillies and Daffadils blow in the same Season.

But the better to discover the Merits of our two Contemporary Pastoral Writers, I shall endeavour to draw a Parallel of them, by setting several of their particular Thoughts in the same light, whereby it will be obvious how much *Philips* hath the Advantage. With what Simplicity he introduces two Shepherds singing alternately.

Hobb. *Come*, Rosalind, *O come, for without thee*
   What Pleasure can the Country have for me:
   Come, Rosalind, *O come; my brinded Kine,*
   My snowy Sheep, my Farm, and all is thine.
Lanq. *Come* Rosalind, *O come; here shady Bowers*
   Here are cool Fountains, and here springing Flow'rs.
   Come, Rosalind; *Here ever let us stay,*
   And sweetly wast, our live-long Time away.

Our other Pastoral Writer, in expressing the same Thought, deviates into downright Poetry.

Streph. *In Spring the Fields, in Autumn Hills I love,*
   At Morn the Plains, at Noon the shady Grove,
   But Delia *always; forc'd from Delia's Sight,*
   Nor Plains at Morn, nor Groves at Noon delight.
Daph. Sylvia's *like Autumn ripe, yet mild as* May,
   More bright than Noon, yet fresh as early Day;
   Ev'n Spring displeases, when she shines not here.
   But blest with her, 'tis Spring throughout the Year.

In the first of these Authors, two Shepherds thus innocently describe the Behaviour of their Mistresses.

Hobb. *As* Marian *bath'd, by chance I passed by,*
   She blush'd, and at me cast a side-long Eye:
   Then swift beneath the Crystal Wave she try'd
   Her beauteous Form, but all in vain, to hide.
Lanq. *As I to cool me bath'd one sultry Day,*
   Fond Lydia *lurking in the Sedges lay.*
   The Wanton laugh'd, and seem'd in Haste to fly;
   Yet often stopp'd, and often turn'd her Eye.

The other Modern (who it must be confessed hath a knack of Versifying) hath it as follows.

Streph. *Me gentle* Delia *beckons from the Plain,*
   Then, hid in Shades, eludes her eager Swain;
   But feigns a Laugh, to see me search around,
   And by that Laugh the willing Fair is found.

Contributions to *The Guardian*

Daph. *The sprightly* Sylvia *trips along the Green,*
    She runs, but hopes she does not run unseen;
    While a kind Glance at her Pursuer flyes,
    How much at Variance are her Feet and Eyes!

There is nothing the Writers of this kind of Poetry are fonder of, than Descriptions of Pastoral Presents. *Philips* says thus of a Sheephook.

    Of Season'd Elm; where Studs of Brass appear,
    To speak the Giver's Name, the Month and Year.
    The Hook of polish'd Steel, the Handle turn'd,
    And richly by the Graver's Skill adorn'd.

The other of a Bowl embossed with Figures.

    —where wanton Ivy twines,
    And swelling Clusters bend the curling Vines;
    Four Figures rising from the Work appear,
    The various Seasons of the rolling Year;
    And what is That which binds the radiant Sky,
    Where twelve bright Signs in beauteous Order lie.

The Simplicity of the Swain in this Place, who forgets the Name of the *Zodiack*, is no ill Imitation of *Virgil*; but how much more plainly and unaffectedly would *Philips* have dressed this Thought in his *Doric*?

    And what That hight, which girds the Welkin sheen,
    Where twelve gay Signs in meet array are seen.

If the Reader would indulge his Curiosity any farther in the Comparison of Particulars, he may read the first Pastoral of *Philips* with the second of his Contemporary, and the fourth and sixth of the former, with the fourth and first of the latter; where several Parallel Places will occur to every one.

Having now shown some Parts, in which these two Writers may be compared, it is a Justice I owe to Mr. *Philips*, to discover those in which no Man can compare with him. First, That *beautiful Rusticity*, of which I shall only produce two Instances, out of a hundred not yet quoted.

    O woful Day! O Day of Woe, quoth he,
    And woful I, who live the Day to see!

That Simplicity of Diction, the Melancholy Flowing of the Numbers, the Solemnity of the Sound, and the easie Turn of the Words, in this *Dirge* (to make use of our Author's Expression) are extreamly Elegant.

In another of his Pastorals, a Shepherd utters a *Dirge* not much inferior to the former, in the following Lines.

    Ah me the while! ah me! the luckless Day,
    Ah luckless Lad! the rather might I say;

> *Ah silly I ! more silly than my Sheep,*
> *Which on the flowry Plains I once did keep.*

How he still Charms the Ear with these artful Repetitions of the
Epithets; and how significant is the last Verse! I defy the most
common Reader to repeat them, without feeling some Motions of
Compassion.

In the next Place I shall rank his *Proverbs*, in which I formerly
observed he excells: For Example,

> *A rolling Stone is ever bare of Moss;*
> *And, to their Cost, green Years old Proverbs cross.*
> —*He that late lyes down, as late will rise,*
> *And, Sluggard-like, till Noon-day snoaring lyes.*
> *Against Ill-Luck all cunning Fore-sight fails;*
> *Whether we sleep or wake it nought avails.*
> —*Nor fear, from upright Sentence, Wrong.*

Lastly, His *Elegant Dialect*, which alone might prove him the eldest
Born of *Spencer*, and our only true *Arcadian*; I should think it proper
for the several Writers of Pastoral, to confine themselves to their
several *Counties*. *Spencer* seems to have been of this Opinion: for he
hath laid the Scene of one of his Pastorals in *Wales*, where with all
the Simplicity natural to that Part of our Island, one Shepherd bids
the other *Good-morrow* in an unusual and elegant Manner.

> Diggon Davy, *I bid hur God-day:*
> *Or* Diggon *hur is, or I mis-say.*

Diggon answers,

> *Hur was hur while it was Day-light;*
> *But now hur is a most wretched Wight,* &c.[7]

But the most beautiful Example of this kind that I ever met with,
is in a very valuable Piece, which I chanced to find among some old
Manuscripts, entituled, *A Pastoral Ballad*; which I think, for its
Nature and Simplicity, may (notwithstanding the Modesty of the
Title) be allowed a Perfect Pastoral: It is composed in the *Somerset-
shire* Dialect, and the Names such as are proper to the Country
People. It may be observed, as a further Beauty of this Pastoral, the
Words *Nymph, Dryad, Naiad, Fawn, Cupid,* or *Satyr,* are not once
mentioned through the whole. I shall make no Apology for Inserting
some few Lines of this excellent Piece. *Cicily* breaks thus into the
Subject, as she is going a Milking;

Cicily. *Rager go vetch tha Kee*[8], *or else tha Zun,*
   Will quite be go, be vore c'have half a don.
Roger. *Thou shouldst not ax ma tweece, but I've a be*
   To dreave our Bull to Bull tha Parson's Kee.

It is to be observed, that this whole Dialogue is formed upon the

Passion of Jealousie; and his mentioning the Parson's Kine naturally revives the Jealousie of the Shepherdess *Cicily*, which she expresses as follows:

Cicily. *Ah* Rager, Rager, *chez was zore avraid*
    Ween in yond Vield you kiss'd tha Parsons Maid:
    Is this the Love that once to me you zed,
    When from tha Wake thou brought'st me Gingerbread?
Roger. *Cicily thou charg'st me false,—I'll zwear to thee,*
    Tha Parson's Maid is still a Maid for me.

In which Answer of his are express'd at once that *Spirit of Religion*, and that *Innocence of the Golden Age*, so necessary to be observed by all Writers of Pastoral.

At the Conclusion of this Piece, the Author reconciles the Lovers, and ends the Eclogue the most Simply in the World.

    So Rager *parted vor to vetch tha Kee,*
    And vor her Bucket in went Cicily.

I am loath to show my Fondness for Antiquity so far as to prefer this Ancient *British* Author to our present *English* Writers of Pastoral; but I cannot avoid making this obvious Remark, that both *Spencer* and *Philips* have hit into the same Road with this old *West Country* Bard of ours.

After all that hath been said, I hope none can think it any Injustice to Mr. *Pope*, that I forbore to mention him as a Pastoral Writer; since upon the whole, he is of the same Class with *Moschus* and *Bion*,[9] whom we have excluded that Rank; and of whose Eclogues, as well as some of *Virgil's*, it may be said, that according to the Description we have given of this sort of Poetry, they are by no means *Pastorals*, but *something Better*.

61

Thursday, May 21, 1713.

AGAINST BARBARITY TO ANIMALS

—Primoque a cæde ferarum
Incaluisse putem maculatum sanguine ferrum.   Ovid.[1]

I cannot think it extravagant to imagine, that Mankind are no less, in Proportion, accountable for the ill Use of their Dominion over Creatures of the lower Rank of Beings, than for the Exercise of Tyranny over their own Species. The more entirely the Inferior Creation is submitted to our Power, the more answerable we should seem for our Mismanagement of it; and the rather, as the very

45

Condition of Nature renders these Creatures incapable of receiving any Recompence in another Life for their ill Treatment in this.

'Tis observable of those noxious Animals, which have Qualities most powerful to injure us, that they naturally avoid Mankind, and never hurt us unless provoked, or necessitated by Hunger. Man, on the other Hand, seeks out and pursues even the most inoffensive Animals, on purpose to persecute and destroy them.

Montaigne[2] thinks it some Reflection upon Human Nature it self, that few People take Delight in seeing Beasts caress or play together, but almost every one is pleased to see them lacerate and worry one another. I am sorry this Temper is become almost a distinguishing Character of our own Nation, from the Observation which is made by Foreigners of our beloved Pastimes, *Bear-baiting, Cock-fighting*, and the like. We should find it hard to vindicate the destroying of any thing that has Life, meerly out of Wantonness; yet in this Principle our Children are bred up, and one of the first Pleasures we allow them, is the Licence of inflicting Pain upon poor Animals: Almost as soon as we are sensible what Life is our selves, we make it our Sport to take it from other Creatures. I cannot but believe a very good Use might be made of the Fancy which Children have for Birds and Insects. Mr. *Lock*[3] takes Notice of a Mother who permitted them to her Children, but rewarded or punished them as they treated them well or ill. This was no other than entring them betimes into a daily Exercise of Humanity, and improving their very Diversion to a Virtue.

I fancy too, some Advantage might be taken of the common Notion, that 'tis ominous or unlucky to destroy some sorts of Birds, as *Swallows* and *Martins*; this Opinion might possibly arise from the confidence these Birds seem to put in us by building under our Roofs, so that it is a kind of Violation of the Laws of Hospitality to murder them. As for *Robin-red-breasts* in particular, 'tis not improbable they owe their Security to the old Ballad of *the Children in the Wood*. However it be, I don't know, I say, why this Prejudice, well improved and carried as far as it would go, might not be made to conduce to the Preservation of many innocent Creatures, which are now exposed to all the Wantonness of an ignorant Barbarity.

There are other Animals that have the Misfortune, for no manner of Reason, to be treated as common Enemies where-ever found. The Conceit that a *Cat* has *nine Lives* has cost at least nine Lives in ten of the whole Race of 'em: Scarce a Boy in the Streets but has in this Point outdone *Hercules* himself, who was famous for killing a Monster that had but *Three Lives*. Whether the unaccountable

Animosity against this useful Domestick may be any Cause of the general Persecution of *Owles*, (who are a sort of feathered Cats) or whether it be only an unreasonable Pique the Moderns have taken to a serious Countenance, I shall not determine. Tho' I am inclined to believe the former; since I observe the sole Reason alledged for the Destruction of *Frogs* is because they are like *Toads*. Yet amidst all the Misfortunes of these unfriended Creatures, 'tis some Happiness that we have not yet taken a Fancy to eat them: For should our Countrymen refine upon the *French* never so little, 'tis not to be conceived to what unheard of Torments *Owles*, *Cats*, and *Frogs* may be yet reserved.

When we grow up to Men, we have another Succession of Sanguinary Sports; in particular *Hunting*. I dare not attack a Diversion which has such Authority and Custom to support it, but must have leave to be of Opinion, that the Agitation of that Exercise, with the Example and Number of the Chasers, not a little contribute to resist those *Checks*, which Compassion would naturally suggest in behalf of the Animal pursued. Nor shall I say with Monsieur *Fleury*,[4] that this Sport is *a Remain of the* Gothic *Barbarity*; but I must animadvert upon a certain Custom yet in Use with us, and barbarous enough to be derived from the *Goths*, or even the *Scythians*: I mean that Savage Compliment our Huntsmen pass upon Ladies of Quality, who are present at the Death of a Stag, when they put the Knife in their Hands to cut the Throat of a helpless, trembling and weeping Creature.

—Questuque cruentus,
Atque Imploranti similis.—[5]

But if our *Sports* are destructive, our *Glottony* is more so, and in a more inhuman Manner. *Lobsters roasted alive, Piggs whipp'd to Death, Fowls sowed up*, are Testimonies of our outragious Luxury. Those, who (as *Seneca*[6] expresses it) divide their Lives betwixt an Anxious Conscience and a Nauseated Stomach, have a just Reward of their Gluttony in the Diseases it brings with it: For Human Savages, like other wild Beasts, find Snares and Poyson in the Provisions of Life, and are allured by their Appetite to their Destruction. I know nothing more shocking, or horrid, than the Prospect of one of their Kitchins cover'd with Blood, and filled with the Cries of Creatures expiring in Tortures. It gives one an Image of a *Giant's Den* in a Romance, bestrow'd with the scattered Heads and mangled Limbs of those who were slain by his Cruelty.

The excellent *Plutarch*[7] (who has more Strokes of Good-nature in his Writings than I remember in any Author) cites a Saying of *Cato* to this effect, *That 'tis no easie Task to preach to the Belly which has no Ears.*

'Yet if (says he) we are ashamed to be so out of Fashion as not to Offend, let us at least Offend with some Discretion and Measure. If we kill an Animal for our Provision, let us do it with the Meltings of Compassion, and without tormenting it. Let us consider, that 'tis in its own Nature Cruelty to put a living Creature to Death; we at least destroy a Soul that has Sense and Perception'—In the Life of *Cato* the Censor, he takes occasion from the severe Disposition of that Man to Discourse in this manner. 'It ought to be esteemed a Happiness to Mankind, that our Humanity has a wider Sphere to exert itself in, than bare Justice. It is no more than the Obligation of our very Birth to practise Equity to our own kind, but Humanity may be extended thro' the whole Order of Creatures, even to the meanest: Such Actions of Charity are the Over-flowings of a mild Good nature on all below us. It is certainly the part of a well-natured Man to take care of his Horses and Dogs, not only in expectation of their Labour while they are Foals and Whelps, but even when their old Age has made them incapable of Service.'

History tells us of a wise and polite Nation that rejected a Person of the first Quality, who stood for a Judiciary Office, only because he had been observed in his Youth, to take pleasure in tearing and murdering of Birds. And of another that expelled a Man out of the Senate for dashing a Bird against the Ground which had taken shelter in his Bosom. Every one knows how remarkable the *Turks* are for their Humanity in this kind: I remember an *Arabian* Author, who has written a Treatise to show, how far a Man, supposed to have subsisted in a Desart Island, without any Instruction, or so much as the sight of any other Man, may, by the pure Light of Nature, attain the Knowledge of Philosophy and Virtue. One of the first things he makes him observe is, that Universal Benevolence of Nature in the Protection and Preservation of its Creatures. In Imitation of which, the first Act of Virtue he thinks his Self-taught Philosopher would of Course fall into is, to Relieve and Assist all the Animals about him in their Wants and Distresses.

Ovid has some very tender and pathetick Lines applicable to this Occasion.

> *Quid meruistis oves, placidum pecus, inque tegendos*
> *Natum homines, pleno quæ fertis in Ubere nectar?*
> *Mollia quæ nobis vestras velamina lanas*
> *Præbetis; vitaque magis quam morte juvatis.*
> *Quid meruëre boves, animal sine fraude dolisque,*
> *Innocuum, simplex, natum tolerare labores?*
> *Immemor est demum, nec frugum munere dignus,*
> *Qui potuit, curvi dempto modo pondere aratri,*

Ruricolam mactare suum—
Quam malè consuevit, quam se parat ille cruori
Impius humano, Vituli qui guttura cultro
Rumpit, & immotas prêbet mugitibus aures!
Aut qui vagitus similes puerilibus hædum
Edentem jugulare potest!—[8]

Perhaps that Voice or Cry so nearly resembling the Human, with which Providence has endued so many different Animals, might purposely be given them to move our Pity, and prevent those Cruelties we are too apt to inflict on our Fellow Creatures.

There is a Passage in the Book of *Jonas*,[9] when God declares his Unwillingness to destroy *Nineveh*, where methinks that Compassion of the Creator, which extends to the meanest Rank of his Creatures, is expressed with wonderful Tenderness—*Should I not spare Nineveh the great City, wherein are more than six thousand Persons—And also much Cattel?* And we have in *Deuteronomy*[10] a Precept of great Good-nature of this sort, with a Blessing in Form annexed to it in those Words. *If thou shalt find a Birds Nest in the way, thou shalt not take the Damm with the young: But thou shalt in any wise let the Damm go; that it may be well with thee, and that thou may'st prolong thy days.*

To conclude, there is certainly a Degree of Gratitude owing to those Animals that serve us; as for such as are Mortal or Noxious, we have a Right to destroy them; and for those that are neither of Advantage or Prejudice to us, the common Enjoyment of Life is what I cannot think we ought to deprive them of.

This whole Matter, with regard to each of these Considerations, is set in a very agreeable Light in one of the *Persian* Fables of *Pilpay*,[11] with which I shall end this Paper.

A Traveller passing thro' a Thicket, and seeing a few Sparks of a Fire, which some Passengers had kindled as they went that way before, made up to it. On a sudden the Sparks caught hold of a Bush, in the midst of which lay an Adder, and set it in Flames. The Adder intreated the Traveller's Assistance, who tying a Bag to the end of his Staff, reached it, and drew him out: He then bid him go where he pleased, but never more be hurtful to Men, since he owed his Life to a Man's Compassion. The Adder, however, prepared to sting him, and when he expostulated how unjust it was to retaliate Good with Evil, I shall do no more (said the Adder) than what you Men practise every Day, whose Custom it is to requite Benefits with Ingratitude.If you can deny this Truth, let us refer it to the first we meet. The Man consented, and seeing a Tree, put the Question to it in what manner a good Turn was to be recompenced? If you mean according to the

Usage of Men (replied the Tree) by its contrary, I have been standing here these hundred Years to protect them from the scorching Sun, and in requital they have cut down my Branches, and are going to saw my Body into Planks. Upon this the Adder insulting the Man, he appealed to a second Evidence, which was granted, and immediately they met a Cow. The same Demand was made, and much the same Answer given, that among Men it was certainly so. I know it (said the Cow) by woful Experience; for I have served a Man this long time with Milk, Butter and Cheese, and brought him besides a Calf every Year: but now I am old, he turns me into this Pasture, with design to sell me to a Butcher, who will shortly make an end of me. The Traveller upon this stood confounded, but desired, of Courtesie, one Trial more, to be finally judged by the next Beast they should meet. This happened to be the Fox, who upon hearing the Story in all its Circumstances, could not be persuaded it was possible for the Adder to enter in so narrow a Bag. The Adder to convince him went in again; when the Fox told the Man he had now his Enemy in his Power, and with that he fastened the Bag, and crushed him to Pieces.

91

Inest sua gratia Parvis.   Virg.[1]
Thursday, June 25, 1713.

THE CLUB OF LITTLE MEN[2]

I.
To Nestor Ironside, Esq;

SIR,

I remember a Saying of yours concerning Persons in low Circumstances of Stature, that their Littleness would hardly be taken Notice of, if they did not manifest a Consciousness of it themselves in all their Behaviour. Indeed, the Observation that no Man is Ridiculous for being what he is, but only in the Affectation of being something more, is equally true in regard to the Mind and the Body.

I question not but it will be pleasing to you to hear, that a Sett of us have formed a Society, who are sworn to *Dare to be Short*, and boldly bear out the Dignity of Littleness under the Noses of those Enormous Engrossers of Manhood, those Hyperbolical Monsters of the Species, the tall Fellows that overlook us.

The Day of our Institution was the *Tenth* of *December*, being the

Shortest of the Year, on which we are to hold an Annual Feast over a Dish of *Shrimps*.

The Place we have chosen for this Meeting is in the *Little Piazza*, not without an Eye to the Neighbourhood of Mr. *Powel*'s Opera, for the Performers of which we have, as becomes us, a Brotherly Affection.[3]

At our first Resort hither an old Woman brought her Son to the Club Room, desiring he might be Educated in this School, because she saw here were finer Boys than ordinary. However, this Accident no way discouraged our Designs. We began with sending Invitations to those of a Stature not exceeding *five Foot*, to repair to our Assembly; but the greater part returned Excuses, or pretended they were not qualified.

One said he was indeed but five Foot at present, but represented that he should soon exceed that Proportion, his Perriwig-maker and Shoe-maker having lately promised him three Inches more betwixt them.

Another alledged he was so unfortunate as to have one Leg shorter than the other, and whoever had determined his Stature to *five Foot*, had taken him at a Disadvantage; for when he was mounted on the other Leg he was at least *five Foot two Inches and a half.*

There were some who questioned the exactness of our Measures, and others, instead of complying, returned us Informations of People yet shorter than themselves. In a Word, almost every one recommended some Neighbour or Acquaintance, whom he was willing we should look upon to be less than he. We were not a little ashamed that those, who are past the Years of Growth, and whose Beards pronounce them Men, should be guilty of as many unfair Tricks, in this Point, as the most aspiring *Children* when they are measured.

We therefore proceeded to fit up the Club-Room, and provide Conveniencies for our Accommodation. In the first Place we caus'd a total Removal of all the *Chairs, Stools, and Tables*, which had served the *gross of Mankind* for many Years. The Disadvantages we had undergone, while we made use of these, were unspeakable. The President's whole Body was sunk in the Elbow-Chair, and when his Arms were spread over it, he appeared (to the great lessening of his Dignity) like a *Child* in a *Go-cart:* It was also so wide in the Seat, as to give a Wag Occasion of saying, that notwithstanding the President sate in it there was a *Sede Vacante*.[4] The Table was so high that one, who came by chance to the Door, seeing our Chins just above the Pewter Dishes, took us for a Circle of Men that sate ready to be shaved, and sent in half a dozen Barbers. Another time one of the Club spoke contumeliously of the President, imagining he had been Absent, when he was only eclypsed by a *Flask* of *Florence* which stood on the Table in a Parallel Line before his Face. We therefore new furnished the Room in all Respects proportionably to us, and had the Door made lower, so as to admit no Man of above five Foot high, without brushing his Foretop, which whoever does is utterly unqualified to sit among us.

Some of the Statutes of the Club are as follow:

I. If it be proved upon any Member, tho' never so duly qualified, that he strives as much as possible to get above his Size, by Stretching, Cocking, or the like; or that he hath stood on Tiptoe in a Crowd, with design to be taken for as tall a Man as the rest; or hath privily conveyed any large Book, Cricket,[5] or other Device under him, to exalt him on his Seat: Every such Offender shall be sentenced to Walk in Pumps[6] for a whole Month.

II. If any Member shall take Advantage from the Fulness or Length of his Wig, or any part of his Dress, or the immoderate Extent of his Hat, or otherwise, to seem larger or higher than he is; *it is Ordered*, he shall wear *Red Heels* to his Shoes, and a *Red Feather* in his Hat, which may apparently mark and set Bounds to the Extremities of his small Dimension, that all People may readily find him out between his Hat and his Shoes.

III. If any Member shall purchase a Horse for his own Riding, above fourteen Hands and a half in height, that Horse shall forthwith be Sold, a *Scotch* Galloway[7] bought in its stead for him, and the Overplus of the Mony shall treat the Club.

IV. If any Member, in direct Contradiction to the Fundamental Laws of the Society, shall wear the Heels of his Shoes exceeding one Inch and half, it shall be interpreted as an open Renunciation of Littleness, and the Criminal shall instantly be expell'd. *Note.* The Form to be used in expelling a Member shall be in these Words; *Go from among us, and be tall if you can!*

It is the unanimous Opinion of our whole Society, that since the Race of Mankind is granted to have decreas'd in Stature from the beginning to this present, it is the Intent of Nature it self, that Men should be little; and we believe, that all Human Kind shall at last *grow down* to *Perfection*, that is to say, be reduced to our own Measure.

I am, very Litterally,
Your Humble Servant,
Bob Short.

Contributions to *The Guardian*

92

Homunculi quanti sunt, cum recogito!   Plautus.[1]
Friday, June 26, 1713.

THE CLUB OF LITTLE MEN: II

To Nestor Ironside, Esq;

SIR,
The Club rising early this Evening, I have time to finish my Account of it. You are already acquainted with the Nature and Design of our Institution; the Characters of the Members, and the Topicks of our Conversation, are what remain for the Subject of this Epistle. The most eminent Persons of our Assembly are a little Poet, a little Lover, a little Politician, and a little Heroe. The first of these, *Dick Distick* by Name, we have elected President, not only as he is the shortest of us all, but because he has entertain'd so just a Sense of the Stature, as to go generally in Black that he may appear yet Less. Nay, to that Perfection is he arrived, that he *stoops* as he walks. The Figure of the Man is odd enough; he is a lively little Creature, with long Arms and Legs: A Spider is no ill Emblem of him. He has been taken at a Distance for a *small Windmill*. But indeed what principally moved us in his Favour was his Talent in Poetry, for he hath promised to undertake a long Work in *short Verse* to celebrate the Heroes of our Size. He has entertained so great a Respect for *Statius*, on the Score of that Line,

Major in exiguo regnabat corpore virtus,[2]

that he once designed to translate the whole *Thebaid* for the sake of little *Tydeus*.

Tom. Tiptoe, a dapper black Fellow, is the most gallant Lover of the Age. He is particularly nice in his Habiliments; and to the end Justice may be done him that way, constantly employs the same Artist who makes Attire for the neighb'ring Princes and Ladies of Quality at Mr. *Powel's*. The vivacity of his Temper inclines him sometimes to boast of the Favours of the Fair. He was, 'tother Night, excusing his Absence from the Club on Account of an Assignation with a Lady, (and, as he had the Vanity to tell us, a Tall one too) who had consented to the full Accomplishment of his Desires that Evening. But one of the Company, who was his Confident, assured us she was a Woman of Humour, and made the Agreement on this Condition, That his Toe should be tied to hers.

Selected prose of Alexander Pope

Our *Politician* is a Person of *real Gravity*, and *professed Wisdom*. Gravity in a Man of this Size, compared with that of one of ordinary Bulk, appears like the Gravity of a Cat compared with that of a Lion. This Gentleman is accustomed to talk to himself, and was once over-heard to compare his own Person to a *little Cabinet*, wherein are locked up all the Secrets of State, and refined Schemes of Princes. His Face is pale and meager, which proceeds from much watching and studying for the Welfare of *Europe*, which is also thought to have stinted his Growth: For he hath destroyed his own Constitution with taking care of that of the Nation. He is what Mons. *Balzac*[3] calls *a great Distiller of the Maxims of* Tacitus: When he Speaks, it is slowly and Word by Word, as one that is loth to enrich you too fast with his Observations; like a Limbeck that gives you, Drop by Drop, an Extract of the Simples in it.

The last I shall mention is *Tim. Tuck*, the Hero. He is particularly remarkable for the length of his Sword, which intersects his Person in a cross Line, and makes him appear not unlike a Fly, that the Boys have run a Pin thro', and set a walking. He once challenged a tall Fellow for giving him a blow on the Pate with his Elbow as he pass'd along the Street. But what he especially values himself upon is, that in all the Campaigns he has made, he never once *Duck'd* at the whizz of a Cannon Ball. *Tim.* was full as large at fourteen Years old as he is now. This we are tender of mentioning, your little Heroes being generally Cholerick.

These are the Gentlemen that most enliven our Conversation: The Discourse generally turns upon such Accidents, whether Fortunate or Unfortunate, as are daily occasioned by our Size: These we faithfully communicate, either as Matter of Mirth, or of Consolation to each other. The President had lately an unlucky Fall, being unable to keep his Legs on a Stormy Day; whereupon he informed us it was no new Disaster, but the same a certain Ancient Poet had been subject to; who is recorded to have been so light, that he was obliged to poize himself against the Wind with Lead on one side, and his own Works on the other. The *Lover* confest the other Night that he had been cured of Love to a tall Woman, by reading over the Legend of *Ragotine* in *Scarron*,[4] with his Tea, three Mornings successively. Our Hero rarely acquaints us with any of his unsuccessful Adventures: And as for the *Politician*, he declares himself an utter Enemy to all kind of Burlesque, so will never discompose the Austerity of his Aspect by laughing at our Adventures, much less discover any of his own in this ludicrous Light. Whatever he tells of any Accidents that befal him is by way of Complaint, nor is he ever laughed at but in his Absence.

Contributions to *The Guardian*

We are likewise particularly careful to communicate in the Club all such Passages of History, or Characters of Illustrious Personages, as any way reflect Honour on little Men. *Tim. Tuck* having but just Reading enough for a Military Man, perpetually entertains us with the same Stories, of little *David* that conquered the mighty *Goliah*, and little *Luxembourg* that made *Lewis* XIV. a *Grand Monarque*, never forgetting Little *Alexander the Great*. *Dick Distick* celebrates the exceeding Humanity of *Augustus*, who called *Horace, Lepidissimum Homunciolum*;[5] and is wonderfully pleased with *Voiture* and *Scarron*, for having so well described their Diminutive Forms to all Posterity. He is peremptorily of Opinion, against a great Reader, and all his Adherents, that *Æsop* was not a jot properer or handsomer than he is represented by the common Pictures. But the Soldier believes with the Learned Person above-mentioned; for he thinks none but an impudent Tall Author could be guilty of such an unmannerly Piece of Satire on little Warriors, as his Battle of the *Mouse* and the *Frog*. The *Politician* is very proud of a certain King of *Egypt*, called *Bocchor*, who, as *Diodorus* assures us, was a Person of very low Stature, but far exceeded all that went before him *in Discretion and Politicks*.

As I am Secretary to the Club, 'tis my Business whenever we meet to take Minutes of the Transactions: This has enabled me to send you the foregoing Particulars, as I may hereafter other Memoirs. We have Spies appointed in every Quarter of the Town, to give us Informations of the Misbehaviour of such refractory Persons as refuse to be subject to our Statutes. Whatsoever aspiring Practices any of these our People shall be guilty of in their Amours, single Combats, or any indirect means to Manhood, we shall certainly be acquainted with, and publish to the World for their Punishment and Reformation. For the President has granted me the sole Propriety of exposing and showing to the Town all such intractable Dwarfs, whose Circumstances exempt them from being carried about in Boxes: Reserving only to himself, as the Right of a Poet, those *Smart Characters* that will shine in *Epigrams*. Venerable Nestor, I salute you in the Name of the Club.

BOB SHORT, *Secretar.*

132

Quisque suos patimur manes[1] —
Wednesday, August 12, 1713.

ON SICKNESS

Dear Sir,

You formerly observed to me, that nothing made a more ridiculous Figure in a Man's Life, than the Disparity we often find in him Sick and Well. Thus one of an unfortunate Constitution is perpetually exhibiting a miserable Example of the Weakness of his Mind, or of his Body, in their Turns. I have had frequent Opportunities of late to consider my self in these different Views, and hope I have received some Advantage by it. If what Mr. *Waller* says be true, that

> *The Soul's dark Cottage, batter'd and decay'd,*
> *Lets in new Light thro' Chinks that Time has made:*[2]

Then surely Sickness, contributing no less than old Age to the shaking down this Scaffolding of the Body, may discover the inclosed Structure more plainly. Sickness is a sort of early old Age; it teaches us a Diffidence in our Earthly State, and inspires us with the Thoughts of a future, better than a thousand Volumes of Philosophers and Divines. It gives so warning a Concussion to those Props of our Vanity, our Strength and Youth, that we think of fortifying our selves within, when there is so little dependance on our Outworks. Youth, at the very best, is but a Betrayer of Human Life in a gentler and smoother manner than Age: 'Tis like a Stream that nourishes a Plant upon its Bank, and causes it to flourish and blossom to the Sight, but at the same time is undermining it at the Root in secret. My Youth has dealt more fairly and openly with me; it has afforded several Prospects of my Danger, and given me an Advantage not very common to young Men, that the Attractions of the World have not dazzled me very much; and I began where most People end, with a full Conviction of the Emptiness of all sorts of Ambition, and the unsatisfactory Nature of all human Pleasures.

When a smart Fit of Sickness tells me this Scurvy Tenement of my Body will fall in a little time, I am e'en as unconcern'd as was that honest *Hibernian*, who (being in Bed in the great Storm some Years ago, and told the House would tumble over his Head) made Answer, *What care I for the House? I am only a Lodger.*

I fancy 'tis the best time to die when one is in the best Humour, and so excessively weak as I now am, I may say with Conscience, that I'm not at all uneasie at the Thought that many Men, whom I never had

56

any Esteem for, are likely to enjoy this World after me. When I reflect what an inconsiderable little Atome every single Man is, with respect to the whole Creation, methinks 'tis a Shame to be concerned at the Removal of such a trivial Animal as I am. The Morning after my *Exit*, the Sun will rise as bright as ever, the Flowers smell as sweet, the Plants spring as green, the World will proceed in its old Course, People will laugh as heartily, and Marry as fast, as they were used to do. *The Memory of Man* (as it is elegantly exprest in the Wisdom of *Solomon*) [3] *passeth away as the remembrance of a Guest that tarrieth but one Day.* There are Reasons enough, in the fourth Chapter of the same Book, to make any young Man contented with the Prospect of Death. *For honourable Age is not that which standeth in length of Time, or is measured by number of Years. But Wisdom is the gray Hair to Men, and an unspotted Life is old Age.* He was taken away speedily, lest that *Wickedness should alter his Understanding, or Deceit beguile his Soul.*

I am,

Yours.

173

—*Nec sera comantem*
Narcissum, aut flexi tacuissem Vimen Acanthi,
Pallentesque Hæderas, & amantes littora myrtos.   Virg.[1]
Tuesday, September 29, 1713.

ON GARDENS

I lately took a particular Friend of mine to my House in the Country, not without some Apprehension that it could afford little Entertainment to a Man of his Polite Taste, particularly in Architecture and Gardening, who had so long been conversant with all that is beautiful and great in either. But it was a pleasant Surprize to me, to hear him often declare, he had found in my little Retirement that Beauty which he always thought wanting in the most celebrated Seats, or if you will Villa's, of the Nation. This he described to me in those Verses with which *Martial* begins one of his Epigrams:

Baiana nostri Villa, Basse, Faustini,
Non otiosis ordinata myrtetis,
Viduaque platano, tonsilique buxeto,
Ingrata lati spatia detinet campi,
Sed rure vero, barbaroque lætatur.[2]

There is certainly something in the amiable Simplicity of unadorned Nature, that spreads over the Mind a more noble Sort of Tranquility, and a loftier Sensation of Pleasure, than can be raised from the nicer Scenes of Art.

This was the Taste of the Ancients in their Gardens, as we may discover from the Descriptions that are extant of them. The two most celebrated Wits of the World have each of them left us a particular Picture of a Garden; wherein those great Masters, being wholly unconfined, and Painting at Pleasure, may be thought to have given a full Idea of what they esteemed most excellent in this way. These (one may observe) consist intirely of the useful Part of Horticulture, Fruit Trees, Herbs, Water, &c. The Pieces I am speaking of are *Virgil's* Account of the Garden of the old *Corycian*, and *Homer's* of that of *Alcinous*. The first of these is already known to the *English* Reader, by the excellent Versions of Mr. *Dryden* and Mr. *Addison*. The other having never been attempted in our Language with any Elegance, and being the most beautiful Plan of this sort that can be imagined, I shall here present the Reader with a Translation of it.

The Gardens of *Alcinous*, from *Homer's Odyss.* 7.

Close to the Gates a spacious Garden lies,
From Storms defended and inclement Skies:
Four Acres was th' allotted Space of Ground,
Fenc'd with a green Enclosure all around.
Tall thriving Trees confest the fruitful Mold;
The red'ning Apple ripens here to Gold,
Here the blue Figg with luscious Juice o'erflows,
With deeper Red the full Pomegranate glows,
The Branch here bends beneath the weighty Pear,
And verdant Olives flourish round the Year.
The balmy Spirit of the Western Gale
Eternal breathes on Fruits untaught to fail:
Each dropping Pear a following Pear supplies,
On Apples Apples, Figs on Figs arise:
The same mild Season gives the Blooms to blow,
The Buds to harden, and the Fruits to grow.
Here order'd Vines in equal Ranks appear
With all th' United Labours of the Year,
Some to unload the fertile Branches run,
Some dry the black'ning Clusters in the Sun,
Others to tread the liquid Harvest join,
The groaning Presses foam with Floods of Wine.
Here are the Vines in early Flow'r descry'd,
Here Grapes discolour'd on the sunny Side,
And there in Autumn's richest Purple dy'd.
Beds of all various Herbs, for ever green,
In beauteous Order terminate the Scene.

Contributions to *The Guardian*

> *Two plenteous Fountains the whole Prospect crown'd;* ⎤
> *This thro' the Gardens leads its Streams around,* ⎥
> *Visits each Plant, and waters all the Ground:* ⎦
> *While that in Pipes beneath the Palace flows,*
> *And thence its Current on the Town bestows;*
> *To various Use their various Streams they bring,*
> *The People one, and one supplies the King.*

Sir *William Temple*[3] has remark'd, that this Description contains all the justest Rules and Provisions which can go toward composing the best Gardens. Its Extent was four *Acres*, which, in those times of Simplicity, was look'd upon as a large one, even for a Prince: It was inclos'd all round for Defence; and for Conveniency join'd close to the Gates of the Palace.

He mentions next the Trees, which were Standards, and suffered to grow to their full height. The fine Description of the Fruits that never failed, and the eternal Zephyrs, is only a more noble and poetical way of expressing the continual Succession of one Fruit after another throughout the Year.

The *Vineyard* seems to have been a Plantation distinct from the *Garden*; as also the *Beds of Greens* mentioned afterwards at the Extremity of the Inclosure, in the Nature and usual Place of our *Kitchen Gardens*.

The two Fountains are disposed very remarkably. They rose within the Inclosure, and were brought by Conduits or Ducts, one of them to water all Parts of the Gardens, and the other underneath the Palace into the Town, for the Service of the Publick.

How contrary to this Simplicity is the modern Practice of Gardening; we seem to make it our Study to recede from Nature, not only in the various Tonsure of Greens into the most regular and formal Shapes, but even in monstrous Attempts beyond the reach of the Art it self: We run into Sculpture, and are yet better pleas'd to have our Trees in the most awkward Figures of Men and Animals, than in the most regular of their own.

> *Hinc & nexilibus videas e frondibus hortos,*
> *Implexos late muros, & Mænia circum*
> *Porrigere, & latas e ramis surgere turres;*
> *Deflexam & Myrtum in Puppes, atque ærea rostra:*
> *In buxisque undare fretum, atque e rore rudentes.*
> *Parte aliâ frondere suis tentoria Castris;*
> *Scutaque spiculaque & jaculantia citria Vallos.*[4]

I believe it is no wrong Observation that Persons of Genius, and those who are most capable of Art, are always most fond of Nature, as such are chiefly sensible, that all Art consists in the Imitation and

Study of Nature. On the contrary, People of the common Level of
Understanding are principally delighted with the little Niceties and
Fantastical Operations of Art, and constantly think that *finest* which is
least Natural. A Citizen is no sooner Proprietor of a couple of Yews,
but he entertains Thoughts of erecting them into Giants, like those of
Guild-hall. I know an eminent Cook, who beautified his Country Seat
with a Coronation Dinner in Greens, where you see the Champion
flourishing on Horseback at one end of the Table, and the Queen in
perpetual Youth at the other.

For the benefit of all my loving Countrymen of this curious Taste, I
shall here publish a Catalogue of Greens to be disposed of by an
eminent Town-Gardiner, who has lately applied to me upon this
Head. He represents, that for the Advancement of a politer sort of
Ornament in the Villa's and Gardens adjacent to this great City, and in
order to distinguish those Places from the meer barbarous Countries
of gross Nature, the World stands much in need of a Virtuoso
Gardiner who has a Turn to Sculpture, and is thereby capable of
improving upon the Ancients of his Profession in the Imagery of
Ever-greens. My Correspondent is arrived to such Perfection, that he
cuts Family Pieces of Men, Women or Children. Any Ladies that
please may have their own Effigies in Myrtle, or their Husbands in
Horn-beam. He is a Puritan Wag, and never fails, when he shows his
Garden, to repeat that Passage in the Psalms, *Thy Wife shall be as the
fruitful Vine, and thy Children as Olive Branches round thy Table.*[5] I shall
proceed to his Catalogue, as he sent it for my Recommendation.

Adam and *Eve* in Yew; *Adam* a little shatter'd by the fall of the Tree
of Knowledge in the great Storm; *Eve* and the Serpent very
flourishing.

The Tower of *Babel*, not yet finished.

St. *George* in Box; his Arm scarce long enough, but will be in a
Condition to stick the Dragon by next *April*.

A *green Dragon* of the same, with a Tail of Ground Ivy for the
present.

N.B. *These two not to be Sold separately.*

Edward the *Black Prince* in Cypress.

A *Laurustine* Bear in Blossom, with a Juniper Hunter in Berries.

A Pair of Giants, *stunted*, to be sold cheap.

A Queen *Elizabeth* in Phylyræa, a little inclining to the Green
Sickness, but of full growth.

Another Queen *Elizabeth* in Myrtle, which was very forward, but
Miscarried by being too near a Savine.

Contributions to *The Guardian*

An old Maid of Honour in Wormwood.

A topping *Ben. Johnson* in Lawrel.

Divers eminent Modern Poets in Bays, somewhat blighted, to be disposed of a Pennyworth.

A Quick-set Hog shot up into a Porcupine, by its being forgot a Week in rainy Weather.

A Lavender Pigg with Sage growing in his Belly.

Noah's Ark in Holly, standing on the Mount; the Ribs a little damaged for want of Water.

A Pair of *Maidenheads* in Firr, in great forwardness.

4. The Narrative of
Dr. Robert Norris

The Narrative of Dr. Robert Norris (1713) arises from a difference of opinion between Dennis and Addison. On 16 April 1711 Addison published as *Spectator* no. 40 an essay arguing against the notion that tragedy should conform to 'poetical justice' – the principle that virtue should be rewarded and vice punished. Addison wrote that 'Good and Evil happen alike to all Men on this Side the Grave; and as the principal Design of Tragedy is to raise Commiseration and Terror in the Minds of the Audience, we shall defeat this great End, if we always make Virtue and Innocence happy and successful.' *King Lear*, he said, 'is an admirable Tragedy…as *Shakespear* wrote it; but as it is reformed [by Nahum Tate] according to the chymerical Notion of Poetical Justice, in my humble Opinion it has lost half its Beauty'. Dennis replied to this essay in his letter *To the Spectator, upon his paper on the 16th of April* (1712), arguing that whereas man will be punished and rewarded in a future state, the characters in a drama exist only for the duration of that play, 'and consequently, if they offend, they must be punish'd during that Representation' (*Critical Works*, ii 21). In the same year Dennis published his *Essay on the Genius and Writings of Shakespear*, which censured Shakespeare for not conforming to 'poetical justice', as well as for his ignorance of classical literature and neglect of historical accuracy. In accordance with these views Dennis had rewritten Shakespeare's *Coriolanus* (probably in 1710), but he held it back from publication, no doubt because of the failure of his play *Appius and Virginia* in 1709.

Addison's play *Cato* was performed in April 1713 to great applause, and occasioned a phenomenal demand for printed copies. By July Dennis had written his *Remarks upon Cato, a Tragedy*, published by Bernard Lintot. Dennis set out to show the 'Faults and Absurdities' of *Cato* which were occasioned both by Addison's neglect of Aristotle's rules, and by his observance of those rules 'without any manner of Judgment or Discretion' (*Critical Works*, ii 44). Pope admired *Cato* and wrote a prologue for it, but the *Narrative* is not just a rejoinder to Dennis's *Remarks*. As Pope said in a letter supposedly to Addison: ''twas never in my thoughts to have offer'd you my pen in any direct reply to such a Critic, but only in some little raillery; not in defence of you, but in contempt of him' (*Corr.* i 183). Addison himself disapproved of the pamphlet, according to a letter from Steele to Lintot: 'Mr. *Addison* desir'd me to tell you, that he wholly disapproves the Manner of Treating Mr. *Dennis* in a little Pamphlet, by way of Dr. *Norris*'s Account. When he thinks fit to take notice of Mr. *Dennis*'s Objections to his Writings, he will do it in a Way Mr. *Dennis* shall have no just Reason to complain of. But

The Narrative of Dr. Robert Norris

when the Papers above-mentioned, were offer'd to be communicated to him, he said he could not, either in Honour or Conscience, be privy to such a Treatment, and was sorry to hear of it.' (*Critical Works*, ii 371). The *Narrative* repeats some of the topics of ridicule already aired in *The Critical Specimen*, adding references to Dennis's recent work (mentioned above) and to Dennis's confident preference for English over French literature (he had written of the French threat to English liberties: *Critical Works*, i 320). The friend referred to is probably Henry Cromwell, friend of Dennis and sometime associate of Pope. Robert Norris was a well-known doctor whose advertisements appeared frequently in journals of the day: 'Robert Norris at the Pestle and Mortar on Snow Hill, having been many years experienc'd in the Care of Lunaticks, hath Conveniencies and suitable Attendance at his own House for either Sex; any Person applying themselves to him as above, may have unquestionable satisfaction that the Cure shall be speedily and industriously endeavour'd and (by God's Blessing effected) on reasonable Terms.' (George Sherburn, *The Early Career of Alexander Pope* (Oxford, 1934) p. 106).

The authorship of the *Narrative* is established by Ault (pp. xviii-xxxiii). It was published on 28 July 1713.

Text: *The Narrative of Dr. Robert Norris* (1713).

THE
NARRATIVE
OF
DR. *Robert Norris,*
CONCERNING
The STRANGE and DEPLORABLE FRENZY of Mr.
JOHN DENN[IS] an Officer of the Custom-house.

It is an acknowledg'd Truth, that nothing is so dear to an honest Man as his good Name, nor ought he to neglect the just Vindication of his Character, when it is injuriously attack'd by any Man. The Person I have at present Cause to complain of, is indeed in very melancholy Circumstances, it having pleas'd God to deprive him of his Senses, which may extenuate the Crime in Him. But I should be wanting in my Duty, not only to my self, but also to him who hath endu'd me with Talents for the benefit of my Fellow-Creatures, shou'd I suffer my Profession or Honesty to be undeservedly aspers'd. I have therefore resolv'd to give the Publick an account of all that has past between that unhappy Gentleman and my self.

On the 20*th* instant, while I was in my Closet pondering the Case of one of my Patients, I heard a Knocking at my Door; upon opening of which enter'd an old Woman with Tears in her Eyes, and told me, that without my Assistance her Master would be utterly ruin'd. I was forc'd to interrupt her Sorrow by enquiring her Master's Name and Place of Abode. She told me he was one Mr. *Denn[is]* an Officer of the Custom-house, who was taken ill of a violent Frenzy last *April*, and had continu'd in those melancholy Circumstances with few or no Intervals. Upon this I ask'd her some Questions relating to his Humour and Extravagancies, that I might the better know under what Regimen to put him, when the Cause of his Distemper was found out. Alass, Sir, says she, this Day fortnight in the Morning a poor simple Child came to him from the Printer's; the Boy had no sooner enter'd the Room, but he cry'd out *the Devil was come.* He often stares ghastfully, raves aloud, and mutters between his Teeth the Word *Cator,* or *Cato,* or some such thing. Now, Doctor, this *Cator* is certainly a *Witch,* and my poor Master is under an evil Tongue; for I have heard him say *Cator* has bewitch'd the whole Nation. It pitied my very Heart, to think that a Man of my Master's Understanding and great Scholarship, who, as the Child told me, had a Book of his own in Print, should talk so outragiously.

Upon this I went and laid out a Groat for a Horse-shoe, which is at this time nail'd on the Threshold of his Door; but I don't find my Master is at all the better for it; he perpetually starts and runs to the Window when any one knocks, crying out, *S'death! a Messenger from the French King! I shall die in the* Bastile.

Having said this, the old Woman presented me with a Viol of his Urine; upon Examination of which I perceiv'd the whole Temperament of his Body to be exceeding hot. I therefore instantly took my Cane and my Beaver, and repair'd to the Place where he dwelt.

When I came to his Lodgings near *Charing-cross*, up three Pair of Stairs, (which I should not have publish'd in this manner, but that this Lunatick conceals the Place of his Residence on purpose to prevent the good Offices of those charitable Friends and Physicians, who might attempt his Cure) when I came into the Room, I found this unfortunate Gentleman seated on his Bed, with Mr. *Bernard Lintott*, Bookseller, on the one side of him, and a grave elderly Gentleman on the other, who, as I have since learnt, calls himself a Grammarian, the Latitude of whose Countenance was not a little eclips'd by the Fullness of his Peruke. As I am a black lean Man of a pale Visage, and hang my Clothes on somewhat slovenly, I no sooner went in but he frown'd upon me, and cry'd out with violence, *S'Death*, a *French-man!* I am betray'd to the Tyrant! who cou'd have thought the Queen wou'd have deliver'd me up to *France* in this Treaty, and least of all that you, my Friends, wou'd have been in a Conspiracy against me?—Sir, said I, here is neither Plot nor Conspiracy, but for your advantage. The Recovery of your Senses requires my Attendance, and your Friends sent for me on no other account. I then took a particular Survey of his Person, and the Furniture and Disposition of his Apartment. His Aspect was furious, his Eyes were rather fiery than lively, which he roll'd about in an uncommon manner. He often open'd his Mouth, as if he wou'd have utter'd some Matter of Importance, but the Sound seem'd lost inwardly. His Beard was grown, which they told me he would not suffer to be shav'd, believing the modern Dramatick Poets had corrupted all the Barbers in the Town to take the first Opportunity of cutting his Throat. His Eye-brows were grey, long, and grown together, which he knit with Indignation when any thing was spoken, insomuch that he seem'd not to have smoothed his Forehead for many Years. His Flannel Night Cap, which was exceedingly begrim'd with Sweat and Dirt, hung upon his Left Ear; the Flap of his Breeches dangled between his Legs, and the Rolls of his Stockings fell down to his Ankles.

I observ'd his Room was hung with *old Tapestry*, which had several Holes in it, caus'd, as the Old Woman inform'd me, by his having cut out of it the Heads of divers *Tyrants*, the Fierceness of whose Visages had much provoked him.[1] On all sides of his Room were pinned a great many Sheets of a Tragedy called *Cato*, with Notes on the Margin with his own Hand. The Words *Absurd, Monstrous, Execrable*, were every where written in such large Characters, that I could read them without my Spectacles. By the Fire-side lay Three-farthings-worth of Small-coal in a *Spectator*, and behind the Door huge Heaps of Papers of the same Title, which his Nurse inform'd me she had convey'd thither out of his sight, believing they were Books of the Black Art; for her Master never read in them, but he was either quite mop'd, or in raving Fits: There was nothing neat in the whole Room, except some Books on his Shelves very well bound and gilded, whose Names I had never before heard of, nor I believe are any where else to be found; such as *Gibraltar, a Comedy; Remarks on Prince Arthur; the Grounds of Criticism in Poetry; an Essay on publick Spirit.*[2] The only one I had any Knowledge of was a *Paradise Lost*, interleav'd.[3] The whole Floor was cover'd with Manuscripts, as thick as a Pastry Cook's Shop on a Christmas Eve. On his Table were some Ends of Verse and of Candles; a Gallipot of Ink with a yellow Pen in it, and a Pot of half-dead Ale cover'd with a *Longinus*.

As I was casting my Eyes round on all this odd Furniture with some Earnestness and Astonishment, and in a profound Silence, I was on a sudden surpriz'd to hear the Man speak in the following manner:

'Beware, Doctor, that it fare not with you as with your Predecessor the famous *Hippocrates*, whom the mistaken Citizens of *Abdera* sent for in this very manner to cure the Philosopher *Democritus*; he return'd full of Admiration at the Wisdom of that Person whom he had suppos'd a Lunatick. Behold, Doctor, it was thus *Aristotle* himself and all the great Antients spent their Days and Nights, wrapt up in Criticism, and beset all around with their own Writings. As for me, whom you see in the same manner, be assur'd I have none other Disease than a Swelling in my Legs, whereof I say no more, since your Art may further certify you.'

I thereupon seated my self upon his Bed-side, and placing my Patient on my Right Hand, to judge the better in what he affirm'd of his Legs, felt his Pulse.

For it is *Hippocrates*'s Maxim, that if the Pulse have a Dead Motion, with some unequal Beatings, 'tis a Symptom of a Sciatica, or a Swelling in the Thigh or Leg; in which Assertion of his this Pulse confirm'd me.

I began now to be in hopes that his Case had been misrepresented, and that he was not so far gone, but some timely Medicines might recover him. I therefore proceeded to the proper Queries, which with the Answers made to me, I shall set down in Form of Dialogue, in the very Words they were spoken, because I would not omit the least Circumstance in this Narrative; and I call my Conscience to witness, as if upon Oath, that I shall tell the Truth without addition or diminution.

Doct. Pray, Sir, how did you contract this Swelling?

Denn. By a Criticism.

Doct. A Criticism! that's a Distemper I never read of in *Galen.*

Denn. S'Death, Sir, a Distemper! It is no Distemper, but a Noble Art. I have sat fourteen Hours a Day at it; and are you a Doctor, and don't know there's a Communication between the Legs and the Brain?

Doct. What made you sit so many Hours, Sir?

Denn. Cato, Sir.

Doct. Sir, I speak of your Distemper, what gave you this Tumor?

Denn. Cato, Cato, Cato.

Old Wom. For God's sake, Doctor, name not this evil Spirit, 'tis the whole Cause of his Madness: Alass, poor Master's just falling into his Fits.

Mr. *Lintott.* Fit's! Z— what Fits? A Man may well have Swellings in his Legs, that sits writing fourteen Hours in a Day. He got this by the *Remarks.*

Doct. The *Remarks!* what are those?

Denn. S'Death! have you never read my Remarks? I will be damn'd if this Dog *Lintott* ever publish'd my Advertisements.

Mr. *Lint.* Z—! I publish'd Advertisement upon Advertisement; and if the Book be not read, it is none of my fault, but his that made it. By G—, as much has been done for the Book, as cou'd be done for any Book in Christendom.

Doct. We do not talk of Books, Sir; I fear those are the Fuel that feed his *Delirium*; mention them no more. You do very ill to promote this Discourse.

I desire a Word in private with this other Gentleman, who seems a grave and sensible Man: I suppose, Sir, you are his Apothecary.

Gent. Sir, I am his Friend.

Dr. I doubt it not. What Regimen have you observ'd since he has been under your Care? You remember, I suppose, the Passage of

Celsus, which says, if the Patient, on the third Day, have an Interval, suspend the Medicaments at Night; let Fumigations be used to corroborate the Brain; I hope you have upon no Account promoted Sternutation by Hellebore.

Gent. Sir, no such matter, you utterly mistake.

Dr. Am I not a Physician? and shall an Apothecary dispute my *Nostrums*—You may perhaps have fill'd up a Prescription or two of *Ratcliff*'s, which had chance to succeed, and with that very Prescription injudiciously prescrib'd to different Constitutions, have destroy'd a Multitude. *Pharmacopola componat, Medicus solus prescribat,*[4] says *Celsus*. Fumigate him, I say, this very Evening, while he is relieved by an Interval.

Denn. S'Death, Sir, my Friend an Apothecary! a base Mechanic! He who, like my self, professes the noblest Sciences in the Universe, Criticism and Poetry. Can you think I would submit my Writings to the Judgment of an Apothecary? By the Immortals, he himself inserted three whole Paragraphs in my *Remarks*, had a Hand in my *Publick Spirit*, nay, assisted me in my Description of the Furies, and infernal Regions in my *Appius*.

Mr. Lintott. He is an Author; you mistake the Gentleman, Doctor; he has been an Author these twenty Years, to his Bookseller's Knowledge, and no Man's else.

Denn. Is all the Town in a Combination? Shall Poetry fall to the ground? Must our Reputation be lost to all foreign Countries? O Destruction! Perdition! *Opera! Opera!* As Poetry once rais'd a City, so when Poetry fails, Cities are overturn'd, and the World is no more.[5]

Dr. He raves, he raves; Mr. *Lintott*, I pray you pinion down his Arms, that he may do no Mischief.

Denn. O I am sick, sick to Death!

Dr. That is a good Symptom, a very good Symptom. To be sick to Death (say the modern Physicians) is an excellent Symptom. When a Patient is sensible of his Pain, 'tis half a Cure. Pray, Sir, of what are you sick?

Denn. Of every thing, Of every thing. I am sick of the *Sentiments*, of the *Diction*, of the *Protasis*, of the *Epitasis*, and the *Catastrophe*— Alas, what is become of the *Drama*, the *Drama*?

Old Wom. The *Dram*, Sir? Mr. *Lintott* drank up all the Geneva[6] just now; but I'll go fetch more presently!

Denn. O shameful Want, scandalous Omission! By all the Immortals, here is no *Peripætia*, no Change of Fortune in the Tragedy; Z— no Change at all.

The Narrative of Dr. Robert Norris

Old Wom. Pray, good Sir, be not angry, I'll fetch Change.

Dr. Hold your Peace, Woman, his Fit increases; good Mr. *Lintott* hold him.

Mr. Lintott. Plague on't! I am damnably afraid they are in the right of it, and he is mad in earnest, if he should be really mad, who the Devil will buy the *Remarks?*

(*Here Mr.* Lintott *scratched his Head.*)

Dr. Sir, I shall order you the cold Bath to morrow—Mr. *Lintott,* you are a sensible Man; pray send for Mr. *Verdier's* Servant, and as you are a Friend to the Patient, be so kind as to stay this Evening whilst he is cupp'd on the Head. The Symptoms of his Madness seem to be desperate; for *Avicen* says, that if Learning be mix'd with a Brain that is not of a Contexture fit to receive it, the Brain ferments till it be totally exhausted. We must eradicate these undigested Ideas out of the *Perecranium,* and reduce the Patient to a competent Knowledge of himself.

Denn. Caitiffs stand off; unhand me, Miscreants! Is the Man whose whole Endeavours are to bring the Town to Reason mad? Is the Man who settles Poetry on the Basis of Antiquity mad? Dares any one assert there is a *Peripatia* in that vile Piece that's foisted upon the Town for a Dramatick Poem? That Man is mad, the Town is mad, the World is mad. See *Longinus* in my right Hand, and *Aristotle* in my left; I am the only Man among the Moderns that support them. Am I to be assassinated? and shall a Bookseller, who hath liv'd upon my Labours, take away that Life to which he owes his Support?

Gent. By your Leave, Gentlemen, I apprehend you not. I must not see my Friend ill treated; he is no more affected with Lunacy than my self; I am also of the same Opinion as to the *Peripatia*—Sir, by the Gravity of your Countenance and Habit, I should conceive you to be a graduate Physician; but by your indecent and boisterous Treatment of this Man of Learning, I perceive you are a violent sort of *Person,* I am loth to say *Quack,* who, rather than his Drugs should lie upon his own Hands, would get rid of them, by cramming them into the Mouths of others: The Gentleman is of good Condition, sound Intellectuals, and unerring Judgment: I beg you will not oblige me to resent these Proceedings.

THESE were all the Words that pass'd among us at this Time; nor was there need for more, it being necessary we should make use of Force in the Cure of my Patient.

I privately whisper'd the old Woman to go to *Verdier's* in *Long Acre*, with Orders to come immediately with Cupping Glasses; in the mean time, by the Assistance of Mr. *Lintott*, we lock'd his Friend into a Closet, (who 'tis plain from his last Speech was likewise toucht in his Intellects) after which we bound our Lunatick Hand and Foot down to the Bedsted, where he continued in violent Ravings, notwithstanding the most tender Expressions we could use to perswade him to submit to the Operation, till the Servant of *Verdier* arriv'd. He had no sooner clap'd half a dozen Cupping Glasses on his Head, and behind his Ears, but the Gentleman above-mention'd bursting open the Closet, ran furiously upon us, cut Mr. *Denn[is's]* Bandages, and let drive at us with a vast Folio, which sorely bruis'd the Shin of Mr. *Lintott*; Mr. *John Denn[is]* also starting up with the Cupping Glasses on his Head, seized another Folio, and with the same dangerously wounded me in the Skull, just above my right Temple. The Truth of this Fact Mr. *Verdier's* Servant is ready to attest upon Oath, who, taking an exact Survey of the Volumes, found that which wounded my Head to be *Gruterus's Lampas Critica*, and that which broke Mr. *Lintott's* Shin was *Scaliger's Poetices*. After this, Mr. *John Denn[is]* strengthen'd at once by Rage and Madness, snatch'd up a Peruke-Block, that stood by the Bed-side, and weilded it round in so furious a Manner, that he broke three of the Cupping Glasses from the Crown of his Head, so that much Blood trickled down his Visage—He look'd so ghastly, and his Passion was grown to such a prodigious Height, that my self, Mr. *Lintott*, and *Verdier's* Servant, were oblig'd to leave the Room in all the Expedition imaginable.

I took Mr. *Lintott* home with me, in order to have our Wounds drest, and laid hold of that Opportunity of entering into Discourse with him about the Madness of this Person, of whom he gave me the following remarkable Relation:

That on the 17th of *May*, 1712. between the Hours of 10 and 11 in the Morning, Mr. *John Denn[is]* enter'd into his Shop, and opening one of the Volumes of the *Spectator*, in the large Paper, did suddenly, without the least Provocation, tear out that of N° [40] where the Author treats of Poetical Justice, and cast it into the Street. That the said Mr. *John Denn[is]* on the 27th of *March*, 1712. finding on the said Mr. *Lintott's* Counter a Book called an *Essay on Criticism*, just then publish'd, he read a Page or two with much Frowning and Gesticulation, till coming to these two Lines;

Some have at first for Wits, then Poets past,
Turn'd Criticks next, and prov'd plain Fools at last.

70

He flung down the Book in a terrible Fury, and cried out, *By G— he means Me.*

That being in his Company on a certain Time, when *Shakespear* was mention'd as of a contrary Opinion to Mr. *Denn*[*is*] he swore the said *Shakespear* was a *Rascal*, with other defamatory Expressions, which gave Mr. *Lintott* a very ill Opinion of the said *Shakespear.*

That about two Months since, he came again into the Shop, and cast several suspicious Looks on a Gentleman that stood by him, after which he desired some Information concerning that Person. He was no sooner acquainted that the Gentleman was a new Author, and that his first Piece was to be publish'd in a few Days, but he drew his Sword upon him, and had not my Servant luckily catch'd him by the Sleeve, I might have lost one Author upon the spot, and another the next Sessions.

Upon recollecting all these Circumstances, Mr. *Lintott* was entirely of Opinion, that he had been mad for some Time; and I doubt not but this whole Narrative must sufficiently convince the World of the Excess of his Frenzy. It now remains, that I give the Reasons which obliged me in my own Vindication to publish this whole unfortunate Transaction.

In the first place, Mr. *John Denn*[*is*] had industriously caused to be reported that I enter'd into his Room *Vi & Armis*, either out of a Design to deprive him of his Life, or of a new Play called *Coriolanus*, which he has had ready for the Stage these four Years.

Secondly, He hath given out about *Fleetstreet* and the *Temple*, that I was an Accomplice with his Bookseller, who visited him with Intent to take away divers valuable Manuscripts, without paying him Copy-Money.

Thirdly, He hath told others, that I am no Graduate Physician, and that he had seen me upon a Mountebank Stage in *Moorfields*, when he had Lodgings in the College there.

Fourthly, Knowing that I had much Practice in the City, he reported at the *Royal Exchange, Custom-house,* and other Places adjacent, that I was a foreign Spy, employ'd by the *French* King to convey him into *France*; that I bound him Hand and Foot; and that, if his Friend had not burst from his Confinement to his Relief, he had been at this Hour in the *Bastile.*

All which several Assertions of his are so very extravagant, as well as inconsistent, that I appeal to all Mankind whether this Person be not out of his Senses. I shall not decline giving and producing further Proofs of this Truth in open Court, if he drives the Matter so far. In the mean time I heartily forgive him, and pray that the Lord may restore him to the full Enjoyment of his Understanding: So wisheth, as becometh a Christian,

Robert Norris, M.D.

From my House on
   Snow-hill, July
   the 30th.

God Save the Queen.

5. A Key to the Lock

A Key to the Lock was probably a pre-emptive strike by Pope, aimed at warding off hostile reaction to The Rape of the Lock, which had been published in March 1714. In the months preceding the publication of A Key there had already been adverse comments on his Roman Catholicism, and accusations that he was a Jacobite (Guerinot, pp. 18-19, 22-3, 27-8). Moreover, it would have been awkward and even dangerous for Pope if readers had widely interpreted The Rape as a political poem. Bolingbroke (then an acquaintance of Pope, later an intimate friend) had been dismissed from office on the accession of George I in August 1714, and left for France in March 1715, where he rashly joined the Pretender. Parliament met in March 1715, and the Earl of Oxford, a good friend of Pope, was to be arrested and sent to the Tower in July. It was not unlikely that Pope's enemies would attempt to compromise him politically by publishing a distorted reading of The Rape, so Pope anticipated such a move by issuing his own absurd political interpretation of the poem. However, this does not mean that The Rape has no political connotations: most of the allegorising in A Key is so fatuous as to suggest that all political readings of the poem would be just as ridiculous, and yet the identification of Pam with Marlborough, for example, is not only plausible but likely (see Howard Erskine-Hill, 'The Satirical Game at Cards in Pope and Wordsworth', YES, 14 (1984) 183-95). So A Key seems simultaneously to alert readers to The Rape's political implications and to suggest that Pope himself can carry no responsibility for whatever political significance his readers find there.

The political reading of The Rape of the Lock proposed in A Key refers to the ending of the War of the Spanish Succession. This war had been conducted against France by England and her allies – the Dutch and the Holy Roman Empire – in order to secure the throne of Spain for the Austrian claimant Charles rather than the French claimant Philip V, and thus avert the union of the French and Spanish crowns. The armies of the Empire were commanded by Prince Eugene, those of England by the Duke of Marlborough. The war was supported chiefly by the Whigs under the Lord Treasurer Godolphin. In 1709 Lord Townsend represented England at negotiations for a Barrier Treaty, so called because the Dutch would be given key towns in the Spanish Netherlands to act as a barrier to French aggression. Under this treaty, England had agreed not to make a separate peace with France, but in 1711 the Tory ministry under Lord Treasurer Oxford effected a rapprochement with France which was negotiated by Henry St John (later Viscount Bolingbroke); this paved the way for the Congress of Utrecht in 1712. England's action loosened those ties with the allies which had been cemented with the Barrier Treaty, but advocates of peace argued that England's obligations to her allies were reduced by their lack of effective military action in the campaign. This was the line taken by Swift in his pamphlet *The Conduct of the Allies* (1711).

These manoeuvres in foreign policy had important political implications at home. A peace with France brought closer the possibility of a Jacobite rather than a Hanoverian successor to Queen Anne, though this eventuality depended upon James II's son renouncing his Catholicism. So the question of conformity to the established church continued to be an important element in English politics: in 1710 the high-church Tory Dr Henry Sacheverell was tried for a sermon which he had preached against toleration, occasional conformity and the Whigs who attempted to protect dissenters. He was found guilty, but given only a light sentence.

Although the publication of *A Key* may have been timed to respond to ominous political developments in 1715, it had actually been composed earlier, in the period of Pope's Scriblerian associations: Swift had read it before he left England in August 1714, and Arbuthnot refers to it in a letter of 7 September 1714 (*Corr.* i 302, 251). According to Swift, Pope had 'changed it a good deal, to adapt it to the present times'.

Text: *A Key* went through two editions in 1715, the second of which adds some commendatory poems (see *Poems* vi 132-6). The present text follows the first edition.

A
KEY
TO THE
LOCK.
OR,

A TREATISE proving, beyond all Contradiction, the
dangerous Tendency of a late Poem, entituled, *The RAPE
of the LOCK*,
TO
GOVERNMENT and RELIGION.
By ESDRAS BARNIVELT, Apoth.

THE EPISTLE DEDICATORY, TO MR. POPE.

*Though it may seem foreign to my Profession, which is that of making up
and dispensing salutary Medicines to his Majesty's Subjects, (I might say my
Fellow-Subjects, since I have had the Advantage of being naturalized) yet
cannot I think it unbecoming me to furnish an Antidote against the Poyson
which hath been so artfully distilled through your Quill, and conveyed to the
World through the pleasing Vehicle of your Numbers. Nor is my Profession
as an Apothecary so abhorrent from yours as a Poet, since the Ancients have
thought fit to make the same God the Patron of Both. I have, not without
some Pleasure, observ'd the mystical Arms of our Company, wherein is
represented* Apollo *killing the fell Monster* Python; *this in some measure
admonishes me of my Duty, to trample upon and destroy, as much as in me
lies, that Dragon, or baneful Serpent,* Popery.*

*I must take leave to make you my Patient, whether you will or no; though
out of the Respect I have for you, I should rather chuse to apply Lenitive than
Corrosive Medicines, happy, if they may prove an Emetic sufficient to make
you cast up those Errors, which you have imbibed in your Education, and
which, I hope, I shall never live to see this Nation digest.*

*Sir, I cannot but lament, that a Gentleman of your acute Wit, rectified
Understanding, and sublimated Imagination, should misapply those Talents to raise ill Humours in the Constitution of the Body Politick, of which
your self are a Member, and upon the Health whereof your own Preservation depends. Give me leave to say, such Principles as yours would again
reduce us to the fatal Necessity of the Phlebotomy of War, or the Causticks of
Persecution.*

*In order to inform you of this, I have sought your Acquaintance and
Conversation with the utmost diligence; for I hoped in Person to persuade*

you to a publick Confession of your Fault, and a Recantation of these dangerous Tenets. But finding all my Endeavours ineffectual, and being satisfied with the Conscience of having done all that became a Man of an honest Heart and honourable Intention; I could no longer omit my Duty in opening the Eyes of the World by the Publication of this Discourse. It was indeed written some Months since, but seems not the less proper at this Juncture, when I find so universal an Encouragement given by both Parties, to the Author of a libellous Work that is designed equally to prejudice them both. The uncommon Sale of this Book (for above 6000 of 'em have been already vended) was also a farther Reason that call'd aloud upon me to put a stop to its further Progress, and to preserve his Majesty's Subjects by exposing the whole Artifice of your Poem in Publick.

Sir, to address my self to so florid a Writer as you, without collecting all the Flowers of Rhetorick, would be an unpardonable Indecorum; *but when I speak to the World, as I do in the following Treatise, I must use a simple Stile, since it would be absurd to prescribe an universal Medicine, or* Catholicon, *in a Language not universally understood.*

As I have always professed to have a particular Esteem for Men of Learning, and more especially for your self, nothing but the Love of Truth should have engaged me in a Design of this Nature. Amicus Plato, Amicus Socrates, sed magis Amica Veritas.[1] I am

Your most Sincere Friend,
and Humble Servant,
E. Barnivelt.

A
KEY
TO THE
LOCK.

Since this unhappy Division of our Nation into Parties, it is not to be imagined how many Artifices have been made use of by Writers to obscure the Truth, and cover Designs, which may be detrimental to the Publick; in particular, it has been their Custom of late to vent their Political Spleen in Allegory and Fable. If an honest believing Nation is to be made a Jest of, we have a Story of *John Bull* and his Wife; if a Treasurer is to be glanced at, an *Ant* with a *white Straw* is introduced; if a Treaty of Commerce is to be ridiculed, 'tis immediately metamorphosed into a Tale of Count *Tariff*.

But if any of these Malevolents have never so small a Talent in Rhime, they principally delight to convey their Malice in that pleasing way, as it were, gilding the Pill, and concealing the Poyson under the Sweetness of Numbers. Who could imagine that an *Original Canto* of *Spencer* should contain a Satyr upon one Administration[2]; or that *Yarhel's Kitchin*, or the *Dogs of Egypt*, should be a Sarcasm upon another.[3]

It is the Duty of every well designing Subject to prevent, as far as in him lies, the ill Consequences of such pernicious Treatises; and I hold it mine to warn the Publick of the late Poem, entituled, the *RAPE of the LOCK*; which I shall demonstrate to be of this nature. Many of these sort of Books have been bought by honest and well-meaning People purely for their Diversion, who have in the end found themselves insensibly led into the Violence of Party Spirit, and many domestick Quarrels have been occasioned by the different Application of these Books. The Wife of an eminent Citizen grew very noisy upon reading *Bob Hush*[4]; *John Bull*,[5] upon *Change*, was thought not only to concern the State, but to affront the City; and the Poem we are now treating of, has not only dissolved an agreeable Assembly of Beaus and Belles, but (as I am told) has set Relations at as great a distance, as if they were married together.

It is a common and just Observation, that when the Meaning of any thing is dubious, one can no way better judge of the true Intent of it, than by considering who is the Author, what is his Character in general, and his Disposition in particular.

Now that the Author of this Poem is professedly a *Papist*, is well known; and that a Genius so capable of doing Service to that Cause, may have been corrupted in the Course of his Education by *Jesuits* or others, is justly very much to be suspected; notwithstanding that seeming *Coolness* and *Moderation*, which he has been (perhaps artfully) reproached with, by those of his own Profession. They are sensible that this Nation is secured with good and wholesome Laws, to prevent all evil Practices of the Church of *Rome*; particularly the Publication of Books, that may in any sort propagate that Doctrine: Their Authors are therefore obliged to couch their Designs the deeper; and tho' I cannot averr that the Intention of this Gentleman was directly to spread Popish Doctrines, yet it comes to the same Point, if he touch the Government: For the Court of *Rome* knows very well, that the Church at this time is so firmly founded on the State, that the only way to shake the one is by attacking the other.

What confirms me in this Opinion, is an accidental Discovery I made of a very artful Piece of Management among his Popish Friends and Abettors, to hide this whole Design upon the Government, by taking all the Characters upon themselves.

Upon the Day that this Poem was published, it was my Fortune to step into the *Cocoa Tree*, where a certain Gentleman was railing very liberally at the Author, with a Passion extremely well counterfeited, for having (as he said) reflected upon him in the Character of *Sir Plume*. Upon his going out, I enquired who he was, and they told me, *a Roman Catholick Knight*.

I was the same Evening at *Will's*, and saw a Circle round another Gentleman, who was railing in like manner, and showing his Snuff-box and Cane to prove he was satyrized in the same Character. I asked this Gentleman's Name, and was told, he was *a Roman Catholick Lord*.

A Day or two after I was sent for, upon a slight Indisposition, to the young Lady's to whom the Poem is dedicated. She also took up the Character of *Belinda* with much Frankness and good Humour, tho' the Author has given us a Key in his Dedication,[6] that he meant something further. This Lady is also a *Roman Catholick*. At the same time others of the Characters were claim'd by some Persons in the Room; and all of them *Roman Catholicks*.

But to proceed to the Work it self.

In all things which are intricate, as Allegories in their own Nature are, and especially those that are industriously made so, it is not to be expected we should find the Clue at first sight; but when once we have laid hold on that, we shall trace this our Author through all the Labyrinths, Doublings and Turnings of this intricate Composition.

First then let it be observed, that in the most demonstrative Sciences, some *Postulata* are to be granted, upon which the rest is naturally founded. I shall desire no more than one *Postulatum* to render this obvious to the meanest Capacity; which being granted me, I shall not only shew the Intent of this Work in general, but also explain the very *Names*, and expose all his fictitious *Characters* in their true Light; and we shall find, that even his *Spirits* were not meerly contrived for the sake of *Machinary*.

The only Concession which I desire to be made me, is, that by the *Lock* is meant

The BARRIER TREATY.

I. First then I shall discover, that BELINDA represents GREAT BRITAIN, or (which is the same thing) her late MAJESTY. This is plainly seen in his Description of her.

On her white Breast a sparkling Cross she bore.

Alluding to the antient Name of *Albion*, from her *white Cliffs*, and to the *Cross*, which is the Ensign of *England*.

II. The BARON, who cuts off the Lock, or Barrier Treaty, is the E[arl] of O[xfor]d.

III. CLARISSA, who lent the Scissars, my Lady M[ashe]m.

IV. THALESTRIS, who provokes *Belinda* to resent the Loss of the Lock or Treaty, the D[uches]s of M[arlborou]gh.

V. SIR PLUME, who is mov'd by *Thalestris* to redemand it of *Great Britain*, P[rin]ce Eu[ge]ne, who came hither for that purpose.

There are other inferior Characters, which we shall observe upon afterwards; but I shall first explain the foregoing.

The first Part of the *Baron*'s Character is his being *adventrous*, or enterprizing, which is the common Epithet given the E[arl] of O[xfor]d by his Enemies. The Prize he aspires to is the T[reasur]y, in order to which he offers a Sacrifice.

> *—an Altar built*
> *Of twelve vast* French *Romances neatly gilt.*

Our Author here takes occasion maliciously to insinuate this Statesman's *Love to France*; representing the Books he chiefly studies to be vast *French Romances*. These are the vast Prospects from the Friendship and Alliance of *France*, which he satyrically calls *Romances*, hinting thereby, that these Promises and Protestations were no more to be relied on than those idle Legends. Of these he is said to build an Altar; to intimate, that all the Foundation of his Schemes and Honours was fix'd upon the *French Romances* above-mentioned.

> *A Fan, a Garter, Half a Pair of Gloves.*

One of the Things he sacrifices is a *Fan*, which both for its *gaudy Show* and *perpetual Flutt'ring*, has been made the Emblem of *Woman*. This points at the Change of the *Ladies* of the *Bedchamber*; the *Garter* alludes to the Honours he conferr'd on some of his Friends; and we may without straining the Sense, call the Half Pair of Gloves, a *Gauntlet*; the Token of those Military Employments, which he is said to have sacrificed to his Designs. The Prize, as I said before, means the T[reasur]y, which he makes it his Prayers *soon to obtain*, and *long to possess.*

> *The Pow'rs gave ear, and granted half his Pray'r,*
> *The rest the Winds dispers'd in empty Air.*

In the first of these Lines he gives him the T[reasur]y, and in the last suggests that he should not long possess that Honour.

That *Thalestris* is the D[uches]s of M[arlborou]gh, appears both by her Nearness to *Belinda*, and by this Author's malevolent Suggestion, that she is a Lover of War.

> *To Arms, to Arms, the bold* Thalestris *cries.*

But more particularly in several Passages in her Speech to *Belinda*, upon the cutting off the Lock, or Treaty. Among other Things she says, *Was it for this you bound your Locks in Paper Durance?* Was it for this so much Paper has been spent to secure the Barrier Treaty?

> *Methinks already I your Tears survey,*
> *Already hear the horrid Things they say;*
> *Already see you a degraded Toast.*

This describes the Aspersions under which that good Princess suffer'd, and the Repentance which must have followed the Dissolution of that Treaty, and particularly levels at the Refusal some People made to drink Her M[ajest]y's Health.

Sir Plume (a proper Name for a Soldier) has all the Circumstances that agree with P[rin]ce *Eu[ge]ne*.

> Sir Plume *of Amber Snuff-box justly vain,*
> *And the nice Conduct of a clouded Cane,*
> *With earnest Eyes —*

'Tis remarkable, this General is a great Taker of Snuff as well as Towns; his Conduct of the clouded Cane gives him the Honour which is so justly his due, of an exact Conduct in Battle, which is figured by his Truncheon, the Ensign of a General. His earnest Eye, or the Vivacity of his Look, is so particularly remarkable in him that this Character could be mistaken for no other, had not this Author purposely obscur'd it by the fictitious Circumstance of a *round, unthinking Face.*

Having now explained the chief Characters of his *Human Persons* (for there are some others that will hereafter fall in by the by, in the Sequel of this Discourse) I shall next take in pieces his *Machinary*, wherein his Satyr is wholly confined to Ministers of State.

The SYLPHS and GNOMES at first sight appeared to me to signify the two contending Parties of this Nation; for these being placed in the *Air*, and those on the *Earth*, I thought agreed very well with the common Denomination, HIGH and LOW. But as they are made to be the first Movers and Influencers of all that happens, 'tis plain they represent promiscuously the *Heads of Parties*, whom he makes to be the Authors of all those Changes in the State, which are generally imputed to the Levity and Instability of the *British* Nation.

> *This erring Mortals Levity may call,*
> *Oh blind to Truth! The Sylphs contrive it all.*

But of this he has given us a plain Demonstration; for speaking of these Spirits, he says in express Terms,

A Key to the Lock

—The chief the Care of Nations own,
And guard with Arms Divine the British Throne.

And here let it not seem odd, if in this mysterious way of Writing, we find the same Person, who has before been represented by the *Baron*, again described in the Character of *Ariel*; it being a common way with Authors, in this fabulous Manner, to take such a Liberty. As for instance, I have read in the *English St. Evremont*,[7] that all the different Characters in *Petronius* are but *Nero* in so many different Appearances. And in the Key to the curious Romance of *Barclay's Argenis*,[8] that both *Poliarchus* and *Archombrotus* mean only the *King* of *Navarre*.

We observe in the very Beginning of the Poem, that *Ariel* is possess'd of the Ear of *Belinda*; therefore it is absolutely necessary that this Person must be the Minister who was nearest the Queen. But whoever would be further convinc'd, that he meant the late T[reasure]r, may know him by his Ensigns in the following Line.

He rais'd his Azure Wand.—

His sitting on the Mast of a Vessel shows his presiding over the S[ou]th S[e]a Tr[a]de. When *Ariel* assigns to his *Sylphs* all the Posts about *Belinda*, what is more clearly described, than the Tr[easure]r's disposing all the Places of the Kingdom, and particularly about her M[ajest]y? But let us hear the Lines.

—Ye Spirits, to your charge repair,
The flutt'ring Fan be Zephyretta's *Care;*
The Drops to thee, Brillante, *we consign,*
And, Momentilla, *let the Watch be thine;*
Do thou, Crispissa, *tend her fav'rite Lock.*

He has here particularized the Ladies and Women of the Bed-Chamber, the Keeper of the Cabinet, and her M[ajest]y's Dresser, and impudently given Nick-names to each.

To put this Matter beyond all dispute, the *Sylphs* are said to be *wond'rous fond of Place*, in the Canto following, where *Ariel* is perched uppermost, and all the rest take their Places subordinately under him.

Here again I cannot but observe, the excessive Malignity of this Author, who could not leave this Character of *Ariel* without the same invidious Stroke which he gave him in the Character of the *Baron* before.

Amaz'd, confus'd, he saw his Power expir'd,
Resign'd to Fate, and with a Sigh retir'd.

Being another Prophecy that he should resign his Place, which it is probable all Ministers do with a Sigh.

At the Head of the *Gnomes* he sets *Umbriel*, a dusky melancholy

81

Spright, who makes it his Business to give *Belinda* the Spleen; a vile and malicious Suggestion against some grave and worthy Minister. The Vapours, Fantoms, Visions, and the like, are the Jealousies, Fears, and Cries of Danger, that have so often affrighted and alarm'd the Nation. Those who are described in the House of Spleen, under those several fantastical Forms, are the same whom their Ill-willers have so often called the *Whimsical*.

The two foregoing Spirits being the only considerable Characters of the Machinary, I shall but just mention the *Sylph* that is wounded with the Scissars at the Loss of the Lock, by whom is undoubtedly understood my L[or]d To[wnshen]d, who at that time received a Wound in his Character for making the Barrier Treaty, and was cut out of his Employment upon the Dissolution of it: But that Spirit reunites, and receives no Harm; to signify, that it came to nothing, and his L[o]rdsh[i]p had no real Hurt by it.

But I must not conclude this Head of the Characters, without observing, that our Author has run through every Stage of Beings in search of Topicks for Detraction; and as he has characterized some Persons under Angels and Men, so he has others under Animals, and things inanimate. He has represented an eminent Clergy-man as a Dog, and a noted Writer as a Tool. Let us examine the former.

> —But Shock, *who thought she slept too long,*
> *Leapt up, and wak'd his Mistress with his Tongue,*
> *'Twas then,* Belinda, *if Report say true,*
> *Thy Eyes first open'd on a Billet-doux.*

By this *Shock*, it is manifest he has most audaciously and profanely reflected on Dr. *Sach[evere]ll*, who leapt up, that is, into the Pulpit, and awaken'd *Great Britain* with his *Tongue*, that is, with his *Sermon*, which made so much *Noise*; and for which he has frequently been term'd by others of his Enemies, as well as by this Author, a Dog: Or perhaps, by his *Tongue*, may be more literally meant his *Speech* at his *Trial*, since immediately thereupon, our Author says, her Eyes open'd on a *Billet-doux*; *Billets-doux* being Addresses to Ladies from Lovers, may be aptly interpreted those Addresses of Loving Subjects to her M[ajest]y, which ensued that Trial.

The other Instance is at the End of the third Canto.

> *Steel did the Labours of the Gods destroy,*
> *And strike to Dust th' Imperial Tow'rs of Troy.*
> *Steel could the Works of mortal Pride confound,*
> *And hew triumphal Arches to the Ground.*

Here he most impudently attributes the Demolition of *Dunkirk*, not to the Pleasure of her M[ajest]y, or her Ministry, but to the frequent Instigations of his Friend Mr. *Steel*; a very artful Pun to conceal his wicked Lampoonery!

Having now consider'd the general Intent and Scope of the Poem, and open'd the Characters, I shall next discover the Malice which is covered under the Episodes, and particular Passages of it.

The Game at *Ombre* is a mystical Representation of the late War, which is hinted by his making Spades the Trump; Spade in *Spanish* signifying a Sword, and being yet so painted in the Cards of that Nation; to which it is well known we owe the Original of our Cards. In this one Place indeed he has unawares paid a Compliment to the Queen, and her Success in the War; for *Belinda* gets the better of the two that play against her, the Kings of *France* and *Spain*.

I do not question but ev'ry particular Card has its Person and Character assign'd, which, no doubt, the Author has told his Friends in private; but I shall only instance in the Description of the Disgrace under which the D[uke] of M[arlbor]ough then suffer'd, which is so apparent in these Verses.

> *Ev'n mighty* Pam, *that Kings and Queens o'erthrew,*
> *And mow'd down Armies in the Fights of* Lu,
> *Sad Chance of War! now destitute of Aid,*
> *Falls undistinguish'd—*

That the Author here had an Eye to our modern Transactions, is very plain from an unguarded Stroke towards the End of this Game.

> *And now, as oft in some* distemper'd *State,*
> *On one nice Trick depends the gen'ral Fate.*

After the Conclusion of the War, the publick Rejoicings and *Thanksgivings* are ridiculed in the two following Lines.

> *The Nymph exulting fills with Shouts the Sky,*
> *The Walls, the Woods, and long Canals reply.*

Immediately upon which there follows a malicious Insinuation, in the manner of a Prophecy (which we have formerly observ'd this seditious Writer delights in) that the Peace should continue but a short time, and that the Day should afterwards be curst which was then celebrated with so much Joy.

> *Sudden these Honours shall be snatch'd away,*
> *And curst for ever this Victorious Day.*

As the Game at *Ombre* is a satyrical Representation of the late War; so is the Tea-Table that ensues, of the Council-Table and its Consultations after the Peace. By this he would hint, that all the Advantages we have gain'd by our late extended Commerce, are only Coffee and Tea, or Things of no greater Value. That he thought of the Trade in this Place, appears by the Passage where he represents the *Sylphs* particularly careful of the *rich Brocade*; it having been a frequent Complaint of our Mercers, that *French Brocades* were imported in too great Quantities. I will not say, he means those Presents of rich Gold Stuff Suits, which were said to be made her M[ajest]y by the K[ing] of F[*rance*], tho' I cannot but suspect, that he glances at it.

Here this Author, as well as the scandalous *John Dunton*,[9] represents the Mi[nist]ry in plain Terms taking frequent Cups.

> *And frequent Cups prolong the rich Repast.*

Upon the whole, it is manifest he meant something more than common Coffee, by his calling it,

> *Coffee that makes the* Politician *wise.*

And by telling us, it was this Coffee, that

> *Sent up in Vapours to the* Baron's *Brain*
> *New* Stratagems—

I shall only further observe, that 'twas at this Table the Lock was cut off; for where but at the Council Board should the Barrier Treaty be dissolved?

The ensuing Contentions of the Parties upon the Loss of that Treaty, are described in the Squabbles following the Rape of the Lock; and this he rashly expresses, without any disguise in the Words.

> *All side in* Parties—

Here first you have a Gentleman who sinks beside his Chair: a plain Allusion to a Noble Lord, who lost his Chair of Pre[side]nt of the Co[unci]l.

I come next to the *Bodkin*, so dreadful in the Hand of *Belinda*; by which he intimates the *British Scepter* so rever'd in the Hand of our late August Princess. His own Note upon this Place tells us he alludes to a Scepter; and the Verses are so plain, they need no Remark.

> *The same (his antient Personage to deck)*
> *Her great great Grandsire wore about his Neck*
> *In three Seal Rings, which, after melted down,*
> *Form'd a vast Buckle for his Widow's Gown;*
> *Her Infant Grandame's Whistle next it grew,*
> *The Bells she gingled, and the Whistle blew,*
> *Then in a Bodkin grac'd her Mother's Hairs,*
> *Which long she wore, and now* Belinda *wears.*

An open Satyr upon *Hereditary Right*. The three Seal Rings plainly allude to the three Kingdoms.

These are the chief Passages in the Battle, by which, as hath before been said, he means the Squabble of Parties. Upon this Occasion he could not end the Description of them, without testifying his malignant Joy at those Dissentions, from which he forms the Prospect that *both* should be disappointed, and cries out with Triumph, as if it were already accomplished.

> *Behold how oft ambitious Arms are crost,*
> *And Chiefs contend till all the Prize is lost.*

The Lock at length is turn'd into a *Star*, or the Old Barrier Treaty into a new and glorious *Peace*; this no doubt is what the Author, at the time he printed his Poem, would have been thought to mean, in hopes by that Complement to escape Punishment for the rest of his Piece. It puts me in mind of a Fellow, who concluded a bitter Lampoon upon the Prince and Court of his Days, with these Lines.

> *God save the King, the Commons, and the Peers,*
> *And grant the Author long may wear his Ears.*

Whatever this Author may think of that Peace, I imagine it the most *extraordinary Star* that ever appear'd in our Hemisphere. A Star that is to bring us all the Wealth and Gold of the *Indies*; and from whose Influence, not Mr. *John Partridge* alone, (whose worthy Labours this Writer so ungenerously ridicules) but all true *Britains* may, with no less Authority than he, prognosticate the Fall of *Lewis*, in the Restraint of the exorbitant Power of *France*, and the Fate of *Rome* in the triumphant condition of the Church of *England*.

We have now considered this Poem in its Political View, wherein we have shewn that it hath two different Walks of Satyr, the one in the Story it self, which is a Ridicule on the late Transactions in general; the other in the Machinary, which is a Satyr on the Ministers of State in particular. I shall now show that the same Poem, taken in another Light, has a Tendency to Popery, which is secretly insinuated through the whole.

In the first place, he has conveyed to us the Doctrine of Guardian Angels and Patron Saints in the Machinary of his *Sylphs*, which being a Piece of Popish Superstition that hath been endeavoured to be exploded ever since the Reformation, he would here revive under this Disguise. Here are all the Particulars which they believe of those Beings, which I shall sum up in a few Heads.

1st. The Spirits are made to concern themselves with all human Acts in general.

2dly. A distinct Guardian Spirit or Patron is assigned to each Person in particular.

> *Of these am I, who thy Protection claim,*
> *A watchful Sprite—*

3dly. They are made directly to inspire Dreams, Visions, and Revelations.

> *Her Guardian* Sylph *prolong'd her balmy Rest,*
> *'Twas he had summon'd to her silent Bed*
> *The Morning Dream—*

4thly. They are made to be subordinate, in different Degrees, some presiding over others. So *Ariel* hath his several Under-Officers at Command.

> *Superior by the Head was* Ariel *plac'd.*

5thly. They are employed in various Offices, and each hath his Office assigned him.

> *Some in the Fields of purest Æther play,*
> *And bask and whiten in the Blaze of Day.*
> *Some guide the Course,* &c.

6thly. He hath given his Spirits the Charge of the several Parts of Dress; intimating thereby, that the Saints preside over the several Parts of Human Bodies. They have one Saint to cure the Tooth-ach, another cures the Gripes, another the Gout, and so of all the rest.

> *The flutt'ring Fan be* Zephyretta's *Care,*
> *The Drops to thee,* Brillante, *we consign,* &c.

7thly. They are represented to know the Thoughts of Men.

> *As on the Nosegay in her Breast reclin'd,*
> *He watch'd th' Ideas rising in her Mind.*

8thly. They are made Protectors even to Animals and irrational Beings.

> Ariel *himself shall be the Guard of* Shock.

So St. *Anthony* presides over Hogs, *&c.*

9thly. Others are made Patrons of whole Kingdoms and Provinces.

> *Of these the chief the Care of Nations own.*

So St. *George* is imagined by the Papists to defend *England*; St. *Patrick, Ireland*; St. *James, Spain,* &c. Now what is the Consequence of all this? By granting that they have this Power, we must be brought back again to pray to them.

The *Toilette* is an artful Recommendation of the *Mass,* and pompous Ceremonies of the *Church of Rome.* The *unveiling* of the *Altar,* the *Silver Vases* upon it, being *rob'd* in *White,* as the Priests are upon the chief Festivals, and the *Head uncover'd,* are manifest Marks of this.

> *A heav'nly Image in the Glass appears,*
> *To that she bends—*

Plainly denotes *Image-Worship.*

The *Goddess*, who is deck'd with *Treasures, Jewels*, and the *various Offerings of the World*, manifestly alludes to the Lady of *Loretto*. You have Perfumes breathing from the *Incense Pot* in the following Line.

> *And all* Arabia *breaths from yonder Box.*

The Character of *Belinda*, as we take it in this third View, represents the Popish Religion, or the Whore of *Babylon*; who is described in the State this malevolent Author wishes for, coming forth in all her Glory upon the *Thames*, and overspreading the Nation with Ceremonies.

> *Not with more Glories in th' ætherial Plain,*
> *The Sun first rises o'er the purple Main,*
> *Than issuing forth the Rival of his Beams,*
> *Launch'd on the Bosom of the Silver* Thames.

She is dress'd with a *Cross* on her Breast, the Ensign of Popery, the *Adoration* of which is plainly recommended in the following Lines.

> *On her white Breast a sparkling* Cross *she wore,*
> *Which Jews might kiss, and Infidels adore.*

Next he represents her as the *Universal Church*, according to the Boasts of the Papists.

> *And like the Sun she shines on all alike.*

After which he tells us,

> *If to her Share some Female Errors fall,*
> *Look on her Face, and you'll forget them all.*

Tho' it should be granted some Errors fall to her share, look on the pompous Figure she makes throughout the World, and they are not worth regarding. In the Sacrifice following soon after, you have these two Lines.

> *For this, e'er* Phœbus *rose, he had implor'd*
> *Propitious Heav'n, and ev'ry Pow'r ador'd.*

In the first of them, he plainly hints at their *Matins*; in the second, by adoring ev'ry Power, the *Invocation of Saints*.

Belinda's Visits are described with numerous *Wax-Lights*, which are always used in the Ceremonial Parts of the *Romish* Worship.

> *—Visits shall be paid on solemn Days,*
> *When num'rous Wax-lights in bright Order blaze.*

The *Lunar Sphere* he mentions, opens to us their *Purgatory*, which is seen in the following Line.

> *Since all things lost on Earth are treasur'd there.*

It is a Popish Doctrine, that scarce any Person quits this World, but he must touch at Purgatory in his way to Heaven; and it is here also represented as the *Treasury* of the *Romish Church*. Nor is it much to be wonder'd at, that the *Moon* should be *Purgatory*, when a Learn'd

Divine hath in a late Treatise proved *Hell* to be in the *Sun*.[10]

I shall now before I conclude, desire the Reader to compare this Key with those upon any other Pieces, which are supposed to be secret Satyrs upon the State, either antient or modern; as with those upon *Petronius Arbiter, Lucian*'s true History, *Barclay*'s *Argenis*, or *Rablais*'s *Garagantua*; and I doubt not he will do me the Justice to acknowledge, that the Explanations here laid down, are deduced as naturally, and with as little force, both from the general Scope and Bent of the Work, and from the several Particulars, and are every way as consistent and undeniable as any of those; and ev'ry way as candid as any modern Interpretations of either Party on the mysterious State Treatises of our Times.

To sum up my whole Charge against this Author in a few Words: He has ridiculed both the present Mi[nist]ry and the last; abused great Statesmen and great Generals; nay the Treaties of whole Nations have not escaped him, nor has the Royal Dignity it self been omitted in the Progress of his Satyr; and all this he has done just at the Meeting of a new Parliament. I hope a proper Authority may be made use of to bring him to condign Punishment: In the mean while I doubt not if the Persons most concern'd would but order Mr. *Bernard Lintott*, the Printer and Publisher of this dangerous Piece, to be taken into Custody, and examin'd; many further Discoveries might be made both of this Poet's and his Abettor's secret Designs, which are doubtless of the utmost Importance to the Government.

FINIS.

6. From the translation of Homer

Pope's translation of the *Iliad* was published in six volumes from 1715 to 1720, and his *Odyssey* in five volumes in 1725-6. It was a turning point in Pope's career, and indeed in the profession of the man of letters in England, for the strategy of publishing by subscription gave Pope a comfortable income, and helped to establish him as the first English poet to be able to earn a living from his poetry (Dryden, never rich, had relied partly on the theatre). The translation of Homer was accompanied by two important critical essays, the Preface to *The Iliad* and the Postscript to *The Odyssey*. Pope also added many notes; some of these are taken over from previous commentators, and those to the *Odyssey* are largely by William Broome, but throughout the notes to the *Iliad* there are acute observations by Pope on the nature of Homer's genius, and a sample of these is given here.

The critical context and assumptions of Pope's work on Homer are amply discussed in *Poems* vii; but see also Kirsti Simonsuuri, *Homer's Original Genius* (Cambridge, 1979) and H.A. Mason, *To Homer through Pope* (1972).

Text: The following texts are taken from the first editions; for occasional minor revisions, and early drafts of the two essays, see *Poems* vii, viii, x.

The Preface to The Iliad

Homer is universally allow'd to have had the greatest Invention of any Writer whatever. The Praise of Judgment *Virgil* has justly contested with him, and others may have their Pretensions as to particular Excellencies; but his Invention remains yet unrival'd. Nor is it a Wonder if he has ever been acknowledg'd the greatest of Poets, who most excell'd in That which is the very Foundation of Poetry. It is the Invention that in different degrees distinguishes all great Genius's: The utmost Stretch of human Study, Learning, and Industry, which masters every thing besides, can never attain to this. It furnishes Art with all her Materials, and without it Judgment itself can at best but *steal wisely*: For Art is only like a prudent Steward that lives on managing the Riches of Nature. Whatever Praises may be given to Works of Judgment, there is not even a single Beauty in them but is owing to the Invention: As in the most regular Gardens, however Art may carry the greatest Appearance, there is not a Plant or Flower but is the Gift of Nature. The first can only reduce the Beauties of the latter into a more obvious Figure, which the common Eye may better take in, and is therefore more entertain'd with. And perhaps the reason why most Criticks are inclin'd to prefer a judicious and methodical Genius to a great and fruitful one, is, because they find it easier for themselves to pursue their Observations through an uniform and bouhded Walk of Art, than to comprehend the vast and various Extent of Nature.

Our Author's Work is a wild Paradise, where if we cannot see all the Beauties so distinctly as in an order'd Garden, it is only because the Number of them is infinitely greater. 'Tis like a copious Nursery which contains the Seeds and first Productions of every kind, out of which those who follow'd him have but selected some particular Plants, each according to his Fancy, to cultivate and beautify. If some things are too luxuriant, it is owing to the Richness of the Soil; and if others are not arriv'd to Perfection or Maturity, it is only because they are over-run and opprest by those of a stronger Nature.

It is to the Strength of this amazing Invention we are to attribute that unequal'd Fire and Rapture, which is so forcible in *Homer*, that no Man of a true Poetical Spirit is Master of himself while he reads him. What he writes is of the most animated Nature imaginable; every thing moves, every thing lives, and is put in Action. If a Council be call'd, or a Battel fought, you are not coldly inform'd of what was said or done as from a third Person; the Reader is hurry'd out of himself by the Force of the Poet's Imagination, and turns in

From the translation of Homer

one place to a Hearer, in another to a Spectator. The Course of his Verses resembles that of the Army he describes,

Οἱ δ᾽ ἄρ᾽ ἴσαν, ὡσεί τε πυρὶ χθὼν πᾶσα νέμοιτο.   [II 780]

They pour along like a Fire that sweeps the whole Earth before it. 'Tis however remarkable that his Fancy, which is every where vigorous, is not discover'd immediately at the beginning of his Poem in its fullest Splendor: It grows in the Progress both upon himself and others, and becomes on Fire like a Chariot-Wheel, by its own Rapidity. Exact Disposition, just Thought, correct Elocution, polish'd Numbers, may have been found in a thousand; but this Poetical *Fire,* this *Vivida vis animi,*[1] in a very few. Even in Works where all those are imperfect or neglected, this can over-power Criticism, and make us admire even while we dis-approve. Nay, where this appears, tho' attended with Absurdities, it brightens all the Rubbish about it, 'till we see nothing but its own Splendor. This *Fire* is discern'd in *Virgil,* but discern'd as through a Glass, reflected, and more shining than warm, but every where equal and constant: in *Lucan* and *Statius,* it bursts out in sudden, short, and interrupted Flashes: In *Milton,* it glows like a Furnace kept up to an uncommon Fierceness by the Force of Art: In *Shakespear,* it strikes before we are aware, like an accidental Fire from Heaven: But in *Homer,* and in him only, it burns every where clearly, and every where irresistibly.

I shall here endeavour to show, how this vast *Invention* exerts itself in a manner superior to that of any Poet, thro' all the main constituent Parts of his Work, as it is the great and peculiar Characteristick which distinguishes him from all other Authors.

This strong and ruling Faculty was like a powerful Planet, which in the Violence of its Course, drew all things within its *Vortex.* It seem'd not enough to have taken in the whole Circle of Arts, and the whole Compass of Nature; all the inward Passions and Affections of Mankind to supply his Characters, and all the outward Forms and Images of Things for his Descriptions; but wanting yet an ampler Sphere to expatiate in, he open'd a new and boundless Walk for his Imagination, and created a World for himself in the Invention of *Fable.* That which *Aristotle* calls the *Soul of Poetry,*[2] was first breath'd into it by *Homer.* I shall begin with considering him in this Part, as it is naturally the first, and I speak of it both as it means the Design of a Poem, and as it is taken for Fiction.

Fable may be divided into the *Probable,* the *Allegorical,* and the *Marvelous.* The *Probable Fable* is the Recital of such Actions as tho' they did not happen, yet might, in the common course of Nature: Or of such as tho' they did, become Fables by the additional

Episodes and manner of telling them. Of this sort is the main Story of an Epic Poem, *the Return of* Ulysses, *the Settlement of the* Trojans *in* Italy, or the like. That of the *Iliad* is *the Anger of* Achilles, the most short and single Subject that ever was chosen by any Poet. Yet this he has supplied with a vaster Variety of Incidents and Events, and crouded with a greater Number of Councils, Speeches, Battles, and Episodes of all kinds, than are to be found even in those Poems whose Schemes are of the utmost Latitude and Irregularity. The Action is hurry'd on with the most vehement Spirit, and its whole Duration employs not so much as fifty Days. *Virgil*, for want of so warm a Genius, aided himself by taking in a more extensive Subject, as well as a greater Length of Time, and contracting the Design of both *Homer*'s Poems into one, which is yet but a fourth part as large as his. The other Epic Poets have us'd the same Practice, but generally carry'd it so far as to superinduce a Multiplicity of Fables, destroy the Unity of Action, and lose their Readers in an unreasonable Length of Time. Nor is it only in the main Design that they have been unable to add to his Invention, but they have follow'd him in every Episode and Part of Story. If he has given a regular *Catalogue* of an *Army,* they all draw up their Forces in the same Order. If he has funeral Games for *Patroclus, Virgil* has the same for *Anchises,* and *Statius* (rather than omit them) destroys the Unity of his Action for those of *Archemorus.* If *Ulysses* visit the Shades, the *Æneas* of *Virgil* and *Scipio* of *Silius* are sent after him. If he be detain'd from his Return by the Allurements of *Calypso,* so is *Æneas* by *Dido,* and *Rinaldo* by *Armida.*[3] If *Achilles* be absent from the Army on the Score of a Quarrel thro' half the Poem, *Rinaldo* must absent himself just as long, on the like account. If he gives his Heroe a Suit of celestial Armour, *Virgil* and *Tasso* make the same Present to theirs. *Virgil* has not only observ'd this close Imitation of *Homer*, but where he had not led the way, supply'd the Want from other *Greek* Authors. Thus the Story of *Sinon* and the *Taking of Troy* was copied (says *Macrobius*) almost word for word from *Pisander,* as the Loves of *Dido* and *Æneas* are taken from those of *Medæa* and *Jason* in *Apollonius*, and several others in the same manner.

To proceed to the *Allegorical Fable*: If we reflect upon those innumerable Knowledges, those Secrets of Nature and Physical Philosophy which *Homer* is generally suppos'd to have wrapt up in his *Allegories*, what a new and ample Scene of Wonder may this Consideration afford us? How fertile will that Imagination appear, which was able to cloath all the Properties of Elements, the Qualifications of the Mind, the Virtues and Vices, in Forms and

From the translation of Homer

Persons; and to introduce them into Actions agreeable to the Nature of the Things they shadow'd? This is a Field in which no succeeding Poets could dispute with *Homer*; and whatever Commendations have been allow'd them on this Head, are by no means for their Invention in having enlarg'd his Circle, but for their Judgment in having contracted it. For when the Mode of Learning chang'd in following Ages, and Science was deliver'd in a plainer manner, it then became as reasonable in the more modern Poets to lay it aside, as it was in *Homer* to make use of it. And perhaps it was no unhappy Circumstance for *Virgil*, that there was not in his Time that Demand upon him of so great an Invention, as might be capable of furnishing all those Allegorical Parts of a Poem.

The *Marvelous Fable* includes whatever is supernatural, and especially the Machines of the Gods. If *Homer* was not the first who introduc'd the Deities (as *Herodotus* imagines[4]) into the Religion of *Greece*, he seems the first who brought them into a System of *Machinery* for Poetry, and such an one as makes its greatest Importance and Dignity. For we find those Authors who have been offended at the literal Notion of the Gods, constantly laying their Accusation against *Homer* as the undoubted Inventor of them. But whatever cause there might be to blame his *Machines* in a Philosophical or Religious View, they are so perfect in the Poetick, that Mankind have been ever since contented to follow them: None have been able to enlarge the Sphere of Poetry beyond the Limits he has set: Every Attempt of this Nature has prov'd unsuccessful; and after all the various Changes of Times and Religions, his Gods continue to this Day the Gods of Poetry.

We come now to the *Characters* of his Persons, and here we shall find no Author has ever drawn so many with so visible and surprizing a Variety, or given us such lively and affecting Impressions of them. Every one has something so singularly his own, that no Painter could have distinguish'd them more by their Features, than the Poet has by their Manners. Nothing can be more exact than the Distinctions he has observ'd in the different degrees of Virtues and Vices. The single Quality of *Courage* is wonderfully diversify'd in the several Characters of the *Iliad*. That of *Achilles* is furious and intractable; that of *Diomede* forward, yet listening to Advice and subject to Command: We see in *Ajax* an heavy and self-considering Valour, in *Hector* an active and vigilant one: The Courage of *Agamemnon* is inspirited by Love of Empire and Ambition, that of *Menelaus* mix'd with Softness and Tenderness for his People: We find in *Idomeneus* a plain direct Soldier, in *Sarpedon* a gallant and generous one. Nor is this judicious and astonishing Diversity to be found only in the principal Quality which constitutes the Main of each Character, but even in the Under-parts of it, to which he takes care to give a Tincture of that principal one. For Example, the main Characters of *Ulysses* and *Nestor* consist in *Wisdom*, and they are distinct in this; the Wisdom of one is *artificial* and *various*, of the other *natural, open,* and *regular*. But they have, besides, Characters of *Courage;* and this Quality also takes a different Turn in each from the difference of his Prudence: For one in the War depends still upon *Caution*, the other upon *Experience*. It would be endless to produce Instances of these Kinds. The Characters of *Virgil* are far from striking us in this open manner; they lie in a great degree hidden and undistinguish'd, and where they are mark'd most evidently, affect us not in proportion to those of *Homer*. His Characters of Valour are much alike; even that of *Turnus* seems no way peculiar but as it is in a superior degree; and we see nothing that differences the Courage of *Mnestheus* from that of *Sergesthus, Cloanthus,* or the rest. In like manner it may be remark'd of *Statius's* Heroes, that an Air of Impetuosity runs thro' them all; the same horrid and savage Courage appears in his *Capaneus, Tydeus, Hippomedon,* &c. They have a Parity of Character which makes them seem Brothers of one Family. I believe when the Reader is led into this Track of Reflection, if he will pursue it through the *Epic* and *Tragic* Writers, he will be convinced how infinitely superior in this Point the Invention of *Homer* was to that of all others.

The *Speeches* are to be consider'd as they flow from the Characters, being perfect or defective as they agree or disagree with the Manners of those who utter them. As there is more variety of Characters in the *Iliad,* so there is of Speeches, than in any other Poem. *Every thing in it has Manners* (as *Aristotle* expresses it) that is, every thing is acted or spoken. It is hardly credible in a Work of such length, how small a Number of Lines are employ'd in Narration. In *Virgil* the Dramatic Part is less in proportion to the Narrative; and the Speeches often consist of general Reflections or Thoughts, which might be equally just in any Person's Mouth upon the same Occasion. As many of his Persons have no apparent Characters, so many of his Speeches escape being apply'd and judg'd by the Rule of Propriety. We oftner think of the Author himself when we read *Virgil*, than when we are engag'd in *Homer*: All which are the Effects of a colder Invention, that interests us less in the Action describ'd: *Homer* makes us Hearers, and *Virgil* leaves us Readers.

If in the next place we take a View of the *Sentiments*, the same

From the translation of Homer

presiding Faculty is eminent in the Sublimity and Spirit of his Thoughts. *Longinus* has given his Opinion, that it was in this Part *Homer* principally excell'd. What were alone sufficient to prove the Grandeur and Excellence of his Sentiments in general, is that they have so remarkable a Parity with those of the Scripture: *Duport,* in his *Gnomologia Homerica,* has collected innumerable Instances of this sort. And it is with Justice an excellent modern Writer allows, that if *Virgil* has not so many Thoughts that are low and vulgar, he has not so many that are sublime and noble;[5] and that the *Roman* Author seldom rises into very astonishing Sentiments where he is not fired by the *Iliad.*

If we observe his *Descriptions, Images,* and *Similes,* we shall find the Invention still predominant. To what else can we ascribe that vast Comprehension of Images of every sort, where we see each Circumstance and Individual of Nature summon'd together by the Extent and Fecundity of his Imagination; to which all things, in their various Views, presented themselves in an Instant, and had their Impressions taken off to Perfection at a Heat? Nay, he not only gives us the full Prospects of Things, but several unexpected Peculiarities and Side-Views, unobserv'd by any Painter but *Homer.* Nothing is so surprizing as the Descriptions of his Battels, which take up no less than half the *Iliad,* and are supply'd with so vast a Variety of Incidents, that no one bears a Likeness to another; such different Kinds of Deaths, that no two Heroes are wounded in the same manner; and such a Profusion of noble Ideas, that every Battel rises above the last in Greatness, Horror, and Confusion. It is certain there is not near that Number of Images and Descriptions in any Epic Poet; tho' every one has assisted himself with a great Quantity out of him: And it is evident of *Virgil* especially, that he has scarce any Comparisons which are not drawn from his Master.

If we descend from hence to the *Expression,* we see the bright Imagination of *Homer* shining out in the most enliven'd Forms of it. We acknowledge him the Father of Poetical Diction, the first who taught that *Language of the Gods* to Men. His Expression is like the colouring of some great Masters, which discovers itself to be laid on boldly, and executed with Rapidity. It is indeed the strongest and most glowing imaginable, and touch'd with the greatest Spirit. *Aristotle* had reason to say, He was the only Poet who had found out *Living Words;*[6] there are in him more daring Figures and Metaphors than in any good Author whatever. An Arrow is *impatient* to be on the Wing, a Weapon *thirsts* to drink the Blood of an Enemy, and the like. Yet his Expression is never too big for the Sense, but justly great in proportion to it: 'Tis the Sentiment that swells and fills out the Diction, which rises with it, and forms itself about it. For in the same degree that a *Thought* is warmer, an *Expression* will be brighter; and as That is more strong, This will become more perspicuous: Like Glass in the Furnace which grows to a greater Magnitude, and refines to a greater Clearness, only as the *Breath* within is more powerful, and the *Heat* more intense.

To throw his Language more out of Prose, *Homer* seems to have affected the *Compound-Epithets*. This was a sort of Composition peculiarly proper to Poetry, not only as it heighten'd the *Diction*, but as it assisted and fill'd the *Numbers* with greater Sound and Pomp, and likewise conduced in some measure to thicken the *Images*. On this last Consideration I cannot but attribute these to the Fruitful-ness of his Invention, since (as he has manag'd them) they are a sort of supernumerary Pictures of the Persons or Things they are join'd to. We see the Motion of *Hector's* Plumes in the Epithet Κορυθαίολος,[7] the Landscape of Mount *Neritus* in that of Εἰνοσίφυλλος,[8] and so of others; which particular Images could not have been insisted upon so long as to express them in a Description (tho' but of a single Line) without diverting the Reader too much from the principal Action or Figure. As a Metaphor is a short Simile, one of these Epithets is a short Description.

Lastly, if we consider his *Versification*, we shall be sensible what a Share of Praise is due to his Invention in that also. He was not satisfy'd with his Language as he found it settled in any one Part of *Greece,* but search'd thro' its differing *Dialects* with this particular View, to beautify and perfect his Numbers: He consider'd these as they had a greater Mixture of Vowels or Consonants, and according-ly employ'd them as the Verse requir'd either a greater Smoothness or Strength. What he most affected was the *Ionic,* which has a peculiar Sweetness from its never using Contractions, and from its Custom of resolving the Diphthongs into two Syllables; so as to make the Words open themselves with a more spreading and sonorous Fluency. With this he mingled the *Attic* Contractions, the broader *Doric,* and the feebler *Æolic,* which often rejects its Aspirate, or takes off its Accent; and compleated this Variety by altering some Letters with the License of Poetry. Thus his Measures, instead of being Fetters to his Sense, were always in readiness to run along with the Warmth of his Rapture; and even to give a farther Representa-tion of his Notions, in the Correspondence of their Sounds to what they signify'd. Out of all these he has deriv'd that Harmony, which makes us confess he had not only the richest Head, but the finest Ear in the World. This is so great a Truth, that whoever will but consult the Tune of his Verses even without understanding them (with the same sort of Diligence as we daily see practis'd in the Case of *Italian Opera's*) will find more Sweetness, Variety, and Majesty of Sound, than in any other Language or Poetry. The Beauty of his Numbers is allow'd by the Criticks to be copied but faintly by *Virgil* himself, tho' they are so just to ascribe it to the Nature of the *Latine* Tongue. Indeed the *Greek* has some Advantages both from the natural *Sound* of its *Words*, and the Turn and *Cadence* of its *Verse*, which agree with the Genius of no other Language. *Virgil* was very sensible of this, and used the utmost Diligence in working up a more intractable Language to whatsoever Graces it was capable of, and in particular never fail'd to bring the Sound of his Line to a beautiful Agreement with its Sense. If the *Grecian* Poet has not been so frequently celebrated on this Account as the *Roman*, the only reason is, that fewer Criticks have understood one Language than the other. *Dionysius* of *Halicarnassus* has pointed out many of our Author's Beauties in this kind, in his Treatise of the *Composition of Words*, and others will be taken notice of in the Course of the Notes. It suffices at present to observe of his Numbers, that they flow with so much ease, as to make one imagine *Homer* had no other care than to transcribe as fast as the *Muses* dictated; and at the same time with so much Force and inspiriting Vigour, that they awaken and raise us like the Sound of a Trumpet. They roll along as a plentiful River, always in motion, and always full; while we are born away by a Tide of Verse, the most rapid, and yet the most smooth imaginable.

Thus on whatever side we contemplate *Homer*, what principally strikes us is his *Invention*. It is that which forms the Character of each Part of his Work; and accordingly we find it to have made his Fable more *extensive* and *copious* than any other, his Manners more *lively* and *strongly marked*, his Speeches more *affecting* and *transported*, his Sentiments more *warm* and *sublime*, his Images and Descriptions more *full* and *animated*, his Expression more *rais'd* and *daring*, and his Numbers more *rapid* and *various*. I hope in what has been said of *Virgil* with regard to any of these Heads, I have no way derogated from his Character. Nothing is more absurd or endless, than the common Method of comparing eminent Writers by an Opposition of particular Passages in them, and forming a Judgment from thence of their Merit upon the whole. We ought to have a certain Knowledge of the principal Character and distinguishing Excellence of each: It is in *that* we are to consider him, and in proportion to his Degree in *that* we are to admire him. No Author or Man ever excell'd all the World in more than one Faculty, and as *Homer* has done this in Invention, *Virgil* has in Judgment. Not that we are to think *Homer* wanted Judgment, because *Virgil* had it in a more eminent degree; or that *Virgil* wanted Invention, because *Homer* possest a larger share of it: Each of these great Authors had more of both than perhaps any Man besides, and are only said to have less in Comparison with one another. *Homer* was the greater Genius, *Virgil* the better Artist. In one we most admire the *Man*, in the other the *Work*. *Homer* hurries and transports us with a commanding Impetuosity, *Virgil* leads us with an attractive Majesty: *Homer* scatters with a generous Profusion, *Virgil* bestows with a careful Magnificence: *Homer*, like the *Nile*, pours out his Riches with a sudden Overflow; *Virgil* like a River in its Banks, with a gentle and constant Stream. When we behold their Battels, methinks the two Poets resemble the Heroes they celebrate: *Homer*, boundless and irresistible as *Achilles*, bears all before him, and shines more and more as the Tumult increases; *Virgil*, calmly daring like *Æneas*, appears undisturb'd in the midst of the Action, disposes all about him, and conquers with Tranquillity: And when we look upon their Machines, *Homer* seems like his own *Jupiter* in his Terrors, shaking *Olympus*, scattering the Lightnings, and firing the Heavens; *Virgil*, like the same Power in his Benevolence, counselling with the Gods, laying Plans for Empires, and regularly ordering his whole Creation.

But after all, it is with great Parts as with great Virtues, they naturally border on some Imperfection; and it is often hard to distinguish exactly where the Virtue ends, or the Fault begins. As Prudence may sometimes sink to Suspicion, so may a great Judgment decline to Coldness; and as Magnanimity may run up to Profusion or Extravagance, so may a great Invention to Redundancy or Wildness. If we look upon *Homer* in this View, we shall perceive the chief *Objections* against him to proceed from so noble a Cause as the Excess of this Faculty.

Among these we may reckon some of his *Marvellous Fictions*, upon which so much Criticism has been spent as surpassing all the Bounds of Probability. Perhaps it may be with great and superior Souls as with gigantick Bodies, which exerting themselves with unusual Strength, exceed what is commonly thought the due Proportion of Parts, to become Miracles in the whole; and like the old Heroes of that Make, commit something near Extravagance amidst a Series of glorious and inimitable Performances. Thus *Homer* has his *speaking Horses*, and *Virgil* his *Myrtles distilling Blood*, without so much as contriving the easy Intervention of a Deity to save the Probability.

From the translation of Homer

It is owing to the same vast Invention that his *Similes* have been thought too exuberant and full of Circumstances. The Force of this Faculty is seen in nothing more, than its Inability to confine itself to that single Circumstance upon which the Comparison is grounded: It runs out into Embellishments of additional Images, which however are so manag'd as not to overpower the main one. His Similes are like Pictures, where the principal Figure has not only its proportion given agreeable to the Original, but is also set off with occasional Ornaments and Prospects. The same will account for his manner of heaping a Number of Comparisons together in one Breath, when his Fancy suggested to him at once so many various and correspondent Images. The Reader will easily extend this Observation to more Objections of the same kind.

If there are others which seem rather to charge him with a Defect or Narrowness of Genius, than an Excess of it; those seeming Defects will be found upon Examination to proceed wholly from the Nature of the Times he liv'd in. Such are his *grosser Representations* of the *Gods*, and the vicious and *imperfect Manners* of his *Heroes*, which will be treated of in the following *Essay*[9]: But I must here speak a word of the latter, as it is a Point generally carried into Extreams both by the Censurers and Defenders of *Homer*. It must be a strange Partiality to Antiquity to think with Madam *Dacier*, "that those Times and Manners are so much the more excellent, as they are more contrary to ours."[10] Who can be so prejudiced in their Favour as to magnify the Felicity of those Ages, when a Spirit of Revenge and Cruelty reign'd thro' the World, when no Mercy was shown but for the sake of Lucre, when the greatest Princes were put to the Sword, and their Wives and Daughters made Slaves and Concubines? On the other side I would not be so delicate as those modern Criticks, who are shock'd at the *servile Offices* and *mean Employments* in which we sometimes see the Heroes of *Homer* engag'd. There is a Pleasure in taking a view of that Simplicity in Opposition to the Luxury of succeeding Ages; in beholding Monarchs without their Guards, Princes tending their Flocks, and Princesses drawing Water from the Springs. When we read *Homer*, we ought to reflect that we are reading the most ancient Author in the Heathen World; and those who consider him in this Light, will double their Pleasure in the Perusal of him. Let them think they are growing acquainted with Nations and People that are now no more; that they are stepping almost three thousand Years backward into the remotest Antiquity, and entertaining themselves with a clear and surprizing Vision of Things no where else to be found, and the only authentick Picture of that ancient World. By this means alone their greatest Obstacles will vanish; and what usually creates their Dislike, will become a Satisfaction.

This Consideration may farther serve to answer for the constant Use of the same *Epithets* to his Gods and Heroes, such as the *far-darting Phœbus*, the *blue-ey'd Pallas*, the *swift-footed Achilles*, &c. which some have censured as impertinent and tediously repeated. Those of the Gods depended upon the Powers and Offices then believ'd to belong to them, and had contracted a Weight and Veneration from the Rites and solemn Devotions in which they were us'd: They were a sort of Attributes that it was a Matter of Religion to salute them with on all Occasions, and an Irreverence to omit. As for the Epithets of great Men, Mons. *Boileau* is of Opinion; that they were in the Nature of *Surnames*, and repeated as such; for the *Greeks* having no Names deriv'd from their Fathers, were oblig'd when they mention'd any one to add some other Distinction; either naming his Parents expressly, or his Place of Birth, Profession, or the like: As *Alexander* Son of *Philip, Herodotus* of *Halicarnassus, Diogenes* the *Cynic, &c. Homer* therefore complying with the Custom of his Countrey, us'd such distinctive Additions as better agreed with Poetry. And indeed we have something parallel to these in modern Times, such as the Names of *Harold Harefoot, Edmund Ironside, Edward Long-shanks, Edward* the *black Prince, &c.* If yet this be thought to account better for the Propriety than for the Repetition, I shall add a farther Conjecture. *Hesiod* dividing the World into its Ages, has plac'd a fourth Age between the Brazen and the Iron one, of *Heroes distinct from other Men, a divine Race, who fought at* Thebes *and* Troy, *are called Demi-Gods, and live by the Care of* Jupiter *in the Islands of the Blessed.*[11] Now among the divine Honours which were paid them, they might have this also in common with the Gods, not to be mention'd without the Solemnity of an Epithet, and such as might be acceptable to them by its celebrating their Families, Actions, or Qualities.

What other Cavils have been rais'd against *Homer* are such as hardly deserve a Reply, but will yet be taken notice of as they occur in the Course of the Work. Many have been occasion'd by an injudicious Endeavour to exalt *Virgil*; which is much the same, as if one should think to raise the Superstructure by undermining the Foundation: One would imagine by the whole Course of their Parallels, that these Criticks never so much as heard of *Homer's* having written first; a Consideration which whoever compares these two Poets ought to have always in his Eye. Some accuse him for the same things which they overlook or praise in the other; as when they prefer the Fable and

From the translation of Homer

Moral of the *Æneis* to those of the *Iliad*, for the same Reasons which might set the *Odysses* above the *Æneis*: as that the Heroe is a wiser Man; and the Action of the one more beneficial to his Countrey than that of the other: Or else they blame him for not doing what he never design'd; as because *Achilles* is not as good and perfect a Prince as *Æneas*, when the very Moral of his Poem requir'd a contrary Character. It is thus that *Rapin* judges in his Comparison of *Homer* and *Virgil*.[12] Others select those particular Passages of *Homer* which are not so labour'd as some that *Virgil* drew out of them: This is the whole Management of *Scaliger* in his *Poetices*.[13] Others quarrel with what they take for low and mean Expressions, sometimes thro' a false Delicacy and Refinement, oftner from an Ignorance of the Graces of the Original; and then triumph in the Aukwardness of their own Translations. This is the Conduct of *Perault* in his *Parallels*.[14] Lastly, there are others, who pretending to a fairer Proceeding, distinguish between the personal Merit of *Homer*, and that of his *Work*; but when they come to assign the Causes of the great Reputation of the *Iliad*, they found it upon the Ignorance of his Times, and the Prejudice of those that followed. And in pursuance of this Principle, they make those Accidents (such as the Contention of the Cities, *&c.*) to be the Causes of his Fame, which were in Reality the Consequences of his Merit. The same might as well be said of *Virgil*, or any great Author, whose general Character will infallibly raise many casual Additions to their Reputation. This is the Method of Mons. *de la Motte*;[15] who yet confesses upon the whole, that in whatever Age *Homer* had liv'd he must have been the greatest Poet of his Nation, and that he may be said in this Sense to be the Master even of those who surpass'd him.

In all these Objections we see nothing that contradicts his Title to the Honour of the chief *Invention*; and as long as this (which is indeed the Characteristic of Poetry itself) remains unequal'd by his Followers, he still continues superior to them. A cooler Judgment may commit fewer Faults, and be more approv'd in the Eyes of *One Sort* of Criticks: but that Warmth of Fancy will carry the loudest and most universal Applauses which holds the Heart of a Reader under the strongest Enchantment. *Homer* not only appears the Inventor of Poetry, but excells all the Inventors of other Arts in this, that he has swallow'd up the Honour of those who succeeded him. What he has done admitted no Encrease, it only left room for Contraction or Regulation. He shew'd all the Stretch of Fancy at once; and if he has fail'd in some of his Flights, it was but because he attempted every thing. A Work of this kind seems like a mighty Tree which rises from the most vigorous Seed, is improv'd with Industry, flourishes, and produces the finest

Selected prose of Alexander Pope

Fruit; Nature and Art have conspir'd to raise it; Pleasure and Profit join'd to make it valuable: and they who find the justest Faults, have only said, that a few Branches (which run luxuriant thro' a Richness of Nature) might be lopp'd into Form to give it a more regular Appearance.

Having now spoken of the Beauties and Defects of the Original, it remains to treat of the Translation, with the same View to the chief Characteristic. As far as that is seen in the main Parts of the Poem, such as the *Fable, Manners,* and *Sentiments,* no Translator can prejudice it but by wilful Omissions or Contractions. As it also breaks out in every particular *Image, Description,* and *Simile*; whoever lessens or too much softens those, takes off from this chief Character. It is the first grand Duty of an Interpreter to give his Author entire and unmaim'd; and for the rest, the *Diction* and *Versification* only are his proper Province; since these must be his own, but the others he is to take as he finds them.

It should then be consider'd what Methods may afford some Equivalent in our Language for the Graces of these in the *Greek*. It is certain no literal Translation can be just to an excellent Original in a superior Language: but it is a great Mistake to imagine (as many have done) that a rash Paraphrase can make amends for this general Defect; which is no less in danger to lose the Spirit of an Ancient, by deviating into the modern Manners of Expression. If there be sometimes a *Darkness*, there is often a *Light* in Antiquity, which nothing better preserves than a Version almost literal. I know no Liberties one ought to take, but those which are necessary for transfusing the Spirit of the Original, and supporting the Poetical Style of the Translation: and I will venture to say, there have not been more Men misled in former times by a servile dull Adherence to the Letter, than have been deluded in ours by a chimerical insolent Hope of raising and improving their Author. It is not to be doubted that the *Fire* of the Poem is what a Translator should principally regard, as it is most likely to expire in his managing: However it is his safest way to be content with preserving this to his utmost in the Whole, without endeavouring to be more than he finds his Author is, in any particular Place. 'Tis a great Secret in Writing to know when to be plain, and when poetical and figurative; and it is what *Homer* will teach us if we will but follow modestly in his Footsteps. Where his Diction is bold and lofty, let us raise ours as high as we can; but where his is plain and humble, we ought not to be deterr'd from imitating him by the fear of incurring the Censure of a meer *English* Critick. Nothing that belongs to *Homer* seems to have

From the translation of Homer

been more commonly mistaken than the just Pitch of his Style: Some of his Translators having swell'd into Fustian in a proud Confidence of the *Sublime*; others sunk into Flatness in a cold and timorous Notion of *Simplicity*. Methinks I see these different Followers of *Homer*, some sweating and straining after him by violent Leaps and Bounds, (the certain Signs of false Mettle) others slowly and servilely creeping in his Train, while the Poet himself is all the time proceeding with an unaffected and equal Majesty before them. However of the two Extreams one could sooner pardon Frenzy than Frigidity: No Author is to be envy'd for such Commendations as he may gain by that Character of Style, which his Friends must agree together to call *Simplicity*, and the rest of the World will call *Dulness*. There is a *graceful* and *dignify'd* Simplicity, as well as a *bald* and *sordid* one, which differ as much from each other as the Air of a *plain* Man from that of a *Sloven*: 'Tis one thing to be tricked up, and another not to be dress'd at all. Simplicity is the Mean between Ostentation and Rusticity.

This pure and noble Simplicity is no where in such Perfection as in the *Scripture* and our Author. One may affirm with all respect to the inspired Writings, that the *Divine Spirit* made use of no other Words but what were intelligible and common to Men at that Time, and in that Part of the World; and as *Homer* is the Author nearest to those, his Style must of course bear a greater Resemblance to the sacred Books than that of any other Writer. This Consideration (together with what has been observ'd of the Parity of some of his Thoughts) may methinks induce a Translator on the one hand to give into several of those general Phrases and Manners of Expression, which have attain'd a Veneration even in our Language from their use in the *Old Testament*; as on the other, to avoid those which have been appropriated to the Divinity, and in a manner consign'd to Mystery and Religion.

For a farther Preservation of this Air of Simplicity, a particular Care should be taken to express with all Plainness those *Moral Sentences* and *Proverbial Speeches* which are so numerous in this Poet. They have something Venerable, and as I may say *Oracular*, in that unadorn'd Gravity and Shortness with which they are deliver'd: a Grace which would be utterly lost by endeavouring to give them what we call a more ingenious (that is a more modern) Turn in the Paraphrase.

Perhaps the Mixture of some *Græcisms* and old Words after the manner of *Milton*, if done without too much Affectation, might not have an ill Effect in a Version of this particular Work, which most of any other seems to require a venerable *Antique* Cast. But certainly the use of *modern Terms* of *War* and *Government*, such as *Platoon, Cam-*

pagne, Junto, or the like (which some of his Translators have fallen into) cannot be allowable; those only excepted, without which it is impossible to treat the Subjects in any living Language.

There are two Peculiarities in *Homer's* Diction that are a sort of *Marks* or *Moles,* by which every common Eye distinguishes him at first sight: Those who are not his greatest Admirers look upon them as Defects, and those who are seem pleased with them as Beauties. I speak of his *Compound-Epithets* and of his *Repetitions.* Many of the former cannot be done literally into *English* without destroying the Purity of our Language. I believe such should be retain'd as slide easily of themselves into an *English-Compound,* without Violence to the Ear or to the receiv'd Rules of Composition; as well as those which have receiv'd a Sanction from the Authority of our best Poets, and are become familiar thro' their use of them; such as the *Cloud-compelling Jove, &c.* As for the rest, whenever any can be as fully and significantly exprest in a single word as in a compounded one, the Course to be taken is obvious. Some that cannot be so turn'd as to preserve their full Image by one or two Words, may have Justice done them by Circumlocution; as the Epithet εἰνοσίφυλλος to a Mountain would appear little or ridiculous translated literally *Leaf-shaking,* but affords a majestic Idea in the *Periphrasis: The lofty Mountain shakes his waving Woods.* Others that admit of differing Significations, may receive an Advantage by a judicious Variation according to the Occasions on which they are introduc'd. For Example, the Epithet of *Apollo,* ἑκηβόλος, or *far-shooting,* is capable of two Explications; one literal in respect of the Darts and Bow, the Ensigns of that God; the other allegorical with regard to the Rays of the Sun: Therefore in such Places where *Apollo* is represented as a God in Person, I would use the former Interpretation, and where the Effects of the Sun are describ'd, I would make choice of the latter. Upon the whole, it will be necessary to avoid that perpetual Repetition of the same Epithets which we find in *Homer,* and which, tho' it might be accommodated (as has been already shewn) to the Ear of those Times, is by no means so to ours: But one may wait for Opportunities of placing them, where they derive an additional Beauty from the Occasions on which they are employed; and in doing this properly, a Translator may at once shew his Fancy and his Judgment.

As for *Homer's Repetitions;* we may divide them into three sorts; of whole Narrations and Speeches, of single Sentences, and of one Verse or Hemistich. I hope it is not impossible to have such a Regard to these, as neither to lose so known a Mark of the Author on the one hand, nor to offend the Reader too much on the other. The Repetition is not ungraceful in those Speeches where the Dignity of the

From the translation of Homer

Speaker renders it a sort of Insolence to alter his Words; as in the Messages from Gods to Men, or from higher Powers to Inferiors in Concerns of State, or where the Ceremonial of Religion seems to require it, in the solemn Forms of Prayers, Oaths, or the like. In other Cases, I believe the best Rule is to be guided by the Nearness, or Distance, at which the Repetitions are plac'd in the Original: When they follow too close one may vary the Expression, but it is a Question whether a profess'd Translator be authorized to omit any: If they be tedious, the Author is to answer for it.

It only remains to speak of the *Versification*. *Homer* (as has been said) is perpetually applying the Sound to the Sense, and varying it on every new Subject. This is indeed one of the most exquisite Beauties of Poetry, and attainable by very few: I know only of *Homer* eminent for it in the *Greek*, and *Virgil* in *Latine*. I am sensible it is what may sometimes happen by Chance, when a Writer is warm, and fully possest of his Image: however it may be reasonably believed they design'd this, in whose Verse it so manifestly appears in a superior degree to all others. Few Readers have the Ear to be Judges of it, but those who have will see I have endeavour'd at this Beauty.

Upon the whole, I must confess my self utterly incapable of doing Justice to *Homer*. I attempt him in no other Hope but that which one may entertain without much Vanity, of giving a more tolerable Copy of him than any entire Translation in Verse has yet done. We have only those of *Chapman, Hobbes,* and *Ogilby*.[16] *Chapman* has taken the Advantage of an immeasurable Length of Verse, notwithstanding which there is scarce any Paraphrase more loose and rambling than his. He has frequent Interpolations of four or six Lines, and I remember one in the thirteenth Book of the *Odyssos, ver.* 312, where he has spun twenty Verses out of two. He is often mistaken in so bold a manner, that one might think he deviated on purpose, if he did not in other Places of his Notes insist so much upon Verbal Trifles. He appears to have had a strong Affectation of extracting new Meanings out of his Author, insomuch as to promise in his Rhyming Preface, a Poem of the Mysteries he had revealed in *Homer*; and perhaps he endeavoured to strain the obvious Sense to this End. His Expression is involved in Fustian, a Fault for which he was remarkable in his Original Writings, as in the Tragedy of *Bussy d'Amboise,* &c. In a word, the Nature of the Man may account for his whole Performance; for he appears from his Preface and Remarks to have been of an arrogant Turn, and an Enthusiast in Poetry. His own Boast of having finish'd half the *Iliad* in less than fifteen Weeks, shews with what Negligence his Version was performed. But that which is to be allowed him, and which very much contributed to cover his Defects, is a daring fiery Spirit that animates his Translation, which is something like what one might imagine *Homer* himself would have writ before he arriv'd to Years of Discretion. *Hobbes* has given us a correct Explanation of the Sense in general, but for Particulars and Circumstances he continually lopps them, and often omits the most beautiful. As for its being esteem'd a close Translation, I doubt not many have been led into that Error by the Shortness of it, which proceeds not from his following the Original Line by Line, but from the Contractions above-mentioned. He sometimes omits whole Similes and Sentences, and is now and then guilty of Mistakes which no Writer of his Learning could have fallen into, but thro' Carelesness. His Poetry, as well as *Ogilby*'s, is too mean for Criticism.

It is a great Loss to the Poetical World that Mr. *Dryden* did not live to translate the *Iliad*. He has left us only the first Book and a small Part of the sixth;[17] in which if he has in some Places not truly interpreted the Sense, or preserved the Antiquities, it ought to be excused on account of the Haste he was obliged to write in. He seems to have had too much Regard to *Chapman*, whose Words he sometimes copies, and has unhappily follow'd him in Passages where he wanders from the Original. However had he translated the whole Work, I would no more have attempted *Homer* after him than *Virgil*, his Version of whom (notwithstanding some human Errors) is the most noble and spirited Translation I know in any Language. But the Fate of great Genius's is like that of great Ministers, tho' they are confessedly the first in the Commonwealth of Letters, they must be envy'd and calumniated only for being at the Head of it.

That which in my Opinion ought to be the Endeavour of any one who translates *Homer*, is above all things to keep alive that Spirit and Fire which makes his chief Character. In particular Places, where the Sense can bear any Doubt, to follow the strongest and most Poetical, as most agreeing with that Character. To copy him in all the Variations of his Style, and the different Modulations of his Numbers. To preserve in the more active or descriptive Parts, a Warmth and Elevation; in the more sedate or narrative, a Plainness and Solemnity; in the Speeches a Fulness and Perspicuity; in the Sentences a Shortness and Gravity. Not to neglect even the little Figures and Turns on the Words, nor sometimes the very Cast of the Periods. Neither to omit or confound any Rites or Customs of Antiquity. Perhaps too he ought to include the whole in a shorter Compass, than has hitherto been done by any Translator who has tolerably preserved either the Sense or Poetry. What I would farther recommend to him, is to study his

From the translation of Homer

Author rather from his own Text than from any Commentaries, how learned soever, or whatever Figure they make in the Estimation of the World. To consider him attentively in Comparison with *Virgil* above all the Ancients, and with *Milton* above all the Moderns. Next these the Archbishop of *Cambray's Telemachus*[18] may give him the truest Idea of the Spirit and Turn of our Author, and *Bossu's* admirable Treatise of the Epic Poem[19] the justest Notion of his Design and Conduct. But after all, with whatever Judgment and Study a Man may proceed, or with whatever Happiness he may perform such a Work; he must hope to please but a few, those only who have at once a Taste of Poetry, and competent Learning. For to satisfy such as want either, is not in the Nature of this Undertaking; since a meer Modern Wit can like nothing that is not *Modern,* and a Pedant nothing that is not *Greek.*

What I have done is submitted to the Publick, from whose Opinions I am prepared to learn; tho' I fear no Judges so little as our best Poets, who are most sensible of the Weight of this Task. As for the worst, whatever they shall please to say, they may give me some Concern as they are unhappy Men, but none as they are malignant Writers. I was guided in this Translation by Judgments very different from theirs, and by Persons for whom they can have no Kindness, if an old Observation be true, that the strongest Antipathy in the World is that of Fools to Men of Wit. Mr. *Addison* was the first whose Advice determin'd me to undertake this Task, who was pleas'd to write to me upon that Occasion in such Terms as I cannot repeat without Vanity. I was obliged to Sir *Richard Steele* for a very early Recommendation of my Undertaking to the Publick. Dr. *Swift* promoted my Interest with that Warmth with which he always serves his Friend. The Humanity and Frankness of Sir *Samuel Garth* are what I never knew wanting on any Occasion. I must also acknowledge with infinite Pleasure the many friendly Offices as well as sincere Criticisms of Mr. *Congreve,* who had led me the way in translating some Parts of *Homer,* as I wish for the sake of the World he had prevented me in the rest. I must add the Names of Mr. *Rowe* and Dr. *Parnell,* tho' I shall take a farther Opportunity of doing Justice to the last, whose Good-nature (to give it a great Panegyrick) is no less extensive than his Learning. The Favour of these Gentlemen is not entirely undeserved by one who bears them so true an Affection. But what can I say of the Honour so many of the *Great* have done me, while the *First Names* of the Age appear as my Subscribers, and the most distinguish'd Patrons and Ornaments of Learning as my chief Encouragers. Among these it is a particular Pleasure to me to find, that my highest Obligations are to such who have done most Honour to the Name of Poet: That his

Selected prose of Alexander Pope

Grace the *Duke* of *Buckingham* was not displeas'd I should undertake the Author to whom he has given (in his excellent *Essay*) the finest Praise he ever yet receiv'd.

> *Read* Homer once, *and you can read no more;*
> *For all things else appear so mean and poor,*
> *Verse will seem Prose: yet often on him look,*
> *And you will hardly need another Book.* [20]

That the Earl of *Halifax* was one of the first to favour me, of whom it is hard to say whether the Advancement of the Polite Arts is more owing to his Generosity or his Example. That such a Genius as my Lord *Bolingbroke*, not more distinguished in the great Scenes of Business than in all the useful and entertaining Parts of Learning, has not refus'd to be the Critick of these Sheets, and the Patron of their Writer. And that so excellent an Imitator of *Homer* as the noble Author of the Tragedy of *Heroic Love*,[21] has continu'd his Partiality to me from my writing Pastorals to my attempting the *Iliad*. I cannot deny my self the Pride of confessing, that I have had the Advantage not only of their Advice for the Conduct in general, but their Correction of several Particulars of this Translation.

I could say a great deal of the Pleasure of being distinguish'd by the *Earl* of *Carnarvon*, but it is almost absurd to particularize any one generous Action in a Person whose whole Life is a continued Series of them. The Right Honourable Mr. *Stanhope,* the present Secretary of State, will pardon my Desire of having it known that he was pleas'd to promote this Affair. The particular Zeal of Mr. *Harcourt* (the Son of the late Lord Chancellor) gave me a Proof how much I am honour'd in a Share of his Friendship. I must attribute to the same Motive that of several others of my Friends, to whom all Acknowledgments are render'd unnecessary by the Privileges of a familiar Correspondence: And I am satisfy'd I can no way better oblige Men of their Turn, than by my Silence.

In short, I have found more Patrons than ever *Homer* wanted. He would have thought himself happy to have met the same Favour at *Athens,* that has been shewn me by its learned Rival, the University of *Oxford.* If my Author had the *Wits* of After-Ages for his Defenders, his Translator has had the *Beauties* of the present for his Advocates; a Pleasure too great to be changed for any Fame in Reversion. And I can hardly envy him those pompous Honours he receiv'd after Death, when I reflect on the Enjoyment of so many agreeable Obligations, and easy Friendships which make the Satisfaction of Life. This Distinction is the more to be acknowledg'd, as it is shewn to one whose Pen has never gratify'd the Prejudices of particular *Parties,* or the

From the translation of Homer

Vanities of particular *Men*. Whatever the Success may prove, I shall never repent of an Undertaking in which I have experienc'd the Candour and Friendship of so many Persons of Merit; and in which I hope to pass some of those Years of Youth that are generally lost in a Circle of Follies, after a manner neither wholly unuseful to others, nor disagreeable to my self.

SELECTED NOTES FROM THE ILIAD

From the opening note to Book 1:

The Plan of this Poem is form'd upon Anger and its ill Effects, the Plan of *Virgil's* upon pious Resignation and its Rewards: and thus every Passion or Virtue may be the Foundation of the Scheme of an Epic Poem. This Distinction between two Authors who have been so successful, seem'd necessary to be taken notice of, that they who would imitate either may not stumble at the very Entrance, or curb their Imaginations so as to deprive us of noble Morals told in a new Variety of Accidents. Imitation does not hinder Invention: We may observe the Rules of Nature, and write in the Spirit of those who have best hit upon them, without taking the same Track, beginning in the same Manner, and following the Main of their Story almost step by step; as most of the modern Writers of Epic Poetry have done after one of these great Poets.

1 155. *Insatiate King.*] Here, where this Passion of Anger grows loud, it seems proper to prepare the Reader, and prevent his Mistake in the Character of *Achilles*, which might shock him in several Particulars following. We should know that the Poet has rather study'd Nature than Perfection in the laying down his Characters. He resolv'd to sing the Consequences of Anger; he consider'd what Virtues and Vices would conduce most to bring his Moral out of the Fable; and artfully dispos'd them in his chief Persons after the manner in which we generally find them; making the Fault which most peculiarly attends any good Quality, to reside with it. Thus he has plac'd Pride with Magnanimity in *Agamemnon,* and Craft with Prudence in *Ulysses*. And thus we must take his *Achilles,* not as a meer heroick dispassion'd Character, but as one compounded of Courage and Anger; one who finds himself almost invincible, and assumes an uncontroul'd Carriage upon the Self-consciousness of his Worth; whose high Strain of Honour will not suffer him to betray his Friends or fight against them, even when he thinks they have affronted him; but whose inexorable

Resentment will not let him hearken to any Terms of Accommodation. These are the Lights and Shades of his Character, which *Homer* has heighten'd and darkned in Extreams; because on the one side Valour is the darling Quality of Epic Poetry, and on the other, Anger the particular Subject of his Poem. When Characters thus mix'd are well conducted, tho' they be not morally beautiful quite through, they conduce more to the end, and are still poetically perfect.

Plutarch takes occasion from the Observation of this Conduct in *Homer,* to applaud his just Imitation of Nature and Truth, in representing Virtues and Vices intermixed in his Heroes: contrary to the Paradoxes and strange Positions of the Stoicks, who held that no Vice could consist with Virtue, nor the least Virtue with Vice. Plut. *de aud. Poetis.*

II 552. *Or thick as Insects play.*] This Simile translated literally runs thus; *As the numerous Troops of Flies about a Shepherd's Cottage in the Spring, when the Milk moistens the Pails; such Numbers of* Greeks *stood in the Field against the* Trojans, *desiring their Destruction.* The Lowness of this Image in Comparison with those which precede it, will naturally shock a modern Critick, and would scarce be forgiven in a Poet of these Times. The utmost a Translator can do is to heighten the Expression, so as to render the Disparity less observable: which is endeavour'd here, and in other Places. If this be done successfully the Reader is so far from being offended at a low Idea, that it raises his Surprize to find it grown great in the Poet's Hands, of which we have frequent Instances in *Virgil's Georgicks.* Here follows another of the same kind, in the Simile of *Agamemnon* to a *Bull* just after he has been compar'd to *Jove, Mars,* and *Neptune.* This, *Eustathius* tells us, was blam'd by some Criticks, and Mr. *Hobbes* has left it out in his Translation. The Liberty has been taken here to place the humbler Simile first, reserving the noble one as a more magnificent Close of the Description: The bare turning the Sentence removes the Objection. *Milton* who was a close Imitator of our Author, has often copy'd him in these humble Comparisons. He has not scrupled to insert one in the midst of that pompous Description of the Rout of the Rebel-Angels in the sixth Book, where the Son of God in all his dreadful Majesty is represented pouring his Vengeance upon them:

> —*As a Herd*
> *Of Goats, or tim'rous Flocks together throng'd,*
> *Drove them before him Thunder-struck—*   [856-8]

From the translation of Homer

III 7. *The Cranes embody'd fly.*] If Wit has been truly describ'd to be a Similitude in Ideas, and is more excellent as that Similitude is more surprizing; there cannot be a truer kind of Wit than what is shewn in apt Comparisons, especially when composed of such Subjects as having the least Relation to each other in general, have yet some Particular that agrees exactly. Of this Nature is the Simile of the *Cranes* to the *Trojan* Army, where the Fancy of *Homer* flew to the remotest Part of the World for an Image which no Reader could have expected. But it is no less exact than surprizing. The Likeness consists in two Points, the *Noise* and the *Order*; the latter is so observable as to have given some of the Ancients occasion to imagine the embatteling of an Army was first learn'd from the close manner of Flight of these Birds. But this Part of the Simile not being directly express'd by the Author, has been overlook'd by some of the Commentators. It may be remark'd that *Homer* has generally a wonderful Closeness in all the Particulars of his Comparisons, notwithstanding he takes a Liberty in his Expression of them. He seems so secure of the main Likeness, that he makes no scruple to play with the Circumstances; sometimes by transposing the Order of them, sometimes by super-adding them, and sometimes (as in this Place) by neglecting them in such a manner as to leave the Reader to supply them himself. For the present Comparison, it has been taken by *Virgil* in the tenth Book, and apply'd to the Clamours of Soldiers in the same manner...[264-6].

III 53. *As God-like* Hector.] This is the first Place of the Poem where *Hector* makes a figure, and here it seems proper to give an Idea of his Character, since if he is not the chief Heroe of the *Iliad*, he is at least the most amiable. There are several Reasons which render *Hector* a favorite Character with every Reader, some of which shall here be offer'd. The chief Moral of *Homer* was to expose the ill Effects of Discord; the *Greeks* were to be shewn disunited, and to render that Disunion the more probable, he has designedly given them *mixt* Characters. The *Trojans* on the other hand were to be represented making all Advantages of the others Disagreement, which they could not do without a strict Union among themselves. *Hector* therefore who commanded them, must be endu'd with all such Qualifications as tended to the Preservation of it; as *Achilles* with such as promoted the contrary. The one stands in Contraste to the other, an accomplish'd Character of Valour unruffled by Rage and Anger, and uniting his People by his Prudence and Example. *Hector* has also a Foil to set him off in his own Family; we are perpetually opposing in

III

our Minds the Incontinence of *Paris,* who exposes his Country, to the Temperance of *Hector* who protects it. And indeed it is this Love of his Country which appears his principal Passion, and the Motive of all his Actions. He has no other Blemish than that he fights in an unjust Cause, which *Homer* has yet been careful to tell us he would not do, if his Opinion were followed. But since he cannot prevail, the Affection he bears to his Parents and Kindred, and his desire of defending them, incites him to do his utmost for their Safety. We may add that *Homer* having so many *Greeks* to celebrate, makes them shine in their turns, and singly in their several Books, one succeeding in the Absence of another: Whereas *Hector* appears in every Battel the Life and Soul of his Party, and the constant Bulwark against every Enemy: He stands against *Agamemnon's* Magnanimity, *Diomed's* Bravery, *Ajax's* Strength, and *Achilles's* Fury. There is besides, an accidental Cause for our liking him from reading the Writers of the *Augustan* Age, especially *Virgil,* whose Favorite he grew more particularly from the time when the *Cæsars* fancy'd to derive their Pedigree from *Troy.*

IV 478. *As when the Winds.*] Madam *Dacier* thinks it may seem something odd, that an Army going to conquer should be compared to the Waves going to break themselves against the Shore; and would solve the appearing Absurdity by imagining the Poet laid not the Stress so much upon this Circumstance, as upon the same Waves assaulting a Rock, lifting themselves over its Head, and covering it with Foam as the *Trophy of their Victory* (as she expresses it). But to this it may be answer'd, that neither did the *Greeks* get the better in this Battel, nor will a Comparison be allowed intirely beautiful, which instead of illustrating its Subject stands itself in need of so much Illustration and Refinement, to be brought to agree with it. The Passage naturally bears this Sense. *As when, upon the rising of the Wind, the Waves roll after one another to the Shore; at first there is a distant Motion in the Sea, then they approach to break with Noise on the Strand, and lastly rise swelling over the Rocks, and toss their Foam above their Heads: So the* Greeks, *at first, marched in order one after another silently to the Fight* – Where the Poet breaks off from prosecuting the Comparison, and by a *Prolepsis,* leaves the Reader to carry it on; and image to himself the future Tumult, Rage, and Force of the Battel, in Opposition to that Silence in which he describes the Troops at present, in the Lines immediately ensuing. What confirms this Exposition is, that *Virgil* has made use of the Simile in the same Sense in the seventh *Æneid*... [528-30].

From the translation of Homer

Ibid. As when the Winds, &c.] This is the first Battel in *Homer*, and it is worthy Observation with what Grandeur it is described, and raised by one Circumstance above another, 'till all is involved in Horror and Tumult: The foregoing Simile of the Winds, rising by degrees into a general Tempest, is an Image of the Progress of his own Spirit in this Description. We see first an innumerable Army moving in order, and are amus'd with the Pomp and Silence, then waken'd with the Noise and Clamour; next they join, the adverse Gods are let down among them; the Imaginary Persons of *Terror, Flight, Discord* succeed to re-inforce them; then all is undistinguish'd Fury and a Confusion of Horrors, only that at different Openings we behold the distinct Deaths of several Heroes, and then are involv'd again in the same Confusion.

v 641. *So when th' embattel'd Clouds.*] This Simile contains as proper a Comparison, and as fine a Picture of Nature as any in *Homer*: Yet however it is to be fear'd the Beauty and Propriety of it will not be very obvious to many Readers, because it is the Description of a natural Appearance which they have not had an Opportunity to remark, and which can be observed only in a mountainous Country. It happens frequently in very calm Weather, that the Atmosphere is charg'd with thick Vapors, whose Gravity is such, that they neither rise nor fall, but remain poiz'd in the Air at a certain Height, where they continue frequently for several Days together. In a plain Country this occasions no other visible Appearance, but of an uniform clouded Sky; but in a Hilly Region these Vapors are to be seen covering the Tops and stretch'd along the Sides of the Mountains, the clouded Parts above being terminated and distinguish'd from the clear Parts below by a strait Line running parallel to the Horizon, as far as the Mountains extend. The whole Compass of Nature cannot afford a nobler and more exact Representation of a numerous Army, drawn up in Line of Battel, and expecting the Charge. The long-extended even front, the Closeness of the Ranks; the Firmness, Order, and Silence of the whole, are all drawn with great Resemblance in this one Comparison. The Poet adds, that this Appearance is while *Boreas* and the other boisterous Winds which disperse and break the Clouds, are laid asleep. This is as exact as it is Poetical; for when the Winds arise, this regular Order is soon dissolv'd. This Circumstance is added to the Description, as an ominous Anticipation of the Flight and Dissipation of the *Greeks*, which soon ensued when *Mars* and *Hector* broke in upon them.

v 848. *Nor* Hector *to the Chief replies.*] *Homer* is in nothing more admirable than in the excellent Use he makes of the *Silence* of the Persons he introduces. It would be endless to collect all the Instances of this Truth throughout his Poem: yet I cannot but put together those that have already occurr'd in the Course of this Work, and leave to the Reader the Pleasure of observing it in what remains. The Silence of the two Heralds when they were to take *Briseis* from *Achilles* in *Lib*.I. of which see *Note* 39. In the third Book, when *Iris* tells *Helen* the two Rivals were to fight in her Quarrel, and that all *Troy* were standing Spectators; that guilty Princess makes no Answer, but casts a Veil over her Face and drops a Tear; and when she comes just after into the Presence of *Priam*, she speaks not, till after he has in a particular manner encourag'd and commanded her. *Paris* and *Menelaus* being just upon the Point to encounter, the latter declares his Wishes and Hopes of Conquest to Heaven, the former being engag'd in an unjust Cause, says not a word. In the fourth Book, when *Jupiter* has express'd his Desire to favour *Troy, Juno* declaims against him, but the *Goddess of Wisdom,* tho' much concern'd, holds her Peace. When *Agamemnon* too rashly reproves *Diomed,* that Hero remains silent, and in the true Character of a rough Warrior, leaves it to his Actions to speak for him. In the present Book when *Sarpedon* has reproach'd *Hector* in an open and generous manner, *Hector* preserving the same warlike Character, returns no Answer, but immediately hastens to the Business of the Field; as he also does in this Place, where he instantly brings off *Sarpedon,* without so much as telling him he will endeavour his Rescue. *Chapman* was not sensible of the Beauty of this, when he imagined *Hector's* Silence here proceeded from the Pique he had conceiv'd at *Sarpedon* for his late Reproof of him. That Translator has not scrupled to insert this Opinion of his in a groundless Interpolation altogether foreign to the Author. But indeed it is a Liberty he frequently takes, to draw any Passage to some new, far-fetch'd Conceit of his Invention; insomuch, that very often before he translates any Speech, to the Sense or Design of which he gives some fanciful Turn of his own; he prepares it by several additional Lines purposely to prepossess the Reader of that Meaning. Those who will take the Trouble may see Examples of this in what he sets before the Speeches of *Hector, Paris,* and *Helena* in the sixth Book, and innumerable other Places.

v The Allegory of this whole Book lies so open, is carry'd on with such Closeness, and wound up with so much Fulness and Strength,

From the translation of Homer

that it is a wonder how it could enter into the Imagination of any Critick, that these Actions of *Diomed* were only a daring and extravagant Fiction in *Homer*, as if he affected the *Marvellous* at any rate. The great Moral of it is, that a brave Man should not contend against Heaven, but resist only *Venus* and *Mars,* Incontinence and ungovern'd Fury. *Diomed* is propos'd as an Example of a great and enterprizing Nature, which would perpetually be venturing too far, and committing Extravagancies or Impieties, did it not suffer itself to be check'd and guided by *Minerva* or Prudence: For it is this *Wisdom* (as we are told in the very first Lines of the Book) that raises a Hero above all others. Nothing is more observable than the particular Care *Homer* has taken to shew he designed this Moral. He never omits any Occasion throughout the Book, to put it in express Terms into the Mouths of the Gods or Persons of the greatest Weight. *Minerva*, at the beginning of the Battel, is made to give this Precept to *Diomed; Fight not against the Gods, but give way to them, and resist only* Venus. The same Goddess opens his Eyes, and enlightens him so far as to perceive when it is Heaven that acts immediately against him, or when it is Man only that opposes him. The Hero himself, as soon as he has perform'd her Dictates in driving away *Venus*, cries out, not as to the *Goddess*, but as to the *Passion, Thou hast no Business with Warriors, is it not enough that thou deceiv'st weak Women?* Even the Mother of *Venus* while she comforts her Daughter, bears Testimony to the Moral: *That Man* (says she) *is not long-liv'd who contends with the Gods.* And when *Diomed*, transported by his Nature, proceeds but a Step too far, *Apollo* discovers himself in the most solemn manner, and declares this Truth in his own Voice, as it were by direct Revelation: *Mortal, forbear! consider, and know the vast difference there is between the Gods and Thee. They are immortal and divine, but Man a miserable Reptile of the Dust.*

VI 390 *Himself the Mansion rais'd.*] I must own my self not so great an Enemy to *Paris* as some of the Commentators. His blind Passion is the unfortunate Occasion of the Ruine of his Country, and he has the ill Fate to have all his fine Qualities swallowed up in that. And indeed I cannot say he endeavours much to be a better Man than his Nature made him. But as to his Parts and Turn of Mind, I see nothing that is either weak, or wicked, the general Manners of those Times considered. On the contrary, a gentle Soul, patient of good Advice, tho' indolent enough to forget it; and liable only to that Frailty of Love which methinks might in his Case as well as *Helen's* be charged upon the *Stars,* and the *Gods.* So very amorous a

Constitution, and so incomparable a Beauty to provoke it, might be Temptation enough even to a wise Man, and in some degree make him deserve Compassion, if not Pardon. It is remarkable, that *Homer* does not paint him and *Helen* (as some other Poets would have done) like Monsters, odious to Gods and Men, but allows their Characters such esteemable Qualifications as could consist, and in Truth generally do, with tender Frailties. He gives *Paris* several polite Accomplishments, and in particular a Turn to those Sciences that are the Result of a fine Imagination. He makes him have a Taste and Addiction to *curious Works* of all sorts, which caus'd him to transport *Sidonian* Artists to *Troy*, and employ himself at home in adorning and finishing his Armour: And now we are told that he assembled the most skilful Builders from all Parts of the Country, to render his Palace a compleat Piece of *Architecture*. This, together with what *Homer* has said elsewhere of his Skill in the *Harp*, which in those Days included both *Musick* and *Poetry*, may I think establish him a *Bel-Esprit* and a *fine Genius*.

VI 595. *Stretch'd his fond Arms.*] There never was a finer Piece of Painting than this. *Hector* extends his Arms to embrace his Child; the Child affrighted at the glittering of his Helmet and the shaking of the Plume, shrinks backward to the Breast of his Nurse; *Hector* unbraces his Helmet, lays it on the Ground, takes the Infant in his Arms, lifts him towards Heaven, and offers a Prayer for him to the Gods: then returns him to the Mother *Andromache*, who receives him with a Smile of Pleasure, but at the same instant the Fears for her Husband make her burst into Tears. All these are but small Circumstances, but so artfully chosen, that every Reader immediately feels the force of them, and represents the whole in the utmost Liveliness to his Imagination. This alone might be a Confutation of that false Criticism some have fallen into, who affirm that a Poet ought only to collect the great and noble Particulars in his Paintings. But it is in the Images of Things as in the Characters of Persons; where a small Action, or even a small Circumstance of an Action, lets us more into the Knowledge and Comprehension of them, than the material and principal Parts themselves. As we find this in a History, so we do in a Picture, where sometimes a small Motion or Turning of a Finger will express the Character and Action of the Figure more than all the other Parts of the Design. *Longinus* indeed blames an Author's insisting too much on trivial Circumstances; but in the same Place extols *Homer* as "the Poet who best knew how to make use of important and beautiful Circumstances, and to avoid the mean

From the translation of Homer

and superfluous ones." There is a vast difference betwixt a *small* Circumstance and a *trivial* one, and the smallest become important if they are well chosen, and not confused.

XIII 191. *As from some Mountain's craggy Forehead torn,* &c.] This is one of the noblest Simile's in all *Homer,* and the most justly corresponding in its Circumstances to the thing described. The furious Descent of *Hector* from the Wall represented by a Stone that flies from the top of a Rock, the Hero push'd on by the superior Force of *Jupiter,* as the Stone driven by a Torrent, the Ruins of the Wall falling after him, all things yielding before him, the Clamour and Tumult around him, all imag'd in the violent bounding and leaping of the Stone, the crackling of the Woods, the Shock, the Noise, the Rapidity, the Irresistibility, and the Augmentation of Force in its Progress. All these points of Likeness make but the first Part of this admirable Simile. Then the sudden Stop of the Stone when it comes to the Plain, as of *Hector* at the Phalanx of the *Ajaces* (alluding also to the natural Situation of the Ground, *Hector* rushing down the Declivity of the Shore and being stopp'd on the Level of the Sea.) And lastly, the Immobility of both when so stopp'd, the Enemy being as unable to move him back, as he to get forward: This last Branch of the Comparison is the happiest in the World, and tho' not hitherto observ'd, is what methinks makes the principal Beauty and Force of it...[1]

There is yet another Beauty in the Numbers of this Part. As the Verses themselves make us see, the Sound of them makes us hear what they represent, in the noble Roughness, Rapidity, and sonorous Cadence that distinguishes them.

Ῥήξας ἀσπέτῳ ὄμβρῳ ἀναιδέος ἔχματα πέτρης, &c.[2]

The Translation, however short it falls of these Beauties, may yet serve to shew the Reader, that there was at least an Endeavour to imitate them.

XIII 739. *As on some ample Barn's well-harden'd Floor.*] We ought not to be shock'd at the Frequency of these Similes taken from the Ideas of a rural Life. In early Times, before Politeness had rais'd the Esteem of Arts subservient to Luxury, above those necessary to the Subsistence of Mankind, Agriculture was the Employment of Persons of the greatest Esteem and Distinction: We see in sacred History Princes busy at Sheep-shearing; and in the middle Times of the *Roman* Common-wealth, a Dictator taken from the Plough. Wherefore it ought not to be wonder'd that Allusions and Comparisons of this kind are frequently used by ancient heroick Writers, as well to raise, as illustrate their Descriptions. But since these Arts are fallen from their ancient Dignity, and become the Drudgery of the lowest People, the Images of them are likewise sunk into Meanness, and without this Consideration, must appear to common Readers unworthy to have place in Epic Poems. It was perhaps thro' too much Deference to such Tastes, that *Chapman* omitted this Simile in his Translation.

XIV 21. *As when old Ocean's silent Surface sleeps.*] There are no where more finish'd Pictures of Nature, than those which *Homer* draws in several of his Comparisons. The Beauty however of some of these will be lost to many, who cannot perceive the Resemblance, having never had Opportunity to observe the things themselves. The Life of this Description will be most sensible to those who have been at Sea in a Calm: In this Condition the Water is not entirely motionless, but swells gently in smooth Waves, which fluctuate backwards and forwards in a kind of balancing Motion: This State continues till a rising Wind gives a Determination to the Waves, and rolls 'em one certain way. There is scarce any thing in the whole Compass of Nature that can more exactly represent the State of an irresolute Mind, wavering between two different Designs, sometimes inclining to the one, sometimes to the other, and then moving to the Point to which its Resolution is at last determin'd. Every Circumstance of this Comparison is both beautiful and just; and it is the more to be admir'd, because it is very difficult to find sensible Images proper to represent the Motions of the Mind; wherefore we but rarely meet with such Comparisons even in the best Poets. There is one of great Beauty in *Virgil*, upon a Subject very like this, where he compares his Hero's Mind, agitated with a great Variety and quick Succession of Thoughts, to a dancing Light reflected from a Vessel of Water in Motion. ...[VIII 19-25]

XVI 466.   *As when in Autumn* Jove *his Fury pours—*
            —When guilty Mortals, &c.]

The Poet in this Image of an Inundation, takes occasion to mention a Sentiment of great Piety, that such Calamities were the Effects of divine Justice punishing the Sins of Mankind. This might probably refer to the Tradition of an universal Deluge, which was very common among the ancient heathen Writers; most of them ascribing the Cause of this Deluge to the Wrath of Heaven provoked by the Wickedness of Men. *Diodorus Siculus, l.* 15. *c.* 5. speaking of an

From the translation of Homer

Earthquake and Inundation, which destroyed a great part of *Greece* in the 101st *Olympiad*, has these Words. *There was a great Dispute concerning the Cause of this Calamity: The Natural Philosophers generally ascribed such Events to necessary Causes, not to any divine Hand: But they who had more devout Sentiments gave a more probable Account hereof; asserting, that it was the divine Vengeance alone that brought this Destruction upon Men who had offended the Gods with their Impiety.* And then proceeds to give an Account of those Crimes which drew down this Punishment upon them.

This is one, among a thousand Instances, of *Homer's* indirect and oblique manner of introducing moral Sentences and Instructions. These agreeably break in upon his Reader even in Descriptions and poetical Parts, where one naturally expects only Painting and Amusement. We have Virtue put upon us by Surprize, and are pleas'd to find a thing where we should never have look'd to meet with it. I must do a noble *English* Poet[3] the justice to observe, that it is this particular Art that is the very distinguishing Excellence of *Cooper's-Hill*; throughout which, the Descriptions of Places, and Images rais'd by the Poet, are still tending to some Hint, or leading into some Reflection, upon moral Life or political Institution: Much in the same manner as the real Sight of such Scenes and Prospects is apt to give the Mind a compos'd Turn, and incline it to Thoughts and Contemplations that have a Relation to the Object.

XVII 642. *So burns the vengeful Hornet, &c.*] It is literally in the *Greek, she inspir'd the Hero with the Boldness of a Fly.* There is no Impropriety in the Comparison, this Animal being of all others the most persevering in its Attacks, and the most difficult to be beaten off: The Occasion also of the Comparison being the resolute Persistance of *Menelaus* about the dead Body, renders it still the more just. But our present Idea of the Fly is indeed very low, as taken from the Littleness and Insignificancy of this Creature. However, since there is really no Meanness in it, there ought to be none in expressing it; and I have done my best in the Translation to keep up the Dignity of my Author.

POSTSCRIPT TO THE ODYSSEY

I Cannot dismiss this work without a few observations on the true Character and Style of it. Whoever reads the Odyssey with an eye to the Iliad, expecting to find it of the same character, or of the same sort of spirit, will be grievously deceived, and err against the first principle of Criticism, which is to consider the nature of the piece, and the intent of its author. The Odyssey is a moral and political work, instructive to all degrees of men, and filled with images examples and precepts, of civil and domestic life. *Homer* is here a person

> *Qui didicit patriæ quid debeat, & quid amicis,*
> *Quo sit amore parens, quo* frater *amandus, &* hospes:
> *Qui quid sit* pulcrum, *quid* turpe, *quid* utile, *quid* non,
> *Plenius & melius Chrysippo & Crantore dicit.* [1]

The Odyssey is the reverse of the Iliad, in *Moral, Subject, Manner* and *Style*; to which it has no sort of relation, but as the story happens to follow in order of time, and as some of the same persons are actors in it. Yet from this incidental connexion many have been mis-led to regard it as a continuation or second part, and thence to expect a parity of character inconsistent with its nature.

It is no wonder that the common Reader should fall into this mistake, when so great a Critic as *Longinus* seems not wholly free from it. Although what he has said has been generally understood to import a severer censure of the Odyssey than it really does, if we consider the occasion on which it is introduced, and the circumstances to which it is confined.

"The Odyssey (says he) is an instance, how natural it is to a great Genius, when it begins to grow old and decline, to delight it self in *Narrations* and *Fables*. For, that *Homer* composed the Odyssey after the Iliad, many proofs may be given, &c. From hence in my judgment it proceeds, that as the Iliad was written while his *Spirit* was in its greatest vigor, the whole structure of that work is Dramatick and full of action; whereas the greater part of the Odyssey is employ'd in Narration, which is the taste of *Old Age:* So that in this latter piece we may compare him to the setting Sun, which has still the same greatness but not the same ardor, or force. He speaks not in the same strain; we see no more that *Sublime* of the Iliad which marches on with a constant pace, without ever being stopp'd, or retarded: there appears no more that hurry and that strong tyde of motions and passions, pouring one after another: there is no more the same fury, or the same volubility of diction, so suitable to action, and all along drawing in such innumerable images of nature. But *Homer*, like the Ocean, is always great, even when he ebbs and retires; even when he is lowest and loses himself most in Narrations and incredible Fictions: As instances of this, we cannot forget the descriptions of tempests, the adventures of *Ulysses* with the *Cyclops*, and many others. But tho' all this be *Age*, it is the *Age* of *Homer*—And it may be said for the credit of these fictions, that they are *beautiful Dreams*, or if you will, the *Dreams of* Jupiter *himself.* I spoke of the Odyssey only to show, that the greatest Poets when their genius wants strength and warmth for the *Pathetic*, for the most part employ themselves in painting the *Manners*. This *Homer* has done, in characterizing the Suitors, and describing their way of life; which is properly a branch of

From the translation of Homer

Comedy, whose peculiar business it is to represent the manners of men."[2]

We must first observe, it is the *Sublime* of which *Longinus* is writing: That, and not the nature of *Homer's* Poem, is his subject. After having highly extoll'd the sublimity and fire of the Iliad, he justly observes the Odyssey to have less of those qualities, and to turn more on the side of moral, and reflections on human life. Nor is it his business here to determine, whether the *elevated spirit* of the one, or the *just moral* of the other, be the greater excellence in it self.

Secondly, that fire and fury of which he is speaking, can not well be meant of the general Spirit and Inspiration which is to run through a whole Epic Poem, but of that particular warmth and impetuosity necessary in some parts, to image or represent actions or passions, of haste, tumult, and violence. It is on occasion of citing some such particular passages in *Homer*, that *Longinus* breaks into this reflection; which seems to determine his meaning chiefly to that sense.

Upon the whole, he affirms the Odyssey to have less sublimity and fire than the Iliad, but he does not say it wants the sublime or wants fire. He affirms it to be narrative, but not that the narration is defective. He affirms it to abound in fictions, not that those fictions are ill invented, or ill executed. He affirms it to be nice and particular in painting the manners, but not that those manners are ill painted. If *Homer* has fully in these points accomplish'd his own design, and done all that the nature of his Poem demanded or allowed, it still remains perfect in its kind, and as much a master-piece as the Iliad.

The Amount of the passage is this; that in his own particular taste, and with respect to the *Sublime*, *Longinus* preferr'd the Iliad: And because the Odyssey was less active and lofty, he judged it the work of the old age of *Homer*.

If this opinion be true, it will only prove, that *Homer's* Age might determine him in the choice of his subject, but not that it affected him in the execution of it: And that which would be a very wrong instance to prove the decay of his Imagination, is a very good one to evince the strength of his Judgment. For had he (as Madam *Dacier* observes) compos'd the Odyssey in his youth, and the Iliad in his age, both must in reason have been exactly the same as they now stand. To blame *Homer* for his choice of such a subject, as did not admit the same incidents and the same pomp of style as his former; is to take offence at too much variety, and to imagine, that when a man has written one good thing, he must ever after only copy himself.

The *Battle of* Constantine, and the *School of* Athens, are both pieces of *Raphael:* Shall we censure the School of *Athens* as faulty, because it has not the fury and fire of the other? or shall we say, that *Raphael* was grown grave and old, because he chose to represent the manners of old men and Philosophers? There is all the silence, tranquillity and composure in the one, and all the warmth, hurry and tumult in the other, which the subject of either required: both of them had been imperfect, if they had not been as they are. And let the Painter or Poet be young or old, who designs and performs in this manner, it proves him to have made the piece at a time of life when he was master not only of his art, but of his discretion.

Aristotle makes no such distinction between the two Poems: He constantly cites them with equal praise, and draws the rules and examples of Epic writing equally from both. But it is rather to the Odyssey that *Horace* gives the preference, in the Epistle to *Lollius*, and in the Art of Poetry.[3] It is remarkable how opposite his opinion is to that of *Longinus*; and that the particulars he chuses to extoll, are those very *fictions* and *pictures of the manners* which the other seems least to approve. Those fables and manners are of the very essence of the work: But even without that regard, the fables themselves have both more invention and more instruction, and the manners more moral and example, than those of the Iliad.

In some points (and those the most essential to the Epic Poem) the Odyssey is confessed to excel the Iliad; and principally in the great end of it, the *Moral*. The conduct, turn, and disposition of the *Fable* is also what the Criticks allow to be the better model for Epic writers to follow: Accordingly we find much more of the Cast of this Poem than of the other in the *Æneid,* and (what next to that is perhaps the greatest example) in the *Telemachus*. In the *Manners*, it is no way inferior: *Longinus* is so far from finding any defect in these, that he rather taxes *Homer* with painting them too minutely. As to the *Narrations,* although they are more numerous as the occasions are more frequent, yet they carry no more the marks of old age, and are neither more prolix nor more circumstantial, than the conversations and dialogues of the Iliad. Not to mention the length of those of *Phœnix* in the ninth book, and of *Nestor* in the eleventh (which may be thought in compliance to their characters) those of *Glaucus* in the sixth, of *Æneas* in the twentieth, and some others, must be allow'd to exceed any in the whole Odyssey. And that the propriety of style, and the numbers, in the Narrations of each are equal, will appear to any who compare them.

To form a right judgment, whether the Genius of *Homer* had suffer'd any decay; we must consider, in both his poems, such parts as are of a similar nature, and will bear comparison. And it is certain we shall find in each, the same vivacity and fecundity of invention, the same life and strength of imaging and colouring, the particular descriptions as highly painted, the figures as bold, the metaphors as animated, and the numbers as harmonious and as various.

The Odyssey is a perpetual source of Poetry: The stream is not the less full, for being gentle; tho' it is true (when we speak only with regard to the *Sublime*) that a river, foaming and thund'ring in cataracts from rocks and precipices, is what more strikes, amazes and fills the mind, than the same body of water, flowing afterwards thro' peaceful vales and agreeable scenes of pasturage.

The Odyssey (as I have before said) ought to be consider'd according to its own nature and design, not with an eye to the Iliad. To censure *Homer* because it is unlike what it was never meant to resemble, is, as if a Gardiner who had purposely cultivated two beautiful trees of contrary natures, as a specimen of his skill in the several kinds, should be blamed for not bringing them into *pairs*; when in root, stem, leaf, and flower, each was so entirely different, that one must have been spoil'd in the endeavour to match the other.

Longinus, who saw this Poem was "*partly of the nature of Comedy,*" ought not for that very reason to have consider'd it with a view to the Iliad. How little any such resemblance was the intention of *Homer*, may appear from hence, that although the character of *Ulysses* there was already drawn, yet here he purposely turns to another side of it, and shows him not in that full light of glory but in the shade of common life, with a mixture of such qualities as are requisite to all the lowest accidents of it, strugling with misfortunes, and on a level with the meanest of mankind. As for the other persons, none of them are above what we call the higher Comedy: *Calypso,* tho' a Goddess, is a character of intrigue; the *Suitors* are yet more approaching to it; the *Phæacians* are of the same cast; the *Cyclops, Melanthius,* and *Irus,* descend even to droll characters: and the scenes that appear throughout, are generally of the comic kind; banquets, revels, sports, loves, and the pursuit of a woman.

From the Nature of the Poem, we shall form an Idea of the *Style*. The diction is to follow the images, and to take its colour from the complexion of the thoughts. Accordingly the Odyssey is not always cloath'd in the majesty of verse proper to Tragedy, but sometimes descends into the plainer Narrative, and sometimes even to that familiar dialogue essential to Comedy. However, where it cannot support a sublimity, it always preserves a dignity, or at least a propriety.

There is a real beauty in an easy, pure, perspicuous description even of a *low action*. There are numerous instances of this both in *Homer* and *Virgil*; and perhaps those natural passages are not the least pleasing of their works. It is often the same in History, where the representations of common, or even domestic things, in clear, plain, and natural words, are frequently found to make the liveliest impression on the reader.

The question is, how far a Poet, in pursuing the description or image of an action, can attach himself to *little circumstances,* without vulgarity or trifling? what particulars are proper, and enliven the image; or what are impertinent, and clog it? In this matter Painting is to be consulted, and the whole regard had to those circumstances which contribute to form a full, and yet not a confused, idea of the thing.

Epithets are of vast service to this effect, and the right use of these is often the only expedient to render the narration poetical.

The great point of judgment is to distinguish when to speak simply, and when figuratively: But whenever the Poet is oblig'd by the nature of his subject to descend to the lower manner of writing, an elevated style would be affected, and therefore ridiculous; and the more he was forc'd upon figures and metaphors to avoid that lowness, the more the image would be broken, and consequently obscure.

One may add, that the use of the grand style on little subjects, is not only ludicrous, but a sort of transgression against the rules of proportion and mechanicks: 'Tis using a vast force to lift a *feather*.

I believe, now I am upon this head, it will be found a just observation, that the *low actions of life* cannot be put into a figurative style without being ridiculous, but *things natural* can. Metaphors raise the latter into Dignity, as we see in the *Georgicks*; but throw the former into Ridicule, as in the *Lutrin*.[4] I think this may very well be accounted for: Laughter implies censure; inanimate and irrational beings are not objects of censure; therefore these may be elevated as much as you please, and no ridicule follows: but when rational beings are represented above their real character, it becomes ridiculous in Art, because it is vicious in Morality. The *Bees* in *Virgil*,[5] were they rational beings, would be ridiculous by having their actions and manners represented on a level with creatures so superior as men; since it would imply folly or pride, which are the proper objects of Ridicule.

The use of pompous expression for low actions or thoughts is the *true Sublime* of *Don Quixote*. How far unfit it is for Epic Poetry, appears in its being the perfection of the Mock-Epick. It is so far

From the translation of Homer

from being the Sublime of *Tragedy*, that it is the cause of all *Bombaste*; when Poets instead of being (as they imagine) constantly lofty, only preserve throughout a painful equality of fustian: That continu'd swell of language (which runs indiscriminately even thro' their lowest characters, and rattles like some mightiness of meaning in the most indifferent subjects) is of a piece with that perpetual elevation of tone which the Players have learned from it; and which is not *speaking*, but *vociferating*.

There is still more reason for a variation of style in *Epic* Poetry than in *Tragic*, to distinguish between that *Language of the Gods* proper to the *Muse* who sings, and is inspir'd; and that of *Men* who are introduced speaking only according to nature. Farther, there ought to be a difference of style observ'd in the speeches of human persons, and those of Deities; and again, in those which may be called set harangues or orations, and those which are only conversation or dialogue. *Homer* has more of the latter than any other Poet: what *Virgil* does by two or three words of narration, *Homer* still performs by speeches: Not only replies, but even rejoynders are frequent in him, a practice almost unknown to *Virgil*. This renders his Poems more animated, but less grave and majestic; and consequently necessitates the frequent use of a lower style. The writers of Tragedy lye under the same necessity, if they would copy nature; whereas that painted and poetical diction which they perpetually use, would be improper even in Orations design'd to move with all the arts of Rhetorick: This is plain from the practice of *Demosthenes* and *Cicero*; and *Virgil* in those of *Drances* and *Turnus*[6] gives an eminent example, how far remov'd the style of them ought to be from such an excess of figures and ornaments: which indeed fits only that *Language of the Gods* we have been speaking of, or that of a *Muse* under inspiration.

To read thro' a whole work in this strain, is like travelling all along on the ridge of a hill; which is not half so agreeable as sometimes gradually to rise, and sometimes gently to descend, as the way leads, and as the end of the journey directs.

Indeed the true reason that so few Poets have imitated *Homer* in these lower parts, has been the extreme difficulty of preserving that mixture of Ease and Dignity essential to them. For it is as hard for an Epic Poem to stoop to the Narrative with success, as for a Prince to descend to be familiar, without diminution to his greatness.

The *sublime* style is more easily counterfeited than the *natural*; something that passes for it, or sounds like it, is common in all false writers: But nature, purity, perspicuity, and simplicity, never walk in the clouds; they are obvious to all capacities; and where they are not evident, they do not exist.

The most plain Narration not only admits of these, and of harmony (which are all the qualities of style) but it requires every one of them to render it pleasing. On the contrary, whatever pretends to a share of the Sublime, may pass notwithstanding any defects in the rest, nay sometimes without any of them, and gain the admiration of all ordinary readers.

Homer in his lowest narrations or speeches is ever easy, flowing, copious, clear, and harmonious. He shows not less *invention*, in assembling the humbler, than the greater, thoughts and images; nor less *judgment*, in proportioning the style and the versification to these, than to the other. Let it be remember'd, that the same Genius that soar'd the highest, and from whom the greatest models of the *Sublime* are derived, was also he who stoop'd the lowest, and gave to the simple *Narrative* its utmost perfection. Which of these was the harder task to *Homer* himself, I cannot pretend to determine; but to his Translator I can affirm (however unequal all his imitations must be) that of the latter has been much the more difficult.

Whoever expects here the same pomp of verse, and the same ornaments of diction, as in the Iliad; he will, and he ought to be disappointed. Were the original otherwise, it had been an offence against nature; and were the translation so, it were an offence against *Homer*, which is the same thing.

It must be allow'd that there is a majesty and harmony in the *Greek* language which greatly contribute to elevate and support the narration. But I must also observe that this is an advantage grown upon the language since *Homer*'s time; for things are remov'd from vulgarity by being out of use: And if the words we could find in any present language were equally sonorous or musical in themselves, they would still appear less poetical and uncommon than those of a dead one from this only circumstance, of being in every man's mouth. I may add to this another disadvantage to a Translator, from a different cause: *Homer* seems to have taken upon him the character of an Historian, Antiquary, Divine, and Professor of Arts and Sciences; as well as a Poet. In one or other of these characters he descends into many particularities, which as a Poet only perhaps he would have avoided. All these ought to be preserv'd by a faithful Translator, who in some measure takes the place of *Homer*; and all that can be expected from him is to make them as poetical as the subject will bear. Many arts therefore are requisite to supply these

From the translation of Homer

disadvantages, in order to dignify and solemnize these plainer parts, which hardly admit of any poetical ornaments.

Some use has been made to this end, of the style of *Milton*. A just and moderate mixture of old words may have an effect like the working old Abbey stones into a building, which I have sometimes seen to give a kind of venerable air, and yet not destroy the neatness, elegance, and equality requisite to a new work; I mean without rendring it too unfamiliar, or remote from the present purity of writing, or from that ease and smoothness which ought always to accompany Narration or Dialogue. In reading a style judiciously antiquated, one finds a pleasure not unlike that of travelling on an old *Roman* way: but then the road must be as *good*, as the way is *ancient*; the style must be such in which we may evenly proceed, without being put to short stops by sudden abruptnesses, or puzled by frequent turnings and transpositions: No man delights in furrows and stumbling-blocks: And let our love to Antiquity be ever so great, a fine ruin is one thing, and a heap of rubbish another. The imitators of *Milton*, like most other imitators, are not *Copies* but *Caricatura's* of their original; they are a hundred times more obsolete and cramp than he, and equally so in all places: Whereas it should have been observed of *Milton*, that he is not lavish of his exotick words and phrases every where alike, but employs them much more where the subject is marvellous vast and strange, as in the scenes of Heaven, Hell, Chaos, &c. than where it is turn'd to the natural and agreeable, as in the pictures of Paradise, the loves of our first parents, the entertainments of Angels, and the like. In general, this unusual style better serves to awaken our ideas in the descriptions and in the imaging and picturesque parts, than it agrees with the lower sort of narrations, the character of which is simplicity and purity. *Milton* has several of the latter, where we find not an antiquated affected or uncouth word, for some hundred lines together; as in his fifth book, the latter part of the eighth, the former of the tenth and eleventh books, and in the narration of *Michael* in the twelfth. I wonder indeed that he, who ventur'd (contrary to the practice of all other Epic Poets) to imitate *Homer's* Lownesses in the *Narrative*, should not also have copied his plainness and perspicuity in the *Dramatic* parts: Since in his speeches (where clearness above all is necessary) there is frequently such transposition and forced construction, that the very sense is not to be discover'd without a second or third reading: And in this certainly he ought to be no example.

To preserve the true character of *Homer's* style in the present translation, great pains has been taken to be easy and natural. The chief merit I can pretend to, is, not to have been carried into a more plausible and figurative manner of writing, which would better have pleased all readers, but the judicious ones. My errors had been fewer, had each of those Gentlemen who join'd with me shown as much of the severity of a friend to me, as I did to them, in a strict animadversion and correction. What assistance I receiv'd from them, was made known in general to the publick in the original Proposals for this work, and the particulars are specify'd at the conclusion of it; to which I must add (to be punctually just) some part of the tenth and fifteenth books. The Reader will now be too good a judge, how much the greater part of it, and consequently of its faults, is chargeable upon me alone. But this I can with integrity affirm, that I have bestowed as much time and pains upon the whole, as were consistent with the indispensable duties and cares of life, and with that wretched state of health which God has been pleased to make my portion. At the least, it is a pleasure to me to reflect, that I have introduced into our language this other work of the greatest and most ancient of Poets, with some dignity; and I hope, with as little disadvantage as the Iliad. And if, after the unmerited success of that translation, any one will wonder why I would enterprize the Odyssey? I think it is a sufficient answer to say, that *Homer* himself did the same, or the world would never have seen it....[7]

7. Three Attacks on Edmund Curll

Edmund Curll (1675-1747) was an unscrupulous publisher who specialized in poetical miscellanies and instant biographies, with an eye for scandal in both cases. He was behind the publication in 1714 of *Poems and Translations*, edited by the Whig pamphleteer John Oldmixon (1673-1742; see *Dunciad* B ii 283-90) which included an epigram alleging that Pope had a merely mercenary interest in translating Homer; but more seriously for Pope it included his own slightly risqué lines called *Two or Three; or Receipt to make a Cuckold*. On 26 March 1716 Curll issued *Court Poems*, a collection of three pieces which he attributed either to Pope, to Gay, or to 'a Lady of Quality' – a phrase intended to indicate Lady Mary Wortley Montagu, then a close friend of Pope. Pope's revenge upon Curll was perhaps taken to avenge her as much as himself. The revenge took the form of an emetic, administered as described by Pope in *A Full and True Account*, which was published at the end of March 1716. Curll did not retire from the fray. In the course of 1716 he printed two more poems by Pope which were in questionable taste – *The Worms* and *A Roman Catholick Version of the First Psalm* – and he also published attacks on Pope: *The Catholick Poet* by Oldmixon (also attributed by Pope to Mrs Centlivre) and John Dennis's *A True Character of Mr. Pope*. Then on 15 September 1716 Curll announced the publication of *More Court Poems*, which again associated Pope with Lady Mary in the composition of satirical verses. The exact date of *A Further Account* is unknown, but Ault places it in November 1716. This second pamphlet refers to the hack writers employed by Curll, who live in the area of 'Grub Street' (the topography of this passage is discussed by Pat Rogers in *Grub Street: Studies in A Subculture* (1972) pp. 76-83). Curll threatened a reply in an advertisement in *The St. James's Post* for 7-10 December 1716: 'There is preparing for the *Press*, A Satyr, entitled, *Pope* on the Stool of Repentance: Or, the Purge given to *Sir Alexander Knaw-post*, to prepare his Body for the New Madhouse, erected for the cure of Atheists, Blasphemers, Libertines, Punsters, Jacobites, and other prophane Lunaticks' (see Ault, pp. civ-cv). Pope's third satire against Curll, *A Strange but True Relation* survives only in *Miscellanies: The Third Volume* (1732) but Ault found evidence that it had been published as a separate pamphlet in late March or early April 1720. The occasion seems once again to be Curll's publication of a piece linking Pope and Lady Mary, this time a poem addressed to her, called *The Second Eve*, and attributed to Pope. Though Pope published no more pamphlets against Curll, he did not give up the fight, and Curll features in *The Dunciad* (B ii 58ff.). See further, R. Straus, *The Unspeakable Curll* (1927).

Texts: *A Full and True Account* and *A Further Account* are printed from the original pamphlets; *A Strange but True Relation* is printed from *Miscellanies: The Third Volume* (1732).

Three attacks on Edmund Curll

A HORRID AND BARBAROUS REVENGE
BY POISON,
ON THE BODY OF
MR. EDMUND CURLL,
BOOKSELLER;
WITH A FAITHFUL COPY OF
HIS LAST WILL AND TESTAMENT.
PUBLISH'D BY AN EYE WITNESS.

> So when Curll's Stomach the strong Drench o'ercame,
> (Infus'd in Vengeance of insulted Fame)
> Th' Avenger sees, with a delighted Eye,
> His long Jaws open, and his Colour fly;
> And while his Guts the keen Emeticks urge,
> Smiles on the Vomit, and enjoys the Purge.

History furnishes us with Examples of many Satyrical Authors who have fallen Sacrifices to Revenge, but not of any Booksellers that I know of, except the unfortunate Subject of the following Papers; I mean Mr. *Edmund Curll*, at the *Bible* and *Dial* in *Fleetstreet*, who was Yesterday poison'd by Mr. *Pope*, after having liv'd many Years an Instance of the mild Temper of the *British* Nation.

Every Body knows that the said Mr. *Edmund Curll*, on Monday the 26th Instant, publish'd a Satyrical Piece, entituled *Court Poems*, in the Preface whereof they were attributed to a *Lady of Quality*, Mr. *Pope*, or Mr. *Gay*; by which indiscreet Method, though he had escaped one Revenge, there were still two behind in reserve.

Now on the Wednesday ensuing, between the Hours of 10 and 11, Mr. *Lintott*, a neighb'ring Bookseller, desir'd a Conference with Mr. *Curll* about settling the *Title Page* of *Wiquefort's Ambassador*, inviting him at the same Time to take a Whet together. Mr. *Pope*, (who is not the only Instance how Persons of bright Parts may be carry'd away by the Instigations of the Devil) found Means to convey himself into the same Room, under pretence of Business with Mr. *Lintott*, who it seems is the Printer of his *Homer*. This Gentleman with a seeming Coolness, reprimanded Mr. *Curll* for wrongfully ascribing to him the aforesaid Poems: He excused himself, by declaring that one of his Authors (Mr. *Oldmixon* by Name) gave the Copies to the Press, and wrote the *Preface*. Upon this Mr. *Pope* (being to all appearance reconcil'd) very civilly drank a Glass of Sack to Mr. *Curll*, which he as civilly pledged; and tho' the Liquor in Colour and Taste differ'd not from common Sack, yet was it plain by the Pangs this unhappy Stationer felt soon after, that some poisonous Drug had been secretly infused therein.

About Eleven a Clock he went home, where his Wife observing his Colour chang'd, said, *Are you not Sick, my Dear?* He reply'd, *Bloody Sick*; and incontinently fell a vomiting and straining in an uncommon and unnatural Manner, the Contents of his vomiting being as Green as Grass. His Wife had been just reading a Book of her Husband's printing, concerning *Jane Wenham*, the famous Witch of *Hartford*,[1] and her Mind misgave her that he was bewitch'd; but he soon let her know that he suspected *Poison*, and recounted to her, between the Intervals of his Yawnings and Reachings, every Circumstance of his Interview with Mr. *Pope*.

Mr. *Lintott* in the mean Time coming in, was extremely afrighted at the sudden Alteration he observed in him: *Brother* Curll, says he, *I fear you have got the vomiting Distemper, which (I have heard) kills in half an Hour. This comes from your not following my Advice, to drink old Hock as I do, and abstain from Sack.* Mr. *Curll* reply'd, in a moving Tone, *Your Author's Sack I fear has done my Business. Z—ds*, says Mr. *Lintott, My Author! —Why did not you drink old Hock?* Notwithstanding which rough Remonstrance, he did in the most friendly Manner press him to take warm Water; but Mr. *Curll* did with great Obstinacy refuse it; which made Mr. *Lintott* infer, that he chose to die, as thinking to recover greater Damages.

All this Time the Symptoms encreas'd violently, with acute Pains in the lower Belly. *Brother* Lintott, says he, *I perceive my last Hour approaching, do me the friendly Office to call my Partner, Mr.* Pemberton, *that we may settle our Worldly Affairs.* Mr. *Lintott*, like a kind Neighbour, was hastening out of the Room, while Mr. *Curll* rav'd aloud in this Manner, *If I survive this, I will be revenged on* Tonson, *it was he first detected me as the Printer of these Poems, and I will reprint these very Poems in his Name.* His Wife admonish'd him not to think of Revenge, but to take care of his Stock and his Soul: And in the same Instant, Mr. *Lintott* (whose Goodness can never be enough applauded) return'd with Mr. *Pemberton*. After some Tears jointly shed by these Humane Booksellers, Mr. *Curll*, being (as he said) in his perfect Senses though in great bodily Pain, immediately proceeded to make a verbal Will (Mrs. *Curll* having first put on his Night Cap) in the following Manner.

Gentlemen, in the first Place, I do sincerely pray Forgiveness for those indirect Methods I have pursued in inventing new Titles to old Books, putting Authors Names to Things they never saw, publishing private Quarrels for publick Entertainment; all which, I hope will be pardoned, as being done to get an honest livelihood.

I do also heartily beg Pardon of all Persons of Honour, Lords Spiritual and Temporal, Gentry, Burgesses, and Commonalty, to whose Abuse I have any, or every way, contributed by my Publications. Particularly, I hope it will be considered, that if I have vilify'd his Grace the Duke of M[arlborou]gh, I have likewise aspers'd the late Duke of O[rmon]d; if I have abused the honourable Mr. W[alpo]le, I have also libell'd the late Lord B[olingbro]ke; so that I have preserv'd that Equality and Impartiality which becomes an honest Man in Times of Faction and Division.

I call my Conscience to Witness, that many of these Things which may seem malicious, were done out of Charity; I having made it wholly my Business to print for poor disconsolate Authors, whom all other Booksellers refuse: Only God bless Sir Richard Bl[ackmo]re; you know he takes no Copy Money.[2]

The Book of the Conduct of the Earl of N[ottingha]m,[3] is yet unpublished; as you are to have the Profit of it, Mr. Pemberton, you are to run the Risque of the Resentments of all that Noble Family. Indeed I caused the Author to assert several Things in it as Facts, which are only idle Stories of the Town; because I thought it would make the Book sell. Do you pay the Author for Copy Money, and the Printer and Publisher. I heartily beg God's, and my L[or]d N[ottingha]m's Pardon; but all Trades must live.

The second Collection of Poems, which I groundlesly called Mr. Prior's,[4] will sell for Nothing, and hath not yet paid the Charge of the Advertisements, which I was obliged to publish against him: Therefore you may as well suppress the Edition, and beg that Gentleman's Pardon in the Name of a dying Christian.

The French Cato,[5] with the Criticism, showing how superior it is to Mr. Addison's, (which I wickedly inscribed to Madam Dacier) may be suppress'd at a reasonable Rate, being damnably translated.

I protest I have no Animosity to Mr. Rowe, having printed Part of his Callipædia, and an incorrect Edition of his Poems without his Leave, in Quarto.[6] Mr. Gildon's Rehearsal; or Bays the Younger,[7] did more harm to me than to Mr. Rowe; though upon the Faith of an honest Man, I paid him double for abusing both him and Mr. Pope.

Heaven pardon me for publishing the Trials of Sodomy in an Elzevir Letter;[8] but I humbly hope, my printing Sir Richard Bl[ackmo]re's Essays will attone for them. I beg that you will take what remains of these last, which is near the whole Impression, (Presents excepted) and let my poor Widow have in Exchange the sole Propriety of the Copy of Madam *Mascranny*.

Here Mr. Pemberton *interrupted, and would by no Means consent to this Article, about which some Dispute might have arisen, unbecoming a dying Person, if Mr.* Lintott *had not interposed, and Mr.* Curll *vomited.*

What this poor unfortunate Man spoke afterwards, was so indistinct, and in such broken Accents, (being perpetually interrupted by Vomitings) that the Reader is intreated to excuse the Confusion and Imperfection of this Account.

Dear Mr. *Pemberton*, I beg you to beware of the Indictment at *Hicks's-Hall*, for publishing *Rochester's* bawdy Poems; that Copy will otherwise be my best Legacy to my dear Wife, and helpless Child.

The Case of Impotence was my best Support all the last long Vacation.[9]

In this last Paragraph Mr. Curll's *Voice grew more free, for his Vomitings abated upon his Dejections, and he spoke what follows from his Close-stole.*

For the Copies of Noblemen's and Bishop's *Last Wills and Testaments*, I solemnly declare I printed them not with any Purpose of Defamation; but meerly as I thought those Copies lawfully purchased from *Doctors Commons*, at *One Shilling* a Piece. Our Trade in Wills turning to small Account, we may divide them blindfold.

For Mr. *Manwaring's Life*,[10] I ask Mrs. *Old[fiel]d's* Pardon: Neither *His*, nor my Lord *Halifax's* Lives,[11] though they were of great Service to their Country, were of any to me: But I was resolved, since I could not print their Works while they liv'd, to print their Lives after they were dead.

While he was speaking these Words, Mr. *Oldmixon* enter'd. *Ah! Mr.* Oldmixon (said poor Mr. *Curll*) *to what a Condition have your Works reduced me! I die a Martyr to that unlucky Preface. However, in these my last Moments, I will be just to all Men; you shall have your Third Share of the* Court Poems, *as was stipulated. When I am dead, where will you find another Bookseller? Your* Protestant Packet *might have supported you, had you writ a little less scurrilously, There is a mean in all things.*

Then turning to Mr. *Pemberton*, he told him, he had several *Taking Title Pages* that only wanted Treatises to be wrote to them, and earnestly entreated, that when they were writ, his Heirs might have some Share of the Profit of them.

After he had said this he fell into horrible Gripings, upon which Mr. *Lintott* advis'd him to repeat the Lord's Prayer. He desir'd his Wife to step into the Shop for a Common-Prayer-Book, and read it by the Help of a Candle, without Hesitation. He clos'd the Book, fetch'd a Groan, and recommended to Mrs. *Curll* to give Forty Shillings to the Poor of the Parish of St. *Dunstan*'s, and a Week's Wages Advance to each of his Gentlemen Authors, with some small Gratuity in particular to Mrs. *Centlivre*.[12]

The poor Man continued for some Hours with all his disconsolate Family about him in Tears, expecting his final Dissolution; when of a sudden he was surprizingly relieved by a plentiful fœtid Stool, which obliged them all to retire out of the Room. Notwithstanding, it is judged by Sir *Richard Bl[ackmor]e*, that the Poyson is still latent in his Body, and will infallibly destroy him by slow Degrees, in less than a Month. It is to be hoped the other Enemies of this wretched Stationer, will not further pursue their Revenge, or shorten this small Period of his miserable Life.

FINIS.

A FURTHER
ACCOUNT
OF THE MOST
DEPLORABLE CONDITION
OF
Mr. *EDMUND CURLL*,
BOOKSELLER.

Since his being POISON'D on the
28th of *March*.

The Publick is already acquainted with the Manner of Mr. *Curll*'s Impoisonment, by a faithful, tho' unpolite, Historian of *Grubstreet*. I am but the Continuer of his History; yet I hope a due Distinction will be made, between an undignify'd Scribler of a Sheet and half, and the Author of a Three-Penny stitcht Book, like my self.

Wit (saith Sir *Richard Blackmore*) *proceeds from a Concurrence of regular and exalted Ferments, and an Affluence of Animal Spirits rectify'd and refin'd to a degree of Purity.*[13] On the contrary, when the igneous Particles rise with the vital Liquor, they produce an Abstraction of the rational Part of the Soul, which we commonly call *Madness*. The Verity of this Hypothesis, is justify'd by the Symptoms with which the unfortunate Mr. *Edmund Curll*, Bookseller, hath been afflicted ever since his swallowing the Poison at the *Swan* Tavern in *Fleetstreet*. For tho' the *Neck* of his *Retort*, which carries up the Animal Spirits to the Head, is of an extraordinary Length, yet the said Animal Spirits rise muddy, being contaminated with the inflammable Particles of this uncommon Poison.

The Symptoms of his Departure from his usual Temper of Mind, were at first only *speaking civilly to his Customers*, taking a Fancy to *say his Prayers, singeing a Pig with a new purchas'd Libel*, and *refusing Two and Nine Pence for Sir* R[ichard] B[lackmore]*'s Essays*.

As the poor Man's Frenzy increas'd, he began to *void his Excrements in his Bed, read* Rochester*'s bawdy Poems to his Wife*, gave *Oldmixon* a *slap* on the *Chops*, and wou'd have kiss'd Mr. *Pemberton*'s A— *by Violence*.

But at last he came to such a pass, that he wou'd *dine upon nothing but Copper Plates*, took a *Clyster for a whipt Syllabub*, and eat a *Suppository* for a *Raddish* with *Bread* and *Butter*.

We leave it to every tender Wife to imagine how sorely all this afflicted poor Mrs. *Curll*: At first she privately put a *Bill* into several *Churches*, desiring the Prayers of the Congregation for a *wretched Stationer* distemper'd in Mind. But when she was sadly convinc'd that his Misfortune was publick to all the World, writ the following Letter to her good Neighbour Mr. *Lintott*.

A true Copy of Mrs. *Curll*'s Letter to Mr. *Lintott*.

Worthy Mr. Lintott,

'You, and all the Neighbours know too well, the Frenzy with which my poor Man is visited. I never perceiv'd he was out of himself, till that melancholy Day that he thought he was poison'd in a Glass of Sack; upon this, he took a strange Fancy to run a Vomiting all over the House, and in the new wash'd Dining Room. Alas! this is the greatest Adversity that ever befel my poor Man since he lost *one Testicle* at School by the bite of a black Boar. Good Lord! if he should die, where should I dispose of the Stock? unless Mr. *Pemberton* or you would help a distressed Widow; for God knows he never publish'd any Books that lasted above a Week, so that if we wanted *daily Books*, we wanted *daily Bread*. I can write no more, for I hear the Rap of Mr. *Curll*'s *Ivory headed Cane* upon the Counter. –Pray recommend me to your *Pastry Cook*, who furnishes you yearly with Tarts in exchange for your Papers, for Mr. *Curll* has disoblig'd ours since his Fits came upon him; –before that, we generally liv'd upon bak'd Meats. –He is coming in, and I have but just time to put his Son out of the way for fear of Mischief: So wishing you a merry Easter, I remain your

most humble Servant,
C. *Curll*.

Three attacks on Edmund Curll

'*P.S.* As to the Report of my poor Husband's stealing a *Calf*, it is really groundless, for he always binds in *Sheep*.'

But return we to Mr. *Curll*, who all *Wednesday* continued outragiously Mad. On *Thursday* he had a *lucid Interval*, that enabled him to send a general Summons to all *his Authors*. There was but one Porter who cou'd perform this Office, to whom he gave the following Bill of Directions where to find 'em. This Bill, together with Mrs. *Curll*'s Original Letter, lye at Mr. *Lintott*'s Shop to be perus'd by the Curious.

Instructions to a Porter how to find Mr. *Curll*'s Authors.

'At a Tallow-chandlers in *Petty France*, half way under the blind Arch: Ask for the *Historian*.

'At the Bedsted and Bolster, a Musick House in *Morefields*, two Translators in a Bed together.

'At the *Hercules* and *Still* in *Vinegar-yard*, a School-Master with Carbuncles on his Nose.

'At a Blacksmiths Shop in the *Friars*, a Pindarick Writer in red Stockings.

'In the Calendar Mill Room at *Exeter* Change, a Composer of Meditations.

'At the Three *Tobacco Pipes* in *Dog* and *Bitch* Yard, one that has been a Parson, he wears a blue Camblet Coat trim'd with black: my best Writer against *reveal'd Religion*.

'At Mr. *Summers* a Thief-catchers, in *Lewkners* Lane, the Man that wrote against the Impiety of Mr. *Rowe*'s Plays.

'At the Farthing Pye House in *Tooting* Fields, the young Man who is writing my new *Pastorals*.

'At the Laundresses, at the Hole in the Wall in *Cursitors* Alley, up three Pair of Stairs, the Author of my *Church History* – if his Flux be over – you may also speak to the Gentleman who lyes by him in the Flock Bed, my *Index-maker*.

'The *Cook's Wife* in *Buckingham* Court; bid her bring along with her the *Similes* that were lent her for her next new Play.

'Call at *Budge Row* for the Gentleman you use to go to in the Cock-loft; I have taken away the Ladder, but his Landlady has it in keeping.

'I don't much care if you ask at the *Mint* for the old Beetle-brow'd Critick, and the purblind Poet at the Alley over against St. *Andrews Holbourn*. But this as you have time.'

All these Gentlemen appear'd at the Hour appointed, in Mr. *Curll's* Dining Room, two excepted; one of whom was the Gentleman in the Cock-loft, his Landlady being out of the way, and the *Gradus ad Parnassum* taken down; the other happened to be too closely watch'd by the Bailiffs.

They no sooner enter'd the Room, but all of them show'd in their Behaviour some Suspicion of each other; some turning away their Heads with an Air of Contempt; others squinting with a Leer that show'd at once Fear and Indignation, each with a haggard abstracted Mien, the lively Picture of *Scorn, Solitude*, and *short Commons*. So when a Keeper feeds his hungry Charge, of Vultures, Panthers, and of *Lybian* Leopards, each eyes his Fellow with a fiery Glare: High hung, the bloody Liver tempts their Maw. Or as a Housewife stands before her Pales, surrounded by her Geese; they fight, they hiss, they gaggle, beat their Wings, and Down is scatter'd as the Winter's Snow, for a poor Grain of Oat, or Tare, or Barley. Such Looks shot thro' the Room transverse, oblique, direct; such was the stir and din, till *Curll* thus spoke, (but without rising from his Close-stool.)

'*Whores* and *Authors* must be paid beforehand to put them in good Humour; therefore here is half a Crown a piece for you to drink your own Healths, and Confusion to Mr. *Addison*, and all other successful Writers.

'Ah Gentlemen! What have I not done, what have I not suffer'd, rather than the World should be depriv'd of your Lucubrations? I have taken involuntary Purges, I have been vomited, three Times have I been can'd, once was I hunted, twice was my Head broke by a Grenadier, twice was I toss'd in a Blanket; I have had Boxes on the Ear, Slaps on the Chops; I have been frighted, pump'd, kick'd,

Three attacks on Edmund Curll

slander'd and beshitten.—I hope, Gentlemen, you are all convinc'd
that this Author of Mr. *Lintott*'s could mean nothing else but
starving you by poisoning me. It remains for us to consult the best
and speediest Methods of Revenge.'

He had scarce done speaking, but the *Historian* propos'd a
History of his Life. The *Exeter* Exchange Gentleman was for
penning Articles of his Faith. Some pretty smart *Pindarick*, (says the
Red-Stocking Gentleman,) would effectually do his Business. But
the *Index-maker* said there was nothing like an *Index* to his *Homer*.
After several Debates they came to the following Resolutions.

'*Resolv'd*, That every Member of this Society, according to his several
Abilities, shall contribute some way or other to the Defamation of
Mr. *Pope*.

'*Resolv'd*, That towards the Libelling of the said Mr. *Pope*, there be a
Summ employ'd not exceeding Six Pounds Sixteen Shillings and
Nine Pence (not including Advertisements.)

'*Resolv'd*, That Mr. *D[ennis]* make an Affidavit before Mr. *Justice
Tully*, that in Mr. *Pope*'s *Homer*, there are several Passages contrary to
the establish'd Rules of OUR Sublime.

'*Resolved*, That he has on Purpose in several Passages perverted the
true ancient *Heathen* Sense of *Homer*, for the more effectual Prop-
agation of the *Popish* Religion.

'*Resolv'd*, That the Printing of *Homer*'s Battles at this Juncture, has
been the Occasion of all the Disturbances of this Kingdom.

'*Ordered*, That Mr. *Barnivelt* be invited to be a Member of this
Society, in order to make further Discoveries.

'*Resolv'd*, That a number of effective *Errata*'s be raised out of Mr.
Pope's *Homer* (not exceeding 1746.) and that every Gentleman, who
shall send in one Error, for his Encouragement shall have the whole
Works of this Society *Gratis*.

'*Resolv'd*, That a Summ not exceeding Ten Shillings and Six-pence be distributed among the Members of this Society for *Coffee* and *Tobacco*, in order to enable them the more effectually to defame him in *Coffee-Houses*.

'*Resolv'd*, That towards the further lessening the Character of the said Mr. *Pope*, some Persons be deputed to abuse him at Ladies *Tea Tables*, and that in Consideration our Authors are not *well dress'd* enough, Mr. *C—y* be deputed for that Service.

'*Resolv'd*, That a *Ballad* be made against Mr. *Pope*, and that Mr. *Oldmixon*, Mr. *Gildon* and Mrs. *Centlivre* do prepare and bring in the same.

'*Resolv'd*, That above all, some effectual Ways and Means be found to encrease the Joint Stock of the Reputation of this Society, which at present is exceedingly low, and to give their Works the greater Currency; whether by raising the Denomination of the said Works by counterfeit Title Pages, or mixing a greater Quantity of the fine Metal of other Authors, with the Alloy of this Society.

'*Resolv'd*, That no Member of this Society for the future mix *Stout* in his *Ale* in a Morning, and that Mr. *B.* remove from the *Hercules* and *Still*.

'*Resolv'd*, That all our Members, (except the *Cook's* Wife) be provided with a sufficient Quantity of the *vivifying Drops*, Or *Byfield's Sal Volatile*.

'*Resolv'd*, That Sir *R[ichard] B[lackmore]* be appointed to endue this Society with a large Quantity of *regular and exalted Ferments*, in order to *enliven* their *cold Sentiments* (being his true Receipt to make Wits.)

These Resolutions being taken, the Assembly was ready to break up, but they took so near a-part in Mr. *Curll's* Afflictions, that none of them could leave him without giving some Advice to re-instate him in his Health.

Mr. *Gildon* was of Opinion, That in order to drive a *Pope* out of his *Belly*, he should get the Mummy of some deceas'd Moderator of the General Assembly in *Scotland*, to be taken inwardly as an effectual

Three attacks on Edmund Curll

Antidote against Antichrist; but Mr. *Oldmixon* did conceive, that the *Liver* of the Person who administred the Poison, boil'd in Broth, would be a more certain Cure.

While the Company were expecting the Thanks of Mr. *Curll*, for these Demonstrations of their Zeal, a whole Pile of *Essays* on a sudden fell on his Head; the Shock of which in an Instant brought back his Dilirium. He immediately rose up, over-turn'd the Close-stool, and beshit the *Essays* (which may probably occasion a *second Edition*) then without putting up his Breeches, in a most furious Tone, he thus broke out to his Books, which his distemper'd Imagination represented to him as alive, coming down from their Shelves, fluttering their Leaves, and flapping their Covers at him.

Now *G—d damn* all *Folio's, Quarto's, Octavo's* and *Duodecimo's!* ungrateful Varlets that you are, who have so long taken up my House without paying for your Lodging? —Are you not the beggarly Brood of fumbling *Journey-men;* born in *Garrets,* among *Lice* and *Cobwebs,* nurs'd upon *Grey Peas, Bullocks Liver,* and *Porter's Ale?* —Was not the first Light you saw, the *Farthing* Candle I paid for? Did you not come before your Time into *dirty Sheets* of brown Paper? —And have not I cloath'd you in double *Royal,* lodg'd you handsomely on *decent Shelves,* lac'd your *Backs* with *Gold,* equipt you with splendid *Titles,* and sent you into the World with the Names of *Persons of Quality?* Must I be *always* plagu'd with you? —Why flutter ye your Leaves, and flap your Covers at me? Damn ye all, ye *Wolves* in *Sheeps Cloathing; Rags ye were, and to Rags ye shall return.* Why hold you forth your *Texts* to me, ye paltry *Sermons?* Why cry ye – at every Word to me, ye *bawdy Poems?* – To my Shop at *Tunbridge* ye shall go, by G— and thence be drawn like the rest of your Predecessors, bit by bit, to the *Passage-House:* For in this present Emotion of my Bowels, how do I compassionate those who have great need, and nothing to wipe their Breech with?

Having said this, and at the same Time recollecting that his own was yet unwiped, he abated of his Fury, and with great Gravity, apply'd to that Function the unfinish'd Sheets of the Conduct of the E[arl] of N[ottingha]m.

FINIS.

Selected prose of Alexander Pope

A STRANGE BUT TRUE
RELATION
HOW
EDMUND CURLL,
of *Fleetstreet*, Stationer,

Out of an extraordinary Desire of Lucre, went into
Change Alley, and was converted from the Christian
Religion by certain Eminent *Jews*: And how he was
circumcis'd and initiated into their Mysteries.

Avarice (as Sir *Richard* in the Third Page of his Essays hath elegantly observ'd) *is an inordinate Impulse of the Soul towards the amassing or heaping together a Superfluity of Wealth without the least Regard of applying it to its proper Uses.*[14]

And how the Mind of Man is possessed with this Vice, may be seen every Day both in the City and Suburbs thereof. It has been always esteemed by *Plato, Puffendorf*[15] and *Socrates*, as the darling Vice of old Age: But now our young Men are turn'd Usurers and Stock-jobbers; and, instead of lusting after the real Wives and Daughters of our rich Citizens, they covet nothing but their Money and Estates. Strange Change of Vice! when the Concupiscence of Youth is converted into the Covetousness of Age, and those Appetites are now become VENAL which should be VENEREAL.

In the first Place, let us shew you how many of the ancient Worthies and Heroes of Antiquity have been undone and ruin'd by this Deadly Sin of Avarice.

I shall take the Liberty to begin with *Brutus*, that noble *Roman*. Does not *Ætian* inform us that he received Fifty Broad Pieces for the Assassination of that renowned Emperor *Julius Cæsar*, who fell a Sacrifice to the *Jews*, as Sir *Edmund Bury Godfrey* did to the *Papists*?[16]

Did not *Themistocles* let in the *Goths* and *Vandals* into *Carthage* for a Sum of Money, where they barbarously put out the other Eye of the famous *Hannibal?* As *Herodotus* hath it in his ninth Book upon the *Roman* Medals.

Even the great *Cato* (as the late Mr. *Addison* hath very well observ'd) though otherwise a Gentleman of good Sense, was not unsully'd by this pecuniary Contagion: For he sold *Athens* to *Artaxerxes Longimanus* for a hundred *Rix-Dollars*, which in our Money will amount to two *Talents* and thirty *Sestertii*, according to Mr. *Demoiver's* Calculation. *See* Hesiod *in his 7th Chapter of* Feasts *and* Festivals.

Three attacks on Edmund Curll

Actuated by the same Diabolical Spirit of Gain, *Scylla* the *Roman* Consul shot *Alcibiades* the Senator with a Pistol, and robb'd him of several *Bank Bills* and *Chequer Notes* to an immense Value; for which he came to an untimely End, and was deny'd *Christian* Burial. Hence comes the Proverb *incidat in Scyllam.*

To come near to our own Times, and give you one modern Instance (tho' well known, and often quoted by Historians, *viz.* *Echard, Dionysius Halicarnassæus, Virgil, Horace*, and others) 'Tis that, I mean, of the famous *Godfrey* of *Bulloigne*, one of the great Heroes of the Holy War, who rob'd *Cleopatra* Queen of *Egypt* of a Diamond Necklace, Ear-Rings, and a *Tompion*'s Gold Watch (which was given her by *Mark Antony*) all these things were found in *Godfrey*'s Breeches Pocket, when he was kill'd at the Siege of *Damascus*.

Who then can wonder after so many great and illustrious Examples that Mr. *Edmund Curll* the Stationer, should renounce the *Christian Religion* for the *Mammon* of Unrighteousness, and barter his precious Faith for the filthy Prospect of Lucre in the present Fluctuation of *Stocks*.

It having been observ'd to Mr. *Curll* by some of his ingenious Authors, (who I fear are not over-charg'd with any Religion) what immense Sums the *Jews* had got by *Bubbles*, &c. he immediately turned his Mind from the Business in which he was educated, but thriv'd little, and resolv'd to quit his Shop, for *Change Alley*. Whereupon falling into Company with the *Jews* at their Club at the Sign of the *Cross* in *Cornhill*, they began to tamper with him upon the most important Points of the *Christian Faith*, which he for some time zealously, and *like a good Christian obstinately* defended. They promised him *Paradise*, and many other Advantages *hereafter*, but he artfully insinuated that he was more inclinable to listen to *present* Gain. They took the Hint, and promis'd him that immediately upon his Conversion to their Persuasion he should become as rich as a *Jew*.

They made use likewise of several other Arguments, to wit,

That the wisest Man that ever was, and inasmuch the richest, beyond all peradventure, was a *Jew*, videlicet *Solomon*.

That *David*, the Man after God's own Heart, was a *Jew* also. And most of the Children of *Israel* are suspected for holding the same Doctrine.

This Mr. *Curll* at first strenuously deny'd, for indeed he thought them *Roman Catholicks*, and so far was he from giving way to their Temptations, that to convince them of his *Christianity* he call'd for a *Pork-Grisking*.

They now promis'd if he would poison his Wife and give up his

Grisking, that he should marry the rich *Ben Meymon*'s only Daughter. This made some Impression on him.

They then talk'd to him in the *Hebrew* Tongue, which he not understanding, it was observ'd had very great Weight with him.

They, now perceiving that his *Godliness* was only *Gain*, desisted from all other Arguments, and attack'd him on his weak side, namely that of *Avarice*.

Upon which *John Mendez* offer'd him an Eighth of an advantagious Bargain for the *Apostles Creed*, which he readily and wickedly renounced.

He then sold the *Nine and Thirty Articles* for a *Bull*; but insisted hard upon *Black-Puddings*, being a great Lover thereof.

Joshua Perrara engag'd to let him share with him in his *Bottomrye*, upon this he was persuaded out of his *Christian Name*; but he still adher'd to *Black-Puddings*.

Sir *Gideon Lopez* tempted him with *Forty Pound* Subscription in *Ram*'s *Bubble*; for which he was content to give up the *Four Evangelists*, and he was now compleated a perfect *Jew*, all but *Black-Pudding* and *Circumcision*; for both of which he would have been glad to have had a Dispensation.

But on the 17th of *March*, Mr. *Curll* (unknown to his Wife) came to the Tavern aforesaid. At his Entrance into the Room he perceived a meagre Man, with a sallow Countenance, a black forky Beard, and long Vestment. In his Right Hand he held a large Pair of Sheers, and in his Left a red hot Searing-Iron. At Sight of this, Mr. *Curll*'s Heart trembled within him, and feign would he retire; but he was prevented by six Jews, who laid Hands upon him, and unbuttoning his Breeches threw him upon the Table, a pale pitiful Spectacle!

He now entreated them in the most moving Tone of Voice to dispense with that *unmanly* Ceremonial, which if they would consent to, he faithfully promis'd that he would eat a Quarter of *Paschal Lamb* with them the next *Sunday* following.

All these Protestations availed him nothing, for they threatned him that all Contracts and Bargains should be void unless he would submit to bear all the *outward* and *visible* Signs of *Judaism*.

Our Apostate hearing this, stretched himself upon his Back, spread his Legs, and waited for the Operation; but when he saw the High-Priest take up the *Cleft Stick*, he roared most unmercifully, and swore several Christian Oaths, for which the *Jews* rebuked him.

The Savour of the *Effluvia* that issued from him, convinced the

Three attacks on Edmund Curll

Old *Levite* and all his Assistants that he needed no present *Purgation*, wherefore without farther *anointing* him he proceeded in his Office; when by an unfortunate Jerk upward of the impatient Victim, he lost five times as much as ever Jew did before.

They finding that he was too much circumcis'd, which by the *Levitical Law* is worse than not being circumcis'd at all, refused to stand to any of their Contracts: Wherefore they cast him forth from their Synagogue; and he now remains a most piteous, woful and miserable Sight at the Sign of the *Old Testament* and *Dial* in *Fleet-street*, his Wife, (poor Woman) is at this Hour lamenting over him, wringing her Hands and tearing her Hair; for the barbarous Jews still keep, and expose at *Jonathan*'s and *Garraway*'s, the Memorial of her Loss, and her Husband's Indignity.

PRAYER. (*To save the Stamp.*)

KEEP us, we beseech thee, from the Hands of such barbarous and cruel Jews, who, albeit, they abhor the Blood of Black Puddings, yet thirst they vehemently after the Blood of White ones. And that we may avoid such like Calamities, may all good and well-disposed Christians be warn'd by this unhappy Wretch's woful Example to abominate the heinous Sin of Avarice, *which sooner or later will draw them into the cruel Clutches of* Satan, Papists, Jews, *and* Stock-jobbers. *Amen.*

8. Preface to
The Works (1717)

This is the Preface to *The Works of Mr. Alexander Pope* (1717). For a discussion of the importance of this preface, and a text of the manuscript drafts of it, see Maynard Mack, *Collected in Himself* (1982) pp. 159-78, and for later minor revisions see the notes in *Poems* i 3-10.

Text: *Works* (1717).

Preface to *The Works*
PREFACE

I am inclined to think that both the writers of books, and the readers of them, are generally not a little unreasonable in their expectations. The first seem to fancy that the world must approve whatever they produce, and the latter to imagine that authors are obliged to please them at any rate. Methinks as on the one hand, no single man is born with a right of controuling the opinions of all the rest; so on the other, the world has no title to demand, that the whole care and time of any particular person should be sacrificed to its entertainment. Therefore I cannot but believe that writers and readers are under equal obligations, for as much fame, or pleasure, as each affords the other.

Every one acknowledges, it would be a wild notion to expect perfection in any work of man: and yet one would think the contrary was taken for granted, by the judgment commonly past upon Poems. A Critic supposes he has done his part, if he proves a writer to have fail'd in an expression, or err'd in any particular point: and can it then be wonder'd at, if the Poets in general seem resolv'd not to own themselves in any error? For as long as one side despises a well-meant endeavour, the other will not be satisfy'd with a moderate approbation.

I am afraid this extreme zeal on both sides is ill-plac'd; Poetry and Criticism being by no means the universal concern of the world, but only the affair of idle men who write in their closets, and of idle men who read there. Yet sure upon the whole, a bad Author deserves better usage than a bad Critic; a man may be the former merely thro' the misfortune of an ill judgment, but he cannot be the latter without both that and an ill temper.

I think a good deal may be said to extenuate the fault of bad Poets. What we call a Genius, is hard to be distinguish'd by a man himself, from a strong inclination: and if it be never so great, he can not at first discover it any other way, than by that prevalent propensity which renders him the more liable to be mistaken. The only method he has, is to make the experiment by writing, and appealing to the judgment of others: And if he happens to write ill (which is certainly no sin in itself) he is immediately made an object of ridicule. I wish we had the humanity to reflect that even the worst authors might endeavour to please us, and in that endeavour, deserve something at our hands. We have no cause to quarrel with them but for their obstinacy in persisting, and this too may admit of alleviating circumstances. Their particular friends may be either ignorant, or

147

insincere; and the rest of the world too well bred to shock them with a truth, which generally their Booksellers are the first that inform them of. This happens not till they have spent too much of their time, to apply to any profession which might better fit their talents; and till such talents as they have are so far discredited, as to be but of small service to them. For (what is the hardest case imaginable) the reputation of a man generally depends upon the first steps he makes in the world, and people will establish their opinion of us, from what we do at that season when we have least judgment to direct us.

On the other hand, a good Poet no sooner communicates his works with the same desire of information, but it is imagin'd he is a vain young creature given up to the ambition of fame; when perhaps the poor man is all the while trembling with the fear of being ridiculous. If he is made to hope he may please the world, he falls under very unlucky circumstances; for from the moment he prints, he must expect to hear no more truth, than if he were a Prince, or a Beauty. If he has not very good sense, his living thus in a course of flattery may put him in no small danger of becoming a Coxcomb: If he has, he will consequently have so much diffidence, as not to reap any great satisfaction from his praise; since if it be given to his face, it can scarce be distinguish'd from flattery, and if in his absence, it is hard to be certain of it. Were he sure to be commended by the best and most knowing, he is as sure of being envy'd by the worst and most ignorant; for it is with a fine Genius as with a fine fashion, all those are displeas'd at it who are not able to follow it: And 'tis to be fear'd that esteem will seldom do any man so much good, as ill will does him harm. Then there is a third class of people who make the largest part of mankind, those of ordinary or indifferent capacities; and these (to a man) will hate, or suspect him: a hundred honest gentlemen will dread him as a wit, and a hundred innocent women as a satyrist. In a word, whatever be his fate in Poetry, it is ten to one but he must give up all the reasonable aims of life for it. There are indeed some advantages accruing from a Genius to Poetry, and they are all I can think of: the agreeable power of self-amusement when a man is idle or alone; the privilege of being admitted into the best company; and the freedom of saying as many careless things as other people, without being so severely remark'd upon.

I believe, if any one, early in his life should contemplate the dangerous fate of authors, he would scarce be of their number on any consideration. The life of a Wit is a warfare upon earth; and the present spirit of the world is such, that to attempt to serve it (any way) one must have the constancy of a martyr, and a resolution to suffer for its sake. I confess it was want of consideration that made me an author; I writ because it amused me; I corrected because it was as pleasant to me to correct as to write; and I publish'd because I was told I might please such as it was a credit to please. To what degree I have done this, I am really ignorant; I had too much fondness for my productions to judge of them at first, and too much judgment to be pleas'd with them at last. But I have reason to think they can have no reputation which will continue long, or which deserves to do so: for they have always fallen short not only of what I read of others, but even of my own Ideas of Poetry.

If any one should imagine I am not in earnest, I desire him to reflect, that the Ancients (to say the least of them) had as much Genius as we; and that to take more pains, and employ more time, cannot fail to produce more complete pieces. They constantly apply'd themselves not only to that art, but to that single branch of an art, to which their talent was most powerfully bent; and it was the business of their lives to correct and finish their works for posterity. If we can pretend to have used the same industry, let us expect the same immortality: Tho' if we took the same care, we should still lie under a farther misfortune: they writ in languages that became universal and everlasting, while ours are extremely limited both in extent, and in duration. A mighty foundation for our pride! when the utmost we can hope, is but to be read in one Island, and to be thrown aside at the end of one Age.

All that is left us is to recommend our productions by the imitation of the Ancients: and it will be found true, that in every age, the highest character for sense and learning has been obtain'd by those who have been most indebted to them. For to say truth, whatever is very good sense must have been common sense in all times; and what we call Learning, is but the knowledge of the sense of our predecessors. Therefore they who say our thoughts are not our own because they resemble the Ancients, may as well say our faces are not our own, because they are like our Fathers: And indeed it is very unreasonable, that people should expect us to be Scholars, and yet be angry to find us so.

I fairly confess that I have serv'd my self all I could by reading; that I made use of the judgment of authors dead and living; that I omitted no means in my power to be inform'd of my errors, both by my friends and enemies; and that I expect not to be excus'd in any negligence on account of youth, want of leisure, or any other idle allegations: But the true reason these pieces are not more correct, is owing to the consideration how short a time they, and I, have to live: One may be ashamed to consume half one's days in bringing sense and rhyme together; and what Critic can be so unreasonable as not to leave a man time enough for any more serious employment, or more agreeable amusement?

The only plea I shall use for the favour of the publick, is, that I have as great a respect for it, as most authors have for themselves; and that I have sacrificed much of my own self-love for its sake, in preventing not only many mean things from seeing the light, but many which I thought tolerable. I believe no one qualification is so likely to make a good writer, as the power of rejecting his own thoughts; and it must be this (if any thing) that can give me a chance to be one. For what I have publish'd, I can only hope to be pardon'd; but for what I have burn'd, I deserve to be prais'd. On this account the world is under some obligation to me, and owes me the justice in return, to look upon no verses as mine that are not inserted in this collection. And perhaps nothing could make it worth my while to own what are really so, but to avoid the imputation of so many dull and immoral things, as partly by malice, and partly by ignorance, have been ascribed to me. I must farther acquit my self of the presumption of having lent my name to recommend any Miscellanies,[1] or works of other men, a thing I never thought becoming a person who has hardly credit enough to answer for his own.

In this office of collecting my pieces, I am altogether uncertain, whether to look upon my self as a man building a monument, or burying the dead?

If time shall make it the former, may these Poems (as long as they last) remain as a testimony, that their Author never made his talents subservient to the mean and unworthy ends of Party or self-interest; the gratification of publick prejudices, or private passions; the flattery of the undeserving, or the insult of the unfortunate. If I have written well, let it be consider'd that 'tis what no man can do without good sense, a quality that not only renders one capable of being a good writer, but a good man. And if I have made any acquisition in the opinion of any one under the notion of the former, let it be continued to me under no other title than that of the latter.

But if this publication be only a more solemn funeral of my Remains, I desire it may be known that I die in charity, and in my senses; without any murmurs against the justice of this age, or any mad appeals to posterity. I declare I shall think the world in the right, and quietly submit to every truth which time shall discover to the prejudice of these writings; not so much as wishing so irrational a thing, as that every body should be deceiv'd, meerly for my credit. However, I desire it may then be consider'd, that there are very few things in this collection which were not written under the age of five and twenty; so that my youth may be made (as it never fails to be in Executions) a case of compassion. That I was never so concern'd about my works as to vindicate them in print, believing if any thing was good it would defend itself, and what was bad could never be defended. That I used no artifice to raise or continue a reputation, depreciated no dead author I was obliged to, brib'd no living one with unjust praise, insulted no adversary with ill language, or when I could not attack a Rival's works, encourag'd reports against his Morals. To conclude, if this volume perish, let it serve as a warning to the Critics, not to take too much pains for the future to destroy such things as will die of themselves; and a *Memento mori* to some of my vain cotemporaries the Poets, to teach them that when real merit is wanting, it avails nothing to have been encourag'd by the great, commended by the eminent, and favour'd by the publick in general.

9. *A Discourse on Pastoral Poetry*

This essay was first printed in Pope's *Works* (1717), with a half-title claiming that both the *Discourse* and the following four *Pastorals* (first printed in 1709) had been 'Written in the Year 1704', at the age of sixteen. As the opening paragraph makes clear, Pope is consciously drawing on a tradition of pastoral criticism. Two French writers had been particularly influential in establishing the main lines of debate. René Rapin published his *Dissertatio de Carmine Pastorali* in 1659 (abridged and translated by Thomas Creech in 1684), and in 1688 Bernard Le Bouyer de Fontenelle issued his *Poésies pastorales... avec un traité sur la nature de l'églogue*, which offered a rival view of pastoral. Rapin grounded his analysis on the practice of the ancients, drawing on Theocritus and Virgil; Fontenelle, claiming to follow instead the natural light of his own reason, argued that pastoral represents not the golden age but the tranquillity of rural life, hiding its harsher side. Pope draws upon both positions, frequently echoing Rapin, but also agreeing with Fontenelle that pastoral is an illusion which represents only the innocent and tranquil side of a shepherd's life (see further *Poems* i 13-33). But for Pope the proper role and character of pastoral was a question which touched his own practice and reputation. The pastorals of Ambrose Philips, published simultaneously with his own in Tonson's *Poetical Miscellanies: The Sixth Part* (1709), followed a course opposite to the one defined by Rapin and practised by Pope: instead of depicting a classical golden age, Philips used an English setting, and antique quasi-rural diction. This method was supported by Thomas Tickell in a series of *Guardian* essays in April 1713, where Philips was not only quoted and praised, but linked with Spenser. Pope replied with ironic praise of Philips in *Guardian* 40.

Text: *Works* (1717). For minor later revisions see the notes in *Poems* i 23-33.

A DISCOURSE ON
PASTORAL POETRY.

There are not, I believe, a greater number of any sort of verses than of those which are called Pastorals, nor a smaller, than of those which are truly so. It therefore seems necessary to give some account of this kind of Poem, and it is my design to comprize in this short paper the substance of those numerous dissertations the Criticks have made on the subject, without omitting any of their rules in my own favour. You will also find some points reconciled, about which they seem to differ, and a few remarks which I think have escaped their observation.

The original of Poetry is ascribed to that age which succeeded the creation of the world: And as the keeping of flocks seems to have been the first employment of mankind, the most ancient sort of poetry was probably pastoral. 'Tis natural to imagine, that the leisure of those ancient shepherds requiring some diversion, none was so proper to that solitary life as singing; and that in their songs they took occasion to celebrate their own felicity. From hence a Poem was invented, and afterwards improv'd to a perfect image of that happy time; which by giving us an esteem for the virtues of a former age, might recommend them to the present. And since the life of shepherds was attended with more tranquillity than any other rural employment, the Poets chose to introduce their Persons, from whom it receiv'd the name of Pastoral.

A Pastoral is an imitation of the action of a shepherd; the form of this imitation is dramatic, or narrative, or mix'd of both; the fable simple, the manners not too polite nor too rustic: The thoughts are plain, yet admit a little quickness and passion, but that short and flowing: The expression humble, yet as pure as the language will afford; neat, but not florid; easy, and yet lively. In short, the fable, manners, thoughts, and expressions, are full of the greatest simplicity in nature.

The complete character of this poem consists in simplicity, brevity, and delicacy; the two first of which render an eclogue natural, and the last delightful.

If we would copy Nature, it may be useful to take this consideration along with us, that pastoral is an image of what they call the Golden age. So that we are not to describe our shepherds as shepherds at this day really are, but as they may be conceiv'd then to have been; when a notion of quality was annex'd to that name, and the best of men follow'd the employment. To carry this resemblance yet farther, that Air of piety to the Gods should shine thro' the Poem, which so visibly appears in all the works of antiquity: And it ought to preserve some relish of the old way of writing; the connections should be loose, the narrations and descriptions short, and the periods concise. Yet it is not sufficient that the sentences only be brief, the whole Eclogue should be so too. For we cannot suppose Poetry to have been the business of the ancient shepherds, but their recreation at vacant hours.

But with a respect to the present age, nothing more conduces to make these composures natural, than when some Knowledge in rural affairs is discover'd. This may be made to appear rather done by chance than on design, and sometimes is best shewn by inference; lest by too much study to seem natural, we destroy the delight. For what is inviting in this sort of poetry (as *Fontenelle* observes) proceeds not so much from the Idea of a country life itself, as from that of its Tranquillity. We must therefore use some illusion to render a Pastoral delightful; and this consists in exposing the best side only of a shepherd's life, and in concealing its miseries. Nor is it enough to introduce shepherds discoursing together, but a regard must be had to the subject; that it contain some particular beauty in itself, and that it be different in every Eclogue. Besides, in each of them a design'd scene or prospect is to be presented to our view, which should likewise have its variety. This Variety is obtain'd in a great degree by frequent comparisons, drawn from the most agreeable objects of the country; by interrogations to things inanimate; by beautiful digressions, but those short; sometimes by insisting a little on circumstances; and lastly by elegant turns on the words, which render the numbers extremely sweet and pleasing. As for the numbers themselves, tho' they are properly of the heroic measure, they should be the smoothest, the most easy and flowing imaginable.

It is by rules like these that we ought to judge of Pastoral. And since the instructions given for any art are to be deliver'd as that art is in perfection, they must of necessity be deriv'd from those in whom it is acknowledg'd so to be. 'Tis therefore from the practice of *Theocritus* and *Virgil*, (the only undisputed authors of Pastoral) that the Criticks have drawn the foregoing notions concerning it.

Theocritus excels all others in nature and simplicity. The subjects of his *Idyllia* are purely pastoral, but he is not so exact in his persons, having introduced Reapers and fishermen as well as shepherds. He is apt to be long in his descriptions, of which that of the Cup in the first pastoral is a remarkable instance. In the manners he seems a little defective, for his swains are sometimes abusive and immodest, and perhaps too much inclining to rusticity; for instance, in his fourth and fifth *Idyllia*. But 'tis enough that all others learn'd their excellencies from him, and that his Dialect alone has a secret charm in it which no other could ever attain.

Virgil who copies *Theocritus*, refines upon his original: and in all points where Judgment has the principal part, is much superior to his master. Tho' some of his subjects are not pastoral in themselves, but only seem to be such; they have a wonderful variety in them which the *Greek* was a stranger to. He exceeds him in regularity and brevity, and falls short of him in nothing but simplicity and propriety of style; the first of which perhaps was the fault of his age, and the last of his language.

Among the moderns, their success has been greatest who have most endeavour'd to make these ancients their pattern. The most considerable Genius appears in the famous *Tasso*, and our *Spenser*. *Tasso* in his *Aminta*[1] has as far excell'd all the Pastoral writers, as in his *Gierusalemme* he has outdone the Epic Poets of his country. But as this piece seems to have been the original of a new sort of poem, the Pastoral Comedy, in *Italy*, it cannot so well be consider'd as a copy of the ancients. *Spenser's Calender*, in Mr. *Dryden's* opinion,[2] is the most complete work of this kind which any Nation has produc'd ever since the time of *Virgil*. Not but he may be thought imperfect in some few points. His Eclogues are somewhat too long, if we compare them with the ancients. He is sometimes too allegorical, and treats of matters of religion in a pastoral style as *Mantuan*[3] had done before him. He has employ'd the Lyric measure, which is contrary to the practice of the old Poets. His Stanza is not still the same, nor always well chosen. This last may be the reason his expression is sometimes not concise enough: for the Tetrastic has oblig'd him to extend his sense to the length of four lines, which would have been more closely confin'd in the Couplet.

In the manners, thoughts, and characters, he comes near *Theocritus* himself; tho' notwithstanding all the care he has taken, he is certainly inferior in his Dialect: For the *Doric* had its beauty and propriety in the time of *Theocritus*; it was used in part of *Greece*, and frequent in the mouths of many of the greatest persons; whereas the old *English* and country phrases of *Spenser* were either entirely obsolete, or spoken only by people of the basest condition. As there is a difference betwixt simplicity and rusticity, so the expression of simple thoughts should be plain, but not clownish. The addition he has made of a Calendar to his Eclogues is very beautiful: since by this, besides that general moral of innocence and simplicity, which is common to other authors of pastoral, he has one peculiar to himself; he compares human Life to the several Seasons, and at once exposes to his readers a view of the great and little worlds, in their various changes and aspects. Yet the scrupulous division of his Pastorals into Months, has oblig'd him either to repeat the same description, in other words, for three months together; or when it was exhausted before, entirely to omit it: whence it comes to pass that some of his Eclogues (as the sixth, eighth, and tenth for example) have nothing but their Titles to distinguish them. The reason is evident, because the year has not that variety in it to furnish every month with a particular description, as it may every season.

Of the following Eclogues I shall only say, that these four comprehend all the subjects which the Critics upon *Theocritus* and *Virgil* will allow to be fit for pastoral: That they have as much variety of description, in respect of the several seasons, as *Spenser*'s: That in order to add to this variety, the several times of the day are observ'd, the rural employments in each season or time of day, and the rural scenes or places proper to such employments; not without some regard to the several ages of man, and the different passions proper to each age.

But after all, if they have any merit, it is to be attributed to some good old Authors, whose works as I had leisure to study, so I hope I have not wanted care to imitate.

10. Preface to
The Works of Shakespear

The Works of Shakespear. In Six Volumes. Collated and Corrected by the former Editions, By Mr. Pope was published by Jacob Tonson in 1725. Pope began work on the edition in 1721. He was the first editor to collate the quartos for the establishment of a modern text, but he did not use them with much consistency or intelligence, and relied too heavily upon Rowe's edition. He removed some corruptions, continued Rowe's modernization and made many alterations for the sake of the metre. Some 1,560 lines were relegated to the foot of the page because Pope refused to admit them into the text on critical grounds: passages of word-play (e.g. many parts of *Love's Labours Lost*) were particularly affected. His methods received justifiable criticism from Lewis Theobald in his *Shakespeare Restored: Or, a Specimen of the Many Errors, As well Committed, as Unamended, by Mr. Pope In His Late Edition of this Poet* (1726); for his temerity in being a good scholar Theobald was pilloried by Pope in *The Dunciad* (1728). On Pope as an editor, see T.R. Lounsbury, *The First Editors of Shakespeare: Pope and Theobald* (1906), and R.B. McKerrow, 'The Treatment of Shakespeare's Text by his Earlier Editors, 1709-1768', *Proceedings of the British Academy*, 19 (1933) 89-122.

Pope attached a few notes to his edition, but they are without much interest (they are accessible in *Shakespeare: The Critical Heritage, Volume II 1693-1733*, edited by Brian Vickers (1974) 415-18). He also marked passages of which he particularly approved with marginal inverted commas, and outstanding scenes with asterisks. Pope's choice of fine passages has been discussed by John Butt, *Pope's Taste in Shakespeare* (1936), and compared with contemporary opinion by P. Dixon, 'Pope's Shakespeare', *JEGP*, 63 (1964) 191-203.

Pope's Preface develops certain lines of critical thought about Shakespeare which had become common since Dryden's seminal passage in his *Essay of Dramatic Poesy* (1668): Shakespeare's originality, his lack of learning, his relation to Jonson. Pope appears, however, to be breaking new ground when discussing the likely influence of the playhouse upon Shakespeare.

Text: *The Works of Shakespear* (1725).

PREFACE TO
THE WORKS OF SHAKESPEAR

It is not my design to enter into a Criticism upon this Author; tho'
to do it effectually and not superficially, would be the best occasion
that any just Writer could take, to form the judgment and taste of
our nation. For of all *English* Poets *Shakespear* must be confessed to
be the fairest and fullest subject for Criticism, and to afford the most
numerous, as well as most conspicuous instances, both of Beauties
and Faults of all sorts. But this far exceeds the bounds of a Preface,
the business of which is only to give an account of the fate of his
Works, and the disadvantages under which they have been transmitted to us. We shall hereby extenuate many faults which are his, and
clear him from the imputation of many which are not: A design,
which tho' it can be no guide to future Criticks to do him justice in
one way, will at least be sufficient to prevent their doing him an
injustice in the other.

I cannot however but mention some of his principal and characteristic Excellencies, for which (notwithstanding his defects) he is
justly and universally elevated above all other Dramatic Writers. Not
that this is the proper place of praising him, but because I would not
omit any occasion of doing it.

If ever any Author deserved the name of an *Original*, it was
Shakespear. Homer himself drew not his art so immediately from the
fountains of Nature, it proceeded thro' *Ægyptian* strainers and
channels, and came to him not without some tincture of the
learning, or some cast of the models, of those before him. The
Poetry of *Shakespear* was Inspiration indeed: he is not so much an
Imitator, as an Instrument, of Nature; and 'tis not so just to say that
he speaks from her, as that she speaks thro' him.

His *Characters* are so much Nature her self, that 'tis a sort of injury
to call them by so distant a name as Copies of her. Those of other
Poets have a constant resemblance, which shews that they receiv'd
them from one another, and were but multiplyers of the same image:
each picture like a mock-rainbow is but the reflexion of a reflexion.
But every single character in *Shakespear* is as much an Individual, as
those in Life itself; it is as impossible to find any two alike; and such
as from their relation or affinity in any respect appear most to be
Twins, will upon comparison be found remarkably distinct. To this
life and variety of Character, we must add the wonderful Preservation of it; which is such throughout his plays, that had all the
Speeches been printed without the very names of the Persons, I

Preface to *The Works of Shakespear*

believe one might have apply'd them with certainty to every speaker.

The *Power* over our *Passions* was never possess'd in a more eminent degree, or display'd in so different instances. Yet all along, there is seen no labour, no pains to raise them; no preparation to guide our guess to the effect, or be perceiv'd to lead toward it: But the heart swells, and the tears burst out, just at the proper places: We are surpriz'd, the moment we weep; and yet upon reflection find the passion so just, that we shou'd be surpriz'd if we had not wept, and wept at that very moment.

How astonishing is it again, that the passions directly opposite to these, Laughter and Spleen, are no less at his command! that he is not more a master of the *Great*, than of the *Ridiculous* in human nature; of our noblest tendernesses, than of our vainest foibles; of our strongest emotions, than of our idlest sensations!

Nor does he only excell in the Passions: in the coolness of Reflection and Reasoning he is full as admirable. His *Sentiments* are not only in general the most pertinent and judicious upon every subject; but by a talent very peculiar, something between Penetration and Felicity, he hits upon that particular point on which the bent of each argument turns, or the force of each motive depends. This is perfectly amazing, from a man of no education or experience in those great and publick scenes of life which are usually the subject of his thoughts: So that he seems to have known the world by Intuition, to have look'd thro' humane nature at one glance, and to be the only Author that gives ground for a very new opinion, That the Philosopher and even the Man of the world, may be *Born,* as well as the Poet.

It must be own'd that with all these great excellencies, he has almost as great defects; and that as he has certainly written better, so he has perhaps written worse, than any other. But I think I can in some measure account for these defects, from several causes and accidents; without which it is hard to imagine that so large and so enlighten'd a mind could ever have been susceptible of them. That all these Contingencies should unite to his disadvantage seems to me almost as singularly unlucky, as that so many various (nay contrary) Talents should meet in one man, was happy and extraordinary.

It must be allowed that Stage-Poetry of all other, is more particularly levell'd to please the *Populace,* and its success more immediately depending upon the *Common Suffrage.* One cannot therefore wonder, if *Shakespear,* having at his first appearance no other aim in his writings than to procure a subsistance, directed his endeavours solely to hit the taste and humour that then prevailed.

The Audience was generally composed of the meaner sort of people; and therefore the Images of Life were to be drawn from those of their own rank: accordingly we find, that not our Author's only but almost all the old Comedies have their Scene among *Tradesmen* and *Mechanicks:* And even their Historical Plays strictly follow the common *Old Stories* or *Vulgar Traditions* of that kind of people. In Tragedy, nothing was so sure to *Surprize* and cause *Admiration,* as the most strange, unexpected, and consequently most unnatural, Events and Incidents; the most exaggerated Thoughts; the most verbose and bombast Expression; the most pompous Rhymes, and thundering Versification. In Comedy, nothing was so sure to *please,* as mean buffoonry, vile ribaldry, and unmannerly jests of fools and clowns. Yet even in these, our Author's Wit buoys up, and is born above his subject: his Genius in those low parts is like some Prince of a Romance in the disguise of a Shepherd or Peasant; a certain Greatness and Spirit now and then break out, which manifest his higher extraction and qualities.

It may be added, that not only the common Audience had no notion of the rules of writing, but few even of the better sort piqu'd themselves upon any great degree of knowledge or nicety that way; till *Ben Johnson* getting possession of the Stage, brought critical learning into vogue: And that this was not done without difficulty, may appear from those frequent lessons (and indeed almost Declamations) which he was forced to prefix to his first plays, and put into the mouth of his Actors, the *Grex, Chorus,* &c. to remove the prejudices, and inform the judgment of his hearers. Till then, our Authors had no thoughts of writing on the model of the Ancients: their Tragedies were only Histories in Dialogue; and their Comedies follow'd the thread of any Novel as they found it, no less implicitly than if it had been true History.

To judge therefore of *Shakespear* by *Aristotle's* rules, is like trying a man by the Laws of one Country, who acted under those of another. He writ to the *People*; and writ at first without patronage from the better sort, and therefore without aims of pleasing them; without assistance or advice from the Learned, as without the advantage of education or acquaintance among them; without that knowledge of the best models, the Ancients, to inspire him with an emulation of them; in a word, without any views of Reputation, and of what Poets are pleas'd to call Immortality: Some or all of which have encourag'd the vanity, or animated the ambition, of other writers.

Yet it must be observ'd, that when his performances had merited the protection of his Prince, and when the encouragement of the

Court had succeeded to that of the Town; the works of his riper years are manifestly raised above those of his former. The Dates of his plays sufficiently evidence that his productions improved, in proportion to the respect he had for his auditors. And I make no doubt this observation would be found true in every instance, were but Editions extant from which we might learn the exact time when every piece was composed, and whether writ for the Town, or the Court.

Another Cause (and no less strong than the former) may be deduced from our Author's being a *Player,* and forming himself first upon the judgments of that body of men whereof he was a member. They have ever had a Standard to themselves, upon other principles than those of *Aristotle.* As they live by the Majority, they know no rule but that of pleasing the present humour, and complying with the wit in fashion; a consideration which brings all their judgment to a short point. Players are just such judges of what is *right*, as Taylors are of what is *graceful.* And in this view it will be but fair to allow, that most of our Author's faults are less to be ascribed to his wrong judgment as a Poet, than to his right judgment as a Player.

By these men it was thought a praise to *Shakespear,* that he scarce ever *blotted a line.* This they industriously propagated, as appears from what we are told by *Ben Johnson* in his *Discoveries,* and from the preface of *Heminges* and *Condell* to the first folio Edition. But in reality (however it has prevailed) there never was a more groundless report, or to the contrary of which there are more undeniable evidences. As, the Comedy of the *Merry Wives* of *Windsor,* which he entirely new writ; the *History of* Henry *the 6th,* which was first published under the Title of the *Contention of* York *and* Lancaster; and that of *Henry the 5th,* extreamly improved; that of *Hamlet* enlarged to almost as much again as at first, and many others. I believe the common opinion of his want of Learning proceeded from no better ground. This too might be thought a Praise by some, and to this his Errors have as injudiciously been ascribed by others. For 'tis certain, were it true, it could concern but a small part of them; the most are such as are not properly Defects, but Superfœtations:[1] and arise not from want of learning or reading, but from want of thinking or judging: or rather (to be more just to our Author) from a compliance to those wants in others. As to a wrong choice of the subject, a wrong conduct of the incidents, false thoughts, forc'd expressions, &c. if these are not to be ascrib'd to the foresaid accidental reasons, they must be charg'd upon the Poet himself, and there is no help for it. But I think the two Disadvantages which I have mentioned (to be obliged to please the lowest of people, and to keep the worst of company) if the consideration be extended as far as it reasonably may, will appear sufficient to mis-lead and depress the greatest Genius upon earth. Nay the more modesty with which such a one is endued, the more he is in danger of submitting and conforming to others, against his own better judgment.

But as to his *Want of Learning,* it may be necessary to say something more: there is certainly a vast difference between *Learning* and *Languages.* How far he was ignorant of the latter, I cannot determine; but 'tis plain he had much Reading at least, if they will not call it Learning. Nor is it any great matter, if a man has Knowledge, whether he has it from one language or from another. Nothing is more evident than that he had a taste of natural Philosophy, Mechanicks, ancient and modern History, Poetical learning and Mythology: We find him very knowing in the customs, rites, and manners of Antiquity. In *Coriolanus* and *Julius Cæsar,* not only the Spirit, but Manners, of the *Romans* are exactly drawn; and still a nicer distinction is shown, between the manners of the *Romans* in the time of the former, and of the latter. His reading in the ancient Historians is no less conspicuous, in many references to particular passages: and the speeches copy'd from *Plutarch* in *Coriolanus* may, I think, as well be made an instance of his learning, as those copy'd from *Cicero* in *Catiline,* of *Ben Johnson's.* The manners of other nations in general, the *Egyptians, Venetians, French,* &c. are drawn with equal propriety. Whatever object of nature, or branch of science, he either speaks of or describes; it is always with competent, if not extensive knowledge: his descriptions are still exact; all his metaphors appropriated, and remarkably drawn from the true nature and inherent qualities of each subject. When he treats of Ethic or Politic, we may constantly observe a wonderful justness of distinction, as well as extent of comprehension. No one is more a master of the Poetical story, or has more frequent allusions to the various parts of it: Mr. *Waller* (who has been celebrated for this last particular) has not shown more learning this way than *Shakespear.* We have Translations from *Ovid* published in his name, among those Poems which pass for his,[2] and for some of which we have undoubted authority (being published by himself, and dedicated to his noble Patron the Earl of *Southampton*): He appears also to have been conversant in *Plautus,* from whom he has taken the plot of one of his plays: he follows the *Greek* Authors, and particularly *Dares Phrygius*[3], in another (altho' I will not pretend to say in what language he read them). The modern *Italian* writers of Novels he was manifestly acquainted with; and we may conclude him to be no less conversant with the Ancients of his own country, from the use he has made of *Chaucer* in *Troilus* and *Cressida*, and in the *Two Noble Kinsmen*, if that Play be his, as there goes a Tradition it was (and indeed it has little resemblance of *Fletcher*, and more of our Author than some of those which have been received as genuine).

I am inclined to think, this opinion proceeded originally from the zeal of the Partizans of our Author and *Ben Johnson*; as they endeavoured to exalt the one at the expence of the other. It is ever the nature of Parties to be in extremes; and nothing is so probable, as that because *Ben Johnson* had much the most learning, it was said on the one hand that *Shakespear* had none at all; and because *Shakespear* had much the most wit and fancy, it was retorted on the other, that *Johnson* wanted both. Because *Shakespear* borrowed nothing, it was said that *Ben Johnson* borrowed every thing. Because *Johnson* did not write extempore, he was reproached with being a year about every piece; and because *Shakespear* wrote with ease and rapidity, they cryed, he never once made a blot. Nay the spirit of opposition ran so high, that whatever those of the one side objected to the other, was taken at the rebound, and turned into Praises; as injudiciously as their antagonists before had made them Objections.

Poets are always afraid of Envy; but sure they have as much reason to be afraid of Admiration. They are the *Scylla* and *Charybdis* of Authors; those who escape one, often fall by the other. *Pessimum genus inimicorum Laudantes*, says *Tacitus*:[4] and *Virgil* desires to wear a charm against those who praise a Poet without rule or reason.

—*Si ultra placitum laudarit, baccare frontem*
Cingito, ne Vati noceat—[5]

But however this contention might be carried on by the Partizans on either side, I cannot help thinking these two great Poets were good friends, and lived on amicable terms and in offices of society with each other. It is an acknowledged fact, that *Ben Johnson* was introduced upon the Stage, and his first works encouraged, by *Shakespear*. And after his death, that Author writes *To the memory of his beloved Mr.* William Shakespear, which shows as if the friendship had continued thro' life. I cannot for my own part find any thing *Invidious* or *Sparing* in those verses, but wonder Mr. *Dryden* was of that opinion.[6] He exalts him not only above all his Contemporaries, but above *Chaucer* and *Spenser*, whom he will not allow to be great enough to be rank'd with him; and challenges the names of *Sophocles, Euripides,* and *Æschylus,* nay all *Greece* and *Rome* at once, to equal him. And (which is very particular) expresly vindicates him from the imputation of wanting *Art,* not enduring that all his excellencies shou'd be attributed to *Nature.* It is remarkable too, that the praise he gives him in his *Discoveries* seems to proceed from a *personal kindness;* he tells us that he lov'd the man, as well as honoured his memory; celebrates the honesty, openness, and frankness of his temper; and only distinguishes, as he reasonably ought, between the real merit of the Author, and the silly and derogatory applauses of the Players. *Ben Johnson* might indeed be sparing in his Commendations (tho' certainly he is not so in this instance) partly from his own nature, and partly from judgment. For men of judgment think they do any man more service in praising him justly, than lavishly. I say, I would fain believe they were Friends, tho' the violence and ill-breeding of their Followers and Flatterers were enough to give rise to the contrary report. I would hope that it may be with *Parties,* both in Wit and State, as with those Monsters described by the Poets; and that their *Heads* at least may have something humane, tho' their *Bodies* and *Tails* are wild beasts and serpents.

As I believe that what I have mentioned gave rise to the opinion of *Shakespear's* want of learning; so what has continued it down to us may have been the many blunders and illiteracies of the first Publishers of his works. In these Editions their ignorance shines almost in every page; nothing is more common than *Actus tertia. Exit Omnes. Enter three Witches solus.* Their *French* is as bad as their *Latin,* both in construction and spelling; Their very *Welsh* is false. Nothing is more likely than that those palpable blunders of *Hector's* quoting *Aristotle,* with others of that gross kind, sprung from the same root. It not being at all credible that these could be the errors of any man who had the least tincture of a School, or the least conversation with such as had. *Ben Johnson* (whom they will not think partial to him) allows him at least to have had *some Latin;* which is utterly inconsistent with mistakes like these. Nay the constant blunders in proper names of persons and places, are such as must have proceeded from a man, who had not so much as read any history, in any language: so could not be *Shakespear's.*

I shall now lay before the reader some of those almost innumerable Errors, which have risen from one source, the ignorance of the Players, both as his actors, and as his editors. When the nature and kinds of these are enumerated and considered, I dare to say that not *Shakespear* only but *Aristotle* or *Cicero,* had their works undergone the same fate, might have appear'd to want sense as well as learning.

It is not certain that any one of his Plays was published by himself. During the time of his employment in the Theatre, several of his pieces were printed separately in Quarto. What makes me think that most of these were not publish'd by him, is the excessive carelessness of the press: every page is so scandalously false spelled, and almost all the learned or unusual words so intolerably mangled, that it's plain there either was no Corrector to the press at all, or one totally illiterate. If any were supervised by himself, I should fancy the two parts of *Henry the 4th,* and *Midsummer-Night's Dream* might have been so: because I find no other printed with any exactness; and (contrary to the rest) there is very little variation in all the subsequent editions of them. There are extant two Prefaces, to the first quarto edition of *Troilus* and *Cressida* in 1609, and to that of *Othello*; by which it appears, that the first was publish'd without his knowledge or consent, and even before it was acted, so late as seven or eight years before he died: and that the latter was not printed till after his death. The whole number of genuine plays which we have been able to find printed in his life-time, amounts but to eleven. And of some of these, we meet with two or more editions by different printers, each of which has whole heaps of trash different from the other: which I should fancy was occasion'd, by their being taken from different copies, belonging to different Playhouses.

The folio edition (in which all the plays we now receive as his, were first collected) was published by two Players, *Heming* and *Condell,* in 1623, seven years after his decease. They declare, that all the other editions were stolen and surreptitious, and affirm theirs to be purged from the errors of the former. This is true as to the literal errors, and no other; for in all respects else it is far worse than the Quarto's:

First, because the additions of trifling and bombast passages are in this edition far more numerous. For whatever had been added, since those Quarto's, by the actors, or had stolen from their mouths into the written parts, were from thence conveyed into the printed text, and all stand charged upon the Author. He himself complained of this usage in *Hamlet,* where he wishes that *Those who play the Clowns wou'd speak no more than is set down for them* (Act.3. Sc.4).But as a proof that he could not escape it, in the old editions of *Romeo* and *Juliet* there is no hint of a great number of the mean conceits and ribaldries now to be found there. In others, the low scenes of Mobs, Plebeians and Clowns, are vastly shorter than at present: And I have seen one in particular (which seems to have belonged to the playhouse, by having the parts divided with lines, and the Actors names in the margin) where several of those very passages were added in a written hand, which are since to be found in the folio.

In the next place, a number of beautiful passages which are extant in the first single editions, are omitted in this: as it seems, without any other reason, than their willingness to shorten some scenes: These men (as it was said of *Procrustes*) either lopping, or stretching an Author, to make him just fit for their Stage.

This edition is said to be printed from the *Original Copies;* I believe they meant those which had lain ever since the Author's days in the playhouse, and had from time to time been cut, or added to, arbitrarily. It appears that this edition, as well as the Quarto's, was printed (at least partly) from no better copies than the *Prompter's Book,* or *Piece-meal Parts* written out for the use of the actors: For in some places their very[7] names are thro' carelessness set down instead of the *Personæ Dramatis:* And in others the notes of direction to the *Property-men* for their *Moveables,* and to the *Players* for their *Entries,*[8] are inserted into the Text, thro' the ignorance of the Transcribers.

The Plays not having been before so much as distinguish'd by *Acts* and *Scenes,* they are in this edition divided according as they play'd them; often where there is no pause in the action, or where they thought fit to make a breach in it, for the sake of Musick, Masques, or Monsters.

Sometimes the scenes are transposed and shuffled backward and forward; a thing which could no otherwise happen, but by their being taken from seperate and piece-meal-written parts.

Many verses are omitted intirely, and others transposed; from whence invincible obscurities have arisen, past the guess of any Commentator to clear up, but just where the accidental glympse of an old edition enlightens us.

Some Characters were confounded and mix'd, or two put into one, for want of a competent number of actors. Thus in the Quarto edition of *Midsummer-Night's Dream,* Act. 5, *Shakespear* introduces a kind of Master of the Revels called *Philostratus:* all whose part is given to another character (that of *Ægeus*) in the subsequent editions: So also in *Hamlet* and *King Lear.* This too makes it probable that the Prompter's Books were what they call'd the Original Copies.

From liberties of this kind, many speeches also were put into the mouths of wrong persons, where the Author now seems chargeable with making them speak out of character; Or sometimes perhaps for no better reason, than that a governing Player, to have the mouthing of some favourite speech himself, would snatch it from the unworthy lips of an Underling.

Preface to *The Works of Shakespear*

Prose from verse they did not know, and they accordingly printed one for the other throughout the volume.

Having been forced to say so much of the Players, I think I ought in justice to remark, that the Judgment, as well as Condition, of that class of people was then far inferior to what it is in our days. As then the best Playhouses were Inns and Taverns (the *Globe,* the *Hope,* the *Red Bull,* the *Fortune,* &c.) so the top of the profession were then meer Players, not Gentlemen of the stage: They were led into the Buttery by the Steward, not plac'd at the Lord's table, or Lady's toilette: and consequently were intirely depriv'd of those advantages they now enjoy, in the familiar conversation of our Nobility, and an intimacy (not to say dearness) with people of the first condition.

From what has been said, there can be no question but had *Shakespear* published his works himself (especially in his latter time, and after his retreat from the stage) we should not only be certain which are genuine; but should find in those that are, the errors lessened by some thousands. If I may judge from all the disting-uishing marks of his style, and his manner of thinking and writing, I make no doubt to declare that those wretched plays, *Pericles, Locrine, Sir John Oldcastle, Yorkshire Tragedy, Lord Cromwell, The Puritan,* and *London Prodigal,* cannot be admitted as his. And I should conjecture of some of the others (particularly *Love's Labour Lost, The Winter's Tale,* and *Titus Andronicus*) that only some characters, single scenes, or perhaps a few particular passages, were of his hand. It is very probable what occasion'd some Plays to be supposed *Shakespear's* was only this; that they were pieces produced by unknown authors, or fitted up for the Theatre while it was under his administration; and no owner claiming them, they were adjudged to him, as they give Strays to the Lord of the Manor. A mistake, which (one may also observe) it was not for the interest of the House to remove. Yet the Players themselves, *Hemings* and *Condell,* afterwards did *Shakespear* the justice to reject those eight plays in their edition; tho' they were then printed in his name, in every body's hands, and acted with some applause (as we learn from what *Ben Johnson* says of *Pericles* in his Ode on the *New Inn*). That *Titus Andronicus* is one of this class I am the rather induced to believe, by finding the same Author openly express his contempt of it in the *Induction* to *Bartholomew-Fair,* in the year 1614, when *Shakespear* was yet living. And there is no better authority for these latter sort, than for the former, which were equally published in his life-time.

If we give in to this opinion, how many low and vicious parts and passages might no longer reflect upon this great Genius, but appear unworthily charged upon him? And even in those which are really his, how many faults may have been unjustly laid to his account from arbitrary Additions, Expunctions, Transpositions of scenes and lines, confusion of Characters and Persons, wrong application of Speeches, corruptions of innumerable Passages by the Ignorance, and wrong Corrections of 'em again by the Impertinence, of his first Editors? From one or other of these considerations, I am verily perswaded, that the greatest and the grossest part of what are thought his errors would vanish, and leave his character in a light very different from that disadvantageous one, in which it now appears to us.

This is the state in which *Shakespear's* writings lye at present; for since the above-mentioned Folio Edition, all the rest have implicitly followed it, without having recourse to any of the former, or ever making the comparison between them. It is impossible to repair the Injuries already done him; too much time has elaps'd, and the materials are too few. In what I have done I have rather given a proof of my willingness and desire, than of my ability to do him justice. I have discharg'd the dull duty of an Editor, to my best judgment, with more labour than I expect thanks, with a religious abhorrence of all Innovation, and without any indulgence to my private sense or conjecture. The method taken in this Edition will show it self. The various Readings are fairly put in the margin, so that every one may compare 'em; and those I have prefer'd into the Text are constantly *ex fide Codicum,*[9] upon authority. The Alterations or Additions which *Shakespear* himself made, are taken notice of as they occur. Some suspected passages which are excessively bad (and which seem Interpolations by being so inserted that one can intirely omit them without any chasm, or deficience in the context), are degraded to the bottom of the page; with an Asterisk referring to the places of their insertion. The Scenes are mark'd so distinctly that every removal of place is specify'd; which is more necessary in this Author than any other, since he shifts them more frequently: and sometimes without attending to this particular, the reader would have met with obscurities. The more obsolete or unusual words are explained. Some of the most shining passages are distinguish'd by comma's in the margin; and where the beauty lay not in particulars but in the whole, a star is prefix'd to the scene. This seems to me a shorter and less ostentatious method of performing the better half of Criticism (namely the pointing out an Author's excellencies) than to fill a whole paper with citations of fine passages, with *general Applauses,* or *empty Exclamations* at the tail of them. There is also subjoin'd a Catalogue of those first Editions by which the greater part of the various readings and of the corrected passages are authorised (most of which are such as carry their own evidence along with them). These Editions now hold the place of Originals, and are the only materials left to repair the deficiences or restore the corrupted sense of the Author: I can only wish that a greater number of them (if a greater were ever published) may yet be found, by a search more successful than mine, for the better accomplishment of this end.

I will conclude by saying of *Shakespear*, that with all his faults, and with all the irregularity of his *Drama,* one may look upon his works, in comparison of those that are more finish'd and regular, as upon an ancient majestick piece of *Gothick* Architecture, compar'd with a neat Modern building: The latter is more elegant and glaring, but the former is more strong and more solemn. It must be allow'd, that in one of these there are materials enough to make many of the other. It has much the greater variety, and much the nobler apartments; tho' we are often conducted to them by dark, odd, and uncouth passages. Nor does the Whole fail to strike us with greater reverence, tho' many of the Parts are childish, ill-plac'd, and unequal to its grandeur.

11. *The Art of Sinking in Poetry*

In the first half of 1714 Pope was meeting regularly with his friends Swift, Gay, Arbuthnot and Parnell, an association which became known as the Scriblerus club. One of their projects was a satire on pedantry and false taste, which was to be attributed to Martinus Scriblerus. The idea for *The Art of Sinking* and the collection of material probably originated at this date, with further work on it in 1716, and the casting of it into final shape in 1726-7. The question of its authorship is difficult to solve: the most probable explanation is that all the friends had a hand in contributing materials and ideas, and that Pope was responsible for the final composition.

As its Greek title Περὶ Βάθους indicates, the treatise is an ironic counter-part to Περὶ Ὕψους, the first-century work on the sublime, which goes under the name of Longinus. In his preface Longinus asks whether there is an art of the sublime or the profound, and the latter word (Βάθος) is taken up in Pope's work. *The Art of Sinking* has a loose relation to the structure of Longinus' essay: his question in the preface is echoed at the opening of chapter IV, and his summary of the marks and sources of the sublime (6-8) has a counterpart in chapters V-VI. Longinus then discusses greatness of thought (9-15; cp. ch. VIII), figures of thought and speech (16-29; cp. chs. VIII, X-XI), and nobility of diction and composition (30-42; cp. ch. XII). Finally, Longinus has an appendix on the causes of the current decline of literature (44), while Pope has an appendix on the advancement of the bathos (chs. XIII-XVI). Even the lacuna in chapter XII may be an imitation of the lacuna in Longinus (9).

The examples cited by Pope are chiefly from contemporary or late seventeenth-century writers: chief amongst these is Sir Richard Blackmore, whose *Prince Arthur* and *Paraphrases on Job* qualify him for the role of father of the bathos (ch. VI) as Homer was for Longinus the best source of examples of the sublime. Ambrose Philips is also cited frequently, especially for his *Pastorals*, but it is possible that Pope also quotes himself, for the anonymous quotations in chapter VII are probably from his juvenile epic *Alcander*. Other quotations (such as those attributed to 'Vet. Aut.', 'an ancient author') may have been invented for the occasion. In chapter VI there are many initials cited, but certain identification of the victims seems impossible. For further information see the edition by Edna Leake Steeves (1956).

Text: Chapter XV was first printed as *Guardian* no. 78; the whole treatise first appeared in the Pope–Swift miscellanies: *Miscellanies. The Last Volume* (1727), from which the present text is taken.

The Art of Sinking in Poetry
ΠΕΡΙ ΒΑΘΟΥΣ:
OR,
MARTINUS SCRIBLERUS
HIS
TREATISE
OF THE
ART OF SINKING
IN
POETRY.

CHAP. I.

It hath been long (my dear Countrymen[1]) the Subject of my
Concern and Surprize, that whereas numberless Poets, Cricticks and
Orators have compiled and digested the Art of *Ancient Poesie*, there
hath not arisen among us one Person so publick spirited, as to
perform the like for the *Modern*. Altho' it is universally known, that
our every-way-industrious Moderns, both in the Weight of their
Writings, and in the Velocity of their *Judgments*, do so infinitely
excel the said Ancients.

NEVERTHELESS, too true it is, that while a plain and direct Road
is pav'd to their ὕψος, or *sublime*; no Track has been yet chalk'd out,
to arrive at our βάθος, or *profund*. The *Latins*, as they came between
the *Greeks* and Us, make use of the Word *Altitudo*, which implies
equally *Height* and *Depth*. Wherefore considering with no small
Grief, how many promising Genius's of this Age are wandering (as I
may say) in the dark without a Guide, I have undertaken this
arduous but necessary Task, to lead them as it were by the hand, and
step by step, the gentle downhill way to the *Bathos*; the Bottom, the
End, the Central Point, the *non plus ultra* of true Modern Poesie!

WHEN I consider (my dear Countrymen) the Extent, Fertility,
and Populousness of our *Lowlands* of *Parnassus*, the flourishing State
of our Trade, and the Plenty of our Manufacture; there are two
Reflections which administer great Occasion of Surprize; the one,
that all Dignities and Honours should be bestow'd upon the
exceeding few meager Inhabitants of the Top of the Mountain; the
other, that our own Nation should have arriv'd to that Pitch of
Greatness it now possesses, without any regular *System of Laws*. As to
the first, it is with great Pleasure I have observ'd of late the gradual
Decay of Delicacy and Refinement among Mankind, who are

become too reasonable to require that we should labour with infinite Pains to come up to the Taste of those Mountaineers, when they without any, may condescend to ours. But as we have now an *unquestionable Majority* on our side, I doubt not but we shall shortly be able to level the *Highlanders*, and procure a farther Vent for our own Product, which is already so much relish'd, encourag'd, and rewarded, by the Nobility and Gentry of *Great Britain*.

THEREFORE to supply our former Defect, I purpose to collect the scatter'd Rules of our Art into regular Institutes, from the Example and Practice of the deep Genius's of our Nation; imitating herein my Predecessors, the Master of *Alexander*, and the Secretary of the renown'd *Zenobia*:[2] And in this my Undertaking I am the more animated, as I expect more Success than has attended even those great Criticks, since their Laws (tho' they might be good) have ever been slackly executed, and their Precepts (however strict) obey'd only by Fits, and by a very small Number.

AT the same time I intend to do justice upon our Neighbours, Inhabitants of the *upper Parnassus*; who taking advantage of the rising Ground, are perpetually throwing down Rubbish, Dirt, and Stones upon us, never suffering us to live in Peace: These Men, while they enjoy the Chrystal Stream of *Helicon*, envy us our common Water, which (thank our Stars) tho it is somewhat muddy, flows in much greater abundance. Nor is this the greatest injustice we have to complain of; for tho' it is evident that we never made the least *Attempt* or *Inrode* into *their* Territories, but lived contented in our Native Fens; they have often, not only committed *Petty Larcenys* upon our Borders, but driven the Country, and carried off at once *whole Cart-loads* of our *Manufacture*; to reclaim some of which stolen Goods is part of the Design of this Treatise.

FOR we shall see in the course of this Work, that our greatest Adversaries have sometimes descended towards us; and doubtless might now and then have arrived at the *Bathos* itself, had it not been for that mistaken Opinion they all entertained, that the *Rules* of the *Antients* were *equally necessary* to the *Moderns*, than which there cannot be a more grievous Error, as will be amply proved in the following Discourse.

AND indeed when any of these have gone so far, as by the light of their own Genius to attempt upon *new Models*, it is wonderful to observe, how nearly they have approach'd Us in those particular Pieces; tho' in all their others they differ'd *toto cælo*[3] from us.

The Art of Sinking in Poetry
CHAP. II.

That the Bathos, *or* Profund, *is the natural Taste of Man,
and in particular, of the present Age.*

The Taste of the *Bathos* is implanted by Nature itself in the Soul of Man; 'till perverted by Custom or Example he is taught, or rather compell'd, to relish the *Sublime*. Accordingly, we see the unprejudiced Minds of Children delight only in such Productions, and in such Images, as our true modern Writers set before them. I have observ'd how fast the general Taste is returning to this first Simplicity and Innocence; and if the Intent of all Poetry be to divert and instruct, certainly that Kind which diverts and instructs the greatest Number, is to be preferr'd. Let us look round among the Admirers of Poetry, we shall find those who have a Taste of the *Sublime* to be very few, but the *Profund* strikes universally, and is adapted to every Capacity. 'Tis a fruitless Undertaking to write for Men of a nice and foppish *Gusto*, whom, after all, it is almost impossible to please; and 'tis still more Chimerical to write for *Posterity*, of whose Taste we cannot make any Judgment, and whose Applause we can never enjoy. It must be confess'd, our wiser Authors have a present End,

Et prodesse volunt, & delectare Poetæ.[4]

Their true Design is *Profit* or *Gain*; in order to acquire which, 'tis necessary to procure Applause, by administring *Pleasure* to the Reader: From whence it follows demonstrably, that their Productions must be suited to the *present Taste*; and I cannot but congratulate our Age on this peculiar Felicity, that tho' we have made indeed great Progress in all other Branches of Luxury, we are not yet debauch'd with any *high relish* in Poetry, but are in this one Taste, less *nice* than our Ancestors. If an Art is to be estimated by its Success, I appeal to Experience, whether there have not been, in proportion to their Number, as many starving good Poets, as bad ones?

NEVERTHELESS, in making *Gain* the principal End of our Art, far be it from me to exclude any great *Genius's* of *Rank* or *Fortune* from diverting themselves this way. They ought to be praised no less than those Princes, who pass their vacant Hours in some ingenious Mechanical or Manual Art: And to such as these, it would be Ingratitude not to own, that our Art has been often infinitely indebted.

Chap.III.

The Necessity of the Bathos, *Physically consider'd.*

Farthermore, it were great Cruelty and Injustice, if all such Authors as cannot write in the other Way, were prohibited from writing at all. Against this, I draw an Argument from what seems to me an undoubted Physical Maxim, That Poetry is a *natural* or *morbid Secretion from the Brain.* As I would not suddenly stop a Cold in the Head, or dry up my Neighbour's Issue, I would as little hinder him from necessary Writing. It may be affirm'd with great truth, that there is hardly any human Creature past Childhood, but at one time or other has had some Poetical Evacuation, and no question was much the better for it in his Health; so true is the Saying, *Nascimur Poetæ:*[5] Therefore is the Desire of Writing properly term'd *Pruritus,* the *Titillation of the Generative Faculty of the Brain*; and the Person is said to *conceive*; Now such as conceive must *bring forth.* I have known a Man thoughtful, melancholy, and raving for divers days, but forthwith grow wonderfully easy, lightsome and cheerful, upon a Discharge of the peccant Humour, in exceeding purulent Metre. Nor can I question, but abundance of untimely Deaths are occasion'd by want of this laudable Vent of unruly Passions; yea, perhaps, in poor Wretches, (which is very lamentable) for meer Want of Pen, Ink, and Paper! From hence it follows, that a Suppression of the very worst Poetry is of dangerous consequence to the State: We find by Experience, that the same Humours which vent themselves in Summer in *Ballads* and *Sonnets,* are condens'd by the Winter's Cold into *Pamphlets* and *Speeches* for and against the *Ministry*: Nay I know not, but many times a Piece of Poetry may be the most innocent Composition of a *Minister himself.*

It is therefore manifest that *Mediocrity* ought to be allow'd, yea indulg'd, to the good Subjects of *England.* Nor can I conceive how the World has swallow'd the contrary as a Maxim, upon the single Authority of that *Horace?*[6] Why should the *Golden Mean,* and Quintessence of all Virtues, be deem'd so offensive only in this Art? Or *Coolness* or *Mediocrity* be so amiable a Quality in a Man, and so detestable in a Poet?

HOWEVER, far be it from me to compare these Writers with those *Great Spirits,* who are born with a *Vivacité de pesanteur,* or (as an *English* Author calls it) an *Alacrity of sinking*;[7] and who by *Strength of Nature* alone can excell. All I mean is to evince the *Necessity* of Rules to these lesser Genius's, as well as the *Usefulness* of them to the Greater.

CHAP. IV.

That there is an Art of the Bathos, *or* Profund.

We come now to prove, that there is an *Art of Sinking* in Poetry. Is there not an Architecture of Vaults and Cellars, as well as of lofty Domes and Pyramids? Is there not as much Skill and Labour in making of *Dykes*, as in raising of *Mounts*? Is there not an Art of *Diving* as well as of *Flying*? And will any sober Practitioner affirm, That a diving Engine is not of singular Use in making him long-winded, assisting his Sight, and furnishing him with other ingenious means of keeping under Water?

IF we search the Authors of Antiquity, we shall find as few to have been distinguish'd in the *true Profund*, as in the *true Sublime*. And the very same thing (as it appears from *Longinus*) had been imagin'd of that, as now of this; namely, that it was entirely the Gift of Nature. I grant, that to excel in the *Bathos* a Genius is requisite; yet the Rules of Art must be allow'd so far useful, as to add Weight, or as I may say, hang on Lead, to facilitate and enforce our Descent, to guide us to the most advantageous Declivities, and habituate our Imagination to a Depth of thinking. Many there are that can fall, but few can arrive at the Felicity of falling gracefully; much more for a Man who is amongst the lowest of the Creation at the very bottom of the Atmosphere, to descend *beneath himself*, is not so easy a Task unless he calls in Art to his Assistance. It is with the *Bathos* as with small Beer, which is indeed vapid and insipid, if left at large and let abroad; but being by our Rules confin'd, and well stopt, nothing grows so frothy, pert and bouncing.

THE *Sublime* of Nature is the Sky, the Sun, Moon, Stars, &c. The *Profund* of Nature is Gold, Pearls, precious Stones, and the Treasures of the Deep, which are inestimable as unknown. But all that lies between these, as Corn, Flowers, Fruits, Animals, and Things for the meer Use of Man, are of mean price, and so common as not to be greatly esteem'd by the Curious: It being certain, that any thing, of which we know the true Use, cannot be Invaluable: Which affords a Solution, why *common Sense* hath either been totally despis'd, or held in small Repute, by the greatest modern Criticks and Authors.

CHAP. V.

Of the true Genius for the Profund, *and by what it is constituted.*

And I will venture to lay it down, as the first Maxim and Corner-Stone of this our Art, That whoever would excell therein must studiously avoid, detest, and turn his Head from all the Ideas, Ways, and Workings of that pestilent Foe to Wit and Destroyer of fine Figures, which is known by the name of *Common Sense*. His Business must be to contract the true *Gout de travers*;[8] and to acquire a most *happy, uncommon, unaccountable Way of Thinking*.

HE is to consider himself as a *Grotesque* Painter, whose Works would be spoil'd by an Imitation of Nature, or Uniformity of Design. He is to mingle Bits of the most various, or discordant kinds, Landscape, History, Portraits, Animals, and connect them with a great deal of *Flourishing*, by *Heads* or *Tails*, as it shall please his Imagination, and contribute to his principal End, which is to glare by strong Oppositions of Colours, and surprize by Contrariety of Images.

Serpentes avibus geminentur, tigribus agni.[9]   *Hor.*

His Design ought to be like a Labyrinth, out of which no body can get you clear but himself. And since the great Art of all Poetry is to mix Truth and Fiction, in order to join the Credible with the Surprizing; our Author shall produce the *Credible*, by painting Nature in her *lowest Simplicity*; and the *Surprizing*, by contradicting *Common Opinion*. In the very *Manners* he will affect the Marvellous; he will draw *Achilles* with the Patience of *Job*; a Prince talking like a Jack-pudding;[10] a Maid of Honour selling *Bargains*; a Footman speaking like a Philosopher; and a fine Gentleman like a Scholar. Whoever is conversant in *modern Plays*, may make a most noble Collection of this kind, and at the same time, form a compleat Body of *Modern Ethicks and Morality*.

NOTHING seem'd more plain to our great Authors, than that the World had long been weary of natural Things. How much the contrary is form'd to please, is evident from the universal Applause daily given to the admirable Entertainments of *Harlequins* and *Magicians* on our Stage. When an Audience behold a Coach turn'd into a Wheel-barrow, a Conjurer into an Old Woman, or a Man's Head where his Heels should be; how are they struck with Transport and Delight? Which can only be imputed to this Cause, that each

Object is chang'd into That which hath been suggested to them by their own low Ideas before.

HE ought therefore to render himself Master of this happy and antinatural way of thinking to such a degree, as to be able, on the appearance of any Object, to furnish his Imagination with Ideas infinitely below it. And his Eyes should be like unto the wrong end of a Perspective Glass, by which all the Objects of Nature are lessen'd.

FOR example, when a true Genius looks upon the *Sky*, he immediately catches the Idea of a Piece of *Blue Lutestring*, or a *Child's Mantle.*

> *The Skies, whose spreading Volumes scarce have room,*
> *Spun thin, and wove in Nature's finest Loom,*
> *The* new-born *World in* their soft Lap *embrac'd,*
> *And all around their* starry Mantle *cast.* [11]   Pr. *Arthur,* p. 41,42.

IF he looks upon a *Tempest*, he shall have the Image of a tumbled Bed, and describe a succeeding Calm in this manner,

> *The Ocean joy'd to see the Tempest fled,*
> New lays *his Waves and* smooths his ruffled Bed.   p. 14.

THE *Triumphs* and *Acclamations* of the *Angels*, at the Creation of the Universe, present to his Imagination the *Rejoicings of the Lord Mayor's Day*; and he beholds those glorious Beings celebrating the Creator, by Huzzaing, making Illuminations, and flinging Squibbs, Crackers and Sky-rockets.

> *Glorious* Illuminations, *made on high*
> *By all the Stars and Planets of the Sky,*
> *In* just Degrees, *and* shining Order *plac'd,*
> *Spectators charm'd, and the* blest Dwelling *grac'd.*
> *Thro' all th' enlighten'd Air swift* Fireworks *flew,*
> *Which with repeated* Shouts *glad Cherubs* threw.
> *Comets* ascended with their sweeping Train,
> *Then fell in* starry Showers *and* glittering Rain.
> *In Air ten thousand Meteors* blazing hung,
> *Which from th' Eternal* Battlements *were* flung.   page 50.

IF a Man who is violently fond of *Wit*, will sacrifice to that Passion his Friend or his God; would it not be a shame, if he who is smit with the Love of the *Bathos* should not sacrifice to it all other transitory Regards? You shall hear a zealous Protestant Deacon invoke a Saint, and modestly beseech her only to change the Course of Providence and Destiny, for the sake of three or four weighty Lines.

> *Look down, blest Saint, with Pity then look down,*
> *Shed on this Land thy kinder Influence,*

Selected prose of Alexander Pope

And guide us through the Mists of Providence,
In which we stray. —

A. Phil. on the Death of Queen *Mary*.

Neither will he, if a goodly Simile come in his way, scruple to affirm himself an Eye-witness of things never yet beheld by Man, or never in Existence; as thus,

Thus have I seen, *in* Araby *the blest,*
A Phœnix *couch'd upon her Fun'ral Nest.*   *Anon.*

BUT to convince you, that nothing is so great which a marvellous Genius, prompted by this laudable Zeal, is not able to lessen; hear how the most Sublime of all Beings is represented in the following Images.

First he is a PAINTER.

Sometimes the Lord of Nature in the Air,
Spreads forth *his Clouds, his* sable Canvass, *where*
His Pencil, dipt *in heavenly* Colour *bright,*
Paints *his fair Rain-bow, charming to the Sight.*

Blackm. Job. opt. edit. *duod.* 1716. pag. 172.

Now he is a CHYMIST.

Th' Almighty Chymist *does his Work prepare,*
Pours down his Waters *on the thirsty Plain,*
Digests *his Lightning, and* distills *his Rain.*

Black. Ps. 104. p. 263.

Now he is a WRESTLER.

Me in his griping Arms *th' Eternal took,*
And with such mighty Force *my* Body shook,
That the Strong Grasp *my Members* sorely bruis'd,
Broke *all my* Bones, *and all my* Sinews loos'd.   Pag. 75.

Now a RECRUITING OFFICER.

For Clouds the Sun-Beams levy fresh Supplies,
And raise Recruits *of Vapours, which arise,*
Drawn *from the Seas, to* muster *in the Skies.*   Pag. 170.

The Art of Sinking in Poetry

Now a peaceable GUARANTEE.

In Leagues *of* Peace *the* Neighbours *did agree,*
And to maintain them, God was Guarantee. Pag. 70.

Then he is an ATTORNEY.

Job, *as a vile Offender, God* indites,
And terrible Decrees against me writes. —
God will not be my Advocate,
My Cause *to* manage, *or* debate. Pag. 61.

In the following Lines he is a GOLDBEATER.

Who the rich Metal beats, *and then, with Care,*
Unfolds *the* Golden Leaves, *to* gild *the Fields of Air.* Pag. 181.

Then a FULLER.

—th' exhaling Reeks that secret rise,
Born on rebounding Sun-beams thro' the Skies;
Are thicken'd, wrought, *and* whiten'd, *'till they grow*
A Heavenly Fleece. — Pag. 180.

A MERCER, or PACKER.

Didst thou one End *of Air's wide* Curtain *hold,*
And help the Bales *of* Æther *to* unfold;
Say, which cerulian Pile *was by thy Hand* unroll'd? Pag. 174.

A BUTLER.

He measures all the Drops *with* wondrous Skill,
Which the black Clouds, his floating Bottles, fill. page 131.

And a BAKER.

God in the Wilderness his Table spread,
And in his Airy Ovens bak'd their Bread.
Black. Song of *Moses.* p. 218.

CHAP. VI.

Of the several Kinds of Genius's in the Profund, *and the Marks and Characters of each.*

I DOUBT not but the Reader, by this *Cloud* of Examples, begins to be convinc'd of the Truth of our Assertion, that the *Bathos* is an *Art*; and that the Genius of no Mortal whatever, following the meer Ideas of Nature, and unassisted with an habitual, nay laborious Peculiarity of thinking, could arrive at Images so wonderfully low and unaccountable. The great Author, from whose Treasury we have drawn all these Instances (the Father of the *Bathos*, and indeed the *Homer* of it) has like that immortal *Greek*, confin'd his Labours to the greater Poetry, and thereby left room for others to acquire a due share of Praise in inferiour kinds. Many Painters who could never hit a Nose or an Eye, have with Felicity copied a Small-Pox, or been admirable at a Toad or a Red-Herring. And seldom are we without *Genius's* for *Still Life*, which they can work up and stiffen with incredible Accuracy.

AN universal Genius rises not in an Age; but when he rises, Armies rise in him! he pours forth five or six Epick Poems with greater Facility, than five or six Pages can be produc'd by an elaborate and servile Copyer after Nature or the Ancients. It is affirm'd by *Quintilian*, that the same Genius which made *Germanicus* so great a General, would with equal Application have made him an excellent Heroic Poet.[12] In like manner, reasoning from the Affinity there appears between Arts and Sciences, I doubt not but an active Catcher of Butterflies, a careful and fanciful Pattern-drawer, an industrious Collector of Shells, a laborious and tuneful Bagpiper, or a diligent Breeder of tame Rabbits, might severally excel in their respective parts of the *Bathos*.

I SHALL range these confin'd and less copious Genius's under proper Classes, and (the better to give their Pictures to the Reader) under the Names of Animals of some sort or other; whereby he will be enabled, at the first sight of such as shall daily come forth, to know to what *Kind* to refer, and with what *Authors* to compare them.

1. THE *Flying Fishes*; these are Writers who now and then *rise* upon their *Fins*, and fly out of the *Profund*; but their Wings are soon *dry*, and they drop down to the *Bottom*. G. S. A. H. C. G.

2. THE *Swallows* are Authors that are eternally *skimming* and

fluttering up and down, but all their Agility is employ'd to *catch Flies*. *LT. WP.* Lord *R*.

3. THE *Ostridges* are such whose Heaviness rarely permits them to raise themselves from the Ground; their Wings are of no use to lift them up, and their Motion is between *flying* and *walking*; but then they *run* very fast. *D. F. L. E.* The Hon. *E. H.*

4. THE *Parrots* are they that repeat *another's Words*, in such a *hoarse, odd* Voice, that makes them seem *their own. W. B. W. H. C. C.* The Reverend *D. D*.

5. THE *Didappers* are Authors that keep themselves long *out of sight*, under water, and *come up* now and then where you *least expected* them. *L. W. — D.* Esq; The Hon. Sir *W. Y*.

6. THE *Porpoises* are unweildly and big; they put all their Numbers into a great *Turmoil* and *Tempest*, but whenever they appear in *plain Light*, (which is seldom) they are only *shapeless* and *ugly Monsters. I. D. C. G. I. O*.

7. THE *Frogs* are such as can neither *walk* nor *fly*, but can *leap* and *bound* to admiration: They live generally in the *Bottom of a Ditch*, and make a *great Noise* whenever they thrust their *Heads above Water. E. W. I. M.* Esq; *T. D.* Gent.

8. THE *Eels* are obscure Authors, that wrap themselves up in their *own Mud*, but are mighty *nimble* and *pert. L. W. L. T. P. M.* General *C*.

9. THE *Tortoises* are *slow* and *chill*, and like *Pastoral Writers* delight much in *Gardens*: they have for the most part a *fine embroider'd Shell*, and underneath it, a *heavy Lump. A. P. W. B. L. E.* The Rt. Hon. *E.* of *S*.

THESE are the chief Characteristicks of the *Bathos*, and in each of these kinds we have the comfort to be bless'd with sundry and manifold choice Spirits in this our Island.

CHAP. VII.

Of the Profund, *when it consists in the Thought.*

We have already laid down the Principles upon which our Author is to proceed, and the Manner of forming his Thoughts by familiarizing his Mind to the lowest Objects; to which it may be added, that *vulgar Conversation* will greatly contribute. There is no Question but the *Garret* or the *Printer's Boy* may often be discern'd in the Compositions made in such Scenes, and Company; and much of Mr.

Curl himself has been insensibly infused into the Works of his
learned Writers.

THE Physician, by the Study and Inspection of Urine and Ordure,
approves himself in the Science; and in like sort should our Author
accustom and exercise his Imagination upon the Dregs of Nature.

THIS will render his Thoughts truly and fundamentally Low, and
carry him many fathoms beyond Mediocrity. For, certain it is, (tho'
some lukewarm Heads imagine they may be safe by temporizing
between the Extreams) that where there is a Triticalness[13] or
Mediocrity in the *Thought*, it can never be sunk into the genuine and
perfect *Bathos*, by the most elaborate low *Expression*: It can, at most,
be only carefully obscured, or metaphorically debased. But 'tis the
Thought alone that strikes, and gives the whole that Spirit, which we
admire and stare at. For instance, in that ingenious Piece on a Lady's
drinking the *Bath*-Waters.

> *She drinks! She drinks! Behold the matchless Dame!*
> *To her 'tis Water, but to us 'tis Flame:*
> *Thus Fire is Water, Water Fire, by turns,*
> *And the same Stream at once both cools and burns.*   Anon.

WHAT can be more easy and unaffected than the *Diction* of these
Verses? 'Tis the Turn of *Thought* alone, and the Variety of Imagination, that charm and surprize us. And when the same Lady goes into
the Bath, the Thought (as in justness it ought) goes still deeper.

> *Venus beheld her, 'midst her Crowd of Slaves,*
> *And thought* Herself *just risen from the Waves.*   Idem.

How much out of the way of common Sense is this Reflection of
Venus, not knowing herself from the Lady?

OF the same nature is that noble Mistake of a frighted Stag in full
Chace, of which the Poet,

> *Hears his own Feet, and thinks they sound like more;*
> *And fears the hind Feet will o'ertake the fore.*

So astonishing as these are, they yield to the following, which is
Profundity itself,

> *None but* Himself *can be his* Parallel.
>   Theobald, *Double Distress.* [14]

unless it may seem borrow'd from the Thought of that *Master of a
Show* in *Smithfield*, who writ in large Letters, over the Picture of his
Elephant,

> *This is the greatest Elephant in the World, except* Himself.

HOWEVER our next Instance is certainly an Original: Speaking of
a beautiful Infant,

> *So fair thou art, that if great* Cupid *be*

> *A Child, as Poets say, sure thou art He.*
> *Fair* Venus *would mistake thee for her own,*
> *Did not thy Eyes proclaim thee* not *her Son.*
> *There all the Lightnings of thy* Mother's *shine,*
> *And with a fatal Brightness* kill *in* thine. [15]

FIRST he is *Cupid*, then he is not *Cupid*; first *Venus* would mistake him, then she would not mistake him; next his Eyes are his Mother's; and lastly they are not his Mother's, but his own.

ANOTHER Author, describing a Poet that shines forth amidst a Circle of Criticks,

> *Thus* Phœbus *thro' the Zodiack takes his way,*
> *And amid* Monsters *rises into Day.*

WHAT a Peculiarity is here of Invention? The Author's Pencil, like the Wand of *Circe*, turns all into *Monsters* at a Stroke. A great Genius takes things in the Lump, without stopping at minute Considerations: In vain might the Ram, the Bull, the Goat, the Lion, the Crab, the Scorpion, the Fishes, all stand in his way, as mere natural Animals: much more might it be pleaded that a pair of Scales, an old Man, and two innocent Children, were no Monsters: There were only the Centaur and the Maid that could be esteem'd out of Nature. But what of that? with a Boldness peculiar to these daring Genius's, what he found not Monsters, he made so.

CHAP. VIII.

Of the Profund *consisting in the Circumstances, and of Amplification and Periphrase in general.*

What in a great measure distinguishes other Writers from ours, is their chusing and separating such Circumstances in a Description as illustrate or elevate the Subject.

THE Circumstances which are most natural are obvious, therefore not astonishing or peculiar. But those that are far-fetch'd, or unexpected, or hardly compatible, will surprize prodigiously. These therefore we must principally hunt out; but above all, preserve a laudable *Prolixity*; presenting the Whole and every Side at once of the Image to view. For Choice and Distinction are not only a Curb to the Spirit, and limit the Descriptive Faculty, but also lessen the Book, which is frequently of the worst consequence of all to our Author.

WHEN *Job* says in short, *He wash'd his Feet in Butter*, (a Circumstance some Poets would have soften'd, or past over) hear how it is spread out by the Great Genius.

> With Teats distended with their milky Store,
> Such num'rous lowing Herds, before my Door,
> Their painful Burden to unload did meet,
> That we with Butter might have wash'd our Feet.

Blackm. Job. p. 133

How cautious! and particular! He had (says our Author) so many Herds, which Herds thriv'd so well, and thriving so well, gave so much Milk, and that Milk produc'd so much Butter, that if he *did not*, he *might* have wash'd his Feet in it.

THE ensuing Description of Hell is no less remarkable in the Circumstances.

> In flaming Heaps the raging Ocean rolls,
> Whose livid Waves involve despairing Souls;
> The liquid Burnings dreadful Colours shew,
> Some deeply red, and others faintly blue.   Pr. Arth. p. 89.

COULD the most minute *Dutch* Painter have been more exact? How inimitably circumstantial is this also of a War-Horse!

> His Eye-Balls burn, he wounds the smoaking Plain,
> And knots of scarlet Ribbond deck his Mane.   Anon.

Of certain Cudgel-Players:

> They brandish high in Air their threatning Staves,
> Their Hands a woven Guard of Ozier saves,
> In which, they fix their hazel weapon's end.   Pr. Arth. p. 197.

WHO would not think the Poet had past his whole Life at Wakes in such laudable Diversions? He even teaches us how to hold, and to make, a Cudgel!

Periphrase is another great Aid to *Prolixity*; being a diffus'd circumlocutory Manner of expressing a known Idea, which should be so misteriously couch'd, as to give the Reader the Pleasure of guessing what it is that the Author can possibly mean; and a Surprize when he finds it.

THE Poet I last mention'd is incomparable in this Figure.

> A waving Sea of Heads was round me spread,
> And still fresh Streams the gazing Deluge fed.   Job p. 78.

HERE is a waving Sea of Heads, which by a fresh Stream of Heads, grows to be a gazing Deluge of Heads. You come at last to find it means a *great Crowd*.

How pretty and how genteel is the following.

> Natures Confectioner, —
> Whose Suckets are moist Alchimy:

The Art of Sinking in Poetry

> *The Still of his refining Mold,*
> *Minting the Garden into Gold.*   *Cleveland.*[16]

What is this, but a *Bee* gathering Honey?

> *Little Syren of the Stage*
> *Empty warbler, breathing Lyre,*
> *Wanton Gale of fond desire,*
> *Tuneful mischief, vocal Spell—.*   Ph. to C—.[17]

Who would think this was only a poor Gentlewoman that sung finely?

WE may define *Amplification* to be making the most of a *Thought*; it is the spinning Wheel of the *Bathos*, which draws out and spreads it in the finest Thread. There are Amplifiers who can extend half a dozen thin Thoughts over a whole Folio; but for which, the Tale of many a vast Romance, and the Substance of many a fair Volume might be reduced into the size of a *Primmer.*

IN the Book of *Job*, are these Words, *Hast thou commanded the Morning, and caused the Day Spring to know his Place?* How is this extended by the most celebrated Amplifier of our Age?

> *Canst thou set forth th' etherial* Mines *on high,*
> *Which the refulgent* Ore *of Light supply?*
> *Is the Celestial* Furnace *to thee known,*
> *In which I* melt *the golden* Metal *down?*
> *Treasures, from whence I* deal *out Light as fast,*
> *As all my Stars and* lavish *Suns can* waste.   *Job* p. 180.

THE same Author hath amplified a Passage in the 104th Psalm; *He looks on the Earth, and it trembles. He touches the Hills, and they smoke.*

> *The Hills* forget they're fix'd, *and in their Fright,*
> Cast off their Weight, *and* ease *themselves for flight:*
> *The Woods, with* Terror *wing'd, out-fly the Wind,*
> *And leave the* heavy, panting *Hills behind.*   p. 267

YOU here see the Hills not only trembling, but shaking off their Woods from their Backs, to run the faster: After this you are presented with a Foot Race of Mountains and Woods, where the Woods distance the Mountains, that like corpulent pursy Fellows, come puffing and panting a vast way behind them.

CHAP. IX.

Of Imitation, and the manner of Imitating.

That the true Authors of the *Profund* are to imitate diligently the Examples in their own Way, is not to be question'd, and that divers

Selected prose of Alexander Pope

have by this Means attain'd to a Depth whereunto their own Weight could not have carried them, is evident by sundry Instances. Who sees not that *DeF[oe]* was the Poetical Son of *Withers*, *T[a]te* of *Ogilby*, *E. W[a]rd* of *John Taylor*, and *E[usde]n* of *Bl[ac]k[mo]re*?[18] Therefore when we sit down to write, let us bring some great Author to our Mind, and ask our selves this Question; How would Sir *Richard* have said this? Do I express myself as simply as *A. Ph[ilips]*? or flow my Numbers with the quiet thoughtlessness of Mr. *W[el]st[ea]d*?[19]

BUT it may seem somewhat strange to assert, that our Proficient should also read the Works of those famous Poets who have excell'd in the Sublime: Yet is not this a Paradox. As *Virgil* is said to have read *Ennius*, out of his Dunghil to draw Gold; so may our Author read *Shakespear, Milton*, and *Dryden*, for the contrary End, to bury their Gold in his own Dunghil. A true Genius, when he finds any thing lofty or shining in them, will have the Skill to bring it down, take off the Gloss, or quite discharge the Colour, by some ingenious Circumstance, or Periphrase, some Addition, or Diminution, or by some of those Figures the use of which we shall shew in our next Chapter.

THE Book of *Job* is acknowledg'd to be infinitely sublime, and yet has not our Father of the *Bathos* reduc'd it in every Page? Is there a Passage in all *Virgil* more painted up and labour'd than the Description of *Ætna* in the Third *Æneid*.

> —*Horrificis juxta tonat Ætna ruinis,*
> *Interdumque atram prorumpit ad æthera nubem,*
> *Turbine fumantem piceo, & candente favilla,*
> *Attollitque globos flammarum, & sidera lambit.*
> *Interdum scopulos avulsaque viscera montis*
> *Erigit eructans, liquefactaque saxa sub auras*
> *Cum gemitu glomerat, fundoque exæstuat imo.*[20]

(I beg Pardon of the gentle *English* Reader, and such of our Writers as understand not *Latin*) But lo! how this is taken down by our *British* Poet, by the single happy Thought of throwing the Mountain into a Fit of the *Cholic*.

> *Ætna, and all the burning Mountains, find*
> *Their kindled Stores with* inbred *Storms of* Wind
> Blown up *to Rage, and* roaring out, *complain,*
> *As* torn *with* inward Gripes, *and* torturing Pain:
> *Lab'ring, they cast their dreadful* Vomit *round,*
> *And with their* melted Bowels, spread *the Ground.*
>
> Pr. Arth. Pag. 75.

HORACE, in search of the *Sublime*, struck his Head against the Stars;[21] but *Empedocles*, to fathom the *Profund*, threw himself into

Ætna:[22] And who but would imagine our excellent Modern had also been there, from this Description?

IMITATION is of two Sorts; the First is when we force to our own Purposes the Thoughts of others; The Second consists in copying the Imperfections, or Blemishes of celebrated Authors. I have seen a Play professedly writ in the Stile of *Shakespear*, wherein the greatest Resemblance lay in one single Line,

    And so good Morrow t'ye, good Master Lieutenant.[23]

And sundry Poems in Imitation of *Milton*, where with the utmost Exactness, and not so much as one Exception, nevertheless was constantly *nathless*, embroider'd was *broider'd*, Hermits were *Eremites*, disdain'd was *'sdeign'd*, shady *umbrageous*, Enterprize *Emprize*, Pagan *Paynim*, Pinions *Pennons*, sweet *dulcet*, Orchards *Orchats*, Bridge-work *Pontifical*; nay, her was *hir*, and their was *thir* thro' the whole Poem. And in very Deed, there is no other Way by which the true modern Poet could read to any purpose the Works of such Men as *Milton* and *Shakespear*.

IT may be expected, that like other Criticks, I should next speak of the PASSIONS: But as the main End and principal Effect of the *Bathos* is to produce *Tranquillity of Mind*, (and sure it is a better Design to promote Sleep than Madness) we have little to say on this Subject. Nor will the short Bounds of this Discourse allow us to treat at large of the *Emollients* and *Opiats* of *Poesy*, of the *Cool*, and the Manner of producing it, or of the *Methods* us'd by our Authors in *managing* the *Passions*. I shall but transiently remark, that nothing contributes so much to the *Cool*, as the Use of *Wit* in expressing Passion: The true Genius rarely fails of *Points, Conceits*, and proper *Similies* on such Occasions: This we may term the *Pathetic epigrammatical*, in which even Puns are made use of with good Success. Hereby our best Authors have avoided throwing themselves or their Readers into any indecent Transports.

BUT forasmuch as it is sometimes needful to excite the Passions of our Antagonist in the Polemic way, the true Students in the *Low* have constantly taken their Methods from *Low*-Life, where they observ'd, that to move *Anger*, use is made of *scolding* and *railing*; to move *Love*, of *Bawdry*; to beget *Favour* and Friendship, of gross *Flattery*; and to produce *Fear*, by calumniating an Adversary with *Crimes* obnoxious to the *State*. As for *Shame*, it is a silly Passion, of which as our Authors are incapable themselves, so they would not produce it in others.

Chap. X.

Of Tropes *and* Figures: *and first of the variegating, confusing, and reversing* Figures.

But we proceed to the *Figures*. We cannot too earnestly recommend to our Authors the Study of the *Abuse of Speech*. They ought to lay it down as a Principle, to say nothing in the usual way, but (if possible) in the direct contrary. Therefore the Figures must be so turn'd, as to manifest that intricate and wonderful *Cast* of *Head*, which distinguishes all Writers of this Genius; or (as I may say) to refer exactly the *Mold* in which they were form'd, in all its *Inequalities, Cavities, Obliquities*, odd *Crannies*, and *Distortions*.

It would be endless, nay impossible to enumerate all *such Figures*; but we shall content ourselves to range the Principal which most powerfully contribute to the *Bathos*, under three Classes.

I. The Variegating, Confusing, or Reversing *Tropes* and *Figures*.

II. The Magnifying, and

III. The Diminishing.

We cannot avoid giving to these the *Greek* or *Roman* Names; but in Tenderness to our Countrymen and fellow Writers, many of whom, however exquisite, are wholly ignorant of those Languages, we have also explained them in our Mother Tongue.

Of the First Sort, nothing so much conduces to the *Abuse* of *Speech*, as the

Catachresis.

A Master of this will say,
  Mow the Beard,
  Shave the Grass,
  Pin the Plank,
  Nail my Sleeve.
From whence results the same kind of Pleasure to the Mind, as doth to the Eye when we behold *Harlequin* trimming himself with a Hatchet, hewing down a Tree with a Rasor, making his Tea in a Cauldron, and brewing his Ale in a Tea-pot, to the incredible Satisfaction of the *British* Spectator. Another Source of the *Bathos* is

The Art of Sinking in Poetry

The Metonymy,

the Inversion of Causes for Effects, of Inventors for Inventions, &c.

> *Lac'd in her *Cosins new appear'd the Bride,*
> *A *Bubble-boy and *Tompion at her Side,*
> *And with an Air divine her *Colmar ply'd.*
> *And oh! she cries, what Slaves I round me see?*
> *Here a bright Redcoat, there a smart *Toupee.*[24]

The Synechdoche

Which consists, in the Use of a *Part* for the *Whole*; you may call a young Woman sometimes Pretty-*face* and Pigs-*eyes*, and sometimes Snotty-*nose* and Draggle-*tail*. Or of *Accidents* for *Persons*; as a Lawyer is call'd *Split-cause*, a Taylor *Prick-louse*, &c. Or of things belonging to a Man, for the Man himself; as a *Sword*-Man, a *Gown*-man, a *T[o]m-T[ur]d-man*; a *White Staff*, a *Turn-key*, &c.

The Aposiopesis.

An excellent Figure for the Ignorant, as, *What shall I say?* when one has nothing to say; or *I can no more*, when one really can no more: Expressions which the gentle Reader is so good, as never to take in earnest.

The Metaphor.

The first Rule is to draw it from the lowest things, which is a certain way to sink the highest; as when you speak of the Thunder of Heaven, say,

> *The* Lords above *are* angry *and* talk big.   *Lee Alex.*[25]

  If you would describe a rich Man refunding his Treasures, express it thus,

> *Tho' he (as said) may Riches gorge, the Spoil*
> *Painful in massy Vomit shall recoil.*
> *Soon shall he perish with a swift Decay,*
> *Like his own Ordure, cast with Scorn away.*
>   *Black.* Job. p. 91. 93.

  The Second, that whenever you *start* a Metaphor, you must be sure to *Run it down*, and pursue it as far as it can go. If you get the Scent of a State Negotiation, follow it in this manner.

> *The Stones and all the Elements with thee*

> *Shall* ratify *a* strict Confederacy;
> *Wild Beasts their savage Temper shall forget,*
> *And for a* firm Alliance *with thee* treat;
> *The finny Tyrant of the spacious Seas*
> *Shall send a scaly* Embassy *for* Peace:
> *His* plighted Faith *the* Crocodile *shall keep,*
> *And seeing thee, for Joy sincerely weep.*   Job. p. 22.

OR if you represent the Creator denouncing War against the Wicked, be sure not to omit one Circumstance usual in proclaiming and levying War.

> Envoys *and* Agents, *who by my Command*
> Reside *in* Palestina's *Land,*
> *To whom* Commissions *I have given,*
> *To* manage *there the* Interests *of Heaven.*
> *Ye holy* Heralds *who proclaim*
> *Or* War *or* Peace, *in mine* your Master's *Name.*
> *Ye* Pioneers *of Heaven, prepare a* Road,
> *Make it plain, direct and broad;—*
> *For I in person will my People* head;
> *—For the divine Deliverer*
> *Will* on his March *in Majesty appear,*
> *And needs the* Aid *of no* Confederate Pow'r.
>   Blackm. Isaiah. chap. 40.

UNDER the Article of the *Confusing*, we rank

The MIXTURE OF FIGURES,

which raises so many Images, as to give you no Image at all. But its principal Beauty is when it gives an Idea just opposite to what it seem'd meant to describe. Thus an ingenious Artist painting the *Spring*, talks of a *Snow* of Blossoms, and thereby raises an unexpected Picture of *Winter*. Of this Sort is the following:

> *The gaping Clouds pour Lakes of Sulphur down,*
> *Whose livid flashes sickning Sunbeams drown.*   Pr.*Arthur,* p. 73.

WHAT a noble Confusion? Clouds, Lakes, Brimstone, Flames, Sun-beams, gaping, pouring, sickning, drowning! all in two Lines.

The JARGON,

> *Thy Head shall rise, tho' buried in the Dust,*
> *And 'midst the Clouds his glittering Turrets thrust.*   Job. p. 107.

Quære, what are the glittering Turrets of a Man's Head?

> *Upon the* Shore, *as* frequent *as the* Sand,

To meet the Prince, the glad Dimetians *stand.*

Pr. *Arthur*, p. 157.

Quære, where these *Dimetians* stood? and of what Size they were?

Destruction*'s Empire shall no longer* last,
And Desolation *lye for ever* waste. *Job*. p. 89.

BUT for Variegation and Confusion of Objects, nothing is more useful than

The ANTITHESIS, or SEE-SAW,

Whereby Contraries and Oppositions are ballanc'd in such a way, as to cause a Reader to remain suspended between them, to his exceeding Delight and Recreation. Such are these, on a Lady who made herself appear out of size, by hiding a young Princess under her Cloaths.

While the kind Nymph changing her faultless Shape
Becomes unhandsome, handsomely *to scape*. *Waller.* [26]

On the Maids of Honour in Mourning:

Sadly they charm, and dismally they please.

St-. on Q. *Mary.* [27]

——*His Eyes so bright*
Let in *the Object; and* let out *the Light*. *Quarles*. [28]

The Gods look pale *to see us look so* red. *Lee* Alex.

——*The Fairies and their Queen*
In Mantles blue *came tripping o'er the* Green. *Phil.* Past.

All Nature felt a reverential Shock,
The Sea stood still *to see the Mountains* rock.

Black. Job. p. 176.

CHAP. XI.

The Figures continued: Of the Magnifying and diminishing Figures.

A Genuine Writer of the Profund will take Care never to *magnify* any Object without *clouding* it at the same time; His Thought will appear in a true *Mist*, and very unlike what it is in Nature. It must always be remember'd that *Darkness* is an essential Quality of the *Profund*, or if there chance to be a Glimmering, it must be as *Milton* expresses it,

> *No Light, but rather Darkness visible.* [29]

The chief Figure of this sort is,

> The HYPERBOLE, or *Impossible*,

For Instance, of a Lion;

> *He roar'd so loud, and look'd so wondrous grim,*
> *His very Shadow durst not follow him.*　　　　Vet. Aut.

Of a Lady at Dinner.

> *The silver Whiteness that adorns thy Neck,*
> *Sullies the Plate, and makes the Napkin black.*

Of the same.

> *—Th' obscureness of her Birth*
> *Cannot eclipse the Lustre of her Eyes,*
> *Which make her all one Light.*　　　Theob. *Double Distress.*

Of a Bull-baiting.

> *Up to the Stars the sprawling Mastives fly,*
> *And add new Monsters to the frighted Sky.*　　　Blackm.

Of a Scene of Misery.

> *Behold a Scene of Misery and Woe!*
> *Here* Argus' *soon might weep himself quite blind,*
> *Ev'n tho' he had* Briareus' *hundred Hands*
> *To wipe those hundred Eyes—*　　　Anon.

And that modest Request of two absent Lovers,

> *Ye Gods! annihilate but* Space *and* Time,
> *And make two Lovers happy. —*

The PERIPHRASIS, which the Moderns call the *Circumbendibus*, whereof we have given Examples in the ninth Chapter, and shall again in the twelfth.

To the same Class of the *Magnifying* may be referr'd the following, which are so excellently Modern, that we have yet no Name for them. In describing a Country Prospect

I'd call them Mountains, but can't call them so,
For fear to wrong them with a Name too low;
While the fair Vales beneath so humbly lie,
That even humble seems a Term too high.   Anon. [30]

III. THE third Class remains, of the *Diminishing* Figures: And first, The ANTICLIMAX, where the second Line drops quite short of the first, than which nothing creates greater Surprize.

On the Extent of the *British* Arms.

Under the Tropicks is our Language spoke,
And Part of Flanders hath received our Yoke.   Wall. [31]

On a Warrior.

And thou *Dalhoussy* the great God of War,
Lieutenant Colonel to the Earl of Mar.   Anon.

On the Valour of the *English.*

Nor Death, nor Hell it self can keep them out,
—*Nor* fortify'd Redoubt.   Denn. *on* Namur[32]

AT other times this Figure operates in a larger Extent; and when the gentle Reader is in Expectation of some great Image, he either finds it surprizingly *imperfect*, or is presented with something very *low*, or quite *ridiculous*. A Surprize resembling that of a curious Person in a Cabinet of antique Statues, who beholds on the Pedestal the Names of *Homer*, or *Cato*; but looking up, finds *Homer* without a Head, and nothing to be seen of *Cato* but his privy Member. Such are these Lines on a *Leviathan* at Sea.

His Motion works, and beats the oozy Mud,
And with its Slime incorporates the Flood,
'Till all th' encumber'd, thick, fermenting Stream
Does one vast Pot of boiling Ointment seem.
Where'er he swims, he leaves along the Lake
Such frothy Furrows, such a foamy Track,
That all the Waters of the Deep appear
Hoary – *with* Age, *or* grey *with sudden* Fear.   *Black.* Job. p. 197.

BUT perhaps even these are excell'd by the ensuing.

Now the resisted Flames and fiery Store, ⎫
By winds assaulted, in wide Forges roar, ⎬
And raging Seas flow down of melted Oar. ⎭
Sometimes they hear long Iron Bars remov'd,

And to *and* fro *huge* Heaps of Cynders shov'd.   Pr. *Arthur*. p. 157.

The VULGAR

Is also a Species of the *Diminishing*; By this a Spear flying in the Air is compar'd to a Boy whistling as he goes on an Errand.

> *The mighty* Stuffa *threw a massy Spear,*
> *Which, with its* Errand pleas'd, sung *thro' the Air*.   Pr. *Arthur.*

A Man raging with Grief to a Mastiff Dog.

> *I cannot stifle this gigantic Woe,*
> *Nor on my raging Grief a* Muzzle *throw.*   *Job.* p. 41.

And Clouds big with water to a Woman in great Necessity.

> Distended *with the* Waters *in 'em pent,*
> *The Clouds* hang deep *in Air, but* hang unrent.

The INFANTINE.

THIS is when a Poet grows so very simple, as to think and talk like a Child. I shall take my Examples from the greatest Master in this way. Hear how he fondles, like a meer Stammerer.

> Little Charm *of placid Mien,*
> Miniature *of Beauty's Queen,*
> *Hither* British *Muse* of mine,
> *Hither, all ye* Græcian Nine,
> *With the lovely Graces* Three,
> *And your* pretty Nurseling *see.*
> *When the Meadows next are seen,*
> *Sweet Enamel, white and green.*
> *When again the Lambkins play,*
> *Pretty Sportlings full of* May,
> *Then the Neck so white and round,*
> (Little Neck *with Brilliants bound.*)
> *And thy* Gentleness *of Mind,*
> (Gentle *from a* gentle *Kind*) &c.
> Happy *thrice, and* thrice agen,
> Happiest *he of* happy *Men*, &c.   *A. Phil.* on Miss C—[33]

With the rest of those excellent *Lullabies* of his Composition.
How prettily he asks the Sheep to teach him to bleat?

> *Teach me to grieve with bleating Moan, my Sheep.*   *Phil.* Past.

Hear how a Babe would reason on his Nurse's Death:

> *That ever she* could *dye! Oh most* unkind!
> *To die, and leave poor* Colinet *behind?*
> *And yet,* —*Why blame I her?*—   Phil. Past.

His Shepherd reasons as much like an Innocent, in Love:

> *I love in secret all a beauteous Maid,*
> *And have my Love in secret all repay'd:*
> *This coming* Night *she does* reserve *for me.*   Ibid.

THE Love of this Maiden to him appears by her allowing him the Reserve of one Night from her other Lovers; which you see he takes extreamly kindly.

WITH no less Simplicity does he suppose that Shepherdesses tear their Hair and beat their Breasts, at their own Deaths:

> *Ye brighter Maids, faint Emblems of my Fair,*
> *With Looks cast down, and with dishevel'd Hair,*
> *In bitter Anguish beat your Breasts, and moan*
> *Her Death untimely,* as it were your own.   Ibid.

The INANITY, or NOTHINGNESS.

OF this the same Author furnishes us with most beautiful Instances:

> *Ah silly I, more silly than my Sheep,*
> *(Which on the flow'ry Plain I once did keep.)*   Phil. Past.

> *To the grave Senate she could Counsel give,*
> *(Which with Astonishment they did receive.)*   Phil. on Q. Mary.

> *He whom loud Cannon could not terrify,*
> *Falls (from the Grandeur of his Majesty.)*   Ibid.

> *The* Noise *returning with returning* Light,

What did it?

> —*Dispers'd the* Silence, *and dispell'd the* Night.   Anon.

> *The Glories of proud* London *to survey,*
> *The Sun himself shall rise* — *by break of Day.*
>   Autor Vet.

The EXPLETIVE,

admirably exemplified in the Epithets of many Authors.

Selected prose of Alexander Pope

Th' umbrageous Shadow, and the verdant Green,
The running Current, and odorous Fragrance,
Chear my lone Solitude with joyous Gladness.

The MACROLOGY and PLEONASM,

are as generally coupled, as a lean Rabbit with a fat one; nor is it a
wonder, the Superfluity of Words and Vacuity of Sense, being just the
same thing. I am pleas'd to see one of our greatest Adversaries employ
this Figure.

The Growth of Meadows, and the Pride of Fields;
The Food of Armies and Support of Wars.
Refuse of Swords, and Gleanings of a Fight;
Lessen his Numbers, and contract his Host.
Where'er his Friends retire, or Foes succeed.
Cover'd with Tempests, and in Oceans drown'd,   *Camp.* [34]

Of all which the Perfection is

The TAUTOLOGY.

Break thro' the Billows, and — divide the Main.
In smoother Numbers, and — in softer Verse.
                    Tons. Misc. *duod.* vol. 4. p. 291. Fourth Edition.

Divide — *and* part — *the* sever'd *World* — in two.
                                        Ibid. vol. 6. p. 121.

WITH ten thousand others equally musical, and plentifully flowing
thro' most of our celebrated modern Poems.

CHAP. XII.

Of Expression, *and the several Sorts of* Style *of the present*
Age.

The *Expression* is adequate, when it is proportionally low to the
Profundity of the Thought. It must not be always *Grammatical*, lest it
appear pedantic and ungentlemanly; nor too *clear*, for fear it become
vulgar; for Obscurity bestows a Cast of the Wonderful, and throws an
oracular Dignity upon a Piece which hath no meaning.

FOR example, sometimes use the wrong Number; *The Sword and*
Pestilence at once devours, instead of *devour.* Sometimes the wrong

The Art of Sinking in Poetry

Case; *And who more fit to sooth the God than* thee, instead of *thou*: And rather than say, *Thetis saw Achilles* weep, she *heard* him weep.

Ti. *Hom*. Il. i. [35]

WE must be exceeding careful in two things; first, in the *Choice* of *low Words*; secondly, in the *sober* and *orderly* way of *ranging* them. Many of our Poets are naturally bless'd with this Talent, insomuch that they are in the Circumstance of that honest Citizen, who had made *Prose* all his Life without knowing it.[36] Let Verses run in this manner, just to be a Vehicle to the Words. (I take them from my last cited Author, who tho' otherwise by no means of our Rank, seem'd once in his Life to have a mind to be simple.)

> *If not, a Prize I will my self decree,*
> *From him, or him, or else perhaps from thee.*
>
> Ti. Hom. Il. i. p. ii.

> —— *full of Days was he;*
> *Two Ages past, he liv'd the third to see.*   Idem. p. 17.

> *The King of forty Kings, and honour'd more*
> *By mighty* Jove *than e'er was King before.*   p. 19.

> *That I may know, if thou my Prayer deny,*
> *The most despis'd of all the Gods am I.*   p. 34.

> *Then let my Mother once be rul'd by me,*
> *Tho' much more wise than I pretend to be.*   p. 38.

Or these of the same hand. [37]

> *I leave the Arts of Poetry and Verse*
> *To them that practice them with more success:*
> *Of greater Truths I now prepare to tell,*
> *And so at once, dear Friend and Muse, farewel.*
>
> Tons. Misc. 12ves. vol. 4. p. 292. fourth Edition.

Sometimes a single *Word* will familiarize a poetical Idea; as where a Ship set on fire owes all the Spirit of the *Bathos* to one choice Word that ends the Line.

> *And his scorch'd Ribs the hot Contagion* fry'd.
>
> Pr. *Arthur*. p. 151.

And in that Description of a World in Ruins.

> *Should the whole Frame of Nature round him break,*

197

Selected prose of Alexander Pope

He unconcern'd would hear the mighty Crack.

Tons. Misc. vol. 6. 119.

So also in these:

Beasts tame and savage to the River's Brink
Come from the fields and wild Abodes - to drink.　　*Job*. p. 263.

FREQUENTLY two or three Words will do it effectually.

He from the Clouds does the sweet Liquor squeeze,
That chears the Forest and the Garden *Trees*.　　*Id*. Job. p. 264.

IT is also useful to employ *Technical Terms*, which estrange your Stile from the great and general Ideas of Nature: And the higher your Subject is, the lower should you search into Mechanicks for your Expression. If you describe the Garment of an Angel, say that his *Linnen* was *finely spun*, and *bleach'd on the happy Plains*. Call an Army of Angels, *Angelic Cuirassiers*, and if you have Occasion to mention a Number of Misfortunes, stile them　　　　　　　*Pr. Arth*. p. 19.

Ibid. p. 139.

Fresh Troops *of Pains, and* regimented *Woes*.　　*Job*. p. 86.

STILE is divided by the Rhetoricians into the Proper and the Figured. Of the Figur'd we have already treated, and the Proper is what our Authors have nothing to do with. Of Stiles we shall mention only the Principal, which owe to the *Moderns* either their *chief Improvement*, or entire *Invention*.

1. The FLORID,

Than which none is more proper to the *Bathos*, as Flowers which are the *Lowest* of Vegetables are the most *Gaudy*, and do many times grow in great Plenty at the bottom of *Ponds* and *Ditches*.

A fine Writer in this kind presents you with the following Posie:

The Groves appear all drest with Wreaths of Flowers,
And from their Leaves drop aromatic Showers,
Whose fragrant Heads in mystic Twines above,
Exchang'd their sweets, and mix'd with thousand Kisses,
As if the willing Branches strove
To beautify and shade the Grove. —　　*Behn*'s Poems. p. 2.

(Which indeed most Branches do) But this is still excell'd by our Laureat.

Branches in Branches twin'd compose the Grove,
And shoot and spread, and blossom into Love.

The trembling Palms their mutual Vows repeat,
And bending Poplars bending Poplars meet.
The distant Platanes seems to press more nigh,
And to the sighing Alders, Alders sigh.

Guardian. 12ves. 127. [38]

Hear also our *Homer*.

His Robe of State *is form'd of Light refin'd,*
An endless Train *of Lustre* spreads behind.
His Throne's of bright compacted Glory *made,*
With Pearl *celestial, and with Gems* inlaid:
Whence Floods *of Joy, and* Seas *of Splendor flow,*
On all th' Angelic gazing Throng below.

Black. Ps. 104.

2. The PERT *Stile.*

This does in as peculiar a manner become the low in Wit, as a Pert Air does the low in Stature. Mr. *Thomas Brown,*[39] the Author of the *London Spy,* and all the *Spies* and *Trips* in general, are herein to be diligently study'd: In Verse, Mr. *Cibber's Prologues.* [40]

BUT the Beauty and Energy of it is never so conspicuous, as when it is employ'd in *Modernizing* and *Adapting* to the *Taste of the Times* the Works of the Antients. This we rightly phrase *Doing* them *into English,* and *making* them *English;* two Expressions of great Propriety, the one denoting our *Neglect* of the *Manner how,* the other the *Force* and *Compulsion* with which, it is brought about. It is by Virtue of this Stile that *Tacitus* talks like a *Coffee-House Politician, Josephus* like the *British Gazeteer, Tully* is as short and smart as *Seneca* or Mr. *Asgill, Marcus Aurelius* is excellent at *Snipsnap,* and honest *Thomas a Kempis* as *Prim* and *Polite* as any Preacher at Court. [41]

3. THE ALAMODE Stile,

Which is fine by being *new,* and has this Happiness attending it, that it is as durable and extensive as the Poem itself. Take some Examples of it, in the Description of the Sun in a Mourning Coach upon the Death of Q. *Mary.*

See Phœbus *now, as once for* Phaeton,
Has mask'd *his Face; and put* deep Mourning *on;*
Dark Clouds his sable Chariot *do surround,*
And the dull Steeds stalk o'er *the* melancholy Round.

A. Phil.

199

Selected prose of Alexander Pope

Of Prince *Arthur*'s Soldiers drinking.

While rich Burgundian *Wine, and bright* Champaign,
Chase from their Minds the Terrors of the Main.   Pr. *Ar.* p. 16.

(Whence we also learn, that *Burgundy* and *Champaign* make a Man on
Shore despise a Storm at Sea.)

Of the Almighty encamping his Regiments.

—He sunk a vast capacious deep,
Where he his liquid Regiments *does keep.*
Thither the Waves file off, *and make their way,*
To form the mighty Body *of the Sea;*
Where they incamp, and in their Station stand,
Entrench'd *in* Works *of Rock, and* Lines *of Sand.*
                                          Blackm. Ps. 104. p. 261.

Of two Armies on the Point of engaging.

Yon' Armies are the Cards *which both must play;*
At least come off a Saver *if you may:*
Throw boldly *at the* Sum *the Gods have* set;
These on your Side will all their Fortunes bet.   Lee *Sophon.*[42]

All perfectly agreeable to the present Customs and best Fashions of
this our Metropolis.

BUT the principal Branch of the *Alamode* is the PRURIENT, a Stile
greatly advanc'd and honour'd of late by the practise of Persons of the
first Quality, and by the encouragement of the *Ladies* not unsuccessful-
ly introduc'd even into the *Drawing-Room.* Indeed its *incredible Progress* and *Conquests* may be compar'd to those of the great *Sesostris*, and
are every where known by the *same Marks*, the Images of the Genital
Parts of Men or Women. It consists wholly of Metaphors drawn from
two most fruitful Sources or Springs, the very *Bathos* of the human
Body, that is to say * * * and * * * * * * * * * * * * * * * * *Hiatus Magnus
lachrymabilis.* [43] *.
And *selling of Bargains*, and *double Entendre*, and Κιββερισμος, and
Ολφιελδισμος,[44] all derived from the said Sources.

4. THE FINICAL, which consists of the most curious, affected,
mincing Metaphors, and partakes of the last mentioned.

As this, of a Brook dry'd by the Sun.

Won *by the Summer's* importuning *Ray.*
Th' eloping *Stream did from her Channel stray.*
And with enticing *Sun-beams* stole away.　　*Bl. Job.* p. 26.

Of an easy Death.

When watchful Death shall on his Harvest look,
And see thee ripe with Age, invite *the Hook;*
He'll gently *cut thy* bending *Stalk, and thee*
Lay kindly *in the* Grave, *his* Granary.　　*Ibid.* p. 23.

Of Trees in a Storm.

Oaks with extended Arms the Winds defy,
The Tempest sees *their Strength*, and sighs, and passes by.　　*Denn.*[45]

Of Water simmering over the Fire.

The sparkling Flames raise Water to a Smile,
Yet the pleas'd *Liquor* pines, *and lessens all the while.*
　　　　Anon. in *Tonson's* Misc. Part 6. p. 234.

5. LASTLY, I shall place the CUMBROUS, which moves heavily under a Load of Metaphors, and draws after it a long Train of Words.

AND the BUSKIN, or *Stately,* frequently and with great Felicity mix'd with the Former. For as the first is the proper Engine to depress what is High, so is the second to raise what is Base and Low to a ridiculous Visibility: When both these can be done at once, then is the *Bathos* in Perfection; as when a Man is set with his Head downward, and his Breech upright, his Degradation is compleat: One End of him is as high as ever, only that End is the wrong one. Will not every true Lover of the *Profund* be delighted to behold the most vulgar and low Actions of life exalted in this Manner?

Who knocks at the Door?

For whom thus rudely pleads my loud-tongu'd Gate,
That he may enter? —

See who is there?

Advance the fringed Curtains of thy Eyes,
And tell me who comes yonder.—　　*Temp.*[46]

Selected prose of Alexander Pope

Shut the Door.

The woodden Guardian of our Privacy
Quick on its Axle turn. —

Bring my Cloaths.

Bring me what Nature, Taylor to the Bear,
To Man *himself deny'd: She gave me Cold,*
But would not give me Cloaths. —

Light the Fire.

Bring forth some Remnant of Promethean *Theft,*
Quick to expand th' inclement Air congeal'd
By Boreas's *rude Breath.* —

Snuff the Candle.

Yon Luminary Amputation needs,
Thus shall you save its half-extinguish'd Life.

Open the Letter.

Wax! render up thy Trust. — *Theob.* Double Distress.

Uncork the Bottle, and chip the Bread.

Apply thine Engine to the spungy Door,
Set Bacchus *from his glassy Prison free,*
And strip white Ceres *of her nut-brown Coat.*

APPENDIX.

Chap. XIII.

A Project for the Advancement of the Bathos.

Thus have I (my dear Countrymen) with incredible Pains and Diligence, discover'd the hidden sources of the *Bathos*, or as I may say broke open the Abysses of this *Great Deep*. And having now establish'd the good and wholesome *Laws*, what remains but that all true Moderns with their utmost Might do proceed to put the same in execution? In order whereto, I think I shall in the second place highly deserve of my Country, by proposing such a *Scheme*, as may facilitate this great End.

As our Number is confessedly far superior to that of the Enemy, there seems nothing wanting but Unanimity among our selves. It is therefore humbly offer'd, that all and every Individual of the *Bathos* do enter into a firm *Association*, and incorporate into *one Regular Body*, whereof every Member, even the meanest, will some way contribute to the Support of the whole; in like manner as the weakest Reeds when join'd in one Bundle, become infrangible. To which end our Art ought to be put upon the same foot with other Arts of this Age. The vast Improvement of modern Manufactures ariseth from their being divided into several Branches, and parcel'd out to several *Trades*: For instance, in *Clock-making*, one Artist makes the Balance, another the Spring, another the Crown-Wheels, a fourth the Case, and the principal Workman puts all together; To this OEconomy we owe the Perfection of our modern Watches; and doubtless we also might that of our modern Poetry and Rhetoric, were the several Parts branched out in the like manner.

NOTHING is more evident than that divers Persons, no other way remarkable, have each a strong Disposition to the Formation of some particular Trope or Figure. *Aristotle* saith, that the *Hyperbole* is an Ornament of Speech fit for *young Men of Quality*; accordingly we find in those Gentlemen a wonderful Propensity toward it, which is marvellously improv'd by *travelling*. *Soldiers* also and *Seamen* are very happy in the same Figure. The *Periphrasis* or *Circumlocution* is the peculiar Talent of *Country Farmers*, the Proverb and Apologue of *old Men* at their Clubs, the *Ellipsis* or Speech by half-words of *Ministers* and *Politicians*, the *Aposiopesis* of *Courtiers*, the *Litotes* or Diminution of *Ladies*, *Whisperers* and *Backbiters*; and the *Anadyplosis* of Common *Cryers* and *Hawkers*, who by redoubling the same Words, persuade People to buy their Oysters, green Hastings, or new Ballads. *Epithets* may be found in great plenty at *Billingsgate*, *Sarcasm* and *Irony* learn'd upon the *Water*, and the *Epiphonema* or *Exclamation* frequently from the *Bear-garden*, and as frequently from the *Hear him* of the House of Commons.

Now each man applying his whole Time and Genius upon his particular Figure, would doubtless attain to Perfection; and when each became incorporated and sworn into the Society, (as hath been propos'd;) a Poet or Orator would have no more to do, but to send to the particular Traders in each Kind; to the *Metaphorist* for his *Allegories*, to the *Simile-maker* for his *Comparisons*, to the *Ironist* for his *Sarcasmes*, to the *Apothegmatist* for his *Sentences, &c.* whereby a *Dedication* or *Speech* would be compos'd in a Moment, the superior Artist having nothing to do but to put together all the Materials.

I THEREFORE propose that there be contrived with all convenient Dispatch, at the publick Expence, a *Rhetorical Chest of Drawers*, consisting of three Stories, the highest for the *Deliberative*, the middle for the *Demonstrative*, and the lowest for the *Judicial*.[47] These shall be divided into *Loci* or *Places*, being Repositories for Matter and Argument in the several Kinds of Oration or Writing; and every Drawer shall again be sub-divided into Cells, resembling those of Cabinets for Rarities. The Apartment for *Peace* or *War*, and that of the *Liberty* of the *Press*, may in a very few Days be fill'd with several Arguments *perfectly new*; and the *Vituperative Partition* will as easily be replenish'd with a most choice Collection, entirely of the Growth and Manufacture of the present Age. Every Composer will soon be taught the Use of this Cabinet, and how to manage all the Registers of it, which will be drawn out much in the Manner of those of an Organ.

THE Keys of it must be kept in honest Hands, by some *Reverend Prelate*, or *Valiant Officer*, of unquestion'd Loyalty and Affection to every present Establishment in *Church* and *State*; which will sufficiently guard against any Mischief which might otherwise be apprehended from it.

AND being lodg'd in such Hands, it may be at discretion *let out* by the *Day*, to several great Orators in both Houses; from whence it is to be hop'd much *Profit* or *Gain* will also accrue to our Society.

CHAP. XIV.

How to make Dedications, Panegyricks *or* Satyrs, *and of the* Colours *of Honourable and Dishonourable.*

Now of what Necessity the foregoing Project may prove, will appear from this single Consideration, that nothing is of equal consequence to the Success of our Works, as *Speed* and *Dispatch*. Great pity it is, that solid Brains are not, like other solid Bodies, constantly endow'd with a *Velocity* in sinking, proportion'd to their *Heaviness*: For it is with the *Flowers* of the *Bathos* as with those of Nature, which if the careful Gardener brings not hastily to the Market in the *Morning*, must unprofitably perish and wither before *Night*. And of all our Productions none is so short-liv'd as the *Dedication* and *Panegyric*, which are often but the *Praise of a Day*, and become by the next, utterly useless, improper, indecent and false. This is the more to be lamented, in-asmuch as they are the very two Sorts whereon in a manner depends that *Gain* or *Profit*, which must still be remember'd to be the whole end of *our Writers* and *Speakers*.

WE shall therefore employ this Chapter in shewing the *quickest* Method of composing them; after which we will teach a *short Way* to *Epick Poetry*. And these being confessedly the Works of most Import-ance and Difficulty, it is presum'd we may leave the rest to each Author's own Learning or Practice.

FIRST of *Panegyrick*: Every Man is *honourable*, who is so by *Law*, *Custom* or *Title*; The Publick are better Judges of what is honourable, than private Men. The Virtues of great Men, like those of Plants, are *inherent* in them whether they are *exerted* or not; and the more strongly inherent the less they are exerted; as a Man is the more rich the less he spends.

ALL great Ministers, without either private or œconomical Virtue, are virtuous by their *Posts*; liberal and generous upon the *Publick Money*, provident upon *Parliamentary Supplies*, just by paying *Publick Interest*, couragious and magnanimous by the *Fleets* and *Armies*, mag-nificent upon the *Publick Expences*, and prudent by *Publick Success*. They have by their *Office*, a Right to a share of the *Publick Stock* of Virtues; besides they are by *Prescription immemorial* invested in all the celebrated Virtues of their *Predecessors* in the same *Stations*, especially those of their own *Ancestors*.

As to what are commonly call'd the *Colours* of *Honourable* and *Dishonourable*, they are various in different Countries: In this they are *Blue*, *Green* and *Red*. But forasmuch as the Duty we owe to the Publick doth often require that we should put some things in a strong Light, and throw a Shade over others, I shall explain the Method of turning a vicious Man into a Hero.

THE first and chief Rule is *the Golden Rule* of *Transformation*, which consists in converting Vices into their *bordering* Virtues. A man who is a Spendthrift and will not pay a just Debt, may have his Injustice *transform'd* into Liberality; Cowardice may be metamorphos'd into Prudence; Intemperance into good Nature and good Fellowship, Corruption into Patriotism, and Lewdness into Tenderness and Facil-ity.

THE Second is the *Rule of Contraries*: It is certain the less a Man is endu'd with any Virtue, the more need he has to have it plentifully bestow'd, especially those good Qualities of which the World generally believes he hath none at all: For who will thank a Man for giving him that which he *has*?

THE Reverse of these Precepts will serve for *Satire*, wherein we are ever to remark, that whoso loseth his Place, or becomes out of Favour with the Government, hath forfeited his Share of *Publick Praise* and *Honour*. Therefore the truly-publick-spirited Writer ought in Duty to strip him whom the Government has stripp'd: Which is the real *poetical Justice* of this Age. For a full Collection of Topics and Epithets to be used in the Praise and Dispraise of Ministerial and Unministerial Persons, I refer to our *Rhetorical Cabinet*; concluding with an earnest Exhortation to all my Brethren, to observe the Precepts here laid down; the Neglect of which hath cost some of them their *Ears* in a *Pillory*.

CHAP. XV.

A Receipt to make an Epic Poem.

An Epic Poem, the Criticks agree, is the greatest Work Human Nature is capable of. [48] They have already laid down many mechanical Rules for Compositions of this Sort, but at the same time they cut off almost all Undertakers from the Possibility of ever performing them; for the first Qualification they unanimously require in a Poet, is a *Genius*. I shall here endeavour (for the Benefit of my Countrymen) to make it manifest, that Epick Poems may be made *without a Genius*, nay without Learning or much Reading. This must necessarily be of great Use to all those who confess they never *Read*, and of whom the World is convinc'd they never *Learn*. What *Moliere* observes of making a Dinner, that any Man can do it *with Money*, and if a profess'd Cook cannot do it *without* he has his Art for nothing; [49] the same may be said of making a Poem, 'tis easily brought about by him that *has* a Genius, but the Skill lies in doing it without one. In pursuance of this End, I shall present the Reader with a plain and certain *Recipe*, by which any Author in the *Bathos* may be qualified for this grand Performance.

For the *Fable*.

TAKE out of any old Poem, History-book, Romance, or Legend, (for Instance *Geffry of Monmouth* or *Don Belianis of Greece*) those Parts of Story which afford most Scope for *long Descriptions*: Put these Pieces together, and throw all the Adventures you fancy into *one Tale*.

Then take a Hero, whom you may chuse for the Sound of his Name, and put him into the midst of these Adventures: There let him *work*, for twelve Books; at the end of which you may take him out, ready prepared to *conquer* or to *marry*; it being necessary that the Conclusion of an Epick Poem be *fortunate*.

To make an Episode.

TAKE any remaining Adventure of your former Collection, in which you could no way involve your Hero; or any unfortunate Accident that was too good to be thrown away; and it will be of Use, apply'd to any other Person; who may be lost and *evaporate* in the Course of the Work, without the least Damage to the Composition.

For the Moral and Allegory.

THESE you may extract out of the Fable afterwards, at your leisure: Be sure you *strain* them sufficiently.

For the Manners.

FOR those of the *Hero*, take all the best Qualities you can find in the most celebrated Heroes of Antiquity; if they will not be reduced to a *Consistency*, lay 'em *all on a Heap* upon him. But be sure they are Qualities which your *Patron* would be thought to have; and to prevent any Mistake which the World may be subject to, select from the Alphabet those Capital Letters that compose his Name, and set them at the Head of a Dedication before your Poem. However, do not absolutely observe the exact Quantity of these Virtues, it not being determin'd whether or no it be necessary for the Hero of a Poem to be an *honest Man*. For the *Under-Characters*, gather them from *Homer* and *Virgil*, and change the Names as occasion serves.

For the Machines.

TAKE of *Deities*, Male and Female, as many as you can use. Separate them into two equal Parts, and keep *Jupiter* in the middle. Let *Juno* put him in a Ferment, and *Venus* mollify him. Remember on all occasions to make use of Volatile *Mercury*. If you have need of Devils, draw them out of *Milton's Paradise*, and extract your *Spirits* from *Tasso*. The Use of these Machines is evident; for since no Epick Poem can possibly subsist without them, the wisest way is to reserve them for your greatest Necessities. When you cannot extricate your Hero by any human means, or your self by your own Wit, seek Relief from Heaven, and the Gods will do your business very readily. This is according to the direct Prescription of *Horace* in his Art of Poetry.

Nec Deus intersit, nisi dignus vindice Nodus *Inciderit.* —[50]

That is to say, *A Poet should never call upon the Gods for their Assistance, but when he is in great Perplexity.*

For the Descriptions.

FOR a *Tempest.* Take *Eurus, Zephyr, Auster* and *Boreas,* and cast them together in one Verse: Add to these of Rain, Lightning and of Thunder (the loudest you can) *quantum sufficit.* [51] Mix your Clouds and Billows well together 'till they foam, and thicken your Description here and there with a Quicksand. Brew your Tempest well in your Head, before you set it a blowing.

FOR a *Battle.* Pick a large Quantity of Images and Descriptions from *Homer's* Iliads, with a Spice or two of *Virgil,* and if there remain any Overplus, you may lay them by for a *Skirmish.* Season it well with *Similes,* and it will make an *Excellent Battle.*

FOR a *Burning Town.* If such a Description be necessary, (because it is certain there is one in *Virgil,*) Old *Troy* is ready burnt to your Hands. But if you fear that would be thought borrow'd, A Chapter or two of the Theory of the *Conflagration,*[52] well circumstanced, and done into Verse, will be a good *Succedaneum.* [53]

As for *Similes* and *Metaphors,* they may be found all over the Creation; the most ignorant may *gather* them, but the Danger is in *applying* them. For this advise with your *Bookseller.*

CHAP. XVI.

A Project for the Advancement of the Stage.

It may be thought that we should not wholly omit the *Drama,* which makes so great and so lucrative a Part of Poetry. But this Province is so well taken care of, by the present *Managers* of the Theatre, that it is perfectly needless to suggest to them any other Methods than they have already practis'd for the Advancement of the *Bathos.*

HERE therefore, in the name of all our Brethren, let me return our sincere and humble Thanks to the Most August Mr. *B[ar]t[o]n*

B[oo]th, the Most Serene Mr. *W[i]ll[ia]m W[i]lks*, and the Most Undaunted Mr. *C[o]ll[e]y C[i]bb[e]r*;[54] of whom, let it be known *when the People of this Age shall be Ancestors*, and to all *the Succession of our Successors*, that to this present day they continue to *Out-do* even their *own Out-doings*:[55] And when the inevitable Hand of sweeping *Time* shall have brush'd off all the Works of *To-day*, may this Testimony of a *Co-temporary Critick* to their Fame, be extended as far as *To-morrow!*

YET, if to so wise an Administration it be possible any thing can be added, it is that more ample and comprehensive Scheme which Mr. *D[e]nn[i]s* and Mr. *Gildon*, (the two greatest Criticks and Reformers then living) made publick in the Year 1720. in a Project sign'd with their Names, and dated the 2d of *February*. I cannot better conclude than by presenting the Reader with the Substance of it.

1. IT is propos'd that the two *Theatres* be incorporated into one Company; that the *Royal Academy* of *Musick* be added to them as an *Orchestra*; and that Mr. *Figg* with his Prize-fighters, and *Violante* with the Rope-dancers, be admitted in Partnership.

2. THAT a spacious Building be erected at the Publick Expence, capable of containing at least ten thousand Spectators, which is become absolutely necessary by the great addition of Children and Nurses to the Audience, since the new Entertainments. That there be a Stage as large as the *Athenian*, which was near ninety thousand Geometrical Paces square, and separate Divisions for the two *Houses* of *Parliament*, my *Lords* the *Judges*, the honourable the *Directors* of the *Academy*, and the *Court of Aldermen*, who shall all have their Places frank.

3. IF *Westminster Hall* be not allotted to this Service, (which by reason of its Proximity to the two Chambers of Parliament above mention'd, seems not altogether improper;) it is left to the Wisdom of the Nation whether *Somerset House* may not be demolish'd, and a *Theatre* built upon that Scite, which lies convenient to receive Spectators from the County of *Surrey*, who may be wafted thither by Water-Carriage, esteem'd by all Projectors the cheapest whatsoever. To this may be added, that the River *Thames* may in the readiest manner convey those eminent Personages from Courts beyond the Seas, who may be drawn either by Curiosity to behold some of our most celebrated Pieces, or by Affection to see their Countrymen the Harlequins and Eunuchs; Of which convenient notice may be given for two or three Months before, in the Publick Prints.

4. THAT the *Theatre* abovesaid be environ'd with a fair Quadrangle of Buildings, fitted for the Accommodation of decay'd *Criticks* and

Poets; out of whom *Six* of the most Aged (their Age to be computed from the Year wherein their first Work was publish'd) shall be elected to manage the Affairs of the Society, provided nevertheless that the *Laureat* for the time being, may be always one. The Head or President over all, (to prevent Disputes, but too frequent among the Learned) shall be the *oldest Poet* and *Critick* to be found in the whole Island.

5. THE *Male-Players* are to be lodg'd in the Garrets of the said Quadrangle, and to attend the Persons of the *Poets*, dwelling under them, by brushing their Apparel, drawing on their Shoes, and the like. The *Actresses* are to make their Beds, and wash their Linnen.

6. A LARGE Room shall be set apart for a *Library*, to consist of all the modern Dramatick Poems, and all the Criticisms extant. In the midst of this Room shall be a round Table for the *Council of* SIX to sit and deliberate on the Merits of *Plays*. The *Majority* shall determine the Dispute; and if it should happen that *three* and *three* should be of each Side, the President shall have a *casting Voice*, unless where the Contention may run so high as to require a Decision by *Single Combat*.

7. IT may be convenient to place the *Council of* SIX in some conspicuous Situation in the Theatre, where after the manner usually practised by Composers in Musick, they may give *Signs* (before settled and agreed upon) of Dislike or Approbation. In consequence of these Signs the whole Audience shall be requir'd to *clap* or *hiss*, that the Town may learn certainly when and how far they ought to be pleas'd.

8. IT is submitted whether it would not be proper to distinguish the *Council of* SIX by some particular Habit or Gown of an honourable Shape and Colour, to which might be added a square Cap and a white Wand.

9. THAT to prevent unmarried Actresses making away with their Infants, a competent Provision be allow'd for the Nurture of them, who shall for that reason be deem'd the *Children of the Society*; and that they may be educated according to the Genius of their Parents, the said Actresses shall declare upon Oath (as far as their Memory will allow) the true Names and Qualities of their several Fathers. A private Gentleman's Son shall at the Publick Expence be brought up a Page to attend the *Council of* SIX. A more ample Provision shall be made for the Son of a *Poet*; and a greater still for the Son of a *Critick*.

10. IF it be discover'd that any Actress is got with Child, during the Interludes of any Play, wherein she hath a part, it shall be reckon'd a neglect of her Business, and she shall *forfeit* accordingly. If any Actor for the future shall commit *Murder*, except upon the Stage, he shall be left to the Laws of the Land; the like is to be understood of *Robbery* and *Theft*. In all other Cases, particularly in those of *Debt*, it is

propos'd that this, like the other Courts of *Whitehall* and *St. James's*, may be held a *Place of Priviledge*. And whereas it has been found, that an Obligation to satisfy *paultry Creditors* has been a Discouragement to *Men of Letters*, if any Person of Quality or others shall send for any *Poet* or *Critick* of this Society to any remote Quarter of the Town, the said *Poet* or *Critick* shall freely pass and repass without being liable to an *Arrest*.

11. THE fore-mention'd Scheme in its several Regulations may be supported by Profits arising from every third Night throughout the Year. And as it would be hard to suppose that so many Persons could live without any Food (tho' from the former Course of their Lives, a *very little* will be sufficient) the Masters of Calculation will, we believe, agree, that out of those Profits, the said Persons might be subsisted in a sober and decent manner. We will venture to affirm farther, that not only the proper Magazines of Thunder and Lightning, but *Paint, Diet-Drinks, Spitting-Pots*, and all other *Necessaries* of *Life*, may in like manner fairly be provided for.

12. IF some of the Articles may at first view seem liable to Objections, particularly those that give so vast a Power to the *Council of* SIX (which is indeed larger than any intrusted to the Great Officers of State) this may be obviated, by swearing those *Six* Persons of his Majesty's Privy Council, and obliging them to pass every thing of Moment *previously* at that most honourable Board.

Vale & Fruere. [56]

MAR. SCRIB.

CONTENTS
TO THE
BATHOS.

Selected prose of Alexander Pope

12. Of the Poet Laureate

The *Grub-street Journal*, which ran from 1730 to 1737, devoted itself largely to literary news and controversy. Its editors were John Martyn and Richard Russel, but in its early stages Pope had a guiding hand: the journal took his side in the current literary feuds, and he provided some of the material (see further James T. Hillhouse, *The Grub-Street Journal* (Boston, 1928)). The present piece is almost certainly by Pope; it is one of those assigned, under the letter 'A', to Pope and his friends in the anthology *The Memoirs of Grub-Street* (1737) and it was added to the 1743 edition of *The Dunciad*.

The death of the poet laureate, Laurence Eusden, in September 1730 occasioned much speculation about his successor. Pope's account of the elevation of 'a plain Country-man' to be poet laureate is a satire on Stephen Duck (1705-56), the agricultural labourer and poet who was 'discovered' in 1729-30 and patronized by the court. In a letter to Gay of 23 October 1730, Pope (not knowing yet of Eusden's death) writes of Eusden and Duck as emblems of the state of poetry: 'a drunken sot of a *Parson* holds forth the emblem of *inspiration,* and an honest industrious *Thresher* not unhappily represents *Pains* and *Labour*' (*Corr.* iii 143). In the event, the laureateship was given to Colley Cibber. Pope's account of the ceremonies for the installation of the laureate may have been prompted partly by the recent accounts in *The Grub-street Journal* (nos.43,44) of the ancient ceremonies for celebrating the Lord Mayor's Day.

The Renaissance ceremonies described here took place in the pontificate of Leo X (1475-1521), a pope who was pleasure-loving and recklessly liberal with money and offices, some of which benefitted poets and artists (cp. *Essay on Criticism*, 697). Leo enjoyed the company of buffoons, two of whose stories are conflated here by Pope. Camillo Querno came from Apulia to Rome to make his fortune, and was invited to a symposium at which he was made to drink and sing alternately. He was then crowned with a wreath of vine leaves, cabbage and laurel, and given the title of arch-poet. Leo invited him to drink and declaim his verses at his own table. Another poetaster, Baraballo of Gaeta, considered himself a second Petrarch, and claimed the right to be crowned poet on the Capitol. He rode through the streets in the garb of a Roman conqueror, mounted on an elephant which the King of Portugal had presented to Leo. After reciting his verses to the Pope, he was led away to the sound of drums and trumpets, but on the return journey the elephant shied on the bridge of St Angelo and threw the poet on to the pavement. Pope uses the historian Paulo Giovio's *Elogia Doctorum Virorum* (1557); for a modern account see Ludvig Pastor, *The History of the Popes*, 40 vols. (1891-1953) viii 153-5.

Text: When printed in *The Grub-street Journal* no.46 (19 November 1730), this piece opened with the editorial comment that 'many of our Members are excercising their wit, in hopes of obtaining that honour'; nevertheless the editor says that he will 'humbly beg leave to recommend one against whom there can be no objection'. When preparing the piece to stand as a separate essay in 1743, Pope abridged this introduction to form the new opening sentence. This revision is followed here, but otherwise the text is that of 1730; the 1743 text is printed in *Poems* v 412-7.

OF THE POET LAUREATE

The time of the election of a Poet Laureate being now at hand, it may
be proper to give some account of the *Rites* and *Ceremonies* anciently
used at that solemnity, and only discontinued thro' the neglect and
degeneracy of later times. These we have extracted from an Historian
of undoubted credit, and a Reverend Bishop, the learned *Paulus
Jovius;* and are the same that were practised under the Pontificate of
Leo X. the great restorer of learning.

As we now see an Age and a Court, that for the encouragement of
Poetry rivals, if not exceeds, that of this famous Pope; we cannot but
wish a restoration of all its honours to Poesy; the rather, since there are
so many parallel circumstances in the *person* who was then honoured
with the Laurel, and in *him,* who (in all probability) is now to wear it.

I shall translate my Author exactly, as I find it in the 82d Chapter of
his *Elogia Vir. Doct.* He begins with the character of the Poet himself,
who was the original and father of all Laureates, and called *Camillo.*
He was a plain Country-man of *Apulia,* (whether a *Shepherd* or
Thresher, is not material). 'This man (says *Jovius*) excited by the fame of
the great encouragement given to Poets at Court, and the high
honour in which they were held, came to the City, bringing with him a
strange kind of lyre in his hand, and at least some *twenty thousand of
verses.* All the Wits and Criticks of the Court flock'd about him,
delighted to see a *Clown,* with a ruddy hale complexion, and in his own
long hair, so top-full of Poetry, and at the first sight of him, all agreed,
he was born to be *Poet Laureate.*[1] He had a most hearty welcome in an
Island of the river *Tyber,* (an agreeable place, not unlike our
Richmond[2]) where he was first made to *eat* and *drink plentifully,* and *to
repeat his verses to every body.* Then they adorn'd him with a new and
elegant garland composed of *Vine leaves, Laurel,* and *Brassica,* (a sort
of cabbage) so composed (says my Author) emblematically, *ut tam
salsè, quam lepidè, ejus Temulentia* Brassicae *remedio cohibenda
notaretur.*[3] He was then saluted by common consent with the title of
Archi-poeta or *Arch-poet,* in the style of those days, in ours, *Poet
Laureate.* This honour the poor man received with the most sensible
demonstrations of joy, his eyes drunk with tears of gladness.[4] Next,
the publick acclamation was express'd in a Canticle, which is yet
transmitted to us, as follows.

> Salve, brassicea virens corona
> Et Lauro, Archipoeta, pampinoque,
> Dignus principis auribus Leonis.'

Selected prose of Alexander Pope

> All hail, Arch-poet without peer!
> Vine, Laurel, Cabbage fit to wear,
> And worthy of thy *Prince's* ear.

From hence, he was conducted in pomp to the *Capitol* of *Rome,* mounted on an *Elephant,* thro' the shouts of the populace, where the ceremony ended.

The Historian tells us farther, 'that at his introduction to *Leo,* he not only poured forth verses innumerable, like a torrent, but also *sung* them with *open mouth.* Nor was he only once introduced, or on stated days (like our Laureates) but made a *Companion* to his *Master,* and entertained as one of the instruments of his *most elegant pleasures.* When the Prince was at table, the Poet had his place at the window. When the Prince had[5] half eaten his meat, he gave with his own hands the rest to his poet. When the Poet drank, it was out of the Prince's own flaggon, insomuch (says the Historian), that thro' so great good eating and drinking he contracted a most terrible *Gout.*' Sorry I am to relate what follows, but that I cannot leave my Reader's curiosity unsatisfy'd in the catastrophe of this extraordinary man. To use my Author's words, which are remarkable, *mortuo Leone, profligatisque Poetis,* &c. when Leo dy'd, and Poets were no more, (for I would not understand *profligatis* literally, as if Poets then were *profligate*) this unhappy Laureate was forthwith reduced to return to his Country, where, oppress'd with *old age* and *want,* he miserably perish'd in a *common hospital.*

We see from this sad conclusion, which may be of example to the Poets of our time, that it were happier to meet with no encouragement at all, to remain at the plough, or other lawful occupation, than to be elevated above their condition, and taken out of the common means of life, without a surer support, than the *temporary,* or, at best, *mortal* favours of the Great. It was doubtless for this consideration, that when the Royal Bounty was lately extended to a *Rural Genius,* care was taken to *settle it upon him for life.* And it hath been the practice of our Princes, never to remove from the station of Poet Laureate any Man who hath once been chosen, tho' never so much greater Genius's might arise in his time. A noble instance, how much the *charity* of our Monarchs hath exceeded their *love* of *fame!*

To come now to the intent of this Paper. We have here the whole ancient *ceremonial* of the Laureate. In the first place the Crown is to be mix'd with *Vine leaves,* as the Vine is the plant of *Bacchus,* and full as essential to the honour, as the *butt of sack,* to the salary.

Secondly, the *Brassica* must be made use of, as a qualifier of the former. It seems the *cabbage* was anciently accounted a remedy for *drunkenness*, (a power the French now ascribe to the onion, and style a soupe made of it, *Soupe d' Ivrogne*.) I would recommend a large mixture of the *Brassica*, if Mr. D[ENNI]s be chosen; but if Mr. TIBBALD,[6] it is not so necessary, unless the cabbage be supposed to signify the same thing, with respect to the *Poets* as to *Taylors*, viz. *stealing*.[7] I should judge it not amiss to add another plant to this garland, to wit, *Ivy*: not only as it anciently belonged to Poets in general; but as it is emblematical of the three virtues of a Court Poet in particular, it is *creeping, dirty* and *dangling*.

In the next place, a *Canticle* must be composed, and sung in laud and praise of the new Poet. If Mr. C[IBBE]R be laureated, it is my opinion no man can *write* this but himself: and no man, I am sure, can *sing* it so affectingly.[8] But what this Canticle should be, either in his or the other Candidates case, I shall not pretend to determine.

Thirdly, there ought to be a *publick show*, or *entry* of the Poet: to settle the order or procession of which, Mr. ANSTIS[9] and Mr. D[E-NNI]s ought to have a conference. I apprehend here two difficulties: one, of procuring an *Elephant*; the other, of teaching the Poet to ride him: none that I know (except Mr. BUD[GELL][10] who is no Candidate) having been used to the *menage*, and the rest never set even on horseback. Therefore I should imagine the next animal in size or dignity would do best; either a Mule or a large Ass; particularly if that noble one could be had, whose portraiture makes so great an ornament of the *Dunciad*, and which (unless I am misinform'd) is yet in the park of a Nobleman near this City:–[11] Unless Mr. C[IBBE]R be the man, who may, with great propriety and beauty, ride on a *Dragon*, if he goes by land; or, if he chuse the water, upon one of his own *Swans* from *Caesar in Egypt*.

We have spoken sufficiently of the ceremony; let us now speak of the qualifications and privileges of the Laureate. First, we see he must be able to make verses extempore, and to pour forth innumerable, if requir'd: In this, I doubt Mr. TIBBALD. Secondly, he ought to *sing*, and intrepidly, *patulo ore*:[12] here, I confess the excellency of Mr. C[IBBE]R. Thirdly, he ought to carry a *lyre* about with him: If a large one be thought too cumbersom, a small one may be contrived to hang about the neck, like an Order; and be very much a grace to the person. Fourthly, he ought to have a good *stomach* to eat and drink, whatever his betters think fit; and therefore it is in this high office, as in many others, no puny constitution can discharge it. I do not think C[IBBE]R or TIBBALD here so happy, but rather a stanch, vigorous, season'd, and dry, old Gentleman, whom I have in my eye.

I could also wish at this juncture, such a person, as is truly jealous of the honour and dignity of Poetry; no Joker, or Trifler; but a Bard in good earnest; nay, not amiss, if a Critic, and the better if a little obstinate. For when we consider what great privileges have been lost from this office, (as we see from the fore-cited authentic record of *Jovius*) namely those of *feeding* from the *Prince's table, drinking* out of his *own flaggon,* becoming even his *domestic* and *companion;* it requires a man warm and resolute, to be able to claim and obtain the restoring of these high honours. I have cause to fear the most of the Candidates would be liable, either through the influence of Ministers, or for rewards or favours, to give up the glorious rights of the Laureate: yet I am not without hopes, there is *one,* from whom a *serious* and *steady* assertion of these privileges may be expected; and, if there be such a one, I must do him the justice to say, it is Mr. D[ENNI]s, the worthy President of our Society.

13. A Letter to
a Noble Lord

A *Letter to a Noble Lord* was addressed by Pope to John, Lord Hervey (1696-1743). The origins of the quarrel between them are obscure, as are the reasons for Pope's estrangement from Lady Mary Wortley Montagu (1689-1762), with whom he had once had a close friendship (see Robert Halsband, *The Life of Lady Mary Wortley Montagu* (1956), Mack, and *Corr., passim*). In 1728 Lady Mary appeared briefly in *The Dunciad* (A ii 128; see *Poems* iv xv-xx). In February 1733 Pope published the first of his *Imitations of Horace,* a version of *Satire* II i, which included a slighting reference to Lady Mary (ll. 83-4), while line 6 ('Lord *Fanny* spins a thousand such a Day') was taken by Hervey to refer to himself. A rejoinder appeared in March 1733 entitled *Verses address'd to the Imitator of the First Satire of the Second Book of Horace. By a Lady.* This may well have been the work of Lady Mary and Hervey jointly, and it was followed in August by Hervey's verses, *An Epistle from a Nobleman to a Doctor of Divinity,* which was printed in November 1733. These two attacks (reprinted below in Appendix B) are quoted and alluded to throughout Pope's reply, the *Letter to a Noble Lord* dated 30 November 1733. Pope decided not to print this letter; on 6 January 1734 he wrote to Swift: 'There is a Woman's war declar'd against me by a certain Lord, his weapons are the same which women and children use, a pin to scratch, and a squirt to bespatter. I writ a sort of answer, but was ashamed to enter the lists with him, and after shewing it to some people, suppress it: otherwise it was such as was worthy of him and worthy of me.' (*Corr.* iii 401). Several other writers took up the cudgels against Hervey in some indifferent verses (see Guerinot, 336-7, 339-41; and *The Knight and the Prelate* (1734)). Later that year the question of how to conduct himself in public as a satirist arose in exchanges with Dr Arbuthnot, first in prose letters (see no. 29 below) and then in the verse *Epistle to Dr. Arbuthnot,* composed in August 1734 and printed the following January. This is in some respects a companion piece to the present *Letter,* and includes the famous characterization of Hervey as Sporus.

Text: The *Letter* was first printed by Warburton in volume eight of *The Works of Alexander Pope Esq.,* 9 vols (1751).

Selected prose of Alexander Pope

A
LETTER
TO A
NOBLE LORD.

on occasion of some Libels written and propagated at
Court, in the Year 1732-3.

My Lord, Nov. 30, 1733.

Your Lordship's Epistle has been publish'd some days, but I had
not the pleasure and pain of seeing it till yesterday: Pain, to think your
Lordship should attack me at all; Pleasure, to find that you can attack
me so weakly. As I want not the humility, to think myself in every way
but *one* your inferiour, it seems but reasonable that I should take the
only method either of self-defence or retaliation, that is left me,
against a person of your quality and power. And as by your choice of
this weapon, your pen, you generously (and modestly too, no doubt)
meant to put yourself upon a level with me; I will as soon believe that
your Lordship would give a wound to a man unarm'd, as that you
would deny me the use of it in my own defence.

I presume you will allow me to take the same liberty, in my answer
to so *candid, polite,* and *ingenious* a Nobleman, which your Lordship
took in yours, to so *grave, religious* and *respectable* a Clergyman: As you
answered his *Latin* in *English,* permit me to answer your *Verse* in *Prose.*
And tho' your Lordship's reasons for not writing in *Latin,* might be
stronger than mine for not writing in *Verse,* yet I may plead *Two good*
ones, for this conduct: the one that I want the Talent of spinning *a
thousand lines in a* Day (which, I think, is as much *Time* as this subject
deserves) and the other, that I take your Lordship's *Verse* to be as
much *Prose* as this letter. But no doubt it was your choice, in writing to
a friend, to renounce all the pomp of Poetry, and to give us this
excellent model of the familiar.

When I consider the *great difference* betwixt the rank your *Lordship*
holds in the *World,* and the rank which your *writings* are like to hold in
the *learned world,* I presume that distinction of style is but necessary,
which you will see observ'd thro' this letter. When I speak of *you,* my
Lord, it will be with all the deference due to the inequality which
Fortune has made between you and myself: but when I speak of your
writings, my Lord, I must, I can do nothing but trifle.

I should be obliged indeed to lessen this *Respect,* if all the Nobility
(and especially the elder brothers) are but so many hereditary fools, if
the privilege of Lords be to want brains, if noblemen can hardly write

or read, if all their business is but to dress and vote, and all their employment in court, to tell lies, flatter in public, slander in private, be false to each other, and follow nothing but self-interest. Bless me, my Lord, what an account is this you give of them? and what would have been had said of me, had I immolated, in this manner, the whole body of the Nobility, at the stall of a well-fed Prebendary?

Were it the mere *Excess* of your Lordship's *Wit*, that carried you thus triumphantly over all the bounds of decency, I might consider your Lordship on your *Pegasus,* as a sprightly hunter on a mettled horse; and while you were trampling down all our works, patiently suffer the injury, in pure admiration of the *Noble Sport*. But should the case be quite otherwise, should your Lordship be only like a *Boy* that is *run away with*; and run away with by a *Very Foal*; really common charity, as well as respect for a noble family, would oblige me to stop your carreer, and to *help you down* from *this Pegasus*.

Surely the little praise of a *Writer* should be a thing below your ambition: You, who were no sooner born, but in the lap of the Graces; no sooner at school, but in the arms of the Muses; no sooner in the World, but you practis'd all the skill of it; no sooner in the Court, but you possess'd all the art of it! Unrivall'd as you are, in making a figure, and in making a speech, methinks, my Lord, you may well give up the poor talent of turning a Distich. And why this fondness for Poetry? Prose admits of the two excellencies you most admire, Diction and Fiction: It admits of the talents you chiefly possess, a most fertile invention, and most florid expression; it is with prose, nay the plainest prose, that you best could teach our nobility to vote, which, you justly observe, is half at least of their business: And, give me leave to prophesy, it is to your talent in prose, and not in verse, to your speaking, not your writing, to your art at court, not your art of poetry, that your Lordship must owe your future figure in the world.

My Lord, whatever you imagine, this is the advice of a Friend, and one who remembers he formerly had the honour of some profession of Friendship from you: Whatever was his *real share* in it, whether small or great, yet as your Lordship could never have had the least *Loss* by continuing it, or the least *Interest* by withdrawing it; the misfortune of losing it, I fear, must have been owing to his own *deficiency* or *neglect*. But as to any *actual fault* which deserved to forfeit it in such a degree, he protests he is to this day guiltless and ignorant. It could at most be but a fault of *omission*; but indeed by omissions, men of your Lordship's uncommon merit may sometimes think themselves so injur'd, as to be capable of an inclination to injure another; who, tho' very much below their quality, may be above the injury.

Selected prose of Alexander Pope

I never heard of the least displeasure you had conceived against me, till I was told that an imitation I had made of *Horace* had offended some persons, and among them your Lordship. I could not have apprehended that a few *general strokes* about a *Lord scribling carelesly,* a *Pimp,* or a *Spy* at Court, a *Sharper* in a gilded chariot, &c. that these, I say, should be ever applied as they have been, by *any malice* but that which is the greatest in the world, *the Malice of Ill people to themselves.*

Your Lordship so well knows (and the whole Court and town thro' your means so well know) how far the resentment was carried upon that imagination, not only in the *Nature* of the *Libel* you propagated against me, but in the extraordinary *manner, place,* and *presence* in which it was propagated; that I shall only say, it seem'd to me to exceed the bounds of justice, common sense, and decency.

I wonder yet more, how a *Lady,* of great wit, beauty, and fame for her poetry (between whom and your Lordship there is a *natural,* a *just,* and a *well-grounded esteem*) could be prevail'd upon to take a part in that proceeding. Your resentments against me indeed might be equal, as my offence to you both was the same; for neither had I the least misunderstanding with that Lady, till after I was the *Author* of my own misfortune in discontinuing her acquaintance. I may venture to own a truth, which cannot be unpleasing to either of you; I assure you my reason for so doing, was merely that you had both *too much wit* for me; and that I could not do, with *mine,* many things which you could with *yours.* The injury done you in withdrawing myself could be but small, if the value you had for me was no greater than you have been pleas'd since to profess. But surely, my Lord, one may say, neither the Revenge, nor the Language you held, bore any *proportion* to the pretended offence: The appellations of *Foe* to *humankind,* an *Enemy* like the *Devil* to all that have *Being; ungrateful, unjust,* deserving to be *whipt, blanketed, kicked,* nay *killed;* a *Monster,* an *Assassin,* whose conversation every man ought to *shun,* and against whom *all doors* should be shut; I beseech you, my Lord, had you the least right to give, or to encourage or justify any other in giving such language as this to me? Could I be treated in terms more strong or more atrocious, if, during my acquaintance with you, I had been a *Betrayer,* a *Backbiter,* a *Whisperer,* an *Eves-dropper,* or an *Informer?* Did I in all that time ever throw a *false Dye,* or palm *a foul Card* upon you? Did I ever *borrow, steal,* or accept, either *Money, Wit,* or *Advice* from you? Had I ever the honour to join with either of you in one *Ballad, Satire, Pamphlet,* or *Epigram,* on any person *living* or *dead?* Did I ever do you so great an injury as to put off *my own Verses* for *yours,* especially on *those Persons* whom they might *most offend?* I am confident you cannot answer in the affirmative; and I can truly affirm, that, ever since I lost the happiness of your conversation I have not published or written, one syllable of, or to either of you; never hitch'd your *names* in a *Verse*, or trifled with your *good names* in *company*. Can I be honestly charged with any other crime but an *Omission* (for the word *Neglect*, which I us'd before, slip'd my pen unguardedly) to continue my admiration of you all my life, and still to contemplate, face to face, your many excellencies and perfections? I am persuaded you can reproach me truly with no great *Faults*, except my *natural ones*, which I am as ready to own, as to do all justice to the contrary *Beauties* in you. It is true, my Lord, I am short, not well shap'd, generally ill-dress'd, if not sometimes dirty: Your Lordship and Ladyship are still in bloom; your Figures such, as rival the *Apollo* of *Belvedere*, and the *Venus* of *Medicis*; and your faces so finish'd, that neither sickness nor passion can deprive them of *Colour*; I will allow your own in particular to be the finest that ever *Man* was blest with: preserve it, my Lord, and reflect, that to be a Critic, would cost it too many *frowns*, and to be a Statesman, too many *wrinkles!* I further confess, I am now somewhat old; but so your Lordship and this excellent Lady, with all your beauty, will (I hope) one day be. I know your Genius and hers so perfectly *tally*, that you cannot but join in admiring each other, and by consequence in the contempt of all such as myself. You have both, in my regard, been like – (your Lordship, I know, loves a *Simile*, and it will be one suitable to your *Quality*) you have been like *Two Princes*, and I like a *poor Animal* sacrificed between them to cement a lasting League: I hope I have not bled in vain; but that such an amity may endure for ever! For tho' it be what common *understandings* would hardly conceive, Two *Wits* however may be persuaded, that it is in Friendship as in Enmity, The more *danger*, the more *honour*.

Give me the liberty, my Lord, to tell you, why I never replied to those *Verses* on the *Imitator* of *Horace?* They regarded nothing but my *Figure*, which I set no value upon; and my *Morals*, which, I knew, needed no defence: Any honest man has the pleasure to be conscious, that it is out of the power of the *Wittiest*, nay the *Greatest Person* in the kingdom, to lessen him *that way*, but at the expence of his own *Truth*, *Honour*, or *Justice*.

But tho' I declin'd to explain myself just at the time when I was sillily threaten'd, I shall now give your Lordship a frank account of the offence you imagined to be meant to you. *Fanny* (my Lord) is the plain English of *Fannius*, a real person, who was a foolish Critic, and an enemy of *Horace:* perhaps a Noble one; for so (if your Latin be gone in earnest) I must acquaint you, the word *Beatus* may be construed.

Selected prose of Alexander Pope

Beatus Fannius! ultro
Delatis capsis et imagine.[1]

This *Fannius* was, it seems, extremely fond both of his *Poetry* and his *Person,* which appears by the pictures and *Statues* he caused to be made of himself, and by his great diligence to propagate *bad Verses* at *Court,* and get them admitted into the library of *Augustus.* He was moreover of a delicate or *effeminate complexion,* and constant at the Assemblies and Opera's of those days, where he took it into his head to *slander poor Horace.*

Ineptus
Fannius, *Hermogenis* lædat *conviva Tigelli.*[2]

till it provoked him at last just to *name* him, give him a *lash,* and send him whimpering to the *Ladies.*

Discipularum *inter jubeo plorare cathedras.*[3]

So much for *Fanny,* my Lord. The word *spins* (as Dr. *Freind* or even Dr. *Sherwin* could assure you) was the literal translation of *deduci;* a metaphor taken from a *Silk-worm,* my Lord, to signify any *slight, silken,* or (as your Lordship and the Ladies call it) *flimzy* piece of work. I presume your Lordship has enough of this, to convince you there was nothing *personal* but to *that Fannius,* who (with all his fine accomplishments) had never been heard of, but for *that Horace* he injur'd.

In regard to the right honourable Lady, your Lordship's friend, I was far from designing a person of her condition by a name so derogatory to her, as that of *Sappho;* a name prostituted to every infamous Creature that ever wrote Verses or Novels. I protest I never *apply'd* that name to her in any verse of mine, *public* or *private;* and (I firmly believe) not in any *Letter* or *Conversation.* Whoever could invent a Falsehood to support an accusation, I pity; and whoever can believe such a Character to be theirs, I pity still more. God forbid the Court or Town should have the complaisance to *join* in that opinion! Certainly I meant it only of such modern *Sappho's,* as imitate much more the *Lewdness* than the *Genius* of the ancient one; and upon whom their wretched brethren frequently bestow both the *Name* and the *Qualification* there mentioned.

There was another reason why I was silent as to that paper – I took it for a *Lady's* (on the printer's word in the title page,) and thought it too presuming, as well as indecent, to contend with one of that *Sex* in *altercation:* For I never was so mean a creature as to commit my Anger against a *Lady* to *paper,* tho' but in a *private Letter.* But soon after, her denial of it was brought to me by a Noble person of *real Honour* and *Truth.* Your Lordship indeed said you had it from a Lady, and the Lady said it was your Lordship's; some thought the beautiful by-blow had *Two Fathers,* or (if one of them will hardly be allow'd a man) *Two*

Mothers; indeed I think *both Sexes* had a share in it, but which was *uppermost*, I know not: I pretend not to determine the exact method of this *Witty Fornication:* and, if I call it *Yours,* my Lord, 'tis only because, whoever *got* it, you *brought it forth.*

Here, my Lord, allow me to observe the different proceeding of the *Ignoble poet,* and his *Noble Enemies.* What he has written of *Fanny, Adonis, Sappho,* or who you will, he own'd he publish'd, he set his name to: What they have *publish'd* of him, they have deny'd to have *written*; and what they have *written* of him, they have deny'd to have *publish'd.* One of these was the case in the past Libel, and the other in the present. For tho' the parent has own'd it to a few choice friends, it is such as he has been obliged to deny in the most particular terms, to the great Person whose opinion *concern'd him most.*

Yet, my Lord, this Epistle was a piece not written in *haste,* or in a *passion,* but many months after all pretended provocation; when you was at *full leisure* at Hampton-Court, and I the object *singled,* like a *Deer out of Season,* for so ill-timed, and ill-placed a diversion. It was a *deliberate* work, directed to a *Reverend Person,* of the most *serious* and *sacred* character, with whom you are known to cultivate a *strict correspondence,* and to whom it will not be doubted, but you open your *secret Sentiments,* and deliver your *real judgment* of men and things. This, I say, my Lord, with submission, could not but awaken all my *Reflection* and *Attention.* Your Lordship's opinion of me as a *Poet,* I cannot help; it is yours, my Lord, and that were enough to mortify a poor man; but it is not yours *alone,* you must be content to share it with the *Gentlemen* of the *Dunciad,* and (it may be) with many *more innocent* and *ingenious men.* If your Lordship destroys my *poetical* character, *they* will claim their part in the glory; but, give me leave to say, if my *moral* character be ruin'd, it must be *wholly* the work of *your Lordship*; and will be hard even for you to do, unless I *myself co-operate.*

How can you talk (my most worthy Lord) of all *Pope's* Works as so many *Libels,* affirm, that *he has no invention* but in *Defamation,* and charge him with *selling another man's labours printed with his own name?* Fye, my Lord, you forget yourself. He printed not his name before a line of the person's you mention; that person himself has told you and all the world in the book itself, what part he had in it, as may be seen at the conclusion of his notes to the Odyssey. I can only suppose your Lordship (not having at that time *forgot your Greek*) despis'd to look upon the *Translation*; and ever since entertain'd too mean an Opinion of the Translator to cast an eye upon it. Besides, my Lord, when you said he *sold* another man's works, you ought in justice to have added that he *bought* them, which very much *alters the Case.* What he gave him was five hundred pounds: his receipt can be produced to your Lordship. I dare not affirm that he was as *well paid* as *some Writers* (much his inferiors) have been since; but your Lordship will reflect that I am no man of Quality, either to *buy* or *sell* scribling so high: and that I have neither *Place, Pension,* nor Power to reward for *secret Services.* It cannot be, that one of your rank can have the least *Envy* to such an author as I: but were that possible, it were much better gratify'd by employing *not your own,* but some of *those low and ignoble pens* to do you this *mean office.* I dare engage you'll have them for less than I gave Mr. Broom, if your friends have not rais'd the market: Let them drive the bargain for you, my Lord; and you may depend on seeing, every day in the week, as many (and now and then as pretty) Verses, as these of your Lordship.

And would it not be full as well, that my poor person should be abus'd by them, as by one of your rank and quality? Cannot *Curl* do the same? nay, has he not done it before your Lordship, in the same *kind of Language,* and almost the *same words?* I cannot but think, the worthy and *discreet Clergyman* himself will agree, it is *improper,* nay *unchristian*, to expose the *personal* defects of our brother: that both such perfect forms as yours, and such unfortunate ones as mine, proceed from the hand of the same *Maker,* who *fashioneth his Vessels* as he pleaseth, and that it is not from their *shape* we can tell whether they are made for *honour* or *dishonour*. In a word, he would teach you Charity to your greatest enemies; of which number, my Lord, I cannot be reckon'd, since, tho' a Poet, I was never your flatterer.

Next, my Lord, as to the *Obscurity of my Birth,* (a reflection copy'd also from Mr. *Curl* and his brethren,) I am sorry to be obliged to such a presumption as to name my *Family* in the same leaf with your Lordship's: but my Father had the honour in one instance to resemble you, for he was a *younger Brother.* He did not indeed think it a happiness to bury his *elder Brother,* tho' he had one, who wanted some of those good qualities which *yours* possess. How sincerely glad could I be, to pay to that young Nobleman's memory the debt I ow'd to his friendship,[4] whose early death depriv'd your family of as much *Wit* and *Honour* as he left behind him in any branch of it. But as to my Father, I could assure you, my Lord, that he was no mechanic (neither a hatter, nor, which might please your Lordship yet better, a Cobler) but in truth, of a very tolerable family: And my Mother of an ancient one, as well born and educated as that Lady, whom your Lordship made choice of to be the *Mother of your own Children*;[5] whose merit, beauty, and vivacity (if transmitted to your posterity) will be a *better present* than even the noble blood they derive *only* from *you.* A Mother, on whom I was never oblig'd so far to reflect, as to say she *spoiled me*. And a Father, who never found himself oblig'd to say of me, that he *disapprov'd my Conduct*. In a word, my Lord, I think it enough, that my Parents, such as they were, never cost me a *Blush*; and that their Son, such as he is, never cost them a *Tear*.

I have purposely omitted to consider your Lordship's Criticisms on my *Poetry*. As they are exactly the same with those of the *foremention'd Authors,* I apprehend they would justly charge me with partiality, if I gave to *you* what belongs to *them*; or paid more distinction to the *same things* when they are in your mouth, than when they were in theirs. It will be shewing both them and you (my Lord) a *more particular respect,* to observe how much they are honour'd by *your Imitation of them,* which indeed is carried thro' your whole Epistle. I have read somewhere at *School*, (tho' I make it no *Vanity* to have forgot where) that *Tully* naturaliz'd a few phrases at the instance of some of his friends. Your Lordship has done more in honour of these Gentlemen; you have authoriz'd not only their *Assertions,* but their *Style*. For example, *A* Flow *that* wants skill *to restrain its* ardour, – *a* Dictionary *that gives us nothing at* its own expence. – *As luxuriant branches* bear *but little fruit, so Wit unprun'd is but raw fruit – While you* rehearse ignorance, *you still* know enough *to do it in Verse – Wits* are *but glittering* ignorance. – The *account of* how *we pass our time –* and, *The weight on Sir R.W.—'s* brain. *You can* ever *receive from* no *head more than such a head* (as no head) *has to give:* Your Lordship would have said *never* receive instead of *ever*, and *any head* instead of *no head:* but all this is perfectly new, and has greatly enrich'd our language.

You are merry, my Lord, when you say, *Latin* and *Greek*
> *Have quite deserted your poor* John Trot-head,
> *And left plain native English in their stead,*

for (to do you justice) this is nothing less than *plain English*. And as for your *John Trot-head,* I can't conceive why you should give it that name; for by some papers I have seen sign'd with that name, it is certainly a head *very different* from your Lordship's.[6]

˙ Your Lordship seems determined to fall out with every thing you have learn'd at school: you complain next of a *dull Dictionary*,
> *That gives us nothing at its own expence,*
> *But a few modern words for ancient Sense.*

Your Lordship is the first man that ever carried the love of Wit so far, as to expect a *witty Dictionary*. A Dictionary that gives us *any thing but words,* must not only be an *expensive* but a very *extravagant Dictionary*. But what does your Lordship mean by its giving us but *a few modern words* for *ancient Sense*? If by *Sense* (as I suspect) you mean *words (a mistake not unusual)* I must do the Dictionary the justice to say, that it gives us *just as many modern words as ancient ones.* Indeed, my Lord, you have more need to complain of a bad Grammar, than of a dull Dictionary.

Doctor *Freind,* I dare answer for him, never taught you to talk
of Sapphic, Lyric, and Iambic Odes.

Your Lordship might as well bid your present Tutor, your Taylor, make you a *Coat, Suit of Cloaths,* and *Breeches*; for you must have forgot your Logic, as well as Grammar, not to know, that Sapphic and Iambic are both included in Lyric; that being the *Genus,* and those the *Species.*

For all cannot invent who can translate,
No more than those who cloath us, can create.

Here your Lordship seems in labour for a meaning. Is it that you would have Translations, *Originals?* for 'tis the common opinion, that the *business* of a Translator is to *translate,* and not to *invent,* and of a Taylor to *cloath,* and not to *create.* But why should you, my Lord, of all mankind, abuse a Taylor? not to say *blaspheme* him; if he can (as some think) at least go halves with God Almighty in the formation of a *Beau.* Might not Doctor *Sherwin* rebuke you for this, and bid you *Remember your* Creator *in the days of your Youth?*[7]

From a *Taylor,* your Lordship proceeds (by a beautiful gradation) to a *Silkman.*

Thus P—pe we find
The gaudy Hinchcliff of a beauteous mind.

Here too is some ambiguity. Does your Lordship use *Hinchcliff* as a *proper name?* or as the Ladies say a *Hinchcliff* or a *Colmar,* for a *Silk* or a *Fan?* I will venture to affirm, no Critic can have a perfect taste of your Lordship's works, who does not understand both your *Male Phrase* and your *Female Phrase.*

Your Lordship, to finish your Climax, advances up to a *Hatter;* a Mechanic, whose Employment you inform us, is not (as was generally imagined) to *cover people's heads,* but to *dress their brains.* A most useful Mechanic indeed! I can't help wishing to have been one, for some people's sake. – But this too may be only another *Lady-Phrase:* Your Lordship and the Ladies may take a *Head-dress* for a *Head,* and understand, that to *adorn the Head* is the same thing as to *dress the Brains.*

Upon the whole, I may thank your Lordship for this high Panegyric: For if I have but *dress'd* up *Homer,* as your *Taylor, Silkman,* and *Hatter,* have *equipp'd your Lordship,* I must be own'd to have dress'd him *marvellously indeed,* and no wonder if he is *admir'd by the Ladies.*

A Letter to a Noble Lord

After all, my Lord, I really wish you would learn your *Grammar*. What if you put yourself awhile under the Tuition of your Friend *W—m?*[8] May not I with all respect say to you, what was said to *another Noble Poet*[9] by Mr. Cowley, *Pray, Mr.* Howard, *if you did read your* Grammar, *what harm would it do you?* You yourself wish all Lords would *learn to write;* tho' I don't see of what use it could be, if their whole business is to *give their Votes:* It could only be serviceable in *signing their Protests.* Yet surely this small portion of learning might be indulged to your Lordship, without any *Breach* of that *Privilege* you so generously assert to all those of your rank, or too great an Infringement of that *Right* which you claim as *Hereditary,* and for which, no doubt, your noble Father will thank you. Surely, my Lord, no Man was ever so bent upon depreciating himself!

All your Readers have observ'd the following Lines:

> *How oft we hear some Witling pert and dull,*
> *By fashion Coxcomb, and by nature Fool,*
> *With hackney Maxims, in dogmatic strain,*
> *Scoffing Religion and the Marriage chain?*
> *Then from his Common-place-book he repeats,*
> *The Lawyers all are rogues, and Parsons cheats,*
> *That Vice and Virtue's nothing but a jest,*
> *And all Morality Deceit well drest:*
> *That Life itself is like a wrangling game,* &c.

The whole Town and Court (my good Lord) have heard *this Witling*; who is so much every body's acquaintance but his own, that I'll engage *they all name* the *same Person*. But to hear *you* say, that this is only — *of whipt Cream* a *frothy Store,* is a sufficient proof, that never mortal was endued with so humble an opinion both of himself and his own Wit, as your Lordship: For, I do assure you, these are by much the best Verses in your whole Poem.

How unhappy is it for me, that a Person of your Lordship's *Modesty* and *Virtue,* who manifests so tender a regard to *Religion, Matrimony,* and *Morality*; who, tho' an Ornament to the Court, cultivate an exemplary Correspondence with the *Clergy*; nay, who disdain not charitably to converse with, and even assist, some of the very worst of Writers (so far as to cast a few *Conceits,* or drop a few *Antitheses* even among the *Dear Joys* of the *Courant*) that you, I say, should look upon Me alone as reprobate and unamendable! Reflect what *I was,* and what *I am.* I am even *Annihilated* by your Anger: For in these Verses you have robbed me of *all power to think,* and, in your others, of the very *name* of a *Man!* Nay, to shew that this is wholly your own doing, you have told us that before I wrote my *last Epistles* (that is, before I unluckily mention'd *Fanny* and *Adonis*, whom, I protest, I knew not to be your Lordship's Relations,) *I might have lived and died in glory.*

What would I not do to be well with your Lordship? Tho', you observe, I am a mere *Imitator* of *Homer, Horace, Boileau, Garth,* &c. (which I have the less cause to be asham'd of, since they were *Imitators of one another*) yet what if I should solemnly engage never to imitate *your* Lordship? May it not be one step towards an accommodation, that while you remark my *Ignorance in Greek,* you are so good as to say, you have *forgot your own?* What if I should confess I translated from *D'Acier?*[10] That surely could not but oblige your Lordship, who are known to prefer *French* to all the learned Languages. But allowing that in the space of *twelve years* acquaintance with *Homer,* I might unhappily contract as much *Greek,* as your Lordship did in *Two* at the University, why may not I forget it again, as happily?

Till such a reconciliation take effect, I have but one thing to intreat of your Lordship. It is, that you will not decide of my *Principles* on the same grounds as you have done of my *Learning:* Nor give the same account of my *Want of Grace,* after you have lost all acquaintance with my *Person,* as you do of my *Want of Greek,* after you have confessedly lost all acquaintance with the *Language.* You are too generous, my Lord, to follow the *Gentlemen* of the *Dunciad* quite so far, as to seek my *utter Perdition:* as *Nero* once did *Lucan's,* merely for presuming to be a *Poet,* while one of so much greater quality was a *Writer.* I therefore make this humble request to your Lordship, that the next time you please *to write of me, speak of me,* or even *whisper of me,* you will recollect it is full *eight Years* since I had the honour of *any conversation* or *correspondence* with your Lordship, except *just half an hour* in a Lady's Lodgings at Court, and then I had the happiness of her being present all the time. It would therefore be difficult even for your Lordship's penetration to tell, to what, or from what *Principles, Parties,* or *Sentiments,* Moral, Political, or Theological, I may have been converted, or perverted in all that time. I beseech your Lordship to consider, the Injury a Man of your *high Rank* and *Credit* may do to a *private Person* under *Penal Laws* and many other disadvantages, not for want of *honesty* or *conscience,* but merely perhaps for having too *weak a head,* or too *tender a heart.* It is by *these alone* I have hitherto liv'd excluded from all *posts* of *Profit* or *Trust:* As I can interfere with the *Views* of *no man,* do not deny me, my Lord, *all that is left,* a little *Praise,* or the common Encouragement due, if not to my *Genius,* at least to my *Industry.*

Above all, your Lordship will be careful not to wrong my *Moral Character* with THOSE under whose *Protection* I live, and thro' whose

A Letter to a Noble Lord

Lenity alone I can live with Comfort.[11] Your Lordship, I am confident, upon consideration will think, you inadvertently went a little *too far* when you recommended to THEIR perusal, and strengthened by the weight of your Approbation, a *Libel,* mean in its reflections upon my poor *figure,* and scandalous in those on my *Honour* and *Integrity:* wherein I was represented as *"an Enemy* to Human Race, a *Murderer* of Reputations, and a *Monster* mark'd by God like *Cain,* deserving to wander accurs'd thro' the World."

A strange Picture of a Man, who had the good fortune to enjoy many friends, who will be always remember'd as the first Ornaments of their Age and Country; and no Enemies that ever contriv'd to be heard of, except Mr. *John Dennis,* and your Lordship: A Man, who never wrote a Line in which the *Religion* or *Government* of his Country, the *Royal Family,* or their *Ministry* were disrespectfully mention'd; the Animosity of any one Party gratify'd at the expence of another; or any Censure past, but upon *known Vice, acknowledg'd Folly,* or *aggressing Impertinence.* It is with infinite pleasure he finds, that *some Men* who seem *asham'd* and *afraid* of *nothing else,* are so very sensible of *his Ridicule:* And 'tis for that very reason he resolves (by the grace of God, and your Lordship's good leave)

> *That while he breathes, no rich or noble knave*
> *Shall walk the world in credit to his grave.*

This, he thinks, is rendering the best Service he can to the Publick, and even to the good Government of his Country; and for this, at least, he may deserve some Countenance, even from the GREATEST PERSONS in it. Your Lordship knows of WHOM I speak. Their NAMES I should be as sorry, and as much asham'd, to place near *yours,* on such an occasion, as I should be to see *You,* my Lord, placed so near *their* PERSONS, if you could ever make so ill an Use of their Ear as to asperse or misrepresent any one innocent Man.

This is all I shall ever ask of your Lordship, except your pardon for this tedious letter. I have the honour to be, with equal *Respect* and *Concern,*

My Lord,
Your truly devoted Servant,
A. POPE.

14. Selections from the Correspondence

Pope was a prolific letter writer (his collected correspondence runs to more than 2,200 pages, Dryden's barely to 140). His letters to Henry Cromwell were printed by the unscrupulous Curll in 1726, while Pope himself published his correspondence with Wycherley in 1729. But Pope wanted a collection of his letters printed, and in 1735 managed to trick Curll into publishing such a work, which he then denounced as a piracy. This gave Pope the chance to issue a definitive edition. The complex story of the publication of Pope's letters is set out by Sherburn in *Corr.* i xi-xxv. Sherburn's editorial practice was to print from manuscripts, or from the printed texts which seemed closest to the letter as originally written. This method gives us the letters primarily as biographical documents; the practice adopted here is, for the most part, to treat the letters as literary works, and to give them in the form in which Pope wanted his public to read them. Pope frequently revised (or even fabricated) letters for publication, and this process can be studied in the apparatus to *Corr.*

Text: Of the letters printed here, nos. 1-3, 5, 8, 10, 12-17, 19, 21-4 are taken from Pope's official edition, the *Letters of Mr. Alexander Pope* (1737); nos. 20, 25, 26, 28, 30, 31, 32 from his later collection, *The Works of Alexander Pope Esq;* volume IV (1742); no. 4 from British Library MS Add 36270; nos. 6, 7, 11 from British Library MS Add 28618; no. 9 from Harvard University Library MS Eng. 218.2, by permission of the Houghton Library; no. 18 from *Letters of Mr. Pope, and Several Eminent Persons* (1735); no. 27 from *The Gentleman's Magazine* 159 (1836) 29; and no. 33 from *The Quarterly Review* 139 (1875) 383-4.

Selections from the Correspondence

I

To William Walsh, 2 July 1706.

Walsh (1663-1708), poet and critic and friend of Dryden, was one of the earliest of Pope's influential literary friends. He commented on Pope's *Pastorals* in manuscript, and possibly on his *Essay on Criticism*, where his good judgment is commemorated in lines 729-36. Pope's letters to Walsh exhibit his precocious command of literary history and criticism. This letter already broaches several subjects which will be of continual interest to Pope: the advocacy of variety (cp. *Essay on Criticism* 239-42 and *Epistle to Burlington* 47-70), of simplicity rather than extravagance as the hallmark of true wit (cp. *Essay on Criticism* 289ff. and *Dunciad, passim*), and of the liberal use of one's predecessors (cp. *Essay on Criticism* 297-98).

I Cannot omit the first opportunity of making you my Acknowledgments for reviewing those Papers of mine. You have no less right to correct me, than the same hand that rais'd a tree has to prune it. I am convinc'd, as well as you, that one may correct too much; for in Poetry, as in Painting, a man may lay colours one upon another, till they stiffen and deaden the piece. Besides, to bestow heightning on every part is monstrous: some parts ought to be lower than the rest, and nothing looks more ridiculous, than a work where the thoughts, however different in their own nature, seem all on a level: 'Tis like a meadow newly mown, where weeds, grass, and flowers are all laid even, and appear undistinguish'd. I believe too, that sometimes our first thoughts are the best, as the first squeezing of the grapes makes the finest and richest wine.

I have not attempted any thing of a Pastoral Comedy, because I think the taste of our age will not relish a poem of that sort. People seek for what they call Wit, on all subjects, and in all places; not considering that nature loves truth so well, that it hardly ever admits of flourishing. Conceit is to nature what paint is to beauty; it is not only needless, but impairs what it wou'd improve. There is a certain majesty in simplicity which is far above all the quaintness of wit: insomuch that the Critics have excluded it from the loftiest poetry, as well as the lowest, and forbid it to the Epic no less than the Pastoral. I should certainly displease all those who are charm'd with Guarini and Bonarelli, and imitate Tasso not only in the simplicity of his thoughts, but in that of the fable too.[1] If surprizing Discoveries shou'd have place in the story of a pastoral comedy, I believe it wou'd be more agreeable to probability to make them the effects of chance than of design; intrigue not being very consistent with that innocence which ought to constitute a shepherd's character. There is nothing in all the

Aminta (as I remember) but happens by meer accident; unless it be the meeting of Aminta with Sylvia at the fountain, which is the contrivance of Daphne, and even that is the most simple in the world: The contrary is observable in Pastor Fido, where Corisca is so perfect a mistress of intrigue, that the plot cou'd not have been brought to pass without her. I am inclin'd to think the Pastoral Comedy has another disadvantage, as to the Manners: Its general design is to make us in love with the innocence of a rural life, so that to introduce shepherds of a vicious character must in some measure debase it; and hence it may come to pass, that even the virtuous characters will not shine so much, for want of being opposed to their contraries. – These thoughts are purely my own, and therefore I have reason to doubt them: but I hope your judgment will set me right.

I wou'd beg your opinion too as to another point: It is how far the liberty of *borrowing* may extend? I have defended it sometimes by saying, that it seems not so much the perfection of sense to say things that have never been said before, as to express those best that have been said oftenest; and that writers in the case of borrowing from others, are like trees which of themselves would produce only one sort of fruit, but by being grafted upon others may yield variety. A mutual commerce makes poetry flourish; but then poets, like merchants, should repay with something of their own what they take from others; not like pyrates, make prize of all they meet. I desire you to tell me sincerely, if I have not stretch'd this licence too far in these pastorals? I hope to become a critic by your precepts, and a poet by your example. Since I have seen your Eclogues, I cannot be much pleas'd with my own; however you have not taken away all my vanity, so long as you give me leave to profess my self Your, &c.

2

To Walsh, 22 October 1706.

This letter is in part similar to one which Pope wrote to Henry Cromwell (another of his friendly critics) on 25 November 1710, and Pope may have improved the letter to Walsh when preparing it for publication by adapting material from his letter to Cromwell. Pope's interest in versification is aired again in the *Essay on Criticism* 337-83.

After the thoughts I have already sent you on the subject of English Versification, you desire my opinion as to some farther particulars. There are indeed certain Niceties, which tho' not much observed even by correct versifiers, I cannot but think deserve to be better regarded.

Selections from the Correspondence

1. It is not enough that nothing offends the ear, but a good Poet will adapt the very Sounds as well as Words to the things he treats of, so that there is (if one may express it so) a Style of Sound: as in describing a gliding stream the numbers should run easy and flowing, in describing a rough torrent or deluge sonorous and swelling, and so of the rest. This is evident every where in Homer and Virgil, and no where else that I know of, to any observable degree. The following examples will make this plain, which I have taken from Vida.

> Molle viam tacito lapsu per levia radit.
> Incedit tardo molimine subsidendo.
> Luctantes ventos, tempestatesque sonoras.
> Immenso cum precipitans ruit Oceano Nox.
> Telum imbelle sine ictu, Conjecit.
> Tolle moras, cape saxa manu, cape robora Pastor.
> Ferte citi flammas, date tela, repellite pestem.[1]

This, I think, is what very few observe in practice, and is undoubtedly of wonderful force in imprinting the image on the reader. We have one excellent example of it in our language, Mr. Dryden's Ode on St. Cæcilia's day, entitled, Alexander's Feast.

2. Every nice ear must (I believe) have observ'd, that in any smooth English verse of ten syllables, there is naturally a Pause at the fourth, fifth, or sixth syllable. It is upon these the ear rests, and upon the judicious change and management of which depends the variety of versification. For example,

> At the fifth, Where-e'er thy navy ‖ spreads her canvass wings,
> At the fourth, Homage to thee ‖ and peace to all she brings.
> At the sixth, Like tracts of leverets ‖ in morning snow. [2]

Now I fancy, that to preserve an exact Harmony and Variety, the Pause at the 4th or 6th shou'd not be continu'd above three lines together, without the interposition of another; else it will be apt to weary the ear with one continu'd tone, at least it does mine: That at the 5th runs quicker, and carries not quite so dead a weight, therefore tires not so much, tho' it be continued longer.

3. Another nicety is in relation to Expletives, whether words or syllables, which are made use of purely to supply a vacancy: Do before verbs plural is absolutely such; and it is not improbable but future refiners may explode Did and Does in the same manner, which are almost always used for the sake of rhyme. The same cause has occasioned the promiscuous use of You and Thou to the same person, which can never sound so graceful as either one or the other.

4. I would also object to the irruption of Alexandrine verses, of twelve syllables, which I think should never be allow'd but when some remarkable beauty or propriety in them atones for the liberty: Mr.

Dryden has been too free of these, especially in his latter works. I am of the same opinion as to Triple Rhimes.

5. I could equally object to the Repetition of the same Rhimes within four or six lines of each other, as tiresome to the ear thro' their Monotony.

6. Monosyllable-lines, unless very artfully managed, are stiff, or languishing: but may be beautiful to express Melancholy, Slowness, or Labour.

7. To come to the Hiatus, or Gap between two words, which is caus'd by two vowels opening on each other (upon which you desire me to be particular) I think the rule in this case is either to use the Cæsura, or admit the Hiatus, just as the ear is least shock'd by either: For the Cæsura sometimes offends the ear more than the Hiatus itself, and our language is naturally over-charg'd with consonants: As for example, if in this verse,

The old have Int'rest ever in their eye,

we should say, to avoid the Hiatus,

But th' old have Int'rest—

The Hiatus which has the worst effect is when one word ends with the same vowel that begins the following; and next to this, those vowels whose sounds come nearest to each other are most to be avoided. O, A, or U, will bear a more full and graceful Sound than E, I, or Y. I know some people will think these observations trivial, and therefore I am glad to corroborate them by some great authorities, which I have met with in Tully and Quintilian. In the fourth book of Rhetoric to Herennius, are these words. *Fugiemus crebras vocalium concursiones, quæ vastam atque hiantem reddunt orationem; ut hoc est, "Baccæ æneæ amænissimæ impendebant."* [3] And Quintilian, l. 9. cap. 4. *Vocalium concursus cum accidit, hiat & intersisit, & quasi laborat oratio: pessimi longe quæ easdem inter se literas committunt, sonabunt: præcipuus tamen erit hiatus earum quæ cavo aut patulo ore efferuntur; E plenior litera est, I angustior.* But he goes on to reprove the excess on the other hand of being too sollicitous in this matter, and says admirably, *Nescio an negligentia in hoc, aut solicitudo sit pejor.* [4] So likewise *Tully (Orator ad Brut.) Theopompum reprehendunt, quod eas literas tanto opere fugerit, etsi idem magister ejus Isocrates:* which last author, as Turnebus on Quintilian observes, has hardly one Hiatus in all his works. Quintilian tells us that Tully and Demosthenes did not much observe this nicety, tho' Tully himself says in his Orator, *Crebra ista vocum concursio, quam magna ex parte vitiosam fugit Demosthenes.* [5] If I am not mistaken, Malherbe of all the moderns has been the most scrupulous in this point; [6] and I think Menage in his observations upon him says, he has not one in his poems. To conclude, I believe the Hiatus should be avoided with more care in Poetry than in Oratory; and I would constantly try to prevent it, unless where the cutting it off is more prejudicial to the sound than the Hiatus itself. I am, &c.

3

To William Wycherley, 29 November 1707.

Wycherley (?1641-1716) was another of Pope's distinguished friends in his early years. Pope revised some of Wycherley's poems to accommodate them to modern taste, and these revised texts, together with Pope's letters to Wycherley, were printed in the second volume of Wycherley's *Posthumous Works* (1729).

The compliments you make me, in regard of any inconsiderable service I could do you, are very unkind, and do but tell me in other words, that my friend has so mean an opinion of me, as to think I expect acknowledgments for trifles: which upon my faith I shall equally take amiss, whether made to my self, or to any other. For God's sake, (my dear friend) think better of me, and believe I desire no sort of favour so much, as that of serving you more considerably than I have been yet able to do.

I shall proceed in this manner with some others of your pieces; but since you desire I would not deface your copy for the future, and only mark the repetitions; I must, as soon as I've mark'd these, transcribe what is left on another paper; and in that, blot, alter, and add all I can devise, for their improvement. For you are sensible, the omission of Repetitions is but one, and the easiest part, of yours and my design; there remaining besides to rectify the Method, to connect the Matter, and to mend the Expression and Versification. I will go next upon the poems of Solitude, on the Publick and on the mixt Life, the bill of Fare, the praises of Avarice, and some others.

I must take notice of what you say, of my pains to make your dulness methodical; and of your hint, that the sprightliness of wit despises method. This is true enough, if by wit you mean no more than fancy or conceit; but in the better notion of wit, consider'd as propriety, surely Method is not only necessary for perspicuity and harmony of parts, but gives beauty even to the minute and particular thoughts; which receive an additional advantage from those which precede or follow in their due place. You remember a simile Mr. Dryden us'd in conversation, of feathers in the crowns of the wild Indians, which they not only chuse for the beauty of their colours, but place them in such a manner as to reflect a lustre on each other. I will not disguise any of my sentiments from you: to methodise in your case, is full as necessary as to strike out; otherwise you had better destroy the whole frame, and reduce them into single thoughts in prose, like Rochfoucault,[1] as I have more than once hinted to you.

4

To Ralph Bridges, 5 April [1708].

Bridges was the nephew of Sir William Trumbull, Pope's friend and informal tutor in the classics. This letter refers not to the complete translation of Homer, but to the extracts which Pope was translating in 1707-8. Pope sent the episode of Sarpedon (from *Iliad* XII and XVI) to Bridges for his comments, which still survive: see *Poems* i 352-60. This translation first appeared in part six of Tonson's *Miscellanies* (1709).

Sir,—The favour of your Letter with your Remarks, can never be enough acknowledged; and the speed, with which you Discharg'd so troublesome a Task, doubles the obligation. I must own you have pleased me very much by the commendations so ill bestowed upon me; but I assure you, much more by the frankness of your Censure; which I ought to take the more kindly of the two, as it is more advantageous to a Scribler to be improved in his Judgment, then to be sooth'd in his vanity. The greater part of those deviations from the Greek, which you have observ'd, I was led into by Chapman and Hobbes,[1] who are (it seems) as much celebrated for their knowledge of the Original, as they are decry'd, for the baldness of their Translations. Chapman pretends to have restor'd the genuine Sence of his Author, from the mistakes of all the former Explainers, in several Hundred places: And the Cambridge Editors of the large Homer, in Greek and Latin, attributed so much to Hobbes, that they confess they have corrected the old Latin Interpretation very often by his version. for my part I generally took the Authors meaning to be as you have explain'd it; yet their Authority, join'd to the knowledge of my own imperfectness in the Language, over-ruled me. However, Sir, you may be confident I think you in the right, because you happen to be of my opinion: (for men (let 'em say what they will) never approve any other's sense, but as it squares with their own). But you have made me much more proud of, and positive in my Judgment, since it is strenghthen'd by your's. I think your Criticismes, which regard the Expression, very just, and shall make my profit of them: To give you some proof that I am in earnest, I will alter three verses on your bare objection, tho I have Mr Dryden's Example for each of them. And this I hope you will account no small piece of obedience, from one, who values the Authority of one true Poet above that of twenty Critics or Commentatours. But tho' I speak thus of Commentators, I will continue to read carefully all I can procure, to make up, that way, for my own want of a Critical understanding in the original Beauties of Homer. Though the greatest of them are certainly those of the Invention and Design, which are not at all confin'd to the Language: For the distinguishing Excellencies of Homer are, (by the consent of the best Criticks of all nations) first in the Manners, (which include all the speeches, as being no other than the Representations of each Person's Manners by his words:) and then in that Rapture and Fire, which carries you away with him, with that wonderfull Force, that no man who has a true Poetical spirit is Master of himself, while he reads him. Homer makes you interested and concern'd before you are aware, all at once; whereas Virgill does it by soft degrees. This, I believe, is what a Translator of Homer ought principally to imitate: and it is very hard for any Translator to come up to it, because the chief reason why all Translations fall short of their Originals, is, that the very Constraint they are obliged to, renders 'em heavy and dispirited. The great Beauty of Homer's Language, as I take it, consists in that noble simplicity, which runs through all his works; (and yet his diction, contrary to what one would imagine consistent with simplicity, is at the same time very Copious.) I don't know how I have run into this Pedantry in a Letter, but I find I have said too much, as well as spoken too inconsiderately; what farther Thoughts I have upon this subject, I shall be glad to communicate to you (for my own improvement) when we meet; which is a happiness I very earnestly desire, as I do likewise some opportunity of proving how much I think myself obliged to your Friendship, and how truly I am, | Sir, | Your most faithfull | humble servant, | A: Pope:

5

To Henry Cromwell, 17 December 1710.

Cromwell (1659-1728), was another of Pope's early friends and critics. Pope wrote him many letters which pass judgement on recent poets, and also submitted his own poetry to Cromwell for correction. He once thanked Cromwell for 'dealing plainly with me in the matter of my own Triffles, which I assure you I never valud half so much as I do that Sincerity in you which they were the occasion of discovering to me: & which while I am happy in, I may be trusted with that dangerous weapon, Poetry' (28 October 1710; *Corr.* i 100).

It seems that my late mention of Crashaw, and my quotation from him, has mov'd your curiosity. I therefore send you the whole author, who has held a place among my books for some years; in which time having read him twice or thrice, I find him one of those whose works may just deserve that trouble. I take him to have writ like a Gentleman, that is at leisure hours, and more to keep out of idleness, than to establish a reputation: so that nothing regular or just can be expected from him. All that regards design, form, fable, (which is the Soul of Poetry) all that concerns exactness, or consent of parts, (which is the body) will probably be wanting; only pretty conceptions, fine metaphors, glitt'ring expressions, and something of a neat cast of verse considering the age he liv'd in, (which are properly the dress, gems, or loose ornaments of poetry) may be found in these verses. This is indeed the case of most poetical writers of Miscellanies; nor can it well be otherwise, since no man can be a great Poet, who writes for diversion only. These Authors should be consider'd as Versifiers, and witty men, rather than as Poets; and under this head will only fall the particular thoughts, the expressions, and the numbers: those parts of poetry which may be judg'd of at a view, and comprehended all at once: such whose Colouring only entertains the sight, but the Lines and Life of the picture are not to be inspected too narrowly.

This author form'd himself upon Petrarch, or rather upon Marino.[1] His thoughts one may observe, in the main, are pretty; but oftentimes far-fetch'd, and too often strain'd and stiffned to make them appear the greater: For men are never so apt to think a thing great, as when it is odd or wonderful; and inconsiderate authors would rather be admir'd than understood. This ambition of surprizing a reader, is the true natural cause of all fustian, or bombast in poetry. To confirm what I have said, you need but look into his first Poem call'd the Weeper, where several of the Stanza's are as sublimely dull, as others of the same copy, are soft and pleasing: and if these last want any thing, it is an easier and more unaffected expression: the remaining thoughts in that poem might have been spared, being either but repetitions, or very trivial and mean. And by this example in the first, one may guess at all the rest, to be like this, a mixture of tender gentile thoughts and suitable expressions, of forc'd and inextricable conceits, and of needless fillers-up to the rest. From all which it is plain, this author writ fast, and set down what came uppermost: A reader may skim off the froth, and use the clear underneath; but if he goes too deep, will meet with a mouthful of dregs: either the top or bottom of him are good for little, but what he did in his own natural, middle way is best.

Selections from the Correspondence

To speak of his Numbers is a little difficult, they are so various and irregular, and mostly Pindaric. 'Tis evident his heroic verse (the best example of which is his Music's Duel) is carelesly made up; but one may imagine from what it now is, that had he taken more care it had been musical and pleasing enough, not extremely majestic, but sweet: and the time consider'd of his writing, he was (ev'n as uncorrect as he is) none of the worst Versificators.

I will just observe, that the best pieces of this Author are, a Paraphrase on Psal. xxiii. on Lessius, Epitaph on Mr. Ashton, Wishes to his suppos'd Mistress, and the *Dies Iræ*. I am, &c.

6

To John Caryll, 25 June 1711.

Caryll (1667-1736) was a close friend of Pope over many years, one of the links between them being their Catholicism: see Erskine-Hill, pp. 42-10?. This letter refers to reaction to Pope's *Essay on Criticism*, not only the *Remarks* by Dennis, but also the adverse response by Pope's co-religionists to his praise of Erasmus in ll. 693-6. In this case the original version is preferred, because when Pope printed this letter he omitted the first paragraph and made other revisions.

Besides the two letters you last favored me with, I am yet more in your debt for one to Mr Englefield, where you have defended me with all the spirit of friendship, and the very essence of good nature; but one or two things you have there said of me that I'm ashamed to thank you for, they are so extravagantly above my merit; and they prove it true, that a friend is as blind as a lover. I beg you to be cautious of saying these things to others, for I can't answer for their prudence; if they were only said to myself I would for your sake conceal 'em from all besides; and they would then be less dangerous to me too, for I should take 'em only for complimental civilities, whereas when addressed to other people, I might be so vain as almost to imagine you were partly in earnest. I know too well the vast difference betwixt those who truly deserve the name of poets and men of wit, and one who is nothing but what he owes to them; and I keep the pictures of Dryden, Milton, Shakespear, &c., in my chamber, round about me, that the constant remembrance of 'em may keep me always humble: I wish I had Mr Caryll's there, that I might have something to make me proud, when I reflected on his friendship. The extreme goodness with which you accept the offer I too impudently made you of mine, can never be enough acknowledged: I am like a poor fellow who makes his rich landlord a scurvy and worthless present, on the hopes of receiving one of infinitely a greater value in return. But on second thoughts I'm more like one of those many poor neighbors of yours to whom you have done charities, who offer you a small acknowledgment after receiving great benefits from you; for you have been beforehand with me in the proofs of friendship you speak of, and my heart is a debt, not a present. Let this suffice to be told you, and be assured, sir, if I did not esteem your friendship so very much, I would have said a great deal more.

I send you Mr Dennis's Remarks on the *Essay*, which equally abound in just criticisms and fine railleries: the few observations in my hand in the margin are what only a morning's leisure permitted me to make purely for your perusal, for I am of opinion that such a critic as you will find him by the latter part of his book, is no way to be properly answered but by a wooden weapon: and I should perhaps have sent him a present from Windsor Forest of one of the best and toughest oaken plants between Sunning hill and Oakingham, if he had not informed me in his Preface that he is at this time persecuted by fortune. This I protest I knew not the least of before; if I had, his name had been spared in the *Essay* for that only reason. I can't conceive what ground he has for so excessive a resentment, nor imagine how those three lines can be call'd a reflection on his person, which only describe him subject a little to colour and stare on some occasions,[1] which are revolutions that happen sometimes in the best and most regular faces in Christendom. I have heard of combatants so very furious as to fall down themselves with that very strength, which they designed to lay so heavy on their antagonists. But if Mr Dennis's rage proceeds only from a zeal to discourage young and inexperienced writers from scribbling, he should frighten us with his verse, not prose; for I've often known that when all the precepts in the world would not reclaim a sinner, some very sad example has done the business. Yet to give this man his due, he has objected to one or two lines with reason, and I will alter them in case of another edition: I will make my enemy do me a kindness where he meant an injury, and so serve instead of a friend. What he observes at the bottom of pag. 20th of his reflections, was objected to by yourself, at Ladyholt, and had been mended but for the haste of the press: 'Tis right Hibernian, and I confess it what the English call a bull, in the expression, tho' the sense be manifest enough: Mr Dennis's bulls are seldom in the expression, they are almost always in the sense.[2]

You will see by this, that whoever sets up for wit in these days ought to have the constancy of a primitive Christian, and be prepared to

suffer even martyrdom in the cause of it. But sure this is the first time
that a wit was attacked for his religion, as you'll find I'm most
zealously in this treatise. And you know, sir, what alarms I have had
from the opposite side on this very account? Have I not reason to cry
out with the poor fellow in Virgil,

> —Quid jam misero mihi denique restat?
> Cui neque apud Danaos usquam locus, et super ipsi
> Dardanidæ insensi pœnas cum sanguine poscunt! [3]

'Tis however my happiness that you, sir, are impartial.

> *Jove* was alike to Trojan and to Phrygian,
> For you well know, that wit's of no religion.

The manner in which Mr D. takes to pieces several particular lines
detached from their natural places, may show how easy it is to any one
to give a new sense, or a new nonsense, to what the author intended,
or not intended. And indeed his constructions are not more wrested
from the genuine meaning than theirs, who objected to the heterodox
parts, as they call 'em. Mr Thomas Southcote[4] is not of that number,
who with the utmost candor, and freedom of a friend, has modestly
told me what others thought; and shown himself one (as he expresses
it very well) rather of a *number* than a *party*. I answer'd his obliging
letter some time since, and have received from him a second, to which
I will reply immediately when I have ended this. The only difference
between us in relation to the monks is, that he thinks most sorts of
learning *flourish'd* among 'em, and I am of opinion that only some sort
of learning was barely *kept alive* by 'em. He believes the most natural
and obvious sense of that line (A second deluge *learning* over-run) will
be thought meant of learning in general, and I fancy it will be
understood only, as 'tis meant, of polite learning, criticism, poetry,
&c., which is the only learning concerned in the subject of the *Essay*. I
am highly obliged to Mr Southcote's zeal in my Commendation and
goodness for not concealing what he thinks my errour. And his
testifying some esteem for the book, just at a time when his brethren
raised a clamor against it, is an instance of great generosity and good
nature together, which I shall ever acknowledge. I ventured to give my
most humble service to Mr Southcote when I writ to his brother, and
intreat the favour of you to assure that most worthy gentleman of my
real esteem and hearty respects. If I had the honor of being known to
my Lord Petre, I should be so impudent as to desire his acceptance of a
thing so inconsiderable as my most humble service. I hope my lord
will not, from what Mr Dennis is pleased to say, look upon me as a
despiser of Men of Quality, who as they have the greatest advantages
of all men, so are worse than the rest of mankind if they are not better;

and this may be said (without any danger) to my Lord Petre,[5] who is (by the consent of all who have the happiness to know him) one of those young lords that have wit in our days!...

7

To Caryll, 19 July 1711.

This letter continues the subject of the previous one.

The concern which you more than seem to be affected with for my reputation by the several accounts you have so obligingly given me of what reports and censures the holy Vandals have thought fit to make me the unworthy subject of, makes me desirous of telling so good a friend my whole thoughts of this matter, and of setting before you in a true light the true state of it.

I've ever thought the best piece of service one could do to our religion was openly to expose our detestation and scorn of all those artifices and *pia fraudes*[1] which it stands so little in need of, and which have laid it under so great a scandal among the enemies. Nothing has been so much a scarecrow to them as the too peremptory and seemingly uncharitable assertion of an utter impossibility of salvation to all but ourselves, invincible ignorance excepted, which indeed some people define under so great limitations and with such exclusions, that it seems as if that word were rather invented as a salvo or expedient, not to be thought too bold with the thunderbolts of God (which are hurled about so freely almost on all mankind by the hands of the ecclesiastics) than as a real exceptive to almost universal damnation. For besides the small number of the truly faithful in our Church, we must again subdivide, and the Jansenist is damned by the Jesuit, the Jesuit by the Jansenist, the strict Scotist by the Thomist, &c. There may be errors, I grant, but I can't think 'em of such consequence as to destroy utterly the charity of mankind, the very greatest bond in which we are engaged by God to one another as Christians.

Therefore I own to you I was glad of any opportunity to express our dislike of so shocking a sentiment as those of the religion I profess are charged with, and hoped a slight insinuation,[2] introduced so easily, of a casual similitude only could never have given offense, but on the contrary must needs have done good in a nation and time, wherein we are the smaller party, and consequently the most misrepresented and most wanting vindication from a slander. For the same reason I took occasion to mention the superstition of some ages after the subversion of the Roman Empire, which is too manifest a truth to be denied, and does in no sort reflect upon the present Catholics, who are free from it. Our silence in these points may with some reason make our adversaries think we allow and persist in those bigotries, which in reality all good and sensible men despise, tho' they are persuaded not to speak against them—I can't tell why, since 'tis now no more the interest even of the worst of our priesthood (as it might be then) to have them smothered in silence; for the opposite sects now prevailing, 'tis too late to hinder our Church from being slandered. 'Tis our business now to show it was slandered unjustly, and to vindicate ourselves from being thought abettors of that which they charge us with. This can't be brought about with serious faces: we must laugh with them at what deserves it, and then we need not doubt of being cleared, even in their opinion.

As to the particulars: you can't but have observed that the whole objection against the simile of *wit* and *faith* lay in the word *they:* when that was beyond all contradiction removed, the very grammar seeming to confute them (for it seems at St. Omer's[3] they do not learn the English grammar) then the objection lies against the simile itself: and if that simile will not be objected to, sense and common reason being indeed a little stubborn and not apt to give way to every body, next the mention of superstition must become a crime, as if religion and she were sisters, or else as if it were a scandal upon the family of Christ to say a word against the devil's bastards. Afterwards some more mischief is discovered in a place that seemed very little suspicious at first, and that is in the two lines about schismaticks at the bottom of page 25;[4] for an ordinary man would imagine the author plainly declared against these schismatics for quitting the true faith out of contempt of the understanding of some few of its believers. But these believers are called *Dull*, and because I say that *These schismatics think some believers dull*, therefore these charitable well-disposed interpreters of my meaning say that *I think all believers dull*. I was telling Mrs. Nelson these fine objections, who assured me I had said nothing which a zealous Catholic need to disown: and I've cause to know that that lady's fault (if she has any) is not want of zeal. She put a notion into my head, which I confess I can't but perfectly acquiesce in, and that was, that 'tis observable when a set of people are piqued at any truth which they think to their own disadvantage, their method of revenge on the truth-speaker is to attack his reputation a by-way, and not to object to the place they are really galled by. What these therefore in their own opinion are really angry at is that a man whom their tribe oppressed and persecuted (Erasmus by name) should be vindicated after a whole age of obloquy, by one of their own people who is free and bold enough to utter a generous truth in behalf of the dead, whom no man sure will flatter, and few do justice to. Others you know, were as angry that I mentioned Mr. Walsh with honour, who, as he never refused to any one of merit, of any party, the praise due to him, so honestly deserved it from all others of never so different interests or sentiments. May I ever be guilty of this sort of liberty and latitude of principle, which gives us the hardiness of speaking well of those whom envy oppresses even after death. As I would always speak well of my friends when they are absent, nay, because they are absent, so I would much more of the dead, in that eternal absence, and the rather because I expect no thanks from them for it.

Thus, sir, you see I do in my *conscience* persist in what I have written, yet *in my friendship* I will recant and alter whatever you please in case of a Second Edition,–which I yet think the book will never arrive at, for Tonson's printer told me he drew off a thousand copies in his first impression, and I fancy a treatise of this nature, which not one gentleman in three score even of a liberal education can understand, will hardly exceed the vent of that number. You shall find me a true Trojan in my faith and friendship: in both which I will ever persevere unto the end, and you shall be convinced that both in regard to the determinations of the Church and to your determinations I shall prove a submissive disciple, and renounce all dangerous temptations of the private spirit....

8

To Addison, 30 July 1713.

This letter was fabricated by Pope for publication out of passages from a genuine letter to Caryll of 19 November 1712 (see *Corr.* i 154-6). Representing what Pope would like to have said to Addison, it is an example of Pope's creation of a literary persona. The letter refers to the circumstances which occasioned Pope's *Narrative of Dr. Robert Norris.*

I Am more joy'd at your return than I should be at that of the Sun, so much as I wish for him this melancholy wet season; but 'tis his fate too, like yours, to be displeasing to Owls and obscene animals, who cannot bear his lustre. What put me in mind of these night-birds was John Dennis, whom I think you are best revenged upon, as the Sun was in the fable upon those bats and beastly birds above-mentioned, only by shining on. I am so far from esteeming it any misfortune, that I congratulate you upon having your share in that, of which all the great men and all the good men that ever lived have had their part, Envy and Calumny. To be uncensured and to be obscure, is the same thing. You may conclude from what I here say, that 'twas never in my thoughts to have offered you my pen in any direct reply to such a Critic, but only in some little raillery; not in defence of you, but in contempt of him. But indeed your opinion that 'tis intirely to be neglected, would have been my own, had it been my own case: but I felt more warmth here than I did when first I saw his book against my self, (tho' indeed in two minutes it made me heartily merry.) He has written against every thing the world has approv'd these many years: I apprehend but one danger from Dennis's disliking our sense, that it may make us think so very well of it, as to become proud and conceited upon his disapprobation.

I must not here omit to do justice to Mr. Gay, whose zeal in your concern is worthy a friend and honourer of you. He writ to me in the most pressing terms about it, though with that just contempt of the Critic which he deserves. I think in these days one honest man is obliged to acquaint another, who are his friends; when so many mischievous insects are daily at work to make people of merit suspicious of each other, that they may have the satisfaction of seeing them look'd upon no better than themselves. I am your, &c.

9

To Swift, 8 December 1713.

This is Pope's earliest surviving letter to Swift, whom he had probably met in 1712. In the summer of 1713 Swift had been installed as Dean of St Patrick's, Dublin.

Not to trouble you at present with the Recital of all my Obligations to you, I shall only mention two Things, which I take particularly well of you; your Desire that I should write to you;—and your Proposal of giving me twenty Guineas to change my Religion, which last you must give me Leave to make the Subject of this Letter.

Sure no Clergyman ever offered so much, out of his own Purse, for the Sake of any Religion. 'Tis almost as many Pieces of Gold, as an Apostle could get of Silver from the Priests of old, on a much more valuable Consideration.

I believe it will be better worth my while to propose a Change of my Faith by Subscription, than a Translation of Homer. And to convince you how well disposed I am to the Reformation, I shall be content, if you can prevail with my Lord Treasurer, and the Ministry, to rise to the same Sum, each of them, on this pious Account, as my Lord Halifax has done on the prophane one. I am afraid there is no being at once a Poet, and a good Christian; and I am very much straitned between Two, while the Whigs seem willing to contribute as much to continue me the one, as you would to make me the other. But if you can move every Man in the Government, that has above ten Thousand Pounds a Year, to subscribe as much as your self, I shall become a Convert, as most Men do, when the Lords turn it to my Interest. I know they have the Truth of Religion so much at Heart, that they would certainly give more to have one good Subject translated from Popery to the Church of England, than twenty heathenish Authors out of any unknown Tongue into ours. I therefore commission you, Mr. Dean, with full Authority to transact this Affair in my Name, and to propose as follows.

First,—That as to the Head of our Church, the Pope, I may engage to renounce his Power, whensoever I shall receive any particular Indulgences from the Head of your Church, the Queen.

As to Communion in one Kind, I shall also promise to change it for Communion in both, as soon as the Ministry will allow me where-withal to eat, and to drink.

For Invocations to Saints, mine shall be turned to Dedications to Sinners, when I shall find the Great Ones of this World as willing to do me any Good, as I believe those of the other are.

You see, I shall not be obstinate in the main Points. But there is one Article I must reserve, and which you seemed not unwilling to allow me, Prayer for the Dead. There are People, to whose Souls I wish as well as to my own, and I must crave Leave humbly to lay before them, that tho' the Subscriptions above mentioned will suffice for my self, there are necessary Perquisits, and Additions, which I must demand on the Score of this charitable Article. It is also to be considered, that the greater Part of those, whose Souls I am most concerned for, were unfortunately Heretics, Schismatics, Poets, Painters, or Persons of such Lives, and Manners, as few, or no Churches are willing to save. The Expence will be therefore the greater to make an effectual Provision for the said Souls.

Old Dryden, tho' a Roman Catholick, was a Poet; and 'tis revealed in the Visions of some ancient Saints, that no Poet was ever saved under some Hundreds of Masses. I cannot set his Delivery from Purgatory at less than Fifty Pounds sterling.

Walsh was not only a Socinian, but (what you'll own is harder to be saved) a Whig. He cannot modestly be rated at less than a Hundred.

L'Estrange being a Tory, we compute him but at Twenty Pounds, which I hope no Friend of the Party can deny to give, to keep him from damning in the next Life, considering they never gave him Sixpence to keep him from starving in this.

All this together amounts to 170 Pounds.

In the next Place, I must desire you to represent, that there are several of my Friends yet living, whom I design, God willing, to outlive, in consideration of Legacies, out of which it is a Doctrine in the Reformed Church that not a Farthing shall be allowed, to save their Souls, who gave them.

There is One, who will dye within these few Months, with one Mr. Jervas,[1] who hath grievously offended in making the Likeness of almost all Things in Heaven above, and Earth below. And one Mr. Gay, an unhappy Youth, that writes Pastorals during the Time of Divine Service, whose Case is the more deplorable, as he hath miserably lavished away all that Silver he should have reserved for his Soul's Health, in Buttons and Loops for his Coat.

I cannot pretend to have these People honestly saved under some Hundred Pounds, whether you consider the Difficulty of such a Work, or the extreme Love and Tenderness I bear them, which will infallibly make me push this Charity as far as I am able. There is but One more, whose Salvation I insist upon, and then I have done: But indeed it may prove of so much greater Charge than all the rest, that I will only lay the Case before you, and the Ministry, and leave to their Prudence and Generosity what Summ they shall think fit to bestow upon it.

The Person I mean is Dr. Swift, a dignified Clergyman, but One who, by his own Confession, has composed more Libels than Sermons. If it be true, what I have heard often affirmed by innocent People, that too much Wit is dangerous to Salvation, this unfortunate Gentleman must certainly be damned to all Eternity. But I hope his long Experience in the World, and frequent Conversation with Great Men, will cause him (as it has some others) to have less and less Wit every Day. Be it as it will, I should not think my own Soul deserved to be saved, if I did not endeavour to save his, for I have all the Obligations in Nature to him. He has brought me into better Company than I cared for, made me merrier, when I was sick, than I had a Mind to be, put me upon making Poems on Purpose that he might alter them, &c. I once thought I could never have discharged my Debt to his Kindness, but have lately been informed, to my unspeakable Comfort, that I have more than paid it all. For Monsieur de Montayne has assured me, that the Person, who receives a Benefit, obliges the Giver; for since the chief Endeavour of one Friend is to do Good to the other, He, who administers both the Matter, and Occasion, is the Man that is Liberal. At this Rate it is impossible Dr. Swift should be ever out of my Debt, as matters stand already; and for the future he may expect daily more Obligations from | His most Faithful, Affectionate, | Humble Servant | A. Pope.

I have finished the Rape of the Lock,[2] but believe I may stay here till Christmas without Hindrance of Busyness.

10

To Caryll, 25 July 1714.

I Have no better excuse to offer you, that I have omitted a task naturally so pleasing to me as conversing upon paper with you, but that my time and eyes have been wholly employ'd upon Homer, whom I almost fear I shall find but one way of imitating, which is in his blindness. I am perpetually afflicted with headachs that very much affect my sight; and indeed since my coming hither I have scarce past an hour agreeably, except that in which I read your letter. I would seriously have you think, you have no man who more truly knows to place a right value on your friendship, than he who least deserves it on all other accounts but his due sense of it. Yet let me tell you, you can hardly guess what a task you undertake when you profess your self my friend; there are some Tories who will take you for a Whig, some Whigs who will take you for a Tory, some Protestants who will esteem you a rank Papist, and some Papists who will account you a Heretick.

I find by dear experience, we live in an age where it is criminal to be moderate; and where no one man can be allowed to be just to all men. The notions of right and wrong are so far strain'd, that perhaps to be in the right so very violently, may be of worse consequence than to be easily and quietly in the wrong. I really wish all men so well, that I am satisfied but few can wish me so; but if those few are such as tell me they do, I am content, for they are the best people I know. While you believe me what I profess as to religion, I can bear any thing the bigotted may say: while Mr. Congreve likes my poetry, I can endure Dennis and a thousand more like him; while the most honest and moral of each party think me no ill man, I can easily bear that the most violent and mad of all parties rise up to throw dirt at me.

I must expect an hundred attacks upon the publication of my Homer. Whoever in our times would be a professor of learning above his fellows, ought at the very first to enter the world with the constancy and resolution of a primitive christian, and be prepared to suffer all sort of publick persecution. It is certainly to be lamented, that if any man does but endeavour to distinguish himself, or gratify others by his studies, he is immediately treated as a common enemy, instead of being look'd upon as a common friend; and assaulted as generally, as if his whole design were to prejudice the State or ruin the publick. I will venture to say, no man ever rose to any degree of perfection in writing, but thro' obstinacy, and an inveterate resolution against the stream of mankind: So that if the world has receiv'd any benefit from the labours of the learned, it was in its own despite. For when first they essay their parts, all people in general are prejudiced against new beginners; and when they have got a little above contempt, then some particular persons, who were before unfortunate in their own attempts, are sworn foes to them only because they succeed. —Upon the whole, one may say of the best writers, that they pay a severe Fine for their fame, which it is always in the pow'r of the most worthless part of mankind to levy upon them when they please. I am, &c.

II

To Caryll, 16 August 1714.

Pope printed part of the present extract (down to 'persecution') as a portion of a letter to Edward Blount dated 27 August 1714, but he did not print the subsequent, more personal, comments on his sufferings under the anti-catholic laws. One such law prevented Catholics from owning a horse worth more than £5.

...I could not but take a Trip to London on the Death of the Queen, moved by the Common Curiosity of mankind, who leave their busy-ness to be looking upon other men's. I thank God that as for my Self, I am below all the accidents of State-Changes by my Circumstances, and above them by my Philosophy. Common charity of man to man, and universal Good will to all, are the Points I have most at heart; and I am sure those are not to be broken for the sake of any Governors or Government. I am willing to hope the best and that I more wish than my own or any particular Man's advancement, that this Turn may put an End entierely to the Divisions of Whig and Tory, that those Parties may love each other as well as I love them both, or at least hurt each other as little as I would either; and that our own People may live as quietly as we shall certainly let theirs, that is to say, that want of Power itself in us may not be a surer Prevention of Harm, than want of will in

Selected prose of Alexander Pope

them. I am sure, if all Whigs and all Tories had the spirit of one Roman Catholick that I know, it would be well for all Roman Catholicks; and if all Roman Catholicks had ever had that spirit, it had been well for all others; and we had never been charged with so wicked a Spirit as that of Persecution. It is indeed very unjust to judge of us in this nation by what other members of our communion have done abroad. Our Church Triumphant there is very different from our Church militant here (if I may call that a Church militant which is Every way disarm'd). The greatest fear I have under the Circumstances of a poor Papist is the Loss of my poor Horse; yet if they take it away, I may say with the resignation of Job, tho' not in his very words, *Deus dedit, Diabolus abstulit*,[1] I thank God I can walk. If I had a House and they took it away, I cou'd go into Lodgings: If I had money and they took it away, I cou'd write for my Bread (as much better men than I have been often suffered to do) if my own Works would not do, I cou'd turn writing master at last and set Copies to Children. I remember what Horace said of fortune –

> Si celeres quatit
> Pennas, resigno quae dedit, et mea
> Virtute me involvo, probamque
> Pauperiem sine dote quaero.[2]

Whatever befalls me, I only desire to keep my own Integrity, and your Love. The rest I leave to Heaven....

12

To James Craggs, 15 July 1715.

Craggs (1686-1721) was a friend of both Pope and Addison; see Pope's *Epistle to James Craggs, Esq.*, and *To Mr. Addison*, ll. 63-72. This letter, which seems to have been written when Craggs was in France, refers to Addison's sponsorship of Thomas Tickell's rival translation of Homer, and the court over which he is said to have presided at Button's coffee house. The phrasing is very close to the 'Atticus' portrait of Addison in the *Epistle to Dr. Arbuthnot* (1734) ll. 194-214, which was first drafted by Pope in 1715: see *Poems* vi 142-5.

I Lay hold of the opportunity given me by my Lord Duke of Shrewsbury, to assure you of the continuance of that esteem and affection I have long born you, and the memory of so many agreeable conversations as we have pass'd together. I wish it were a compliment to say, such conversations as are not to be found on this side of the water: for the spirit of dissention is gone forth among us; nor is it a wonder that Button's is no longer Button's, when old England is no longer old

252

Selections from the Correspondence

England, that region of hospitality, society, and good humour. Party affects us all, even the wits, tho' they gain as little by politicks as they do by their wit. We talk much of fine sense, refin'd sense, and exalted sense; but for use and happiness, give me a little common sense. I say this in regard to some gentlemen, profess'd Wits of our acquaintance, who fancy they can make Poetry of consequence at this time of day, in the midst of this raging fit of Politicks. For they tell me, the busy part of the nation is not more divided about Whig and Tory, than these idle fellows of the feather about Mr. T * s and my translation. I (like the Tories) have the town in general, that is the mob, on my side; but 'tis usual with the smaller party to make up in industry what they want in number, and that's the case with the little Senate of Cato. However, if our principles be well consider'd, I must appear a brave Whig, and Mr. T. a rank Tory: I translated Homer for the publick in general, he to gratify the inordinate desires of one Man only. We have it seems, a great Turk in poetry, who can never bear a brother on the throne; and has his Mutes too, a sett of nodders, winkers, and whisperers, whose business is to strangle all other off-spring of wit in their birth. The new translator of Homer is the humblest slave he has, that is to say, his first Minister; let him receive the honours he gives him, but receive them with fear and trembling; let him be proud of the approbation of his absolute Lord; I appeal to the people, as my rightful judges and masters; and if they are not inclin'd to condemn me, I fear no arbitrary high-flying proceedings from the small Court-faction at Button's. But after all I have said of this great man, there is no rupture between us: We are each of us so civil and obliging, that neither thinks he is obliged: And I for my part treat with him, as we do with the Grand Monarch[1]; who has too many great qualities not to be respected, tho' we know he watches any occasion to oppress us....

13
To Sir William Trumbull, 16 December 1715.

Pope writes in the wake of the Jacobite rebellion, suppressed the previous month, which had made the position of English Catholics yet more difficult.

It was one of the Enigma's of Pythagoras, "When the winds rise, worship the Eccho." A modern writer explains this to signify, "When popular tumults begin, retire to solitudes, or such places where Eccho's are commonly found, rocks, woods, &c." I am rather of opinion it should be interpreted, "When rumours increase, and when

253

there is abundance of noise and clamour, believe the second report:" This I think agrees more exactly with the eccho, and is the more natural application of the symbol. However it be, either of these precepts is extreamly proper to be followed at this season; and I cannot but applaud your resolution of continuing in what you call your cave in the forest, this winter; and preferring the noise of breaking ice to that of breaking statesmen, the rage of storms to that of parties, the fury and ravage of floods and tempests, to the precipitancy of some, and the ruin of others, which I fear will be our daily prospects in London.

I sincerely wish my self with you, to contemplate the wonders of God in the firmament, rather than the madness of man on the earth. But I never had so much cause as now to complain of my poetical star, that fixes me at this tumultuous time, to attend the gingling of rymes and the measuring of syllables: to be almost the only trifler in the nation; and as ridiculous as the Poet in Petronius,[1] who while all the rest in the ship were either labouring or praying for life, was scratching his head in a little room, to write a fine description of the tempest.

You tell me, you like the sound of no arms but those of Achilles: for my part I like them as little as any other arms. I listed my self in the battles of Homer, and I am no sooner in war, but like most other folks, I wish my self out again.

I heartily join with you in wishing Quiet to our native country: Quiet in the state, which like Charity in religion, is too much the perfection and happiness of either, to be broken or violated on any pretence or prospect whatsoever. Fire and sword, and fire and faggot, are equally my aversion. I can pray for opposite parties, and for opposite religions, with great sincerity. I think to be a lover of one's country is a glorious elogy, but I do not think it so great an one as to be a lover of mankind.

I sometimes celebrate you under these denominations, and join your health with that of the whole world; a truly catholick health, which far excels the poor narrow-spirited, ridiculous healths now in fashion, to this church, or that church. Whatever our teachers may say, they must give us leave at least to wish generously. These, dear Sir, are my general dispositions, but whenever I pray or wish for particulars, you are one of the first in the thoughts and affections of your, &c.

Selections from the Correspondence

14

To Edward Blount, 10 February 1716.

Blount was another of Pope's Catholic friends. This letter as printed was largely fabricated from one sent to Caryll on 20 September 1713 (*Corr.* i 190-1).

I Am just return'd from the country, whither Mr. Rowe accompanied me, and pass'd a week in the Forest. I need not tell you how much a man of his turn entertain'd me; but I must acquaint you there is a vivacity and gaiety of disposition almost peculiar to him, which make it impossible to part from him without that uneasiness which generally succeeds all our pleasures. I have been just taking a solitary walk by moon-shine, full of reflections on the transitory nature of all human delights; and giving my thoughts a loose in the contemplation of those satisfactions which probably we may hereafter taste in the company of separate spirits, when we shall range the walks above, and perhaps gaze on this world at as vast a distance as we now do on those worlds. The pleasures we are to enjoy in that conversation must undoubtedly be of a nobler kind, and (not unlikely) may proceed from the discoveries each shall communicate to another, of God and of nature; for the happiness of minds can surely be nothing but knowledge.

The highest gratification we receive here from company is Mirth, which at the best is but a fluttering unquiet motion, that beats about the breast for a few moments, and after leaves it void and empty. Keeping good company, even the best, is but a less shameful art of losing time. What we here call science and study, are little better: the greater number of arts to which we apply our selves are meer groping in the dark; and even the search of our most important concerns in a future being, is but a needless, anxious, and uncertain haste to be knowing, sooner than we can, what without all this sollicitude we shall know a little later. We are but curious impertinents in the case of futurity. 'Tis not our business to be guessing what the state of souls shall be, but to be doing what may make our own state happy; we cannot be knowing, but we can be virtuous.

If this be my notion of a great part of that high science, Divinity, you will be so civil as to imagine I lay no mighty stress upon the rest. Even of my darling poetry I really make no other use, than horses of the bells that gingle about their ears (tho' now and then they toss their heads as if they were proud of 'em) only to jogg on, a little more merrily.

Your observations on the narrow conceptions of mankind in the point of friendship, confirm me in what I was so fortunate as at my first knowledge of you to hope, and since so amply to experience. Let me take so much decent pride and dignity upon me, as to tell you, that but for opinions like these which I discover'd in your mind, I had never made the trial I have done; which has succeeded so much to mine, and I believe not less to your satisfaction: for if I know you right, your pleasure is greater in obliging me, than I can feel on my part, till it falls in my power to oblige you.

Your remark, that the variety of opinions in politicks or religion is often rather a gratification, than an objection, to people who have sense enough to consider the beautiful order of nature in her variations; makes me think you have not construed Joannes Secundus wrong, in the verse which precedes that which you quote: *Bene nota Fides*, as I take it, does no way signify the Roman Catholic Religion, tho' Secundus was of it.[1] I think it was a generous thought, and one that flow'd from an exalted mind, that it was not improbable but God might be delighted with the various methods of worshipping him, which divided the whole world: I am pretty sure you and I should no more make good Inquisitors to the modern tyrants in faith, than we could have been qualify'd for Lictors to Procrustes, when he converted refractory members with the rack. In a word, I can only repeat to you what I think I have formerly said; that I as little fear God will damn a man who has Charity, as I hope that any Priest can save him without it. I am, &c.

15

To Lady Mary Wortley Montagu, 18 August 1716.

Lady Mary had just left England to accompany her husband on his embassy to Constantinople. Though she and Pope were on close terms at this date, the friendship later turned to bitter enmity, and Pope printed this letter without any indication of date or recipient.

Madam,
I Can say little to recommend the letters I shall write to you, but that they will be the most impartial representations of a free heart, and the truest copies you ever saw, tho' of a very mean original. Not a feature will be soften'd, or any advantagious light employ'd to make the ugly thing a little less hideous: but you shall find it in all respects, most horribly like. You will do me an injustice if you look upon any thing I shall say from this instant, as a compliment, either to you or to my self:

Selections from the Correspondence

Whatever I write will be the real thought of that hour; and I know you'll no more expect it of me to persevere till death in every sentiment or notion I now set down, than you would imagine a man's face should never change when once his picture was drawn.

The freedom I shall use in this manner of *thinking aloud,* may indeed prove me a fool; but it will prove me one of the best sort of fools, the honest ones. And since what folly we have, will infallibly buoy up at one time or other in spite of all our art to keep it down; methinks 'tis almost foolish to take any pains to conceal it at all, and almost knavish to do it from those that are our friends. If Momus's project had taken, of having windows in our breasts,[1] I shou'd be for carrying it further, and making those windows, casements; that while a man show'd his heart to all the world, he might do something more for his friends; even give it them, and trust it to their handling. I think I love you as well as King Herod did Herodias (tho' I never had so much as one dance with you) and would as freely give you my heart in a dish, as he did another's head. But since Jupiter will not have it so, I must be content to shew my taste in life, as I do my taste in painting, by loving to have as little drapery as possible. Not that I think every body naked altogether so fine a sight, as your self and a few more would be; but because 'tis good to use people to what they must be acquainted with; and there will certainly come some day of judgment or other, to uncover every soul of us. We shall then see that the Prudes of this world ow'd all their fine figure only to their being straiter-laced than the rest; and that they are naturally as arrant squabs as those that went more loose, nay as those that never girded their loins at all. —But a particular reason that may engage you to write your thoughts the more freely to me, is, that I am confident no one knows you better; for I find, when others express their thoughts of you, they fall very short of mine, and I know at the same time, theirs are such as you would think sufficiently in your favour.

You may easily imagine how desirous I must be of a correspondence with a person, who had taught me long ago that it was as possible to esteem at first sight, as to love: and who has since ruin'd me for all the conversation of one sex, and almost all the friendship of the other. I am but too sensible thro' your means, that the company of men wants a certain softness to recommend it, and that of women wants every thing else. How often have I been quietly going to take possession of that tranquility and indolence I had so long found in the Country; when one evening of your conversation has spoil'd me for a Solitaire! Books have lost their effect upon me, and I was convinced since I saw you, that there is one alive wiser than all the sages. A plague of female wisdom! it makes a man ten times more uneasy than his own: what is very strange, Virtue herself (when you have the dressing her) is too amiable for one's repose. You might have done a world of good in your time, if you had allow'd half the fine gentlemen who have seen you, to have conversed with you; they would have been strangely deceiv'd, while they thought only to fall in love with a fair lady, and you had bewitch'd them with Reason and Virtue (two beauties that the very fops pretend to no acquaintance with.)

The unhappy distance at which we correspond, removes a great many of those restrictions and punctilious decorums, that often-times in nearer conversation prejudice truth, to save good breeding. I may now hear of my faults, and you of your good qualities, without a blush; we converse upon such unfortunate generous terms, as exclude the regards of fear, shame, or design, in either of us. And methinks it would be as paltry a part, to impose (even in a single thought) upon each other in this state of separation, as for spirits of a different sphere who have so little intercourse with us, to employ that little (as some would make us think they do) in putting tricks and delusions upon poor mortals.

Let me begin then, Madam, by asking you a question, that may enable me to judge better of my own conduct than most instances of my life. In what manner did I behave the last hour I saw you? what degree of concern did I discover when I felt a misfortune which I hope you will never feel, that of parting from what one most esteems? for if my parting look'd but like that of your common acquaintance, I am the greatest of all the hypocrites that ever decency made.

I never since pass by your house, but with the same sort of melancholy that we feel upon seeing the tomb of a friend, which only serves to put us in mind of what we have lost. I reflect upon the circumstances of your departure which I was there a witness of, (your behaviour in what I may call your last moments) and I indulge a gloomy kind of pleasure in thinking that those last moments were given to me. I would fain imagine this was not accidental, but proceeded from a penetration which I know you have, in finding out the truth of people's sentiments; and that you were willing, the last man that would have parted from you, should be the last that did. I really look'd upon you just as the friends of Curtius might have done upon that Hero, at the instant when he was devoting himself to glory, and running to be lost out of generosity: I was oblig'd to admire your resolution, in as great a degree as I deplored it; and had only to wish, that heaven would reward so much virtue as was to be taken from us, with all the felicities it could enjoy elsewhere! I am, &c.

Selections from the Correspondence

16

To the Earl of Burlington, ?November 1716.

Richard Boyle, third Earl of Burlington (1695-1753) was well known for his interest in architecture. It is not known how or when his friendship with Pope began; this is the first surviving letter to him from Pope, but it was doubtless much improved by Pope for publication. Bernard Lintot was one of Pope's publishers.

My LORD,

If your Mare could speak, she would give you an account of what extraordinary company she had on the road; which since she cannot do, I will.

It was the enterprizing Mr. Lintott, the redoubtable rival of Mr. Tonson, who mounted on a stone-horse, (no disagreeable companion to your Lordship's mare) overtook me in Windsor-forest. He said, he heard I design'd for Oxford, the seat of the muses, and would, as my bookseller, by all means, accompany me thither.

I ask'd him where he got his horse? he answer'd he got it of his Publisher: 'For that rogue, my Printer, (said he) disappointed me: I hoped to put him in good humour by a treat at the tavern, of a brown fricassee of rabbits which cost two shillings, with two quarts of wine, besides my conversation. I thought my self cocksure of his horse, which he readily promis'd me, but said that Mr. Tonson had just such another design of going to Cambridge, expecting there the Copy of a new kind of Horace from Dr. [Bentley] and if Mr. Tonson went, he was preingaged to attend him, being to have the printing of the said copy.

So in short, I borrow'd this stonehorse of my publisher, which he had of Mr. Oldmixon for a debt; he lent me too the pretty boy you see after me: he was a smutty dog yesterday, and cost me near two hours to wash the ink off his face; but the Devil is a fair condition'd Devil, and very forward in his catechise: if you have any more baggs, he shall carry them.'

I thought Mr. Lintot's civility not to be neglected, so gave the boy a small bag, containing three shirts and an Elzevir Virgil; and mounting in an instant proceeded on the road, with my man before, my courteous stationer beside, and the aforesaid devil behind.

Mr. Lintot began in this manner. 'Now damn them! what if they should put it into the news-paper, how you and I went together to Oxford? what would I care? If I should go down into Sussex, they would say I was gone to the Speaker. But what of that? if my son were but big enough to go on with the business, by G-d I would keep as good company as old Jacob.'

Hereupon I enquir'd of his son. 'The lad (says he) has fine parts, but is somewhat sickly, much as you are — I spare for nothing in his Education at Westminster. Pray don't you think Westminster to be the best School in England? most of the late Ministry came out of it, so did many of this Ministry; I hope the boy will make his fortune.'

Don't you design to let him pass a year at Oxford? 'To what purpose? (said he) the Universities do but make Pedants, and I intend to breed him a man of business.'

As Mr. Lintot was talking, I observ'd he sate uneasy on his saddle, for which I express'd some sollicitude: 'Nothing, says he, I can bear it well enough; but since we have the day before us, methinks it would be very pleasant for you to rest a-while under the woods.' When we were alighted, 'See here, what a mighty pretty Horace I have in my pocket! what if you amus'd your self in turning an Ode, till we mount again? if you pleas'd, what a clever Miscellany might you make at leisure hours?' Perhaps I may, said I, if we ride on; the motion is an aid to my fancy, a round trott very much awakens my spirits: then jog on apace, and I'll think as hard as I can.

Silence ensu'd for a full hour; after which Mr. Lintot lugg'd the reins, stopt short, and broke out, 'Well Sir, how far have you gone?' I answer'd, seven miles. 'Lord, Sir, said Lintot, I thought you had done seven stanza's. Oldsworth in a ramble round Wimbleton-hill, would translate a whole Ode in half this time. I'll say that for Oldsworth, (tho' I lost by his Timothy's) he translates an Ode of Horace the quickest of any man in England. I remember Dr. King would write verses in a tavern three hours after he could not speak: and there's Sir Richard in that rumbling old chariot of his, between Fleet-ditch and St. Giles's pound, shall make you half a Job.'[1]

Pray Mr. Lintot (said I) now you talk of Translators, what is your method of managing them? 'Sir (reply'd he) those are the saddest pack of rogues in the world: in a hungry fit, they'll swear they understand all the languages in the universe: I have known one of them take down a Greek book upon my counter and cry, Ay this is Hebrew, I must read it from the latter end. By the Lord, I can never be sure in these fellows, for I neither understand Greek, Latin, French, nor Italian my self. But this is my way; I agree with them for ten shillings per sheet, with a proviso, that I will have their doings corrected by whom I please; so by one or other they are led at last to the true sense of an author; my judgment giving the negative to all my translators.' But how are you secure those correctors may not impose upon you? 'Why I get any civil gentleman, (especially any Scotsman) that comes into my shop, to read the original to me in English; by this I know whether my first translator be deficient, and whether my corrector merits his money or not?

'I'll tell you what happen'd to me last month: I bargain'd with S[ewell] for a new version of Lucretius to publish against Tonson's; agreeing to pay the author so many shillings at his producing so many lines. He made a great progress in a very short time, and I gave it to the corrector to compare with the Latin; but he went directly to Creech's translation,[2] and found it the same word for word, all but the first page. Now, what d'ye think I did, I arrested the translator for a cheat; nay, and I stopt the corrector's pay too, upon this proof that he had made use of Creech instead of the original.'

Pray tell me next how you deal with the Critics? 'Sir (said he) nothing more easy. I can silence the most formidable of them: the rich ones for a sheet a-piece of the blotted manuscript, which costs me nothing: they'll go about with it to their acquaintance, and pretend they had it from the author, who submitted to their correction: this has given some of them such an air, that in time they come to be consulted with, and dedicated to, as the top critics of the town. – As for the poor critics, I'll give you one instance of my management, by which you may guess at the rest. A lean man that look'd like a very good scholar, came to me t'other day; he turn'd over your Homer, shook his head, shrug'd up his shoulders, and pish'd at every line of it; One would wonder (says he) at the strange presumption of some men; Homer is no such easy task, that every stripling, every versifier – he was going on, when my wife call'd to dinner: Sir, said I, will you please to eat a piece of beef with me? Mr. Lintot, said he, I am sorry you should be at the expence of this great book, I am really concern'd on your account – Sir I am much oblig'd to you: if you can dine upon a piece of beef, together with a slice of pudding – Mr. Lintot, I do not say but Mr. Pope, if he would condescend to advise with men of learning – Sir, the pudding is upon the table, if you please to go in – My critic complies, he comes to a taste of your poetry, and tells me in the same breath, that the book is commendable, and the pudding excellent.

'Now Sir (concluded Mr. Lintot) in return to the frankness I have shewn, pray tell me, Is it the opinion of your friends at court that my Lord Lansdown will be brought to the bar or not?'[3] I told him I heard he would not, and I hop'd it, my Lord being one I had particular obligations to. 'That may be (reply'd Mr. Lintot) but if he is not, I shall lose the printing of a very good trial.'

These my Lord are a few traits by which you may discern the genius of Mr. Lintot, which I have chosen for the subject of a letter. I dropt him as soon as I got to Oxford, and paid a visit to Lord Carlton at Middleton.[4]

The conversations I enjoy here are not to be prejudic'd by my pen, and the pleasures from them only to be equal'd when I meet you. I hope in a few days to cast my self from your horse at your feet. I am, &c.

17

To Teresa and Martha Blount, ?September 1717.

(Printed in 1737 as being to an unidentified lady.) These sisters were relatives of Caryll; Pope had an early affectionate relationship with both of them, but that with Teresa cooled, while his feelings for Martha deepened.

Madam,

Nothing could have more of that melancholy which once used to please me, than my last day's journey; for after having pass'd through my favourite woods in the forest, with a thousand reveries of past pleasures, I rid over hanging hills, whose tops were edged with groves, and whose feet water'd with winding rivers, listning to the falls of cataracts below, and the murmuring of the winds above: The gloomy verdure of Stonor succeeded to these; and then the shades of the evening overtook me. The moon rose in the clearest sky I ever saw, by whose solemn light I paced on slowly, without company, or any interruption to the range of my thoughts. About a mile before I reach'd Oxford, all the bells toll'd in different notes; the clocks of every college answer'd one another, and sounded forth (some in a deeper, some a softer tone) that it was eleven at night. All this was no ill preparation to the life I have led since, among those old walls, venerable galleries, stone portico's, studious walks, and solitary scenes of the University. I wanted nothing but a black gown and a salary, to be as meer a bookworm as any there. I conform'd my self to the college hours, was roll'd up in books, lay in one of the most ancient, dusky parts of the University, and was as dead to the world as any hermit of the desart. If any thing was alive or awake in me, it was a little vanity; such as even those good men us'd to entertain, when the monks *of their own order* extoll'd their piety and abstraction. For I found my self receiv'd with a sort of respect, which this idle part of mankind, the learned, pay to their own species; who are as considerable here, as the busy, the gay, and the ambitious are in your world.

Indeed I was treated in such a manner, that I could not but sometimes ask my self in my mind, what college I was founder of, or what library I had built? Methinks I do very ill to return to the world again, to leave the only place where I make a figure, and from seeing my self seated with dignity on the most conspicuous shelves of a library, put my self into the abject posture of lying at a lady's feet in St. James's square....

18

There is no evidence as to the identity of Pope's correspondent (if it were ever a genuine letter) or to the date. Sherburn suggests September 1717, which was one of the occasions when Pope had an opportunity to visit Blenheim.

I will not describe *Bl*— in particular, not to forestall your expectations before you see it: Only take a short account, which I will hazard my little credit is no unjust one. I never saw so great a thing with so much littleness in it: I think the Architect built it entirely in compliance to the taste of its Owners: for it is the most inhospitable thing imaginable, and the most selfish: it has, like their own hearts, no room for strangers, and no reception for any person of superior quality to themselves. There are but just two Apartments, for the Master and Mistress, below; and but two apartments above, (very much inferior to them) in the whole House. When you look upon the Outside, you'd think it large enough for a Prince; when you see the Inside, it is too little for a Subject; and has not conveniency to lodge a common family. It is a house of Entries and Passages; among which there are three Vista's through the whole, very uselessly handsome. There is what might have been a fine Gallery, but spoil'd by two Arches towards the End of it, which take away the sight of several of the windows. There are two ordinary stair-cases instead of one great one. The best things within the house, are the Hall, which is indeed noble and well-proportion'd; and the cellars and offices under-ground, which are the most commodious, and the best contrived, of the whole. At the top of the building are several Cupola's and little Turrets that have but an ill effect, and make the building look at once finical and heavy. What seems of the best taste, is that Front towards the gardens, which is not yet loaded with these turrets. The two Sides of the building are intirely spoil'd by two monstrous bow-windows which stand just in the middle, instead of doors: And as if it were fatal that some trifling littleness should every where destroy the grandeur, there are in the chief front two semi circles of a lower structure than the rest, that cut off the angles, and look as if they were purposely design'd to hide a loftier and nobler piece of building, the top of which appears above them. In a word, the whole is a most expensive absurdity; and the Duke of *Shrewsbury* gave a true character of it, when he said, it was a great *Quarry of Stones above ground.*

We paid a visit to the spring where *Rosamond* bathed herself, on a hill where remains only a piece of a wall of the old Palace of *Henry* the Second. We toasted her shade in the cold water, not without a thought or two, scarce so cold as the liquor we drank it in. I dare not tell you what they were, and so hasten to conclude, | *Your,* &c.

19

To Francis Atterbury, 20 November 1717.

Atterbury (1662-1732) had been Dean of Westminster and Bishop of Roches-ter since 1713. A high churchman, he had both Jacobite sympathies and contacts, for which he was to be arrested in 1722 (see no. 21 below). In the present letter Pope thanks Atterbury for his condolences upon his father's death, which had occurred on 23 October.

My Lord,—I am truly oblig'd by your kind condoleance on my Father's death, and the desire you express that I should improve this incident to my advantage. I know your Lordship's friendship to me is so extensive, that you include in that wish both my Spiritual and my Temporal advantage; and it is what I owe to that friendship, to open my mind unreservedly to you on this head. It is true, I have lost a Parent for whom no gains I could make would be any equivalent: But that was not my only tye: I thank God another still remains (and long may it remain) of the same tender nature: *Genitrix est mihi*–and excuse me if I say with Euryalus,

    —*nequeam lacrymas perferre parentis.*

A rigid Divine may call it a carnal tye, but sure it is a virtuous one. At least I am more certain that it is a Duty of Nature to preserve a good parent's life and happiness, than I am of any Speculative point what-ever.

    —*Ignaram hujus quodcunque pericli*
    Hanc ego, nunc, linquam?[1]

Selections from the Correspondence

For she, my Lord, would think this Separation more grievous than any other; and I, for my part, know as little as poor Euryalus did of the success of such an adventure, (for an Adventure it is, and no small one, in spite of the most positive Divinity.) Whether the change would be to my spiritual advantage, God only knows: this I know, that I mean as well in the Religion I now profess, as I can possibly ever do in any other. Can a man who thinks so, justify a change, even if he thought both equally good? To such an one, the part of *Joyning* with any one body of Christians might perhaps be easy, but I think it would not be so to *Renounce* the other.

Your Lordship has formerly advis'd me to read the best Books of Controversies between the Churches. Shall I tell you a secret? I did so at fourteen years old: for I loved reading, and my father had no other books. There was a collection of all that had been written on both sides in the reign of King James the second: I warm'd my head with them, and the consequence was, that I found my self a Papist and a Protestant by turns, according to the last book I read. I am afraid most Seekers are in the same case, and when they stop, they are not so properly converted, as out-witted. You see how little glory you would gain by my conversion. And after all, I verily believe your Lordship and I are both of the same religion, if we were thoroughly understood by one another; and that all honest and reasonable christians would be so, if they did but talk enough together every day; and had nothing to do together, but to serve God and live in peace with their Neighbour.

As to the *temporal* side of the question, I can have no dispute with you. It is certain, all the beneficial circumstances of life and all the shining ones, lie on the part you would invite me to. But if I could bring myself to fancy what I think you do but fancy, that I have any talents for Active life, I want health for it; and besides it is a real truth, I have less Inclination (if possible) than Ability. Contemplative life is not only my scene, but it is my habit too. I begun my life where most people end theirs, with a dis-relish of all that the world calls Ambition: I don't know why 'tis call'd so, for to me it always seem'd to be rather *stooping* than *climbing*. I'll tell you my politick and religious sentiments in a few words. In my Politicks, I think no further than how to preserve the peace of my life in any Government under which I live; nor in my Religion, than to preserve the peace of my conscience in any Church with which I communicate. I hope all Churches and all Governments are so far of God, as they are rightly understood, and rightly administred: and where they are, or may be wrong, I leave it to God alone to mend or reform them; which whenever he does, it must be by greater Instruments than I am. I am not a Papist, for I renounce the temporal invasions of the Papal power, and detest their arrogated authority over Princes or States. I am a Catholick, in the strictest sense of the word. If I was born under an absolute Prince, I would be a quiet subject; but I thank God I was not: I have a due sense of the excellence of the British constitution. In a word, the things I have always wished to see, are not a Roman Catholick, or a French Catholick, or a Spanish Catholick, but a true Catholick: and not a King of Whigs, or a King of Tories, but a King of England. Which God of his mercy grant his present Majesty may be, and all future Majesties! You see, my Lord, I end like a preacher: but this is *Sermo ad Clerum*, not *ad Populum*.[2] Believe me, with infinite obligation and sincere thanks, ever | Your, &c.

20

To Lord Bathurst, 13 September 1719.

Allen Bathurst (1684-1775), created first Earl Bathurst in 1712, took a particular interest in gardening. Pope published his *Epistle to Bathurst* in 1733.

I Believe you are by this time immers'd in your vast Wood; and one may address to you as to a very abstracted person, like Alexander Selkirk or the Self-taught Philosopher.[1] I should be very curious to know what sort of contemplations employ you? I remember the latter of those I mention'd, gave himself up to a devout exercise of making his head giddy with various circumrotations, to imitate the motions of the cœlestial bodies. I don't think it at all impossible that Mr. L may be far advanced in that exercise, by frequent turns towards the several aspects of the heavens, to which you may have been pleas'd to direct him in search of prospects and new avenues. He will be tractable in time, as birds are tam'd by being whirl'd about; and doubtless come not to despise the meanest shrubs or coppice-wood, tho' naturally he seems more inclin'd to admire God, in his greater works, the tall timber: for as Virgil has it, *Non omnes arbusta juvant, humilesque myricæ*.[2] I wish my self with you both, whether you are in peace or at war, in violent argumentation or smooth consent, over Gazettes in the morning, or over Plans in the evening. In that last article, I am of opinion your Lordship has a loss of me; for generally after the debate of a whole day, we acquiesc'd at night in the best conclusion of which human reason seems capable in all great matters, to fall fast asleep! And so we ended, unless immediate Revelation (which ever must overcome human reason) suggested some new lights to us, by a

Vision in bed. But laying aside Theory, I am told you are going directly to Practice. Alas, what a Fall will that be? A new Building is like a new Church, when once it is set up, you must maintain it in all the forms, and with all the inconveniencies; then cease the pleasant luminous days of inspiration, and there's an end of miracles at once!

That this Letter may be all of a piece, I'll fill the rest with an account of a consultation lately held in my neighbourhood, about designing a princely garden.[3] Several Criticks were of several opinions: One declar'd he would not have too much Art in it; for my notion (said he) of gardening is, that it is only sweeping Nature; Another told them that Gravel walks were not of a good taste, for all of the finest abroad were of loose sand: A third advis'd peremptorily there should not be one Lyme tree in the whole plantation; a fourth made the same exclusive clause extend to Horse-chesnuts, which he affirm'd not to be Trees, but Weeds; Dutch Elms were condemn'd by a fifth; and thus about half the Trees were proscrib'd, contrary to the Paradise of God's own planting, which is expresly said to be planted with *all trees*. There were some who cou'd not bear Ever-greens, and call'd them Never-greens; some, who were angry at them only when cut into shapes, and gave the modern Gardeners the name of Ever-green Taylors; some who had no dislike to Cones and Cubes, but wou'd have 'em cut in Forest-trees; and some who were in a passion against anything in shape, even against clipt-hedges, which they call'd green walls. These (my Lord) are our Men of Taste, who pretend to prove it by tasting little or nothing. Sure such a Taste is like such a stomach, not a good one, but a weak one. We have the same sort of Critics in poetry; one is fond of nothing but Heroicks, another cannot relish Tragedies, another hates Pastorals, all little Wits delight in Epigrams. Will you give me leave to add, there are the same in Divinity? where many leading Critics are for rooting up more than they plant, and would leave the Lord's Vineyard either very thinly furnish'd, or very oddly trimm'd...

21

To Atterbury, 20 April 1723.

Arrested in 1722 on charges of treasonable designs for the restoration of the Stuarts, Atterbury was tried before the House of Lords in May 1723. Pope gave evidence on his behalf. Atterbury was found guilty and exiled, and it became an offence to correspond with him.

It is not possible to express what I think, and what I feel; only this, that I have thought and felt for nothing but you, for some time past: and shall think of nothing so long for the time to come. The greatest comfort I had was an intention (which I would have made practicable) to have attended you in your journey; to which I had brought that person to consent, who only could have hindered me, by a tye, which tho' it may be more tender, I do not think more strong than that of friendship. But I fear there will be no way left me to tell you this great truth, that I remember you, that I love you, that I am grateful to you, that I entirely esteem and value you: no way but that one, which needs no open warrant to authorize it, or secret conveyance to secure it; which no bills can preclude, and no Kings prevent; a way that can reach to any part of the world where you may be, where the very whisper or even the wish of a friend must not be heard, or even suspected: by this way, I dare tell my esteem and affection of you, to your enemies in the gates; and you, and they, and their sons, may hear of it.

You prove your self, my Lord, to know me for the friend I am; in judging that the manner of your Defence, and your Reputation by it, is a point of the highest concern to me: and assuring me it shall be such, that none of your friends shall blush for you. Let me further prompt you to do your self the best and most lasting justice. The instruments of your Fame to posterity will be in your own hands. May it not be, that providence has appointed you to some great and useful work, and calls you to it this severe way? You may more eminently and more effectually serve the publick even now, than in the stations you have so honourably fill'd. Think of Tully, Bacon, and Clarendon: is it not the latter, the disgrac'd part of their lives, which you most envy, and which you would choose to have liv'd?

I am tenderly sensible of the wish you express, that no part of your misfortune may pursue me. But God knows I am every day less and less fond of my native country (so torn as it is by Party-rage) and begin to consider a friend in exile as a friend in death; one gone before, where I am not unwilling nor unprepared to follow after; and where (however various or uncertain the roads and voyages of another world may be) I cannot but entertain a pleasing hope, that we may meet again.

I faithfully assure you, that in the mean time there is no one living or dead, of whom I shall think oftner or better than of you. I shall look upon you as in a state between both, in which you will have from me all the passions and warm wishes that can attend the living, and all the respect and tender sense of loss, that we feel for the dead. And I shall ever depend upon your constant friendship, kind memory, and good offices, tho' I were never to see or hear the effects of them: like the trust we have in benevolent Spirits, who tho' we never see or hear them, we think are constantly serving us, and praying for us.

Whenever I am wishing to write to you, I shall conclude you are intentionally doing so to me: and every time that I think of you, I will believe you are thinking of me. I shall never suffer to be forgotten (nay to be but faintly remember'd) the honour, the pleasure, the pride I must ever have, in reflecting how frequently you have delighted me, how kindly you have distinguish'd me, how cordially you have advis'd me! In conversation, in study, I shall always want you, and wish for you. In my most lively, and in my most thoughtful hours, I shall equally bear about me, the impressions of you: And perhaps it will not be in This life only, that I shall have cause to remember and acknowledge the Friendship of the Bishop of Rochester. I am, &c.

22
To Swift, August 1723.

The two friends had not seen each other since Swift's departure for Ireland in 1714.

I find a Rebuke in a late Letter of yours that both stings and pleases me extreamly. Your saying that I ought to have writ a Postscript to my Friend Gay's, makes me not content to write less than a whole Letter; and your seeming to take his kindly, gives me hopes you will look upon this as a sincere effect of Friendship. Indeed, as I cannot but own the Laziness with which you tax me, and with which I may equally charge you, for both of us have had (and one of us has both had and given) a Surfeit of writing, so I really thought you would know your self to be so certainly intitled to my Friendship, that it was a possession you could not imagine stood in need of any farther Deeds or Writings to assure you of it.

Whatever you seem to think of your withdrawn and separate state, at this distance, and in this Absence, Dean Swift lives still in England, in every place and company where he would chuse to live, and I find him in all the Conversations I keep, and in all the Hearts in which I desire any share.

We have never met these many years without mention of you: Besides my old Acquaintance, I have found that all my friends of a later date are such as were yours before. Lord Oxford, Lord Harcourt, and

Lord Harley, may look upon me as one intailed upon them by you. Lord Bolingbroke is now returned (as I hope) to take Me with all his other Hereditary-Rights; and, indeed, he seems grown so much a Philosopher, as to set his heart upon some of them as little, as upon the Poet you gave him. It is sure my ill fate, that all those I most loved, and with whom I have most lived, must be banished: after both of you left England, my constant Host was the Bishop of Rochester; sure this is a Nation that is cursedly afraid of being over-run with too much Politeness, and cannot regain one great Genius, but at the expence of another. I tremble for my Lord Peterborough (whom I now lodge with) he has too much Wit, as well as Courage, to make a solid General; and if he escapes being banished by others, I fear he will banish himself. This leads me to give you some Account of my manner of Life and Conversation, which has been infinitely more various and dissipated, than when you knew me and cared for me; and among all Sexes, Parties, and Professions. A Glut of Study and Retirement, in the first part of my life, cast me into this; and this I begin to see will throw me again into Study and Retirement.

The Civilities I have met with from opposite Setts of people, have hindred me from being violent or sour to any Party; but at the same time the Observations and Experiences I cannot but have collected, have made me less fond of, and less surprized at, any: I am therefore the more afflicted and the more angry at the Violences and hardships I see practised by either. The merry Vein you knew me in, is sunk into a Turn of Reflection, that has made the World pretty indifferent to me; and yet I have acquired a Quietness of mind which by fits improves into a certain degree of Chearfulness, enough to make me just so good humoured as to wish that World well. My Friendships are increased by new ones, yet no part of the Warmth I felt for the old is diminished. Aversions I have none, but to Knaves (for Fools I have learned to bear with) and such I cannot be commonly civil to; for I think those next to Knaves who converse with them. The greatest Man in power of this sort shall hardly make me bow to him, unless I had a personal obligation to him, and that I will take care not to have. The top pleasure of my life is one I learned from you, both how to gain and how to use; the Freedom of Friendship with men much my Superiors. To have pleased great men, according to Horace, is a praise; but not to have flattered them, and yet not have displeased them, is a greater. I have carefully avoided all Intercourse with Poets and Scriblers, unless where by great chance I have found a modest one. By these means I have had no quarrels with any personally: none have been Enemies but who were also Strangers to me; and as there is no great need of an

Selections from the Correspondence

Eclaircisment with such, whatever they writ or said I never retaliated; not only never seeming to know, but often really never knowing any thing of the matter. There are very few things that give me the Anxiety of a Wish; the strongest I have would be to pass my days with you, and a few such as you: But Fate has dispersed them all about the world; and I find to wish it is as vain, as to wish to live to see the Millennium and the Kingdom of the Just upon Earth.

If I have sinned in my long silence, consider there is one to whom you your self have been as great a sinner. As soon as you see his Hand, you will learn to do me justice, and feel in your Heart how long a man may be silent to those he truly loves and respects.

23

To Blount, 2 June 1725.

You shew your self a just man and a friend in those guesses and suppositions you make at the possible reasons of my silence; every one of which is a true one. As to forgetfulness of you or yours, I assure you the promiscuous conversations of the town serve only to put me in mind of better, and more quiet, to be had in a corner of the world (undisturb'd, innocent, serene, and sensible) with such as you. Let no access of any distrust make you think of me differently in a cloudy day from what you do in the most sunshiny weather. Let the young ladies be assured I make nothing new in my gardens without wishing to see the print of their fairy steps in every part of 'em. I have put the last hand to my works of this kind, in happily finishing the subterraneous way and grotto: I there found a spring of the clearest water, which falls in a perpetual rill, that ecchoes thro' the cavern day and night. From the river Thames, you see thro' my arch up a walk of the wilderness, to a kind of open Temple, wholly compos'd of shells in the rustic manner; and from that distance under the temple you look down thro' a sloping arcade of trees, and see the sails on the river passing suddenly and vanishing, as thro' a perspective glass. When you shut the doors of this grotto, it becomes on the instant, from a luminous room, a *Camera obscura;* on the walls of which all the objects of the river, hills, woods, and boats, are forming a moving picture in their visible radiations: and when you have a mind to light it up, it affords you a very different scene; it is finished with shells interspersed with pieces of looking-glass in angular forms; and in the cieling is a star of the same material, at which when a lamp (of an orbicular figure of thin alabaster) is hung in the middle, a thousand pointed rays glitter and are reflected over the place. There are connected to this grotto by a

271

narrower passage two porches, one towards the river of smooth stones
full of light, and open; the other toward the Garden, shadow'd with
trees, rough with shells, flints, and iron-ore. The bottom is paved with
simple pebble, as is also the adjoining walk up the wilderness to the
temple, in the natural taste, agreeing not ill with the little dripping
murmur, and the aquatic idea of the whole place. It wants nothing to
compleat it but a good statue with an inscription, like that beautiful
antique one which you know I am so fond of,

> Hujus Nympha loci, sacri custodia fontis
> Dormio, dum blandæ sentio murmur aquæ.
> Parce meum, quisquis tangis cava marmora, somnum
> Rumpere, seu bibas, sive lavere, tace. [1]

> Nymph of the grot, these sacred springs I keep,
> And to the murmur of these waters sleep;
> Ah spare my slumbers, gently tread the cave!
> Ah drink in silence, or in silence lave!

You'll think I have been very poetical in this description, but it is
pretty near the truth. I wish you were here to bear testimony how little
it owes to Art, either the place itself, or the image I give of it. I am, &c.

24

To Gay, 16 October 1727.

John Gay (1685-1732), one of the Scriblerus group, had refused the offer of a
place at court as gentleman usher to the two-year-old Princess Louisa.

Dear Sir,
I Have many years ago magnify'd in my own mind, and repeated to
you, a ninth Beatitude, added to the eight in the Scripture; "Blessed is
he who expects nothing, for he shall never be disappointed." I could
find in my heart to congratulate you on this happy dismission from all
Court-dependance. I dare say I shall find you the better and the
honester man for it, many years hence; very probably the healthfuller,
and the chearfuller into the bargain. You are happily rid of many
cursed Ceremonies, as well as of many ill and vicious Habits, of which
few or no men escape the infection, who are hackney'd and tramelled
in the ways of a Court. Princes indeed, and Peers (the lackies of
Princes) and Ladies (the fools of Peers) will smile on you the less; but
men of worth and real friends will look on you the better. There is a
thing, the only thing which Kings and Queens cannot give you (for
they have it not to give) Liberty: But it is worth all they have; and, as
yet I thank God, Englishmen need not ask it from their hands. You

272

will enjoy that, and your own integrity, and the satisfactory consciousness of having *not* merited such graces from Courts as are bestow'd
only on the mean, servile, flattering, interested, and undeserving. The
only steps to the favour of the Great are such complacencies, such
compliances, such distant decorums, as delude them in their vanities,
or engage them in their passions. He is their greatest favourite, who is
the falsest: and when a man by such vile gradations arrives at the
height of grandeur and pow'r, he is then at best but in a circumstance
to be hated, and in a condition to be hanged, for serving their ends: So
many a Minister has found it!

I believe you did not want advice, in the letter you sent by my Lord
Grantham;[1] I presume you writ it not, without: And you cou'd not
have better, if I guess right at the person who agreed to your doing it,
in respect to any decency you ought to observe: for I take that person
to be a perfect judge of decencies and forms. I am not without fears
even on that person's account: I think it a bad omen: but what have I
to do with Court-omens? – Dear Gay, adieu. I can only add a plain
uncourtly speech: while you are no body's servant, you may be any
one's friend; and as such I embrace you, in all conditions of life. While
I have a shilling, you shall have six-pence, nay eight-pence, if I can
contrive to live upon a groat. I am faithfully Yours, &c.

25
To Swift, 28 November 1729.

Swift had made his last visit to England in 1727, and the two friends were never
to meet again.

This letter (like all mine) will be a Rhapsody; it is many years ago since
I wrote as a Wit. How many occurrences or informations must one
omit, if one determin'd to say nothing that one could not say prettily?
I lately receiv'd from the widow of one dead correspondent, and the
father of another, several of my own letters of about fifteen and twenty
years old; and it was not unentertaining to my self to observe, how and
by what degrees I ceas'd to be a witty writer; as either my experience
grew on the one hand, or my affection to my correspondents on the
other. Now as I love you better than most I have ever met with in the
world, and esteem you too the more, the longer I have compar'd you
with the rest of the world; so inevitably I write to you more negligent-
ly, that is more openly, and what all but such as love another will call
writing worse. I smile to think how Curll would be bit, were our

273

Epistles to fall into his hands, and how gloriously they would fall short of ev'ry ingenious reader's expectations?

You can't imagine what a vanity it is to me, to have something to rebuke you for in the way of Oeconomy. I love the man that builds a house *subito ingenio*,[1] and makes a wall for a horse; then cries, "We wise men must think of nothing but getting ready money." I am glad you approve my annuity; all we have in this world is no more than an annuity, as to our own enjoyment: but I will encrease your regard for my wisdom, and tell you, that this annuity includes also the life of another,[2] whose concern ought to be as near me as my own, and with whom my whole prospects ought to finish. I throw my javelin of Hope no farther, *Cur brevi fortes jaculamur ævo*—&c.[3]

The second (as it is called, but indeed the eighth) edition of the Dunciad, with some additional notes and epigrams, shall be sent you if I know any opportunity; if they reprint it with you, let them by all means follow that octavo edition – The Drapier's letters[4] are again printed here, very laudably as to paper, print, &c. for you know I disapprove Irish politicks (as my Commentator tells you) being a strong and jealous subject of England. The Lady you mention, you ought not to complain of for not acknowledging your present; she having lately receiv'd a much richer present from Mr. Knight of the S. Sea;[5] and you are sensible she cannot ever return it to one in the condition of an out-law. It's certain as he can never expect any favour, his motive must be wholly dis-interested. Will not this Reflection make you blush? Your continual deplorings of Ireland, make me wish you were here long enough to forget those scenes that so afflict you: I am only in fear if you were, you would grow such a patriot here too, as not to be quite at ease, for your love of old England. – It is very possible, your journey, in the time I compute, might exactly tally with my intended one to you; and if you must soon again go back, you would not be un-attended. For the poor woman decays perceptibly every week; and the winter may too probably put an end to a very long, and a very irreproachable, life. My constant attendance on her does indeed affect my mind very much, and lessen extremely my desires of long life; since I see the best that can come of it is a miserable benediction. I look upon myself to be many years older in two years since you saw me: The natural imbecility of my body, join'd now to this acquir'd old age of the mind, makes me at least as old as you, and we are the fitter to crawl down the hill together; I only desire I may be able to keep pace with you. My first friendship at sixteen, was contracted with a man of seventy, and I found him not grave enough or consistent enough for me, tho' we lived well to his death. I speak of old

Mr. Wycherley; some letters of whom (by the by) and of mine, the Booksellers have got and printed, not without the concurrence of a noble friend of mine and yours. I don't much approve of it; tho' there is nothing for me to be asham'd of, because I will not be asham'd of any thing I do not do myself, or of any thing that is not immoral but merely dull (as for instance, if they printed this letter I am now writing, which they easily may, if the underlings at the Post-office please to take a copy of it.) I admire on this consideration, your sending your last to me quite open, without a seal, wafer, or any closure whatever, manifesting the utter openness of the writer. I would do the same by this, but fear it would look like affectation to send two letters so together. – I will fully represent to our friend (and I doubt not it will touch his heart) what you so feelingly set forth as to the badness of your Burgundy, &c.[6] He is an extreme honest man, and indeed ought to be so, considering how very indiscreet and unreserved he is: But I do not approve this part of his character, and will never join with him in any of his idlenesses in the way of wit. You know my maxim to keep as clear of all offence, as I am clear of all interest in either party. I was once displeas'd before at you, for complaining to Mr. [Dodington] of my not having a pension, and am so again at your naming it to a certain Lord.[7] I have given proof in the course of my whole life, (from the time when I was in the friendship of Lord Bolingbroke and Mr. Craggs, even to this when I am civilly treated by Sir R. Walpole) that I never thought my self so warm in any Party's cause as to deserve their mony; and therefore would never have accepted it: But give me leave to tell you, that of all mankind the two persons I would least have accepted any favour from, are those very two, to whom you have unluckily spoken of it. I desire you to take off any impressions which that dialogue may have left on his Lordship's mind, as if I ever had any thought of being beholden to him, or any other, in that way. And yet you know I am no enemy to the present Constitution; I believe, as sincere a well-wisher to it, nay even to the church establish'd, as any Minister in, or out of employment, whatever; or any Bishop of England or Ireland. Yet am I of the Religion of Erasmus, a Catholick; so I live, so I shall die; and hope one day to meet you, Bishop Atterbury, the younger Craggs, Dr. Garth, Dean Berkley, and Mr. Hutchenson, in that place, To which God of his infinite mercy bring us, and every body!

Lord B's answer to your letter I have just receiv'd, and join it to this pacquet. The work he speaks of with such abundant partiality, is a system of Ethics in the Horatian way.[8]

26

To Gay, 16 December 1731.

As soon as Pope's *Epistle to Burlington* was published on 13 December 1731, 'Timon' was identified as the Duke of Chandos, and his villa as Cannons. In an attempt to dispel this misapprehension, Pope arranged for an anonymous open letter to Gay to be published in *The Daily Post-Boy* for 22 December, and in *The Daily Journal* the following day. Although in some editions of Pope's letters (including *1742*) it is attributed to 'Mr. Cleland', there can be little doubt that it is Pope's work.

I am astonish'd at the complaints occasion'd by a late Epistle to the Earl of Burlington; and I shou'd be afflicted were there the least just ground for 'em. Had the writer attack'd Vice, at a time when it is not only tolerated but triumphant, and so far from being conceal'd as a Defect, that it is proclaimed with ostentation as a Merit; I should have been apprehensive of the consequence: Had he satirized Gamesters of a hundred thousand pounds fortune, acquir'd by such methods as are in daily practice, and almost universally encouraged; had he over-warmly defended the Religion of his country, against such books as come from every press, are publickly vended in every shop, and greedily bought by almost every rank of men; or had he called our excellent weekly writers by the same names which they openly bestow on the greatest men in the Ministry, and out of the Minstry, for which they are all unpunished, and most rewarded: In any of these cases, indeed, I might have judged him too presumptuous, and perhaps have trembled for his rashness.

I could not but hope better for this small and modest Epistle, which attacks no one Vice whatsoever; which deals only in Folly, and not Folly in general, but a single species of it; that only branch, for the opposite excellency to which, the Noble Lord to whom it is written must necessarily be celebrated. I fancied it might escape censure, especially seeing how tenderly these Follies are treated, and really less accused than apologized for.

> *Yet hence the Poor are cloath'd, the Hungry fed,*
> *Health to himself, and to his Infants Bread*
> *The Lab'rer bears.*[1]

Is this such a crime, that to impute it to a man must be a grievous offence: 'Tis an innocent Folly, and much more beneficent than the want of it; for ill Taste employs more hands, and diffuses expence more than a good one. Is it a moral defect? no, it is but a natural one; a want of taste. It is what the best good man living may be liable to. The worthiest Peer may live exemplarily in an ill-favour'd house, and the best reputed citizen be pleased with a vile garden. I thought (I say) the author had the common liberty to observe a defect, and to compliment a friend for a quality that distinguishes him: which I know not how any quality should do, if we were not to remark that it was wanting in others.

But they say the satire is personal. I thought it could not be so, because all its reflections are on things. His reflections are not on the man, but his house, garden, &c. Nay, he respects (as one may say) the person, of the Gladiator, the Nile, and the Triton: he is only sorry to see them (as he might be to see any of his friends) ridiculous by being in the wrong places and in bad company. Some fancy, that to say a thing, is personal, is the same as to say it is Injust, not considering, that nothing can be just that is not personal. I am afraid that "all such writings and discourses as touch no man, will mend no man." The good-natured, indeed, are apt to be alarmed at any thing like satire; and the guilty readily concur with the weak for a plain reason, because the vicious look upon folly as their Frontier;

—*Jam proximus ardet*
Ucalegon— [2]

No wonder those who know ridicule belongs to them, find an inward consolation in removing it from themselves as far as they can; and it is never so far, as when they can get it fixed on the best characters. No wonder those who are Food for Satirists should rail at them as creatures of prey; every beast born for our use would be ready to call a man so.

I know no remedy, unless people in our age would as little frequent the theatres, as they begin to do the Churches; unless comedy were forsaken, satire silent, and every man left to do what seems good in his own eyes, as if there were no King, no Priest, no Poet, in Israel.

But I find myself obliged to touch a point, on which I must be more serious; it well deserves I should: I mean the malicious application of the Character of Timon, which I will boldly say, they would impute to the person the most different in the world from a Man-hater, to the person whose taste and encouragement of wit have often been shewn in the rightest place. The author of that epistle must certainly think so, if he has the same opinion of his own merit as authors generally have; for he has been distinguished by this very person.

Why, in God's name, must a portrait, apparently collected from twenty different men, be apply'd to one only? Has it his eye? no, it is very unlike. Has it his nose or mouth? no, they are totally differing. What then I beseech you? Why it has the mole on his chin. Very well;

but must the picture therefore be his, and has no other man that blemish?

Could there be a more melancholy instance how much the taste of the publick is vitiated, and turns the most salutary and seasonable physick into poison, than if amidst the blaze of a thousand bright qualities in a great man, they should only remark there is a shadow about him; as what eminence is without; I am confident the author was incapable of imputing any such to one, whose whole life (to use his own expression in print of him) is a *continued series* of *good* and *generous actions*.

I know no man who would be more concerned, if he gave the least pain or offence to any innocent person; and none who would be less concerned, if the satire were challenged by any one at whom he would really aim it. If ever that happens, I dare engage he will own it, with all the freedom of one whose censures are just, and who sets his name to them.

27

To Jacob Tonson, 7 June 1732.

The Man of Ross is the subject of lines 250-80 of the *Epistle to Bathurst*, published the following year. On Pope's concern for factual accuracy in this case see Erskine-Hill, pp. 15-41.

Before I received your last, I intended to write to you my thanks for the great diligence (or let me give it a higher title, zeal) you have shewn in giving me so many particulars of the Man of Ross. They are more than sufficient for my honest purpose of setting up his fame, as an example to greater and wealthyer men, how they ought to use their fortunes. You know, few of these particulars can be made to shine in verse, but I have selected the most affecting, and have added 2 or 3 which I learnd fro' other hands. A small exaggeration you must allow me as a poet; yet I was determined the ground work at least should be *Truth*, which made me so scrupulous in my enquiries; and sure, considering that the world is bad enough to be always extenuating and lessening what virtue is among us, it is but reasonable to pay it sometimes a little over measure, to balance that injustice, especially when it is done for example and encouragement to others. If any man shall ever happen to endeavour to emulate the Man of Ross, 'twill be no manner of harm if I make him think he was something more charitable and more beneficent than really he was, for so much more good it would put the imitator upon doing. And farther I am satisfy'd in my conscience (from the strokes in 2 or 3 accounts I have of his character) that it was in his will, and in his heart, to have done every good a poet can imagine.

My motive for singling out this man, was twofold: first to distinguish real and solid worth from showish or plausible expence, and virtue fro' vanity: and secondly, to humble the pride of greater men, by an opposition of one so obscure and so distant from the sphere of publick glory, this proud town. To send you any of the particular verses will be much to the prejudice of the whole; which if it has any beauty, derives it from the manner in which it is *placed,* and the *contrast* (as the painters call it) in which it stands, with the pompous figures of famous, or rich, or high-born men.

I was not sorry he had no monument, and will put that circumstance into a note, perhaps into the body of the poem itself (unless you entreat the contrary in your own favor, by your zeal to erect one). I would however, in this case, spare the censure upon his heir (so well as he deserves it), because I dare say, after seeing his picture, every body will turn that circumstance to his honour, and conclude the Man of Ross himself would not have any monument in memory of his own good deeds.

I have no thoughts of printing the poem (which is an epistle on the *Use of Riches*) this long time, perhaps not till it is accompanied with many others; and at a time, when telling truths, and drawing exemplary pictures of men and manners can be of no disservice to the author, and occasion no slanderer to mistake them, and apply them falsely, as I was lately serv'd in the character of Timon. But I wish for nothing more than to see you here, on these quiet banks of the Thames, where any of these things should be frankly shewn to you....

28
To Swift, 20[?] April 1733.

You say truly, that death is only terrible to us as it separates us from those we love, but I really think those have the worst of it who are left by us, if we are true friends. I have felt more (I fancy) in the loss of Mr. Gay, than I shall suffer in the thought of going away myself into a state that can feel none of this sort of losses. I wish'd vehemently to have seen him in a condition of living independent, and to have lived in perfect indolence the rest of our days together, the two most idle, most innocent, undesigning Poets of our age. I now as vehemently wish you and I might walk into the grave together, by as slow steps as you please, but contentedly and chearfully: Whether that ever can be, or in what country, I know no more, that into what country we shall walk out of the grave. But it suffices me to know it will be exactly what region or state our Maker appoints, and that whatever *Is, is Right*.[1] Our poor friend's papers are partly in my hands, and for as much as is so, I will take care to suppress things unworthy of him. As to the Epitaph, I'm sorry you gave a copy, for it will certainly by that means come into print, and I would correct it more, unless you will do it for me (and that I shall like as well:) Upon the whole I earnestly wish your coming over hither, for this reason among many others, that your influence may be join'd with mine to suppress whatever we may judge proper of his papers. To be plunged in my neighbours and my papers, will be your inevitable fate as soon as you come. That I am an author whose characters are thought of some weight, appears from the great noise and bustle that the Court and Town make about any I give: and I will not render them less important, or less interesting, by sparing Vice and Folly, or by betraying the cause of Truth and Virtue. I will take care they shall be such, as no man can be angry at but the persons I would have angry. You are sensible with what decency and justice I paid homage to the Royal Family, at the same time that I satirized false Courtiers, and Spies, &c. about 'em. I have not the courage however to be such a Satyrist as you, but I would be as much, or more, a Philosopher. You call your satires, Libels; I would rather call my satires, Epistles: They will consist more of Morality than of Wit, and grow graver, which you will call duller. I shall leave it to my Antagonists to be witty (if they can) and content myself to be useful, and in the right. Tell me your opinion as to Lady M[ary]'s or Lord H[ervey]'s performance?[2] they are certainly the Top-wits of the Court, and you may judge by that single piece what can be done against me; for it was labour'd, corrected, præ-commended and post-disapprov'd, so far as to be dis-own'd by themselves, after each had highly cry'd it up for the others. I have met with some complaints, and heard at a distance of some threats, occasion'd by my verses: I sent fair messages to acquaint them where I was to be found in town, and to offer to call at their houses to satisfy them, and so it dropp'd. It is very poor in anyone to rail and threaten at a distance, and have nothing to say to you when they see you. – I am glad you persist and abide by so good a thing as that Poem, in which I am immortal for my Morality: I never took any praise so kindly, and yet I think I deserve that praise better than I do any other. When does your collection come out, and what will it consist of? I have but last week finished another of my Epistles, in the order of the system; and this week (*exercitandi gratia*)[3] I have translated (or rather parody'd) another of Horace's, in which I introduce you advising me about my expences, housekeeping, &c. But these things shall lye by, till you come to carp at 'em, and alter rhymes, and grammar, and triplets, and cacaphonies of all kinds. Our Parliament will sit till Midsummer, which I hope may be a motive to bring you rather in summer than so late as autumn: you us'd to love what I hate, a hurry of politicks, &c. Courts I see not, Courtiers I know not, Kings I adore, Queens I compliment not; so I am never like to be in fashion, nor in dependance. I heartily join with you in pitying our poor Lady for her unhappiness, and should only pity her more, if she had more of what they at Court call Happiness. Come then, and perhaps we may go all together into France at the end of the season, and compare the Liberties of both kingdoms. Adieu. Believe me dear Sir, (with a thousand warm wishes, mix'd with short sighs) ever yours.

29
To Arbuthnot, 26 July 1734.

Dr John Arbuthnot (1667-1735), one of the Scriblerian group, wrote to Pope on 17 July commenting on their long and untroubled friendship, and adding: 'I make it my Last Request, that you continue that noble *Disdain* and *Abhorrence* of Vice, which you seem naturally endu'd with, but still with a due regard to your own Safety; and study more to reform than chastise, tho' the one often cannot be effected without the other' (*Corr.* iii 417). Pope replied on 2 August (*Corr.* iii 423-4), a letter which he seems to have polished for publication in the form given below. This is one of Pope's most important defences of his satire, and is comparable with the sentiments expressed in the verse *Epistle to Dr. Arbuthnot*, composed at the end of August 1734 and printed in January 1735.

I thank you for your letter, which has all those genuine marks of a good mind by which I have ever distinguish'd yours, and for which I have so long loved you. Our friendship has been constant; because it was grounded on good principles, and therefore not only uninterrupted by any Distrust, but by any Vanity, much less any Interest.

What you recommend to me with the solemnity of a Last Request, shall have its due weight with me. That disdain and indignation against Vice, is (I thank God) the only disdain and indignation I have: It is sincere, and it will be a lasting one. But sure it is as impossible to have a just abhorrence of Vice, without hating the Vicious, as to bear a true love for Virtue, without loving the Good. To reform and not to chastise, I am afraid is impossible, and that the best Precepts, as well as the best Laws, would prove of small use, if there were no Examples to inforce them. To attack Vices in the abstract, without touching Persons, may be safe fighting indeed, but it is fighting with Shadows. General propositions are obscure, misty, and uncertain, compar'd with plain, full, and home examples: Precepts only apply to our Reason, which in most men is but weak: Examples are pictures, and strike the Senses, nay raise the Passions, and call in those (the strongest and most general of all motives) to the aid of reformation. Every vicious man makes the case his own; and that is the only way by which such men can be affected, much less deterr'd. So that to chastise is to reform. The only sign by which I found my writings ever did any good, or had any weight, has been that they rais'd the anger of bad men. And my greatest comfort, and encouragement to proceed, has been to see, that those who have no shame, and no fear, of any thing else, have appear'd touch'd by my Satires.

As to your kind concern for my Safety, I can guess what occasions it at this time. Some Characters I have drawn are such, that if there be any who deserve 'em, 'tis evidently a service to mankind to point those men out: yet such as if all the world gave them, none I think will own they take to themselves. But if they should, those of whom all the world think in such a manner, must be men I cannot fear. Such in particular as have the meanness to do mischiefs in the dark, have seldom the courage to justify them in the face of day; the talents that make a Cheat or a Whisperer, are not the same that qualify a man for an Insulter; and as to private villany, it is not so safe to join in an Assassination, as in a Libel. I will consult my safety so far as I think becomes a prudent man; but not so far as to omit any thing which I think becomes an honest one. As to personal attacks beyond the law, every man is liable to them: as for danger within the law, I am not guilty enough to fear any. For the good opinion of all the world, I know it is not to be had: for that of worthy men, I hope I shall not forfeit it: for that of the Great, or those in power, I may wish I had it, but if thro' misrepresentations (too common about persons in that station) I have it not, I shall be sorry, but not miserable in the want of it.

It is certain, much freer Satyrists than I have enjoy'd the encouragement and protection of the Princes under whom they lived. Augustus and Mecœnas made Horace their companion, tho' he had been in arms on the side of Brutus; and allow me to remark it was out of the suffring Party too, that they favour'd and distinguish'd Virgil. You will not suspect me of comparing my self with Virgil and Horace, nor even with another Court-favourite, Boileau: I have always been too modest to imagine my Panegyricks were Incense worthy of a Court:

and that I hope will be thought the true reason why I have never offer'd any. I would only have observ'd, that it was under the greatest Princes and best Ministers, that moral Satyrists were most encouraged; and that then Poets exercised the same jurisdiction over the Follies, as Historians did over the Vices of men. It may also be worth considering, whether Augustus himself makes the greater figure, in the writings of the former, or of the latter? and whether Nero and Domitian do not appear as ridiculous for their false Taste and Affectation, in Persius and Juvenal, as odious for their bad Government in Tacitus and Suetonius? In the first of these reigns it was, that Horace was protected and caress'd; and in the latter that Lucan was put to death, and Juvenal banish'd.

I wou'd not have said so much, but to shew you my whole heart on this subject; and to convince you, I am deliberately bent to perform that Request which you make your last to me, and to perform it with Temper, Justice, and Resolution. As your Approbation, (being the testimony of a sound head and an honest heart) does greatly confirm me herein, I wish you may live to see the effect it may hereafter have upon me, in something more deserving of that approbation. But if it be the Will of God (which I know will also be yours) that we must separate, I hope it will be better for You than it can be for me. You are fitter to live, or to die, than any man I know. Adieu my dear friend! and may God preserve your life easy, or make your death happy.

30
To Swift, 19 December 1734.

I am truly sorry for any complaint you have, and it is in regard to the weakness of your eyes that I write (as well as print) in folio. You'll think (I know you will, for you have all the candor of a good understanding) that the thing which men of our age feel the most, is the friendship of our equals; and that therefore whatever affects those who are stept a few years before us, cannot but sensibly affect us who are to follow. It troubles me to hear you complain of your memory, and if I am in any part of my constitution younger than you, it will be in my remembring every thing that has pleased me in you, longer than perhaps you will. The two summers we past together dwell always on my mind, like a vision which gave me a glympse of a better life and better company, than this world otherwise afforded. I am now an individual, upon whom no other depends; and may go where I will, if the wretched carcase I am annex'd to did not hinder me. I rambled by very easy journies this year to Lord Bathurst and Lord Peterborow, who upon ev'ry occasion commemorate, love, and wish for you. I now pass my days between Dawley, London, and this place, not studious, nor idle, rather polishing old works than hewing out new. I redeem now and then a paper that hath been abandon'd several years; and of this sort you'll soon see one, which I inscribe to our old friend Arbuthnot.

Thus far I had written, and thinking to finish my letter the same evening, was prevented by company, and the next morning found my self in a fever, highly disorder'd, and so continu'd in bed for five days, and in my chamber till now; but so well recover'd as to hope to go abroad to-morrow, even by the advice of Dr. Arbuthnot. He himself, poor man, is much broke, tho' not worse than for these two last months he has been. He took extremely kind your letter. I wish to God we could once meet again, before that separation, which yet I would be glad to believe shall re-unite us: But he who made us, not for ours but his purposes, knows whether it be for the better or the worse, that the affections of this life should, or should not continue into the other: and doubtless it is as it should be. Yet I am sure that while I am here, and the thing that I am, I shall be imperfect without the communication of such friends as you; you are to me like a limb lost, and buried in another country; tho' we seem quite divided, every accident makes me feel you were once a part of me. I always consider you so much as a friend, that I forget you are an author, perhaps too much, but 'tis as much as I would desire you would do to me. However, if I could inspirit you to bestow correction upon those three Treatises which you say are so near compleated, I should think it a better work than any I can pretend to of my own. I am almost at the end of my Morals, as I've been, long ago, of my Wit; my system is a short one, and my circle narrow. Imagination has no limits, and that is a sphere in which you move on to eternity; but where one is confined to Truth (or to speak more like a human creature, to the appearances of Truth) we soon find the shortness of our Tether. Indeed by the help of a metaphysical chain of Idæas, one may extend the circulation, go round and round for ever, without making any progress beyond the point to which Providence has pinn'd us: But this does not satisfy me, who would rather say a little to no purpose, than a great deal. Lord B.[1] is voluminous, but he is voluminous only to destroy volumes. I shall not live, I fear, to see that work printed; he is so taken up still, (in spite of the monitory Hint given in the first line of my Essay) with particular Men, that he neglects mankind, and is still a creature of this world, not of the Universe: This World, which is a name we give to Europe, to England, to Ireland, to London, to Dublin, to the Court, to the

Castle, and so diminishing, till it comes to our own affairs, and our own persons. When you write (either to him or to me, for we accept it all as one) rebuke him for it, as a Divine if you like it, or as a Badineur, if you think that more effectual.

What I write will show you that my head is yet weak. I had written to you by that gentleman from the Bath, but I did not know him, and every body that comes from Ireland pretends to be a friend of the Dean's. I am always glad to see any that are truly so, and therefore do not mistake any thing I said, so as to discourage your sending any such to me. Adieu.

31
To Swift, 25 March 1736.

If ever I write more Epistles in Verse, one of them shall be address'd to you. I have long concerted it, and begun it, but I would make what bears your name as finished as my last work ought to be, that is to say, more finished than any of the rest. The subject is large, and will divide into four Epistles, which naturally follow the Essay on Man, *viz.* 1. Of the Extent and Limits of Human Reason, and Science. 2. A view of the useful and therefore attainable, and of the un-useful and therefore un-attainable, Arts. 3. Of the Nature, Ends, Application, and Use of different Capacities. 4. Of the Use of *Learning*, of the *Science* of the *World*, and of *Wit*. It will conclude with a Satire against the mis-application of all these, exemplify'd by pictures, characters, and examples.

But alas! the task is great, and *non sum qualis eram!*[1] My understanding indeed, such as it is, is extended rather than diminish'd: I see things more in the whole, more consistent, and more clearly deduced from, and related to, each other. But what I gain on the side of philosophy, I lose on the side of poetry: the flowers are gone, when the fruits begin to ripen, and the fruits perhaps will never ripen perfectly. The climate (under our Heaven of a Court) is but cold and uncertain: the winds rise, and the winter comes on. I find myself but little disposed to build a new house; I have nothing left but to gather up the reliques of a wreck, and look about me to see how few friends I have left. Pray whose esteem or admiration should I desire now to procure by my writings? whose friendship or conversation to obtain by 'em? I am a man of desperate fortunes, that is a man whose friends are dead: for I never aim'd at any other fortune than in friends. As soon as I had sent my last letter, I receiv'd a most kind one from you, expressing great pain for my late illness at Mr. Cheselden's. I conclude

285

you was eased of that friendly apprehension in a few days after you had dispatch'd yours, for mine must have reached you then. I wondered a little at your quære, who Cheselden was? it shews that the truest merit does not travel so far any way as on the wings of poetry; he is the most noted, and most deserving man, in the whole profession of Chirurgery; and has sav'd the lives of thousands by his manner of cutting for the stone. –I am now well, or what I must call so.

I have lately seen some writings of Lord B's, since he went to France. Nothing can depress his Genius: Whatever befals him, he will still be the greatest man in the world, either in his own time, or with posterity.

Every man you know or care for here, enquires of you, and pays you the only devoir he can, that of drinking your health, I wish you had any motive to see this kingdom. I could keep you, for I am rich, that is, I have more than I want. I can afford room for your self and two servants; I have indeed room enough, nothing but myself at home; the kind and hearty house-wife is dead! the agreeable and instructive neighbour is gone! yet my house is inlarg'd, and the gardens extend and flourish, as knowing nothing of the guests they have lost. I have more fruit-trees and kitchen-garden than you have any thought of; nay I have good Melons and Pine-apples of my own growth. I am as much a better Gardiner, as I am a worse Poet, than when you saw me: But gardening is near a-kin to Philosophy, for Tully says *Agricultura proxima sapientiae*.[2] For God's sake, why should not you, (that are a step higher than a Philosopher, a Divine, yet have too much grace and wit than to be a Bishop) e'en give all you have to the Poor of Ireland (for whom you have already done every thing else) so quit the place, and live and die with me? And let *Tales Animae Concordes*[3] be our Motto and our Epitaph.

32
To Swift, 30 December 1736.

Your very kind letter has made me more melancholy, than almost any thing in this world now can do. For I can bear every thing in it, bad as it is, better than the complaints of my friends. Tho' others tell me you are in pretty good health, and in good spirits, I find the contrary when you open your mind to me: And indeed it is but a prudent part, to seem not so concern'd about others, nor so crazy ourselves as we really are: for we shall neither be beloved or esteem'd the more, by our common acquaintance, for any affliction or any infirmity. But to our true friend we may, we must complain, of what ('tis a thousand to one) he complains with us; for if we have known him long, he is old, and if he has known the world long, he is out of humour at it. If you have but as much more health than others at your age, as you have more wit and good temper, you shall not have much of my Pity: But if you ever live to have less, you shall not have less of my Affection. A whole people will rejoyce at every year that shall be added to you, of which you have had a late instance in the publick rejoycings on your birth-day. I can assure you, something better and greater than high birth and quality, must go toward acquiring those demonstrations of publick esteem and love. I have seen a royal birth-day uncelebrated, but by one vile Ode, and one hired bonfire. Whatever years may take away from you, they will not take away the general esteem, for your Sense, Virtue, and Charity.

The most melancholy effect of years is that you mention, the catalogue of those we lov'd and have lost, perpetually increasing. How much that Reflection struck me, you'll see from the Motto I have prefix'd to my Book of Letters, which so much against my inclination has been drawn from me. It is from Catullus,

Quo desiderio veteres revocamus Amores,
Atque olim amissas flemus Amicitias![1]

I detain this letter till I can find some safe conveyance; innocent as it is, and as all letters of mine must be, of any thing to offend my superiors, except the reverence I bear to true merit and virtue. But I have much reason to fear, those which you have too partially kept in your hands will get out in some very disagreeable shape, in case of our mortality: and the more reason to fear it, since this last month Curll has obtain'd from Ireland two letters, (one of Lord Bolingbroke and one of mine, to you, which we wrote in the year 1723,) and he has printed them, to the best of my memory, rightly, except one passage concerning Dawley which must have been since inserted, since my Lord had not that place at that time. Your answer to that letter he has not got; it has never been out of my custody; for whatever is lent is lost (Wit as well as Money) to these needy poetical Readers.

The world will certainly be the better for his change of life. He seems in the whole turn of his letters, to be a settled and principled Philosopher, thanking Fortune for the Tranquility he has been led into by her aversion, like a man driven by a violent wind, from the sea into a calm harbour. You ask me if I have got any supply of new Friends to make up for those that are gone? I think that impossible, for not our friends only, but so much of our selves is gone by the mere flux and course of years, that were the same Friends to be restored to us, we could not be restored to our selves, to enjoy them. But as when the continual washing of a river takes away our flowers and plants, it throws weeds and sedges in their room; so the course of time brings us something, as it deprives us of a great deal; and instead of leaving us what we cultivated, and expected to flourish and adorn us, gives us only what is of some little use, by accident. Thus I have acquired, without my seeking, a few chance-acquaintance, of young men, who look rather to the past age than the present, and therefore the future may have some hopes of them. If I love them, it is because they honour some of those whom I, and the world, have lost, or are losing. Two or three of them have distinguish'd themselves in Parliament, and you will own in a very uncommon manner, when I tell you it is by their asserting of Independency, and contempt of Corruption. One or two are link'd to me by their love of the same studies and the same authors: but I will own to you, my moral capacity has got so much the better of my poetical, that I have few acquaintance on the latter score, and none without a casting weight on the former. But I find my heart harden'd and blunt to new impressions, it will scarce receive or retain affections of yesterday; and those friends who have been dead these twenty years, are more present to me now, than these I see daily. You, dear Sir, are one of the former sort to me in all respects, but that we can, yet, correspond together. I don't know whether 'tis not more vexatious, to know we are both in one world, without any further intercourse. Adieu. I can say no more, I feel so much...

33

To William Borlase, 8 June 1740.

Borlase had supplied Cornish diamonds for Pope's grotto.

Sir, —As soon as I received your very obliging present and letter, I writ to Dr. Oliver, designing him to prepare the way for my thanks, by assuring you I wanted words to express them, and by taking to himself a part of an obligation which is really above any Merit I can claim to it. I fear, by a Paper I found in the Box, that you have robb'd your own Collection to enrich me, and the same paper gave me an excellent Motto for my Grot, in some part of which I must fix your name, if I can contrive it, agreeably to your Modesty and Merit, in a Shade but shining. I deferr'd writing to you 'till I should form a guess how far your materials would go in the work, which is now half finished, the ruder parts entirely so; in its present condition it is quite natural, and can only admit of more beauties by the Glitter of more minerals, not the disposition or manner of placing them, with which I am quite satisfy'd. I have managed the Roof so as to admit of the larger as well as smaller pendulous [crystals]; the sides are strata of various, beautiful, but rude Marbles, between which run the Loads of Metal, East and West, and in the pavement also, the direction of the Grotto happening to lie so. And I have opened the whole into one Room, groin'd above from pillar to pillar (not of a regular Architecture, but like supporters left in a Quarry), by which means there is a fuller Light cast into all but the narrow passage (which is cover'd with living and long Mosse), only behind the 2 largest Pillars there is a deep recess of dark stone, where two Glasses artfully fix'd reflect the Thames, and almost deceive the Eye to that degree as to seem two arches opening to the River on each side, as there is one real in the middle. The little well is very light, ornamented with Stalactites above, and Spars and Cornish Diamonds on the Edges, with a perpetual drip of water into it from pipes above among the Icicles. I have cry'd help to some other friends, as I found my Want of materials, and have stellifyed some of the Roof with Bristol stone of a fine lustre. I am in hopes of some of the Red transparent Spar from the Lead mines, which would vastly vary the colouring. If you will be extravagant, indeed, in sending anything more, I wish it were glittering tho' not curious; as equally proper in such an Imitation of Nature, who is not so Profuse as you, tho' ever most kind to those who cultivate her. As I procure more Ores or Spars, I go on enriching the Crannies and Interstices, which, as my Marbles are in large pieces, cramp'd fast with iron to the walls, are pretty spacious and unequal, admitting Loads and Veins of 2, 3, or 4 inches broad, and running up and down thro' Roof, Sides, and Pavement. The perpendicular Fissures I generally fill with spar. I have run into such a detail, that I had forgot to tell you this whole Grotto makes the communication between my Garden and the Thames. I hope I shall live to see you there.... I have neither room nor words to tell you how much you oblige your Humble Servant, | A. Pope.

APPENDIX A

The Notes for *Brutus*

In March 1743 Pope told Spence that he had plans for an epic poem which turned 'wholly on civil and ecclesiastical government':

> The hero is a prince who establishes an empire. That prince is our Brutus from Troy, and the scene of the establishment, England.
>
> The plan of government is much like our old original plan, supposed so much earlier, and the religion introduced by him is the belief in one God and the doctrines of morality.
>
> Brutus is supposed to have travelled into Egypt, and there to have learned the unity of the Deity, and the other purer doctrines, afterwards kept up in the mysteries.[1]

The poem was thought of as part of Pope's *Opus Magnum,* a large philosophical work; *Brutus* was to form the third stage of this project, treating man 'in his Social, Political, and Religious Capacity'. Warburton summarized Pope's plan in this way:

> In pursuance of this design, he plan'd out a Poem on the subject of the fabulous BRUTUS, the great Grandson of Æneas: whose first and predominant principle he makes to be Benevolence; from this Ruling Passion arises a strong desire to redeem the remains of his countrymen, then captives amongst the Greeks, from slavery and misery, and to establish their freedom and felicity on a just form of Civil Government. He had seen how false Policy, and Superstitions and Vices proceeding from it, had caused the ruin of Troy; and he was enabled to avoid the *one* by the lights his countrymen, whom he had now gathered from their dispersion, could afford him from their observations on the various policies of the Grecian Cities; and to reform the *other* by the Wisdom he himself had gained in Italy, where Evander, as we are told by Virgil, had reformed the reigning Superstitions; ...Thus qualified for the office of Legislation, he puts to sea with a number of brave followers; enters the Atlantic Ocean; and after various traverses (each of which produces some new lesson of Politics) he arrives in Britain, where having surmounted many successive difficulties, which bring him still nearer and nearer to the point the poet aims at, he at length establishes for his Trojans that perfect form of Civil Government which it was our author's purpose to recommend. The poem opens (of which very few lines of the introduction only were written) with Brutus at the Straits of Calpé, in sight of the *ne plus ultra* on Hercules's Pillars, debating in counsel whether he should enter the great ocean.   (*Poems* iii(2) xix-xx)

Text: Pope's notes for his unwritten epic survive, in his own hand, in

Appendix A

British Library MS Egerton 1950 ff. 4^r, 5^{r-v}. The correct order of the passages is not always clear, and some words are illegible. In the following transcript angled brackets mark Pope's deletions, square brackets denote editorial insertions, and three dots indicate illegible material. Note that Pope frequently uses the abbreviation 'y' for 'th'.

Pope's plans for *Brutus* are discussed by Donald T. Torchiana, 'Brutus: Pope's last hero', *JEGP* 61 (1962) 853-67; and Miriam Leranbaum, *Alexander Pope's 'Opus Magnum' 1729-1744* (Oxford, 1977) pp. 155-74.

BRUTUS
Great Grandson of Æneas.

Benevolence ye First Principle & Predominant in Brutus. Thence a strong Desire to <free> redeem ye Remains of his Countrymen* (ye descendts frō Troy) now captives in Greece: & To establish their freedom & felicity in a Just Form of Governmt <& Religion the First to [...]> avoiding y^t. false Policy y^t caused ye Ruin of Troy, (Superstition, & y^e. Vices arising frō it.) <Then> & Taking in ye Good of ye several States wch They had experiencd in Greece as well as He in Italy.

[*margin:*]66 years after ye Destr. of Troy. *A Nestor among these who had seen 2 generations. Thucyd lib.1.

The Love of his Country induces his Voyage. He travels to <Brutus> gather<s> together ye descendts of ye Trojans, who were dispers'd ab^t Greece (& consequently had learnd ye Policies & Customs of different States) after he has collected these, he <puts to Sea & Enters ye Atlantic Ocean> consults ye oracle to incourage them – wch promises him a land in the said Ocean, mark'd out by some circumstances to be Britain. He then puts to Sea & enters the Atlantic Ocean.

<1. Brutus ye Grandson of Eneas Knowing ye true Cause of ye Ruin of Troy, to be Superstition & Vice, &> Experienc'd <by ye abode in Italy.> after Eneas a better Policy in Italy brought up in ye Court of Evander, who condemnd ye comon superstitions, non caeca relligio – &c. Quis Decus incertes, among ye Tuscans, of the unknown God. &c.

<Fird with a Desire of forming a policy & Religion to bless mankind, Promisd by y^e [...] to [...] a Land where in y^e [...]> He observes when he comes to Britain a climate equally free from ye Effeminacy and Softness of ye Southern Clymes, & ye Ferocity and Savageness of ye Northern. <The> a people whose natural Genius & temper <of ye people wd be> in ye medium between these was suited to all <y^e> Improvements & Virtues: <in ye medium between these> There too he finds ye Druids Doctrine tending to a <truer> nobler Religion, & better Morall suited to His Purposes.

How came the Arts & Civility he introduced into Britain to be lost again?

A Prophecy deliverd to him by an Old Druid that the Britons shou'd Degener in an Age or Two, and Relapse into a degree of Barbarism, but that they shou'd be Redeemd again by a Descendant of his Family out of Italy, Julius Caesar, under whose successors they shou'd be Repolishd and that the Love of Liberty he had introduced, the Martial spirit, and other Moral Virtues shou'd never be lost. With

Appendix A

Observations upon the Impossibility of any Institution being Perpetual without some Changes.

Lib 1.

Open ye Poem with Brutus at ye Straits of Calpe, in sight of Hercules Pillars, ne plus ultra, debating in council with his captains whether to enter ye Great Ocean. An Enterprise on a par wth Columbus.

1.<Encouraged by a Vision, shewing ye Prospect of his> Brutus's Opinion, not to Conquer & destroy ye natives, but polish<ing> ye People, & introducing true Religion void of Superstition & false Notions of ye Gods, <incouraging> leading to Vice & Misery, among^t a <Savage> people yet uncorrupted in their manners, & only wanting Arts & Governmt, worthy to be made happy.

2.<wch he had small prospect of, in any of ye then known world in ye me—> The Reasons why he tempts ye great Ocean in search of New Lands: having no prospect of introducing pure manners in the then known mediterranean world; but had learnd in Egypt great Ideas of. This <last> he may tell his Council. <to incourage 'em to proceed. after w^{ch}> yet yy [*i.e.* they] continue afraid, <till ye Vision> pleading ye Example of Hercules for going no farther ye Presumption of going beyond a *God*– He answers he was but a Mortal like them, & if their Virtue were superior to his, they w^d be <as much> as much Gods, <or more y^n he> as He. ye Way is open to Heaven by Virtue. Lastly he resolves to go in a single ship, & reject all cowards. Some then out of Love to him will go, it is determind to set sail to morrow, & y^t night he has <y^e> a Vision incouraging him. Hercules appears, confirming his sentiments deliverd y^t day in Council as tutelary God of the Tuscans & Evander. Hercules & Prodicus

Lib 2.

[*margin:*]Dampier

First carried Westward by ye Winds to ye Canary Islands. [*margin:* The Fortunate Islands./Teneriff/Volcano's] land there, a most delicious Iland describd, but without Inhabitants. a g.^{t} p.^{t} of his people are for setling there. w^t more can be wishd for our selves, an End of our Labors, &c thank ye Gods & rest. [*margin:* The Land of Laziness – Capua – inarata] He refuses, because it dos not answer his purpose of

293

Extending Benevolence, & polishing & teaching Nations, despises y^r mean thought of making only themselves happy, & sets before 'em ye Great Promises of Heaven Vidi ipse, vidi, &c. Good omens attend. Yet they leave ye Old Men & Women & ye fearful, & those unfit for service, to find their Quiet there; & build ym a City, &c. & sail away <with> only with Resolute Men.

The Passion of some old friend or Woman, who will not stay behind. The old sage thinks he can advise & exhort. &c. &c.

(Providence or y^e *God* orders ye wind to blow <sails> Northward – sends his spirit – to raise & direct ye wind – the vessel touches at Lisbon, Ulyssipont, <w>There he finds ye Son of a Trojan Captive of Ulysses, who relates his setling there & building Lisbon. <an episode – He flies from ye detested name of Ulysses, & takes with him ye Captive, who relates> telling on w^t wicked Principles of Policy & Superstition Ulysses had founded his City, & was <murtherd> driven away himself by ye discontented People he had inslaved. <Brutus <restores> gives em a better Form & leaves ym one of their own people to govern 'em, & abolishes ye new Gods introduced by Ulysses, & leaves y^m to worship ye Only One.>

Lib. 3.

Comes to Britain or Ireland either first. finds in ye west of Britain a kind reception, like ye Savages in Peru well disposed, no bloody sacrifices [*margin:* worshippers of ye Sun & fire.] Druids. meets y^m at an Altar of Turf in an open place offering fruits & flowers to Heaven[.] Copy ye Manners of ye best Savages. Picture of ye Haven, Coasts, &c lands by Torbay, <or Wales> ye Western p.^{t} or Southwest, other parts infested by <Giants> Tyrants, of whom Stories are told by Britains as Giants: whom he helps y^m to conquer. <The Hebrides Elades, &c. Isles.> The People of ye Giants dominion. Islands <some> near y^m <are> overrun with Superstition, tell him there are <believed to be> possest by Titans, or Hero's Ghosts, frō wch Thunders & Tempests guard all access. <Storms> <Stories of ym told Brutus by Natives or Britains.> [*margin:* <Plut.> Plut. Fonten. of oracles.] He undertakes these adventures to disperse Tyrrany & Error & spread Truth & good Governm^t.

Moralize ye old Fables concerning Brutus Gogmagog, &c. the Fables being made ye Peoples acc^t of y^m; When Brutus goes, ye Enchantments vanish.

Priests, Conjurers, Magic, resist him. as Priests of delphi <were>

Appendix A

had secrets y^r. past for supernatural. Gunpowder, &c. The Machines of Good & Evil spirits permitted by God, admit of all Magic & Inspiration. [*margin*: The machinery/ names of good spirits/ names of Evil frō Milton]

Scripture & Com̄on Opinion agree in authorising ye operations of spirits: Guardian angels of Heathen Kingdomes taught in Daniel &: These concerned for Good ends to advance ye worship of ye deity, & Virtue, ye Devils angels for Evil, to pro<tect>mote Superstition & Vice. Equally under any dispensation, Ethnic or Xtian.

Human characters) 1. The Achilles, Alex^r Rinaldo.
2. an Old Cautious Counsellor, to contraste him
3. a Soldier seeking only Plunder & <[...]> lust Destroyed by a Woman.
4. a bloody, cruel Hero, always for violent Measures. killd by ye Giants.
5.

False Policies

1. The Island Mona und^r Superstition governd by *Priests* Tacit. <Claudius> ann. 14, 30.
2. Others und^r dismal *Anarchy*, the Buildings, Laws like ye Peruvians at first, & Cyclops of old, infesting their Neighbors & eating Captives, carrying away Virgins. an episode of a Lover carrying Brutus to reconquer<ing> one.
3. The third und^r. *Tyrrany*, stronger y^n others taken for Giants, living in Castles, high Rocks <[...]> these 2 in Britain <y^e [...]ment of Island>, ye Giants in Cornwall. Corinaeus, Gogmagog. Goffarius allied to them. These being finally reduced, ye whole Iland submits to good Government wch ends ye Poem.

*add Difficulties with his own people during this time, a Character of a Kinsman of Brutus young fierce, ambitious & brave to excess, an Achilles
1. eager for passing ye straits.
2. Furious agst setling in ye Fortunate Islands, declare first of all, meerly for Glory, & impatience of Ease
3. In Britain, for conquering all by force & treating ye people who submitted as slaves, indangers a Revolt, by taking away a Woman betrothed to a Britain. (Scipio & Masinissa) some of Brutus people side with him & raise a faction which his wisdom & firmness suppress, & bring him back to his duty, agst ye Giants, a com̄on Enemy, where

he dos great actions after his secession ashamed y^r Brutus left him to his Woman, & went to war with^t him

**Among ye Giants a Minister of Gogmagog persuading him to all injustice/ hangd before some Town, for example

APPENDIX B

Two attacks on Pope by Lady Mary Wortley Montagu and John, Lord Hervey

These two pamphlets are among the most important of the many attacks which Pope was subjected to throughout his career (for which see Guerinot, *passim*). They were the occasion of Pope's *Letter to a Noble Lord*. The *Verses*, published on 9 March 1733, were probably the work of both Lady Mary and Hervey; the *Epistle*, published on 10 November 1733, was Hervey's alone. Both were reprinted several times (see Guerinot 224-6, 239-41).

Selected prose of Alexander Pope

VERSES
ADDRESS'D TO THE
IMITATOR
OF THE
FIRST SATIRE
OF THE
SECOND BOOK OF HORACE.
BY A LADY

TO THE
IMITATOR
OF THE
FIRST SATIRE OF THE SECOND BOOK OF HORACE.

In two large Columns, on thy motly Page,
Where *Roman* Wit is stripe'd with *English* Rage;
Where Ribaldry to Satire makes pretence,
And modern Scandal rolls with ancient Sense:
Whilst on one side we see how *Horace* thought;
And on the other, how he never wrote:
Who can believe, who view the bad and good,
That the dull Copist better understood
That *Spirit*, he pretends to imitate,
Than heretofore that *Greek* he did translate?
   Thine is just such an Image of *his* Pen,
As thou thy self art of the Sons of Men:
Where our own Species in Burlesque we trace,
A Sign-Post Likeness of the noble Race;
That is at once Resemblance and Disgrace.
   Horace can laugh, is delicate, is clear;
You, only coarsely rail, or darkly sneer:
His Style is elegant, his Diction pure,
Whilst none thy crabbed Numbers can endure;
Hard as thy Heart, and as thy Birth obscure.
   If *He* has Thorns, they all on Roses grow;
Thine like rude Thistles, and mean Brambles show;
With this Exception, that tho' rank the Soil,
Weeds, as they are, they seem produc'd by Toil.
Satire shou'd, like a polish'd Razor keen,
Wound with a Touch, that's scarcely felt or seen.
Thine is an Oyster-Knife, that hacks and hews;
The Rage, but not the Talent of Abuse;
And is in *Hate*, what *Love* is in the Stews.

298

Appendix B

'Tis the gross *Lust* of Hate, that still annoys,
Without Distinction, as gross Love enjoys:
Neither to Folly, nor to Vice confin'd;
The Object of thy Spleen is Human Kind:
It preys on all, who yield, or who resist;
To Thee 'tis Provocation to exist.
　　But if thou see'st[1] a great and gen'rous Heart,
Thy Bow is doubly bent to force a Dart.
Nor only Justice vainly we demand,
But even Benefits can't rein thy Hand:
To this or that alike in vain we trust,
Nor find Thee less Ungrateful than Unjust.
　　Not even Youth and Beauty can controul
The universal Rancour of thy Soul;
Charms that might soften Superstition's Rage,
Might humble Pride, or thaw the Ice of Age.
But how should'st thou by Beauty's Force be mov'd,
No more for loving made, than to be lov'd?
It was the Equity of righteous Heav'n,
That such a Soul to such a Form was giv'n;
And shews the Uniformity of Fate,
That one so odious, shou'd be born to hate.
　　When God created Thee, one would believe,
He said the same as to *the Snake of Eve*;
To human Race Antipathy declare,
'Twixt them and Thee be everlasting War.
But oh! the Sequel of the Sentence dread,
And whilst you *bruise their Heel*, beware your Head.
　　Nor think thy Weakness shall be thy Defence;
The Female Scold's Protection in Offence.
Sure 'tis as fair to beat who cannot fight,
As 'tis to libel those who cannot write.
And if thou drawst thy Pen to aid the Law,
Others a Cudgel, or a Rod, may draw.
　　If none with Vengeance yet thy Crimes pursue,
Or give thy manifold Affronts their due;
If Limbs unbroken, Skin without a Stain, ⎫
Unwhipt, unblanketed, unkick'd, unslain; ⎬
That wretched little Carcass you retain: ⎭
The Reason is, not that the World wants Eyes;
But thou'rt so mean, they see, and they despise.
When fretful *Porcupines*, with rancorous Will,
From mounted Backs shoot forth a harmless Quill,
Cool the Spectators stand; and all the while,
Upon the angry little Monster smile.
Thus 'tis with thee: —whilst impotently safe,
You strike unwounding, we unhurt can laugh.
Who but must laugh, this Bully when he sees,

A little Insect shiv'ring at a Breeze?
One over-match'd by ev'ry Blast of Wind,
Insulting and provoking all Mankind.
   Is this the *Thing* to keep Mankind in awe,
To make those tremble who escape the Law?
Is this *the Ridicule* to live so long,
The deathless Satire, and *immortal Song?*
No: like thy self-blown Praise, thy Scandal flies;
And, as we're told of Wasps, it stings and dies.
   If none do yet return th' intended Blow;
You all your Safety, to your Dullness owe:
But whilst that Armour thy poor Corps defends,
'Twill make thy Readers few, as are thy Friends;
Those, who thy Nature loath'd, yet lov'd thy Art,
Who lik'd thy Head, and yet abhor'd thy Heart;
Chose thee, to read, but never to converse,
And scorn'd in Prose, him whom they priz'd in Verse.
Even they shall now their partial Error see,
Shall shun thy Writings like thy Company;
And to thy Books shall ope their Eyes no more,
Than to thy Person they wou'd do their Door.
   Nor thou the Justice of the World disown,
That leaves Thee thus an Out-cast, and alone;
For tho' in Law, to murder be to kill,
In Equity the Murder's in the Will:
Then whilst with Coward Hand you stab a Name,
And try at least t'assassinate our Fame;
Like the first bold Assassin's be thy Lot,
Ne'er be thy Guilt forgiven, or forgot;
But as thou hate'st, be hated by Mankind,
And with the Emblem of thy crooked Mind,
Mark'd on thy Back, like *Cain,* by God's own Hand;
Wander like him, accursed through the Land.

FINIS.

Appendix B

AN
EPISTLE
FROM A
NOBLEMAN
TO A
DOCTOR OF DIVINITY:

In Answer to a *Latin* Letter in Verse.
Written from *H–n–C–t, Aug*. 28. 1733.

Suppliant your Pardon first I must implore,
(Dear Doctor!) that I've never wrote before:
But in the constant Bustle of a Court,
Betwixt our Forms, our Bus'ness, and our Sport;
Tho' you may think whole Days are unenjoy'd,
Yet scarce one Moment passes unemploy'd.

   In the next place, when I declare how long
I've taken leave of *Greek* or *Latin* Song;
That all I learn'd from *Doctor Freind* at School,
By *Gradus, Lexicon,* or Grammar-Rule;
Of Saphic, Lyric, or Iambic Odes,
Or *Doctor King*'s Machinary of Gods,
Has quite deserted this poor *John-Trot* Head,
And left plain native *English* in its stead:
I'm sure your courteous Rev'rence will forgive
The homely Way, in which you now receive
These hearty Thanks, from an illiterate Hand,
For Favours which I barely understand.

   You know the Proverb says, That of a Cat,
The Creature's Skin is all that you can get;
So from no Head you ever can receive
More Wit, than such a Head has got to give:
Let for this Reason then, my learned Friend,
Gracious, accept the All I have to send;
Nor wonder that my Brain no more affords,
But recollect the Privilege of L---ds;
And when you see me fairly write my Name,
For *England's Sake* wish all could do the same.
Nay, I perhaps could not so much have done,
Had I been bred and born an eldest Son.
A Noble Father's Heir, spoil'd by his Mother,
Leaves Learning always to his younger Brother;
Who at the Bar must prate to earn a Groat,
Whilst all *our* Bus'ness is to dress and vote.

301

The very Moment therefore I grew Great,
A lazy, titled Heir to an Estate;
For fear my Education might bely,
By some mean Badge of Sense, my Quality;
That to good Blood, by old prescriptive Rules,
Gives Right hereditary to be Fools;
I streight began upon a quite new Score,
Neglected all that I had learn'd before,
And not to seem a Novice in my State,
Or ignorant what belong'd to being great,
With little Judgment, and good Store of Pride,
I took upon me always to decide:
In every Company was bold and loud, ⎫
Behav'd myself as rudely as I could, ⎬
And ne'er discours'd of what I understood. ⎭
'Tis thus among *the Great*: If any one ⎫
By chance has *Wit*, so aukwardly 'tis shown, ⎬
That 'tis a less Misfortune to have none. ⎭
For still he goes on this erroneous Rule,
That no body with *Wit* can be a *Fool*;
Yet by Example, at his own Expence,
Proves one may have it without *common Sense*.
For, void of Prudence, and too vain of Parts,
How oft good Heads have plainer shewn bad Hearts?
When in Obscurity perhaps the *Last*,
Without the *First*, had fortunately past.
Thus whilst to Wit their sole Ambition tends,
(Whilst for one Joke they give up fifty Friends)
Tho' ne'er adapted to a manly Use,
But still on trifles squander'd, or Abuse;
They think the World so blind, and to admit,
All Understanding is compris'd in *Wit*.
That dang'rous Flow of a licentious Brain, ⎫
Which wanting Skill it's Ardour to restrain, ⎬
Converts to Ill, like Nourishment to Pain. ⎭
Perhaps you'll say, to its Excuse inclin'd,
If 'tis an Ill, 'tis of a pleasing kind.
I grant it such, but still 'tis a Disease.
Are Calentures not Ills because they please?
Or who will call the Gout, or Stone a Good,
Because engender'd by the richest Blood?
Luxuriant Branches show a fertile Root,
But unrestrain'd, they bear but little Fruit:
So Wit unprun'd, and wanting Judgment's Aid,
Is the crude Fruit of a good useless Head.
Such Wits are nought but glittering Ignorance:
What *Monkeys* are to Men, they are to Sense;
Imperfect Mimicks, ludicrous and mean,

Appendix B

Who often bite that Fool they entertain.
Their Tricks may please, their Quickness may surprise;
At first we wonder, but at last despise.
The Wise avoid such Animals with Care,
And he who laughs the loudest, laughs in Fear.
True Wit is Reason in her gayest Strain;
That can at once inform and entertain:
Her lively Truths attentive we explore,
Pleas'd we commend, instructed we adore.

But of this rare, this estimable Kind,
In the great World, few Instances we find:
Tho' aiming at it, dissolute and loud,
And of the Faults, they ought to blush for, proud.
How oft we hear some Witling pert and dull,
By Fashion *Coxcomb*, and by Nature *Fool*:
With hackney Maxims, in dogmatic Strain,
Scoffing *Religion* or the *Marriage-Chain*.
Then from his Common-place Book he repeats,
"That Lawyers all are Rogues, and Parsons Cheats;
"Physicians ignorant, and Courtiers Slaves;
"Great Kings but Actors, and great Statesmen Knaves;
"That Vice and Virtue's nothing but a Jest,
"And all Morality Deceit well drest;
"That Life itself is like a wrangling Game,
"Where some for Int'rest play, and some for Fame;
"Whilst ev'ry Gamester at this Board we meet,
"Must either be the Bubble or the Cheat.
And when this Catalogue he has run o'er,
And empty'd of whipt Cream his frothy Store,
Thinks he's so wise no *Solomon* knows more:
That the weak Texture of his flimsy Brain,
Is fit the Weight on *Walpole*'s to sustain;
In *Senates* to preside, to mold *the State*,
And fix in *England*'s Service, *Europe*'s Fate.

Since such you'll find most Men of our Degree,
Excuse the Ignorance appears in me.
Nor marvel whilst that Ign'rance I rehearse,
That still I know enough to do't in Verse:
Guiltless of Thought, each Blockhead may compose
This nothing-meaning Verse, as fast as Prose.
And *P—e* with Justice of such Lines may say,
His Lordship spins a thousand in a Day.
Such *P—e* himself might write, who ne'er could think:
He who at *Crambo* plays with Pen and Ink;
And is call'd Poet, 'cause in Rhyme he wrote
What *Dacier* construed, and what *Homer* thought:

But in Reality this Jingler's Claim,
Or to an Author's, or a Poet's Name,
A Judge of writing would no more admit,
Than each dull *Dictionary*'s Claim to Wit;
That nothing gives you at its own Expence,
But a few modern Words for ancient Sense.
'Tis thus, whene'er *P—pe* writes, he's forc'd to go
And *beg a little Sense*, as School-boys do.
"For all cannot invent, who can translate;
No more than those who cloath us can create.
When we see *Celia* shining in Brocade,
Who thinks 'tis *Hinchlif* all that Beauty made?
And *P—pe*, in his best Works, we only find
The gaudy *Hinchlif* of some beauteous Mind.
To bid his Genius work without that Aid,
Would be as much mistaking of his Trade,
As 'twould to bid your *Hatter* make a *Head*.
Since this Mechanic's, like the other's Pains,
Are all for dressing other Peoples Brains.

But had he not, to his eternal Shame,
By trying to deserve a Sat'rist's Name,
Prov'd he can ne'er invent but to defame:
Had not his *Taste* and *Riches* lately shown,
When he would talk of Genius to the Town,
How ill he chuses, if he trusts his own.
Had he, in modern Language, only wrote
Those Rules which *Horace*, and which *Vida* taught;
On *Garth* or *Boileau*'s Model built his Fame,
Or sold *Broome*'s Labours printed with *P—pe*'s Name:
Had he ne'er aim'd at any Work beside,
In Glory then he might have liv'd and dy'd;
And ever been, tho' not with Genius fir'd,
By *School-boys* quoted, and by *Girls* admir'd.

So much for *P—pe* —And were I not afraid,
Tho' I wrote more, that you no more would read,
I now would try to jumble into Rhyme,
Th' Account you ask of how we pass our Time:
But by the manner of your spending yours,
Guess— and you'll not be very wide of ours.
For *C—ts* are only larger Families,
The Growth of each, few Truths, and many Lies:
Like you we *lounge*, and feast, and play, and chatter;
In private satirize, in publick flatter.
Few to each other, all to one Point true;
Which one I sha'n't, nor need explain.   Adieu.

FINIS.

Textual notes

The texts printed here follow the original editions as specified in the headnotes. All are given in full, except for some of the material from the translation of Homer, and some of the letters, where omissions are indicated in the usual way. Some names which in the originals are printed as an initial letter followed by a dash have been spelt out, and these additions are placed within square brackets. Titles have been supplied for the contributions to *The Spectator* and *The Guardian*. Other departures from the copy-texts are as follows:

21:15 made] *om.*
33:21 *Tam*] *Tum*
48:40 *dolisque*] *dobisque*
58:5 that] *om.*
100:37 raise] praise
144:21 unknown] unkown
179:16 180.] 18
203:31 *Litotes*] *Littole*
215:1 title] *1743*; *om. 1730*
215:2-5 The...times.] *1743, abridged from 1730*
223:22 like] alike
227:32 seen] *om.*
242:21 so] *om.*
243:37 If] *om.*
243:38 impudent as to] *om.*
244:33 insinuation] *MS unclear*
251:29-30 Common...universal] *1735; om. MS*
251:34 those] *1735*; they *MS*
252:19 resigno] *1735*; refigio *MS*
289:3 [crystals]] *sic 1875*
289:31 there...I] *sic 1875*

Notes

1. *The Critical Specimen*

1 'It was itself a large tree, very similar in appearance to laurel, and had it not given off a different odour it would have been a laurel' (Virgil, *Georgics* II 131-3).
2 Vid. Tatler, 160. [Pope's note]
3 Folly
4 *See the Battle of* Ramellies, *or the* Power *of* Union, *a Poem.* [Pope's note]. Published by Dennis in 1706.

2. Contributions to *The Spectator*

1 'They love shade so much that they think that whatever is in the light is in confusion' (adapted from Seneca, *Epistulae Morales* iii 6).
2 In the lines at the end of his essay 'Of Obscurity' in his *Works* (1668).
3 Plutarch, 'On Tranquillity of Mind' (*Moralia* 467a-b).
4 These lines are attributed to the Roman Emperor Hadrian (AD 76-138) by Aelius Spartianus in *De Vita Hadriani* 25. Pope translated the lines as 'The Heathen to his departing Soul' and also imitated them as 'The Dying Christian to his Soul' (see *Poems* vi 91-5).

3. Contributions to *The Guardian*

No.4
1 Samuel Butler, *Hudibras* II i 627-34.

No.40
1 'Corydon and Thyrsis had driven their flocks together. From that day it is Corydon, Corydon, with us' (Virgil, *Eclogue* vii 2, 70).
2 For the background to this essay, see the headnote to the *Discourse on Pastoral*.
3 *See* Rapin *de* Carm. Past. *pars* 3. [Pope's note]
4 Quintus Ennius (239-169 BC), early Roman poet and dramatist.
5 Philips' fifth pastoral is based on the second of Faminius Strada's academic prolusions (1617).
6 Spenser, *The Shepheardes Calendar*, November, 141.
7 ibid., September, 1-4.
8 That is the *Kine* or Cows. [Pope's note]
9 Moschus (fl. c. 150 BC) and Bion (fl. c. 100 BC), two Greek Bucolic poets.

No.61

1 'In the first place, with the killing of wild beasts the steel was warmed and stained with blood' (Ovid, *Metamorphoses* xv 106-7).

2 Montaigne, 'De la cruauté', *Essais* II xi.

3 John Locke, *Some Thoughts Concerning Education* (1693), pp. 130-33.

4 Claude Fleury, in *Les Moeurs des Israélites* (1681).

5 'Bleeding and suppliant-like [he filled all the house with] his groan' (Virgil, *Aeneid* VII 501-2).

6 Seneca, *Epistulae Morales* 21.

7 Plutarch, *Marcus Cato* viii 1; iv 2.

8 'What have you done to deserve death, you sheep, a peaceful flock, born for man's service, who bring us sweet milk to drink in your full udders, who give us your wool for soft clothing, and who help more by your life than by your death? What have the oxen done, faithful, guileless beasts, harmless and simple, born to a life of toil? He is truly inconsiderate and not worthy of the gift of grain, who could take off the heavy weight of the curved plough and kill his husbandman....What an evil habit he is forming, how surely is he impiously preparing to shed human blood, who cuts a calf's throat with the knife, and listens unmoved to its piteous cries! Or who can slay a kid which cries just like a little child' (Ovid, *Metamorphoses* xv 116-24, 463-7).

9 Jonah iv 11.

10 Deuteronomy xxii 6-7.

11 *The Fables of Pilpay*, translated from the French version of the Persian original, appeared in 1699.

No.91

1 Not in Virgil; a proverbial tag: 'little things have their graces'.

2 Pope was himself only about four foot six in height, and was pilloried throughout his life by his enemies for his small stature and deformity (see Guerinot, *passim*).

3 Martin Powell had established a theatre for his puppets in the galleries of Covent Garden.

4 'the chair being empty': used of a papal interregnum.

5 a low wooden stool

6 low-heeled shoes

7 a small but strong breed of horses peculiar to Galloway

No.92

1 'What little men they are, when I stop to reflect!' (Plautus, *Captivi*, prologue 51).

2 'Greater vigour reigned in the smaller body' (Statius, *Thebaid* i 417)

3 Jean-Louis Guez de Balzac (1594-1654), in *Politics in Select Discourses of Monsieur Balzac* (1709).

4 In the *Roman Comique* (1651-7) by Paul Scarron (1610-60).

5 'most charming little man' (Suetonius, *Vita Horati*).

No.132

1 'We must each bear our punishments' (Virgil, *Aeneid* VI 743).

2 Edmund Waller, 'On the foregoing Divine Poems', ll. 13-14.
3 Wisdom of Solomon v 14; iv 8-11.

No.173

1 'Nor had I been silent about the late-blooming narcissus, or the curling acanthus-stem, the pale ivy or the shore-loving myrtle' (Virgil, *Georgics* IV 122-4).
2 'The Baian villa, Bassus, of our friend Faustinus keeps no unfruitful spaces of wide fields, laid out in idle myrtle-beds, with widowed planes and clipped clumps of box, but rejoices in a farm, honest and artless' (Martial, III lviii 1-5).
3 Sir William Temple, 'Upon the Gardens of Epicurus' in *Miscellanea: the Second Part* (1690), p.26.
4 'Here you may also see walls made from branches woven together and plaited, and ramparts stretching round, and great turrets rising from the branches; myrtle bent into ships, and copper prows: the sea moves in waves of box, and creaks under the dew. In another part tents grow leafy in their encampments; the citrons hurl shields and arrows at the walls.' (Source unknown; perhaps Pope's own verses)
5 Psalm cxxviii 3.

4. The Narrative of Dr. Robert Norris

1 Cp. Pope's earlier reference to Dennis as Appius, 'Like some *fierce Tyrant* in *Old Tapestry!*' (*Essay on Criticism* 587).
2 Dennis's *Gibraltar* (1705), *Remarks on a Book Entituled, Prince Arthur* (1704), *The Grounds of Criticism in Poetry* (1704) and *Essay upon Publick Spirit* (1711).
3 *The Grounds of Criticism in Poetry* includes a substantial discussion of *Paradise Lost*.
4 'The pharmacist compounds [the drugs], the doctor alone prescribes'.
5 Dennis's *Essay on the Opera's after the Italian Manner, which are about to be establish'd on the English Stage* (1706) argued that the opera 'is a Diversion of more pernicious Consequence, than the most licentious Play that ever has appear'd upon the Stage' (*Critical Works* i 383).
6 Gin.

5. A Key to the Lock

1 'Plato is my friend, Socrates is my friend, but Truth is my greater friend' (a traditional tag, adapted from Aristotle, *Nicomachean Ethics* i 6).
2 In 1714 Samuel Croxall, under the name Nestor Ironside, published *An Original Canto of Spencer: Design'd as Part of his Fairy Queen, but never Printed*, followed by *Another Original Canto of Spencer*. Both were attacks upon the Earl of Oxford.
3 *Yarhell's-Kitchen: Or, The Dogs of Egypt. An Heroic Poem* (1713); in praise of Oxford ('Yarhel' is an anagram of 'Harley').
4 *The Present State of Fairy-Land. In several Letters from Esquire Hush, An Eminent Citizen of Fickle-Borough, To the King of Slave-onia* (1713); a Tory pamphlet.

5 Arbuthnot's *The History of John Bull* (1712), a group of pamphlets attacking the war policy of the Whigs.
6 *The Character of* Belinda (*as it is here manag'd*) *resembles you in nothing but in Beauty.* Dedication to the *Rape of the Lock*. [Pope's note]
7 In his 'A Judgment upon Seneca, Plutarch, and Petronius', *Works of Monsieur De St. Evremond*, 3 vols. (1714) i 170.
8 John Barclay's romance *Argenis* (1621) appeared with a key in 1627.
9 John Dunton (1659-1733), a notorious bookseller and Whig pamphleteer who attacked Oxford and Bolingbroke in *Neck or Nothing* (1713).
10 *The Reverend Dr.* Swinden. [Pope's note] Tobias Swinden (d.1719), author of *An Enquiry into the Nature and Place of Hell* (1714).

6. From the translation of Homer

Preface to *The Iliad*
1 'lively strength of mind'
2 *Poetics* 1450a.
3 In Tasso's *Gerusalemme Liberata*.
4 Herodotus, II 53.
5 Addison, *Spectator* 279.
6 *Poetics* 1460a.
7 'with quick-moving helmet'
8 'quivering with leaves'
9 *An Essay on the Life, Writings, and Learning of Homer*, by Thomas Parnell, follows this Preface in the original.
10 In the preface to her French translation of the *Iliad* (1711).
11 Hesiod, lib. I. v.155, &c. [Pope's note]
12 René Rapin, *Comparaison des poèmes d'Homère et de Virgile* (1674).
13 J.C. Scaliger, *Poetices Libri Septem* (1561).
14 Charles Perrault, *Parallèle des Anciens et des Modernes* (1688-96).
15 Antoine Houdar de La Motte published a French translation of the *Iliad*, with a critical essay, in 1714.
16 George Chapman, *Iliad* 1598-1611, *Odyssey* 1614-15; Thomas Hobbes, *Odyssey* 1675, *Iliad* 1676; John Ogilby, *Iliad* 1660, *Odyssey* 1665.
17 Repectively in *Fables* (1700) and *Examen Poeticum* (1693).
18 François Fénelon, *Les avantures de Télémaque* (1699).
19 René Le Bossu, *Traité du poëme épique* (1675).
20 John Sheffield, *An Essay on Poetry* (1682).
21 Lord Lansdowne.

Notes from *The Iliad*
1 Here Pope quotes less effective imitations of this in Virgil and Tasso.
2 *Iliad* XIII 139; Pope translates the passage thus:
As from some Mountain's craggy Forehead torn,
A Rock's round Fragment flies, with Fury born,
(Which from the stubborn Stone a Torrent rends)
Precipitate the pond'rous Mass descends:
From Steep to Steep the rolling Ruin bounds;

At ev'ry Shock the crackling Wood resounds;
Still gath'ring Force, it smoaks; and, urg'd amain,
Whirls, leaps, and thunders down, impetuous to the Plain:
There stops— So *Hector*: (XIII 191-9)
3 Sir John Denham

Postscript to *The Odyssey*
1 'Who has learned what he owes his country and his friends, what love is due to a parent, a brother, and a guest: who tells us what is fair, what is foul, what is helpful, what is not, more plainly and better than Chrysippus or Crantor' (Horace, *Ars Poetica* 312-3; *Epist.* I ii 3-4).
2 *Of the Sublime* ix 11-15.
3 *Epist.* I ii 17-31, and *Ars Poetica* 140-52.
4 *Le Lutrin* (1674-83) by Boileau, a mock-heroic poem on disputes in a chapel.
5 *Georgics* IV.
6 *Aeneid* XI 343-444.
7 In a final section Pope goes on to take issue with Mme Dacier on various points.

7. Three attacks on Edmund Curll

1 Jane Wenham (d.1730) was condemned to death for witchcraft in 1712, but pardoned by the Queen. The case occasioned a flurry of pamphlets, of which Curll published two by Francis Bragge.
2 Curll published Blackmore's *Essays upon Several Subjects* in March 1716.
3 Daniel Finch, Earl of Nottingham (1647-1730), Tory statesman, but opponent of Oxford and Bolingbroke; in February 1716 he supported a motion in the Lords that the rebel Jacobite peers should be pardoned. In 1713 a pamphlet had been published in his name, called *Observations on the State of the Nation*, which occasioned two replies by George Sewell published by Curll in 1713 and 1714.
4 *A Second Collection of Poems on Several Occasions* was fathered on Prior by Curll in March 1716.
5 Des Champs, *Cato of Utica*, translated by John Ozell, published by Curll in May 1716.
6 Rowe's *Poetical Works*, published by Curll in 1715.
7 Charles Gildon's *A New Rehearsal, Or Bays the Younger*, published by Roberts in 1714, reissued 1715, attacked Rowe's plays, and Pope's *The Rape of the Lock*. Pope evidently thought that Curll, not Roberts, was the real culprit.
8 *The Case of Sodomy, in the Tryal of Mervin, Lord Audley* [1707], and *The Case of Bishop Atherton* (1710).
9 *The Case of Impotency Debated, in the late Famous Tryal at Paris, between the Marquis de Gesvres...and...his Lady*, 2 vols (1714), translated by Ozell. Curll published other similar material, and in 1715 issued *The Cases of Impotency and Divorce* in a collected edition.
10 Oldmixon edited the *Life and Posthumous Works of Arthur Maynwaring*, Whig propagandist, for Curll in 1715.
11 Halifax's *Works and Life* were published by Curll in 1715.
12 Susannah Centlivre (1667-1723), actress and dramatist; an outspoken anticatholic. She was the wife of the royal cook, Joseph Centlivre.

13 Sir Richard Blackmore, 'An Essay upon Wit', in his *Essays upon Several Subjects* (1716) p. 193.
14 There are several such platitudes about avarice in Blackmore's 'Essay upon False Virtue', ibid.
15 Samuel Pufendorf (1632–94), German writer on natural law.
16 Godfrey was the magistrate to whom Titus Oates first gave details of the 'Popish Plot' in September 1678; his murder the following month was widely attributed to papists.

8. Preface to *The Works*

1 A reference to *Pope's Miscellany*, published in January 1717, a re-issue by Curll of *Court Poems*.

9. *A Discourse on Pastoral Poetry*

1 Torquato Tasso (1544–95) author of the pastoral play *Aminta* and the epic *Gerusalemme Liberata*.
2 In his dedication to the *Pastorals* in *The Works of Virgil* (1697).
3 Giovanni Battista Spagnuoli (c.1447–1516), born in Mantua, author of eclogues.

10. Preface to *The Works of Shakespear*

1 accretions, superabundant additions
2 Translations from Ovid's *Heroides* were included in *Poems: Written by Wil. Shak-speare. Gent*, published by John Benson in 1640, and in subsequent editions of Shakespeare's poems until Malone rejected them in 1790.
3 Dares Phrygius is the priest of Hephaestus in the *Iliad*; the sixth-century *De Excidio Troiae Historiae*, which tells the story of the war from the Trojan viewpoint, was attributed to him. The verse paraphrase of it by Joseph of Exeter was known to Chaucer, and thus it indirectly influenced Shakespeare's *Troilus and Cressida*.
4 'Those who praise are the worst kind of enemies' (*Agricola* 41).
5 'If [Codrus] should praise me unduly, wreathe my brow with foxglove, lest [his evil tongue] harm the bard' (*Eclogue* vii 27–8).
6 Dryden called Jonson's verses 'An Insolent, Sparing, and Invidious Panegyrick' (*Discourse concerning Satire* (1693)).
7 Much Ado about Nothing. Act 2. *Enter Prince* Leonato, Claudio, *and* Jack Wilson instead of Balthasar. *And in Act* 4. Cowley, *and* Kemp, *constantly thro' a whole Scene*. Edit. Fol. of 1623, and 1632. [Pope's note]
8 *Such as*
—My Queen is murder'd! *Ring the little Bell*—
—His nose grew as sharp as a pen, and *a table of Greenfield's*, &c. [Pope's note]. The first of these examples is not Shakespearean; perhaps it is a distorted recollection of *Macbeth*. As for the second, Pope's note on this passage (*Henry V* II iii 17) is as follows: '*his nose was as sharp as a pen, and a table of green fields.* These words *and a table of green fields* are not to be found in the old editions of 1600 and 1608. This nonsense got into all the following editions by a pleasant mistake of the Stage-editors, who printed from the common piecemeal-

written Parts in the Play-house. A Table was here directed to be brought in, (it being a scene in a tavern where they drink at parting) and this direction crept into the text from the margin. *Greenfield* was the name of the Property man in that time who furnish'd implements &c. for the actors. A *Table* of *Greenfield*'s.' This nonsense is sheer fantasy on Pope's part. Lewis Theobald's subsequent emendation of 'Table' to 'babeld' has been generally accepted.

9 'on the authority of the codices [*sc.* early editions]'

II. *The Art of Sinking in Poetry*

1 *Martinus Scriblerus*, tho' of *German* Extraction, was born in *England*. *Vid.* his *Life* and *Memoirs*, which will speedily be publish'd. [Pope's note]

2 Aristotle and Longinus

3 widely (lit. 'by a whole sky')

4 'Poets wish both to profit and to please' (Horace, *Ars Poetica* 333; correctly 'aut...aut', 'either...or').

5 'We are born poets'

6 —*Mediocribus esse poetis/Non dii, non homines*, &c. Hor. [Pope's note] ('Neither men, nor gods, [nor booksellers] ever allowed that poets should be of middle rank': *Ars Poetica* 372-3).

7 The phrase is used by Falstaff of himself in *The Merry Wives of Windsor* (III v 12), and later by the Earl of Dorset in his lines *On Mr. Edward Howard* (1669): 'So in this way of writing without thinking/ Thou hast a strange alacrity in sinking' (ll. 23-24).

8 'taste for the askew'

9 'serpents couple with birds, lambs with tigers' (*Ars Poetica* 13).

10 a clown attending a mountebank

11 N.B. In order to do justice to these great Poets, our citations are taken from the best, the last, and most correct Editions of their Works. That which we use of Prince *Arthur*, is in *duodecimo*, 1714. The fourth Edition, *revised*. [Pope's note]

12 Quintilian, x i 91.

13 'Tritical' (trite, commonplace) was coined by Swift in his *Tritical Essay upon the Faculties of the Mind* (1711).

14 Lewis Theobald's play *Double Falsehood*, performed in 1727, published 1728.

15 This and the following quotation are from William Broome, 'On the Birthday of Mr. Robert Trefusis' and 'Epistle to My Friend Mr. Elijah Fenton'.

16 John Cleveland (1613-58), 'Fuscara; or, The Bee Errant'.

17 Ambrose Philips, 'To Signora Cuzzoni'.

18 Daniel Defoe (1661-1731), George Wither (1588-1667), Nahum Tate (1652-1715), John Ogilby (1600-76), Edward Ward (1667-1731), John Taylor (1580-1653), Laurence Eusden (1688-1730).

19 Leonard Welsted (1688-1747); see *Dunciad* A iii 163 and Pope's note there.

20 *Aeneid* III 571-7; Dryden translates it thus:
The Port capacious, and secure from Wind,
Is to the foot of thundring *Etna* joyn'd.
By turns a pitchy Cloud she rowls on high;
By turns hot Embers from her entrails fly;
And flakes of mounting Flames, that lick the Skie.

Oft from her Bowels massy Rocks are thrown,
And shiver'd by the force come piece-meal down.
Oft liquid Lakes of burning Sulphur flow,
Fed from the fiery Springs that boil below.
(III 746-54)

21 *Sublimi feriam sidera vertice.* [Pope's note] 'I shall strike the stars with my lofty head' (Horace, *Carm.* 1 i 36).

22 Horace says that Empedocles, eager to be thought an immortal god, leapt into Etna (*Ars Poetica* 465).

23 From Nicholas Rowe's *Lady Jane Grey* (1715).

24 *****Stays, Tweezer-case, Watch, Fan,* and a sort of *Perriwig*: All Words in use this present Year 1727. [Pope's note]

25 Nathaniel Lee, *The Rival Queens: or, Alexander the Great* (1677).

26 Edmund Waller, 'To my Lady Morton on New-years-day'.

27 Richard Steele, *The Procession* (1695).

28 Francis Quarles, 'On the Body of Man'.

29 *Paradise Lost* 1 63.

30 The second line is adapted from a line in John Oldham's 'To the Memory of Mrs Katherine Kingscourt': see K. Robinson, *Notes and Queries*, 219 (1974) 48.

31 Waller, 'Upon the Death of the Lord Protector'.

32 Dennis, 'A Pindarick Ode on the King'.

33 Conflated from Philips, 'To Miss Georgiana, Youngest Daughter to the Lord Carteret' and 'To the Honourable Miss Carteret'.

34 Addison, *The Campaign* (1705).

35 Thomas Tickell's translation of the first book of the *Iliad* (1715).

36 M. Jourdain in Molière's *Le Bourgeois Gentilhomme*.

37 These lines are by Addison, so this remark implies that Tickell's *Iliad* was really the work of Addison.

38 Laurence Eusden's translation of Claudian's 'The Court of Venus'.

39 Tom Brown (1663-1704), satirical writer.

40 Colley Cibber (1671-1757), dramatist.

41 Tacitus was translated by the Whig pamphleteer Thomas Gordon (1728-31); Josephus (1702), Cicero (1680), and Seneca (1678) by Sir Roger L'Estrange, (1616-1704). John Asgill (1659-1738) was an eccentric pamphleteer with a pithy, abrupt style, who in 1700 published *An Argument proving that according to...the Scriptures, man may be translated from hence into that eternal life without passing through death*, which brought upon him the charge of blasphemy and the nickname 'translated Asgill'. Marcus Aurelius was translated by Jeremy Collier (1701) and Thomas à Kempis by George Stanhope (1698). 'Snipsnap' is sharp repartee.

42 Nathaniel Lee, *Sophonisba* (1676).

43 'Here there is unfortunately a large gap'.

44 'Cibberisms' and 'Oldfieldisms'. Anne Oldfield acted in Cibber's plays, and her roles included ribaldry.

45 Dennis, *Upon our Victory at Sea* (1692).

46 *The Tempest* I ii 411-2, but the phrasing is closer to that of the adaptation by Dryden and Davenant (1670): 'Advance the fringed Curtains of thine Eyes, and say what thou seest yonder' (p.44).

47 This idea is based on Aristotle's division of rhetoric into the deliberative, the forensic and the ceremonial (*Rhetoric* 1 3). (Steeves)

48 Cp. 'A Heroick Poem, truly such, is undoubtedly the greatest Work which the Soul of Man is capable to perform' (Dryden, *Dedication of the Aeneis* (1697)).

49 Molière, *L'Avare* III i.

50 'And let no god intervene, unless there is a knot worthy of such a deliverer' (191-2).

51 'as much as is necessary'

52 Thomas Burnet's *The Theory of the Earth* (1684); the third book is concerned with the final conflagration of the earth. (Steeves)

53 'substitute'

54 Barton Booth, Robert Wilks and Colley Cibber were actor–managers at Drury Lane; William Wilks (Robert's nephew) had a career as an actor from 1715-23.

55 This phrase from the preface to Cibber's *Provoked Husband* (1728) was much parodied at the time.

56 'farewell and enjoy yourself'

12. Of the Poet Laureate

1 Appulus praepingui vultu alacer, & prolixè comatus, omnino dignus festa Laurea videretur. [Pope's note] ('The eager Apulian, with a fat face and long hair, seemed to everyone to be worthy of the festive laurel').

2 The Queen had given Duck a small house at Richmond.

3 'so that, both wittily and charmingly, it was signified that his drunkenness was alleviated by the remedy of cabbage'.

4 Manantibus prae gaudio oculis. [Pope's note] ('his eyes streaming for joy').

5 Semesis opsoniis. [Pope's note] ('his food half-eaten').

6 i.e. Lewis Theobald

7 Cabbage is the name given to the pieces of cloth cut off by tailors when cutting out clothes, and appropriated by them as a perquisite.

8 Cibber's voice was notoriously squeaky: cp. *Dunciad* B iii 306.

9 John Anstis, the Garter King-at-Arms, who was responsible for processions.

10 Eustace Budgell (1686-1737) a writer much attacked by the *Journal*.

11 Perhaps a glance at Lord Hervey, who drank ass's milk: cp. *Epistle to Dr. Arbuthnot* 306.

12 'with open mouth'

13. A Letter to a Noble Lord

1 'Happy Fannius, who has delivered his books and bust unasked!' (Horace, *Satires* I iv 21-2).

2 '[Am I to be troubled because] that silly Fannius, who sponges on Hermogenes Tigellius, slanders me?' (Horace, *Satires* I x 79-80).

3 'I tell you to go and whine amidst the comfortable chairs of your lady pupils' (Horace, *Satires* I x 91).

4 Hervey's elder half-brother Carr (1691-1723) was admired by Pope, who presented him with a set of his translation of Homer (*Corr.* i 295).

5 Mary, Lady Hervey (1700-68), daughter of Brigadier-General Nicholas Lepell; a famous beauty, and sometime maid of honour to Princess Caroline.

6 'John Trothead' is the signature on some papers appended to *The Craftsman*, an opposition journal sponsored by William Pulteney and Bolingbroke. Hervey, a supporter of Walpole, was partly responsible for the pamphlet *Sedition and Defamation Display'd*, an attack on *The Craftsman* which led to a duel with Pulteney in 1731. (For Pope's association with Bolingbroke and *The Craftsman* see Brean S. Hammond, *Pope and Bolingbroke* (1984).)

7 Ecclesiastes xii 1.

8 'Windham, tutor to the Duke of Cumberland, who was supposed by Pope to have had a hand in the *Verses to the Imitator of Horace*' (*E-C*).

9 Edward Howard, Restoration poet and dramatist.

10 Many notes in Pope's Homer are translated from those by Mme Dacier.

11 Hervey was an intimate and influential friend of the Queen.

14. Selections from the Correspondence

Letter 1

1 Three Italian writers of pastoral drama: Giovanni Battista Guarini (1538-1612), author of *Il Pastor Fido*; Guido Ubaldo Bonarelli della Rovere (1563-1608), author of *Filli di Sciro*; and Torquato Tasso (1544-95), author of *Aminta* and of the epic *Gerusalemme Liberata*.

Letter 2

1 Some of these lines are from the *Ars Poetica* by Marco Girolamo Vida (?1485-1566), others from Virgil's *Aeneid*: '[one verse] skims more easily over the road in silent flight through the plains' (*AP* III 374); '[another] lags, slouching to a halt from ponderous exertion' (*AP* III 376); 'the contending winds, and loud storms' (*Aen.* I 53); 'when night descends with a rush to the measureless sea' (*AP* III 425); 'and threw his unwarlike spear without a blow' (*Aen.* II 544-5); 'away with delays, seize stones in your hand, shepherd, seize staves of oak, hurry, bring flaming brands, hurl your darts, repulse the plague' (*AP* III 422-3). For Vida, cp. *Essay on Criticism* 705-8.

2 Edmund Waller (1606-87); the first two lines come from 'To the King on His Navy', the third from 'Of a Tree cut in Paper'.

3 'We shall avoid the frequent collision of vowels, which makes the style harsh and gaping, as the following: The copper-coloured berries hung most invitingly' (*Ad Herennium* iv 2).

4 'When it happens that vowels clash, the language is broken by gaps and interstices, and seems to labour. The most unpleasant effects of sound will be produced by the juxtaposition of the same long vowels, while the worst hiatus occurs between vowels which are pronounced hollow- or open-mouthed. *E* has a flatter, *i* a narrower sound...I do not know whether carelessness or a pedantic solicitude for correctness is the worst fault in this connexion' (Quintilian, IX iv 33-4).

5 'Some criticise Theopompus for too careful avoidance of such vowels, though the same is true of his master Isocrates...There is a frequent clash of vowels, which Demosthenes generally avoided as vicious' (Cicero, *Orator* xliv 151).

6 François Malherbe (1555-1628), credited by Boileau with introducing a proper cadence into French verse (*Art Poétique* i 131-2). The Soames–Dryden translation of Boileau assigns the equivalent role in English to Waller.

Letter 3

1 François, Duc de La Rochefoucauld (1613-80), author of *Maximes* (1665).

Letter 4

1 The translation of the *Iliad* by George Chapman (?1559-1634) was published 1598-1611; that by Thomas Hobbes (1588-1679) appeared in 1676.

Letter 5

1 Giambattista Marino (1569-1625), whose poetry abounds in extravagant conceits.

Letter 6

1 *Essay on Criticism* 585-7.
2 *Essay on Criticism* 503 originally read: 'Where *wanted*, scorn'd, and envy'd where *acquir'd*'. Dennis remarked: 'how can Wit be scorn'd where it is not? Is not this a Figure frequently employ'd in Hibernian Land?' For Pope's revisions to this line see *Poems* i 295.
3 'What finally remains now for me in my misery? There is no place for me among the Greeks, and the enraged Trojans themselves demand vengeance with my blood!' (*Aeneid* ii 70-2).
4 A Catholic priest.
5 Robert, Lord Petre, a distant relation of Caryll, who was to figure in *The Rape of the Lock*.

Letter 7

1 'pious deceptions'
2 *Essay on Criticism* 396-9.
3 The Jesuit college at St Omer was a principal training centre for English recusant clergy.
4 *Essay on Criticism* 689-90.

Letter 9

1 Charles Jervas (1675-1739), portrait painter, who gave Pope lessons.
2 The five-canto version, published in 1714.

Letter 11

1 'God has given, the Devil has taken away'; cp. Job i 21.
2 'If she beats her swift wings, I give up what she has given, and wrap myself in my own virtue, and seek honest poverty without any endowment' (Horace, *Carm.* iii xxix 53-6).

Letter 12

1 Louis xiv.

Letter 13

1 *Satyricon* 115.

Letter 14
1 Johannes Secundus, *Epistle* XI i 29.

Letter 15
1 Lucian, *Hermotimus* 20.

Letter 16
1 William Oldsworth, author of the three-volume *Dialogue between Timothy and Philatheus* (1709-11) and of a translation of Horace (1712-13) which included Bentley's notes; Dr William King; Sir Richard Blackmore, author of *A Paraphrase on the Book of Job* (1700), who confessed that his epic *Prince Arthur* had been largely written in coffee houses and when going through the streets.
2 Thomas Creech's translation of Lucretius, published by Tonson, first appeared in 1682 and remained popular.
3 Lord Lansdowne was eventually confined in the Tower as a suspected Jacobite.
4 Lord Carlton was Burlington's uncle.

Letter 19
1 'My mother is still mine'; 'it will be impossible for me to finish my tears for my parents'; 'can I now leave her, ignorant of whatever danger?' (adapted from *Aeneid* IX 284-9, where Euryalus asks Ascanius to take care of his mother for him).
2 An address to the clergy, not to the people.

Letter 20
1 The Title of an Arabic Treatise of the Life of Hai Ebn Yocktan [Pope's note].
2 'Vineyards and the humble tamarisk do not please all' (*Eclogues* iv 2).
3 That of the Prince of Wales at Richmond.

Letter 23
1 The source of the Latin is doubtful: see *Poems* vi 249.

Letter 24
1 The Earl of Grantham, Chamberlain to Queen Caroline, would have received Gay's letter of refusal.

Letter 25
1 'with a sudden fit of genius'
2 His mother's
3 'Why do we aim so high, when life is so short?' (Horace, *Carm.* II xvi 17).
4 Pamphlets written by Swift in 1724 against William Wood's patent for minting copper coins in Ireland, which was seen as a threat to Irish finances and nationhood. Swift was instrumental in defeating the plan and embarrassing Walpole.
5 Queen Caroline; Robert Knight, outlawed after the South Sea scandal.
6 Sent by Dr Arbuthnot's brother Robert.

7 Lord Carteret, Lord Lieutenant of Ireland.
8 The *Essay on Man*.

Letter 26
 1 *Epistle to Burlington* 169-171.
 2 'The house of Ucalegon next door is already in flames' (Virgil, *Aeneid* II 311-12).

Letter 28
 1 Cp. *Essay on Man* i 294
 2 See *A Letter to a Noble Lord*, and Appendix B.
 3 'for the sake of exercise'

Letter 30
 1 Bolingbroke, whose philosophical writings in prose were used by Pope in composing the *Essay on Man*.

Letter 31
 1 'I am not as I used to be!'
 2 'Agriculture is next to wisdom'
 3 'Such united minds'

Letter 32
 1 'with grief let us recall old loves, and let us weep our former friendships, now lost' (Catullus, xcvi 3-4; correctly, 'renovamus', 'let us renew').

Appendix A

1 Joseph Spence, *Observations, Anecdotes, and Characters of Books and Men*, edited by James M. Osborn, 2 vols. (Oxford, 1966) i 153.

Appendix B

1 See *Taste*, an Epistle. [Author's note, referring to Pope's supposed attack on the Duke of Chandos in the *Epistle to Burlington*; cp. Letter 26 above.]

Index

Addison, Joseph 32, 58, 62-3, 95, 107, 133, 138, 142, 196, 197, 252-3, 313; letter to, 246-7
Adrian, *see* Hadrian
Aeschylus 30, 163
Aesop 55
Alexander the Great 55
Anne, Queen 74, 78, 80, 251
Anstis, John 217
Apollonius of Rhodes 92
Arbuthnot, Dr John 74, 170, 219, 284; letter to, 281-3
Aristotle 66, 69, 91, 94, 95, 122, 160, 161, 164, 203, 312, 314
Asgill, John 199
Atterbury, Francis 270, 275; letters to, 264-6, 267-9
Augustus 55, 224, 282, 283
Aurelius, Marcus 199

Bacon, Francis 268
Balzac, Jean-Louis Guez de 54
Baraballo of Gaeta 213
Barclay, John 81, 88
Bathurst, Allen, Earl Bathurst 283; letter to, 266-7
Behn, Aphra 198
Bentley, Richard 31, 259
Berkeley, George 275
Bible
  and Homer 103
  Deuteronomy 49
  Job 186, 252
  Jonah 49
  Psalms 60
  Wisdom of Solomon 57
Bion 45
Blackmore, Sir Richard 133, 135, 140, 178-9, 186, 190, 192, 199, 200, 260
  Essays 133, 135, 136, 142
  Paraphrase on the Book of Job 170, 178, 184, 185, 189, 190, 191, 193, 194, 198, 201, 260

Prince Arthur 170, 177, 184, 186, 190, 191, 193-4, 197, 198, 200
Blenheim 263-4
Blount, Edward, letters to, 251-2, 255-6, 271-2
Blount, Martha and Teresa, letter to, 262-3
Boileau-Despréaux, Nicolas 100, 124, 230, 282, 304, 315
Bolingbroke, Henry St John, Viscount 73, 108, 133, 270, 275, 286, 287, 309, 315, 318
Bonarelli della Rovere, Guido Ubaldo 233
Booth, Barton 208-9
Borlase, William, letter to, 288-9
Bossu, René Le 107
Bridges, Ralph, letter to, 238-9
Broome, William 89, 225-6, 304, 312
Brown, Thomas 199
Buckinghamshire, John Sheffield, Duke of 108
Budgell, Eustace 217
Burlington, Richard Boyle, Earl of, letter to, 259-62
Burnet, Thomas 314
Butler, Samuel 36

Caesar, Julius 142
Carnarvon, Earl of, *see* Chandos
Caryll, John, letters to, 241-6, 250-2, 255-6
Cato (the Censor) 47-8, 142
Catullus 34, 287
Centlivre, Susannah, 129, 135, 140
Cervantes, Miguel de 22, 23, 24, 124
Chandos, James Brydges, Duke of (and Earl of Carnarvon) 108, 276-8
Chapman, George 105-6, 114, 118, 238
Chaucer, Geoffrey 163
Cheselden, William 285-6
Cibber, Colley 27, 199, 200, 209, 213, 217, 314
Cicero 125, 164, 199, 227, 236, 268, 286

319

Index

Index

Index